INLA

DEADLY DIVISIONS

JACK HOLLAND
HENRY McDONALD

Published in 1994 by
Torc
A division of Poolbeg Enterprises Ltd,
Knocksedan House,
123 Baldoyle Industrial Estate,
Dublin 13, Ireland

A catalogue record for this book is available from the British Library.

ISBN 1 898142 05 X

Cover photograph by *The Irish News*
Cover design by Poolbeg Group Services Ltd/Red Dog Graphics
Set by Poolbeg Group Services Ltd in Garamond 10/13.5
Printed by The Guernsey Press Ltd, Vale, Guernsey, Channel Islands

Acknowledgements

It is inevitable and understandable that the majority of those who helped and guided us in our research for this work prefer to remain anonymous. This is a testimony to the fact that our sources were primary, and, given the nature of the material, no explanation is necessary as to why they cannot be named.

However, we also relied on the assistance of librarians, journalists and others, whose collaboration proved at times essential. We would especially like to thank the staff of the Linenhall Library, paticularly Robert Bell and Yvonne Murphy of the Political Collection. Their unstinting co-operation in making available to us the impressive facilities at their disposal was certainly a key factor in helping us complete our research.

We would also like to thank Kathleen Bell of the *Irish News* library, the staff of the *Irish Times* library, and the staff of the BBC Northern Ireland library, for assisting us in our various quests.

Among our fellow reporters who helped us in different ways we would like to thank in paticular David McKittrick, who put at our disposal his formidable files. As well, Jim Cusack, Liam Clarke, Brendan Anderson, Brendan Murphy and Cathy Jonston all gave of their time and experience.

Our thanks go to Terry Robson and Mary Reid, who greatly contributed to our knowledge of the development of the movement in Derry and elsewhere, and to the former IRSP councillor Seán Flynn for all his assistance.

To our editors at Torc our thanks our due for their perseverance at seeing this project to a conclusion. We would especially like to thank Philip MacDermott of Poolbeg, whose enthusiasm played a crucial role in launching it.

Revolutionaries are dead men on leave
(From an epitaph to "Ta" Power and John O'Reilly, murdered in the
Rosnaree Hotel, Drogheda, 20 January 1987.)

Contents

PROLOGUE: THE ROAD TO DARKLEY

The road to Darkley passes through the border lands of County Armagh, where the grey stone bridges and disused factory chimneys add a further touch of desolation to the landscape in winter. It is a curious place, redolent of a past age of industrial prosperity, set down among rolling hills and rushing streams. Now the crows have colonised the tall mill chimneys, and the mills themselves have been converted into shopping malls or community centres. Here the very landscape stands as an epitaph to nineteenth-century capitalism.

The area is full of epitaphs of one kind or another. A few miles from Darkley in a shabby little bus shelter is written: *There are 2 solutions in Northern Ireland. One is to get down on both knees and pray. The other one is to get down on both knees and shoot the other man.* This, surely, is an epitaph to community relations, a product of a place that has been locked for the last quarter of a century in a state of incipient civil war.

Just beyond Keady, heading towards the border, the hamlet of Darkley stands, an isolated, foreboding little cluster of working-class houses dominated by an old linen mill. It looks like a small-scale version of Bradford incongruously set down in a pastoral landscape, a world away from a one-horse south Armagh village. Indeed it is more like a setting for a scene from Dickens's *Hard Times* or an image of Blake's "dark Satanic mills". These days the mill is far from Satanic, having closed down thirty years ago and been converted into an egg production factory. It is also occupied by a community service centre named, apparently without irony, "Crossfire".

Another epitaph of sorts is found on a hill overlooking Darkley. The Mountain Lodge Road, which links it to the hamlet, is in stretches little more than a dirt track. It is one of those places in Northern Ireland where the Protestant siege mentality is physically present. On this hill stands the Mountain Lodge Pentecostal church. It is situated in a cockpit of the Northern conflict. From the church grounds the numerous British army observation posts can be seen perched on hills overlooking the small farms, poor fields and winding dirt roads of south Armagh. In the sky, British army

1

helicopters that look like tiny tadpoles in the distance whiz to and fro from one isolated military base to another. Here republicans like to think that the conflict is at its purest. It is them against the British forces holed up in fortified bases strung along the border.

Darkley is a reminder, however, of another side to the struggle.

Next to the Pentecostal church is a long brown wooden hut, the place where the epitaph of the Irish National Liberation Army was written on a dark November evening in 1983. Three men equipped with INLA guns burst into a prayer service and, as the congregation sang hymn 171, "Have you been to Jesus for the cleansing pow'r … Oh, to be washed in the blood of the lamb," they sprayed the worshippers in a deadly hail of bullets. Three church elders, Victor Cunningham, David Wilson, and Harold Brown, were cut down, mortally wounded. Among the injured were the two daughters of the church's pastor, Bob Pains. The gunmen drove off into the darkness towards Monaghan, leaving the hut awash with the blood of the wounded and dying worshippers.

The church was founded in Monaghan, only three miles distant, in 1915. The spiritual community that worships on the Mountain Lodge Road does not recognise the frontier as a barrier dividing their communion. There are around two thousand Pentecostalists in the Republic, who share their beliefs with eight thousand of their brethren in the North.

Nine years before the massacre, the INLA had been founded by a group of republican socialists dedicated to the politics of James Connolly and the dream of a united, non-sectarian, democratic socialist republic. It denied responsibility for the atrocity at Darkley. A group calling itself the Catholic Reaction Force said that it had carried out the attack. Its statement claimed that the deaths were only a "token" reaction to killings by loyalist gangs. The CRF boasted that if it had wished it could have killed twenty or more Protestants that night.

The CRF was a fiction, a mask behind which to hide. In the fog of sectarian war, paramilitary groups often find it convenient to invent such bogus organisations. But it fooled no-one: the weapons were INLA weapons, and one of the killers was a well-known INLA member seeking revenge for the death of his brother who had earlier been slain by loyalists. The year before, another brother had been shot dead by a police anti-terrorist unit. The name "CRF" was a mask donned to try to hide a shameful act, one that made a grotesque mockery of the ideals of Connolly, Tone and the whole pantheon of republican gods.

How then could members of an organisation that worships at the altar of such republican deities become involved in a blatant sectarian atrocity carried out against defenceless people during a religious service?

INLA volunteers had been involved before in sectarian killings of one sort or another. To the traditional republican role of achieving an independent unitary state has been added that of defending an at times beleaguered Catholic population. On occasion, this has been used as a justification for the retaliatory killings of Protestants. That is, the INLA, like all Northern Ireland's republican groups, straddles the dark gulf of sectarian violence. At times the gulf has consumed them.

The road to Darkley was not direct. When the INLA set out in 1974 it had never intended that it would end up in such a sectarian cul-de-sac. How it arrived at that place is more than just the story of one organisation. It is also the story of violent republicanism in Ireland today, and of the contradictions and conflicts that have developed within it over the last quarter of a century to produce one of its most violent and unpredictable off-shoots: the Irish National Liberation Army.

1

FAULT LINES

In 1974 it seemed as if Northern Ireland was tottering on the edge of the abyss of civil war.

In May the Ulster Workers' Council, backed by the largest of the loyalist paramilitary organisations, the Ulster Defence Association (UDA), had in effect taken over the state, compelling the power-sharing government to resign. That same month thirty-three people were killed in a UVF bombing attack in Dublin and Monaghan. The summer that followed saw a sharp escalation in sectarian killings. Police uncovered a Provisional IRA "doomsday" plan. That autumn the Provisional IRA was drawn into a tit-for-tat murder campaign that for the first time saw more Protestants falling victim to assassination gangs than Catholics. As winter approached, Long Kesh internment camp went up in flames during a rebellion by republican prisoners. A vicious bombing campaign in England culminated in the loss of twenty-one lives in bomb attacks on two Birmingham pubs.

At the beginning of the year the Provisional leadership had proclaimed it the "Year of Victory". But by December 1974, in a year that had seen 216 deaths in Northern Ireland alone, most of them sectarian, only those who were pushing for civil war looked as if they would enjoy a victory.

On Sunday 8 December a group of about eighty republicans gathered at the Spa Hotel in Lucan, outside Dublin. The vast majority of them were former members of the Official republican movement who had either been expelled or had left the organisation in recent months. Their leader was Séamus Costello, a local councillor from Bray and formerly director of operations of the Official IRA and vice-president of Official Sinn Féin. Thirty-five years old, with a lick of black hair hanging over his forehead, Costello's Italianate good looks and charm had stood him in good stead during his days as a car salesman; he had become his company's salesman of the year. But by the early 1960s he had given up selling cars and had devoted all his energies to promoting revolution.

Even his enemies agreed that he was an impressive figure—dynamic and charismatic, a powerful speaker and a non-stop worker who lived off coffee.

And even his friends agreed that at times he was too cunning and secretive, at times over-confident, trusting no-one. In 1974, Costello had embarked on a dangerous venture, one that involved the splitting of the movement to which he had dedicated his life.

He was born in Old Connaught Avenue, Bray, in 1939. He had become a republican at the age of fourteen, when he read an account of the arrest of Cathal Goulding during an IRA arms raid on the Officers' Training Corps School at Felstead in Essex. The raid had been intended to get arms to enable the IRA to launch a campaign against Northern Ireland. Now, twenty-one years later, Costello had decided to make a definitive political break with Goulding, chief of staff of the Official IRA, whose exploits had once inspired him to become involved in republican politics.

Almost exactly five years had passed since the republican movement split into Provisional and Official wings. The fault lines that created the break in 1969 had been laid down in the reaction to the failure of the 1950s campaign. Many republicans had become bitter and disillusioned with physical force and its failure to solve the Northern problem; their attempt to end partition by violent means had met with no popular support among Northern Ireland's nationalists. The campaign ended with a whimper, not a bang. Some drifted away from the IRA in the aftermath of the campaign, like survivors escaping from a sinking ship. Among those who remained, an influential few wanted to pursue broader issues and make republicanism relevant to the 26 Counties.

Costello would have been counted among those members of what was left of the IRA who were keen to open up a new way forward. He thought that the key to this was to fight elections in the south with the goal of entering the Dáil. Couple this with a radical social policy, and republicanism had a chance of filling the left-wing vacuum in Irish political life. Costello's keenness to end abstentionism had got him into trouble with the leadership in 1968. Though still very young, he had outgrown the narrow militarism that so limited its scope in the 1950s. He saw its refusal to recognise the Dáil as self-defeating dogmatism, which had to be discarded if the movement was to advance along a wide front embracing socialism, community activism, parliamentary politics, and the armed struggle. In his time, unlike other prominent leaders such as Cathal Goulding and Seán Garland, he managed to become involved in each, believing that if republicanism had a future it had to combine all four.

As a Sinn Féin member of Bray Urban District Council and Wicklow County Council, he knew the worth of politics as a means to agitate, disrupt and radicalise the electorate. For, unlike Garland and Goulding—those most closely identified with the new strategy—Costello did more than theorise about the creation of a popular republican party: he actually built one, in County Wicklow, where before Sinn Féin as an organisation had not existed. He was actively involved in the setting up of housing action committees, tenants' associations, and community pressure groups.

Many of those who had remained within the Official republican movement after 1969 had done so not because they necessarily agreed with the leadership's views on the future course republicanism might take but because they had suspected the Provisionals of not having any real politics at all. They spoke contemptuously of the Provos as the "Rosary beads brigade". They were attracted to the Officials because it had linked radical ideas to the gun. Many others had remained simply because of personal loyalties, which often play a more crucial role than ideological reasons in deciding who goes with what faction.

The eighty delegates who gathered in Lucan on 8 December 1974 represented the core of supporters that Costello had gathered around him during his disputes with the Official leadership over the previous two years. Among his staunchest allies was a group of Belfast men led by Ronnie Bunting, the son of Rev. Ian Paisley's former ally, Major Ronald Bunting; Vincent Fegan; and the brothers Seán and Harry Flynn.

Belfast had always been a problem with the Dublin leadership. In 1969, Belfast republicans had forcibly taken over the IRA prior to the first split and deposed the area's OC, Billy McMillen, because he was identified too closely with Goulding's new-look movement in the south. Then, they had wanted guns and action. In 1974 the motivation of those ex-Officials who went to Lucan to join Costello was remarkably similar. They suspected Dublin of either not understanding Belfast's needs or of not being sympathetic to them. The southern-based leadership was slow to send them gear. "The Sticks supplied shit to the North," one former Official IRA man put it. Then he added: "Except when the Provos got out of hand." (Interview, 22 April 1993). Men like Bunting and the Flynns suspected that the real enemy of the Official IRA was no longer the British security apparatus but the Provisional IRA.

As the Official IRA kept its guns silent, Belfast was witnessing one of the worst outbreaks of sectarian violence since the troubles had begun. Between 9 and 26 November there were fifteen assassinations in the city, claiming the lives of eight Protestants and seven Catholics. For the first time it looked as if there was a "Catholic backlash", with slightly more Protestants being murdered than Catholics. The Provisional IRA, in theory opposed to sectarian attacks, was in fact actively involved in retaliating against loyalists.

The Provisionals had at the same time launched a vicious bombing campaign in England that autumn. The Birmingham bombs had occurred a few weeks before the IRSP was formed. As the Provos' "Year of Victory" drew to a close they were clearly desperate to win some concession from the British that would justify their extravagant prediction. An all-out bombing campaign in England was designed to force the British government to talks.

The Provisionals were, in fact, in some disarray in Belfast. The young, left-leaning leaders had all been jailed; the organisation was in the hands of less militant men close to the Dublin leadership who were eager to facilitate some sort of face-saving compromise with the British. Most alarming for some, traditional republican goals had been replaced by increasing emphasis on coming to terms with extreme loyalists, many of whom were at that time talking of an independent Ulster. Provisional leaders like Dáithí Ó Conaill were pursuing the idea of a "federal Ireland" with a devolved government in Ulster as a way perhaps of convincing loyalists that they had nothing to fear from republicanism. He had even praised the Ulster Workers' Council strike of the previous May, which had brought down the power-sharing executive. He had called for "an end to the sterile discussion of a United Ireland versus Union with Gt. Britain. Let us have meaningful talks about a New Ulster creating a new Ireland." (*Hibernia*, 6 April 1976.)

So by late 1974 it appeared to many republican activists not only that the Official IRA was betraying the struggle for a united socialist Ireland but that the Provisionals were undergoing an "Ulsterisation" of their politics in a dangerous bid to win over Protestant support and wring concessions from the British. Within two days of the IRSP's formation, Dáithí Ó Conaill met Protestant clergymen from Northern Ireland at Feakle in County Clare. Twelve days later, on 22 December, the Provisionals would declare a truce that would last—after an initial breakdown—for the better part of a year. The consequences this would have for the new organisation that emerged from the 8 December gathering would prove profound. But this lay in the future.

The delegates who arrived in Lucan that Sunday came from all corners of Ireland: as well as Belfast and Derry they came from Armagh, Donegal, Wicklow, Cork, Clare, Dublin, Limerick, and Tipperary. All but a handful shared a common past: membership of the Official republican movement. How they had arrived at the decision to irrevocably break with what many still regarded as *the* IRA and set off on a new course can only be understood in the light of what had happened to the "Stickies"—as they were known in Belfast—between 1970 and 1974.

When the twelve members of the IRA convention trooped out of the meeting in November 1969 to form the Provisional IRA, they left behind them a mixed bag of republican socialists whose ideas on how the "struggle" might develop were far from consistent. Though the members of what soon became known as the Officials agreed on one thing, the need for socialism in Ireland, they differed on how a socialist state with the workers in control of the means of production was to be achieved. Most importantly, there were profound differences on the relationship between this question and the national question. Two tendencies quickly emerged. The first and dominant one saw the march towards a socialist Ireland taking place in three stages: the democratisation of Northern Ireland, during which the Protestant and Catholic working class would unite, followed by national independence, followed by the triumph of socialism. This meant that if the unity of Catholic and Protestant workers had to come before national unity, any act that made that more difficult and retarded its progress was counter-revolutionary. It was, in fact, the theoretical foundation for a policy of gradual withdrawal from the armed struggle in the North.

A smaller tendency within the Officials took the view that the national question and the social question were not to be approached in schematic stages but had to be fought for at the same time. This faction was grouped around Séamus Costello and had the support of many of the most militant members of the Officials in the Northern ghettos.

Since the mid-1960s, Costello had been advocating the joint nature of the struggle the republican movement had to undertake if it were to play a meaningful role as a revolutionary party. Giving the oration in Bodenstown in June 1966 at the republican movement's annual Wolfe Tone commemoration, in a historic speech marking the swing to the left of the IRA and Sinn Féin, Costello emphasised the dual concerns of socialism and armed struggle that characterised his thinking.

"We also believe that the large estates of absentee landlords should be acquired by compulsory acquisition and worked on a co-operative basis, with financial and technical assistance of the state ... Our policy is to nationalise the key industries with the eventual aim of co-operative ownership by the workers. The capital necessary to carry out this programme can be made available by the nationalisation of all banks, insurance companies, loan and investment companies whose present policy is the reinvestment of our hard-earned money in foreign fields.

"This in short is our policy. This is our definition of freedom. It was Tone's definition, Lalor's definition, Mitchel's definition, and the stated aim of Pearse and Connolly. We can expect the same reaction to the implementation of these aims from the forces of exploitation, whether native or foreign-sponsored, as the originators received in '98, '47, '67, and 1916. Therefore, to imagine that we can establish a republic solely by constitutional means is utter folly. The lesson of history shows that in the final analysis the robber baron must be disestablished by the same methods that he used to enrich himself and retain his ill-gotten gains, namely force of arms. To this end we must organise, train and maintain a disciplined armed force which will always be available to strike at the opportune moment." (Quoted in *Séamus Costello, 1939–1977: Irish Republican Socialist*, published by the Séamus Costello Memorial Committee.)

On 29 October 1968, a few weeks after a civil rights march in Derry was batoned by the Royal Ulster Constabulary, thrusting the Northern Ireland problem onto the world's television screens, Costello spoke to the Trinity College Republican Club, founded four years earlier as part of the drive to reach a new audience for republicanism. (It was to become for a time the biggest club in the university.) Costello made plain the centrality of the social struggle in the fight for national independence.

"We have followed false prophets on more than one occasion. We have followed prophets who told us that our job was to achieve political independence and not to concern ourselves with what type of social or economic structure we would have after independence. We have listened to leaders who said that such matters as unemployment, emigration and starvation were not our concern. It is not long ago since we fought a military campaign in the North and failed because of our mistaken beliefs in such policies. We learnt one lesson from that campaign, and I for one feel that the lesson was dearly purchased. We learnt that it is impossible to expect the support of people for a movement that advocates political independence without demonstrating exactly what this independence will mean to the people." (Quoted by Séamus Carraher in "Costello: Scenario for a Nonfiction Film Based on the Life of Séamus Costello", 1986.)

These were the political ambitions that Costello took with him into the Official republican movement after the 1969 split. For two years the impetus of the Northern crisis carried the Official IRA along: it was too powerful for the Goulding leadership to halt. The Provisionals might have grown faster, but the Officials had a more solid following, and in certain areas such as Derry city, Newry and south Down and parts of Belfast they were in fact the dominant group. It was the Officials who first engaged the British in a major shoot-out in Belfast, on 3 July 1970. Three thousand troops were sent into the Lower Falls area, one of the Officials' strongholds, where they had up to 150 volunteers. Rioting developed, and soon the Officials were conducting running gun-battles, forcing the authorities to impose a curfew. During the fighting, Provisionals aided Officials and vice versa. When it was over, four civilians had been killed by the troops and sixty injured.

Near the centre of Belfast lay the Markets area, the base of the legendary Joe McCann, where the Official IRA competed with the Provisionals in firepower. The first British soldier to die at the hands of the Official IRA in the city was killed there on 21 May 1971. McCann and his men opened fire on a British mobile patrol as it passed through Cromac Square, raking it from two sides. (The soldier was the fourth member of the British army to die that year.) The Markets area was to play a vital role not only in the history of the Official IRA but in that of the INLA.

McCann, like Costello, was a charismatic leader. Affable, good-looking, and eager for action, he was perhaps the nearest thing the Northern crisis has produced to a Che Guevara figure. A former bricklayer, McCann had been reared in the Lower Falls area, though he was active mainly in the Markets district. His connection with the IRA went back to 1965, when he was arrested with four others outside a rural police station because he was acting suspiciously. He and his friends were given a year's sentence for possessing bayonets.

When the 1969 split happened, McCann stayed with the Officials, because they were more "political". But his relationship with the Dublin leadership was not a happy one. He was court-martialled on at least two occasions. One of the incidents that led to his appearing before the IRA court is illustrative of the tensions that existed between some of the working-class rank and file of the Officials and a segment of their Dublin supporters. McCann and Seán Flynn were at a party given by the Republican Club in Trinity College—the same one to which Costello had made his speech in October 1968. Drink was taken, and the two Belfast men got into a dispute with what Flynn calls "trendy lefties". It ended in a fight, to the great embarrassment of the leadership, who were vigorously courting socialist and communist intellectuals.

When internment was introduced on 9 August 1971, McCann was OC and operations officer of the Third Battalion in Belfast. He and his men took over Inglis's bakery in Eliza Street in the Markets and, according to legend, held six hundred British troops at bay. The silhouetted image of McCann holding an M1 carbine watching the flames rise over the burning and beleaguered city as the Starry Plough flutters above him is perhaps the most evocative to come out of the internment crisis; it is certainly the most romantic, and marks the high water mark of the Official IRA's revolutionary reputation. The movement's monthly, the *United Irishman*, published this picture of McCann on the front page of its September 1971 issue with the headline "Army of the people" emblazoned across it.

Following Bloody Sunday, the pressure on the Officials to retaliate could not be resisted. Costello, as GHQ operations officer, planned to strike back at the Parachute Regiment, which had been involved in the civil rights massacre. A special six-man active service unit—which included a former member of the Parachute Regiment—was sent to England, where it targeted the regiment's headquarters in Aldershot. On 22 February the ex-para left the bomb in the barracks. It exploded, and killed six cleaning women and a chaplain.

It was the first bombing attack in England during the current Troubles, and it had gone disastrously wrong. It confirmed the fears of those on the Army Council who viewed the "armed campaign" as a political liability. Three days later another active service unit ambushed John Taylor, then Minister of Home Affairs in the Stormont government. Joe McCann and the South Down OC, Paul Tinnelly, along with two other leading Official IRA men who are still alive, were involved in the attack. They opened fire on Taylor with Thompson submachine-guns as he got into his car in Armagh. Five bullets went through his head and jaw, and another ten went past his nose. Though badly wounded, he survived. Yet again it was a case of the Officials' ambition exceeding their reach.

Two months later the Officials' military wing suffered another set-back. On the night of 14 April, McCann, then one of the most wanted men in the North, showed up in the Markets area, much to the concern of his friends, who knew the British army was out to get him. He could not resist stopping off at a pub in Cromac Street for a drink. As usual, he disdained any disguise. The next morning he was spotted by a well-known Special Branch inspector in one of the side streets off Cromac Street. The Special Branch man alerted a patrol of the Parachute Regiment. McCann, known as a gunman and a member of the organisation that had bombed Aldershot, believed he would not be taken alive. When he saw the patrol he made a run for it and tried to get off the street by pushing at doors with his shoulder. None opened. He reached the corner of Joy Street and Hamilton Street when the patrol cut him down. A local shopkeeper counted ten spent cartridges near his body. McCann was unarmed at the time he was shot—allegedly because the Officials' leadership had confiscated his personal protection weapon, a .38. The killing generated one of the earliest "shoot-to-kill" controversies, and an inquiry was demanded but never granted. It also generated allegations that McCann had been deliberately set up by the leadership, who were unhappy at his militancy.

However, in the immediate aftermath of McCann's death there was no lack of militancy. The nationalist ghettos of Belfast and Derry exploded. Three British soldiers were shot dead within hours of McCann's killing, two by the Official IRA in Derry and one by the Divis Flats Officials, part of D Company, Second Battalion, one of the most active units in the city. It was then being led by Jim Sullivan, who later became a Republican Clubs (Official Sinn Féin) city councillor and one of the most outspoken critics of terrorism. According to the report in the *United Irishman* (May 1971), "the intensity of the firing around the flats was so great that British troops were pinned down for several hours." Two other soldiers were seriously injured. Barricades went up in Belfast: in Ballymurphy, Andersonstown, the Falls, and Turf Lodge, which was sealed off from the security forces. In Newry, Official IRA gunmen wounded two soldiers who were on mobile patrol.

On 18 April the Officials' chief of staff, Cathal Goulding, came north to give the oration at McCann's funeral. It proved to be the largest republican gathering to date, with estimates of the number of mourners in attendance varying between six and twenty thousand. Over twenty Official IRA men marched behind the coffin, and more than two hundred women carried wreaths. It was not until the deaths of the hunger strikers nine years later that such crowds were to assemble again at any republican gathering.

On a windswept but mild spring day the vast crowd flooded into Milltown Cemetery, Belfast, to hear Goulding speak. The Official IRA's chief of staff rose to the occasion.

"We come here today to pay tribute to a soldier of the Irish Republican Army who was murdered by the forces of the Crown, to a man who was shot like a dog by the agents of imperialism, by the agents of the Orange junta with the murderous assistance of the political police force of imperialism and Orangism, by the forces of repression and sectarianism, by the forces of evil. It is in itself a tribute to an officer of the Irish Republican Army that his death should have been caused by this combination of corruption and might, that it should have been thought necessary to shoot down, unarmed, in the streets of the city he loved and which honoured him as a man, a volunteer of the IRA who might have been branded a terrorist but who was feared because he had in him the essence of revolutionary spirit and determination.

"We come to pay tribute to Joe McCann, to the man, the soldier, the political activist, the revolutionary, to the Irish republican socialist who personified the struggle of the people for full political and civil rights in the occupied six counties of our land. We are here because we loved him, because we honoured his idealism, because we shared his vision of a country, of a people, free from the vicious shackles of Orange capitalism, free from the corrosive influence of imperialism, free from the repression that has been aimed and ever will be aimed at the working-class people of this country, north and south, Catholic and Protestant—at the working people whose defence was Joe McCann's duty and his pride.

"But in remembering him, let there be *no* doubt that in the days to come the courage, the determination and the political vision of Joe McCann will be remembered by generations of Irishmen with gratitude and pride, and let us keep in our minds the tradition that he so proudly bore. Let us recognise that it was human and humane, let us recognise that it was revolutionary and sympathetic, let us recognise that it was integrally a part of the people's struggle without pause for consideration of religious difference or political sectarianism.

"Joe McCann, lying on the bloodstained ground of this embattled city, made a sacrifice for the people. Let no-one be mistaken that this sacrifice was in vain. Let no-one be mistaken about the reasons why it was made. Let none who come here and none who listen with the ears of Glengall Street or Westminster or Dublin Castle be in any doubt about the existence of a force which is aimed at their masters' destruction, by force of the people's arms, by will of the people's conviction, by the overwhelming need of the people to be free of all and every agent of the imperial demand. Let no-one doubt that the ultimate retribution for the death of Joe McCann will be achieved.

"People of Belfast, who have lost a son, a brother, a defender, let me remind you of the tribute paid to Joe McCann. Let it be your guide and conscience and your motivation. For it was the tribute paid to Volunteer McCann by the people of the place he defended in August 1971, the tribute of emulation. The County Antrim Executive of the Republican Clubs said of him: 'Conscious of the fact that the true liberation of the working classes could only be achieved in the establishment of a socialist republic, Joe had worked constantly to build the revolutionary socialist movement. Much of his time was spent in studying the problems of his area, in educating the members of the movement in his area to the ideals of true republicanism and in working at ground level to change the system which oppresses the ordinary people. He drew his political philosophy from the writings of James Connolly, a man on whose work and ideals he attempted to base his life. It is a measure of the man's greatness that the same authorities who brutally murdered James Connolly meted out the same treatment to Joe McCann for carrying on the same tradition.

"'Joe McCann would never have been satisfied with any type of 32-county gombeen republic. He knew that the answer to Ireland's problems lay in the implementation of socialist ideals. It was to this end that he worked and it was for this reason that he died. His death will not be in vain if we continue to carry on his work, if we continue to build the revolutionary movement, if we continue to organise, educate and agitate until we achieve our final goal, the liberation of Ireland's people and the establishment of a 32-county socialist republic.'

"People of Belfast, there is little need for me to say more to you. You knew his strength, the humanity and the conviction that belonged to Joe McCann. You knew the stress he laid on studying the needs of the area in which he worked; you knew in the bitter month of August 1971 his courage in that area's defence; you knew the vision of the streets, the city and the state that he held within his heart and expressed in action as much as words. And Joe McCann wove words in action with greater power than any dreaming pedagogue with pen and microphone at his command.

"Learn this lesson, and learn it well, because Joe McCann was its master: that action on the streets and in the factories and in the homes of the working people is the best education that a people can have. The lesson of the barricades, the lesson of Inglis's bakery, the lesson of a community thrown upon its own resources—this is the lesson of revolution.

"Remember now, as you stand around his grave, that Joe McCann was not once but doubly and trebly murdered by the forces of the Crown. Once, by the act of shooting him down. Once, by the act of making him and his working people potential slaves to domination. And once, by the strange, impersonal demands that are the military corollary of their territorial imperative. Pearse quoted a French writer saying of the English that they never commit a useless crime. When they hire a man to assassinate an Irish patriot, when they blow a sepoy from the mouth of a cannon, when they produce a famine in one of their own dependencies, they have always had an ulterior motive. They don't do it for entertainment.

"By shooting Joe McCann, their Whitelaws and their Heaths and their Tuzos have shown the colour of their so-called peace initiatives. They have re-declared war on the people. They have spelt out again the rules under which that war will be fought. Our answer to them is to fight them on our terms, not on theirs. We will retaliate against the formulators of that policy. We have given notice, by action that no words can now efface, that those who are responsible for the terrorism that is Britain's age-old reaction to Irish demands will be the victims of that terrorism, paying richly in their own red blood for their crimes and the crimes of their imperial masters.

"Joe McCann goes to his grave, not in defeat but in triumph. Not defeated, but at the moment of victory. A man of courage, of integrity and of vision, essentially an Irish republican and a socialist; a man. At his graveside, we say to those who murdered him: you have the weapons and the strength, but with men like Joe McCann to carry on the struggle of the Irish people, the Irish Republican Army, in the words of Fintan Lalor, will task that strength and break the heart of empire."

This sounded very much like a call to arms; but for some who were listening, its revolutionary rhetoric clashed with what they knew about the leadership's problems with McCann and other militants who followed his example. The romantic image of the urban guerrilla that the Officials were at that time happy to exploit was in conflict with the long-term goals of the movement, and so inevitably there were tensions.

A former IRA man who had been a member of Séamus Costello's active service unit in south Derry in the 1956–62 campaign spoke bitterly about what he saw as the Official IRA leadership's real attitude to McCann.

"Joe McCann was one of the folk heroes of the Official IRA and Joe McCann was very close to Séamus Costello. And when Joe was killed a bit before that he was very out of favour with the leadership of the Officials in Belfast. Because they said he was too kind of militant, he was too on for military action, that he was really a Provo in his outlook. That's what they were saying about him a few nights before he died. They said it in this house. I had a few drinks with them. The people who were down from Belfast were giving out about Joe and they were going to throw Joe out on his ear. And he got killed on the Saturday after that and they had a big fancy funeral and then Goulding got up at the funeral and said they shall pay in their own red blood, that's a quotation from Yeats. And I met Goulding afterwards and I said I hope you meant what you said ... Joe's death hurt Séamus a lot because Joe was the type of person that Séamus liked. He was pretty political Joe was, he was very well read and he was a militant. Now if you saw the big funeral they had for Joe, the way they went on about it and we knew the way they thought about him." (Unpublished interview by Séamus Carraher in "Costello: Scenario for a Nonfiction Film Based on the Life of Séamus Costello".)

Similar allegations were made by another former member of the Officials. He said he was in the Officials' Gardiner Place head office in the week before McCann was shot and noticed that the famous Inglis Bakery poster had been taken down.[1]

"When I asked why, the guy just said he had been ordered to. When I got to speak to one of the leaders I asked him what was the crack about Joe. He told me that Joe was causing a lot of dissension in the north and was in big trouble. I didn't think much of it at the time, but I found out later that they had taken his gun off him and ordered him to stay away from the north." (*Irish News*, 13 March 1992.)

Others have gone as far as suggesting that McCann was not only out of favour with the leadership but was "set up" by them, because they were determined on a cease-fire and saw him as a threat. A man who had hidden McCann while he was on the run claimed he had had a conversation with him six weeks before his death. The man told the *Irish News* that McCann intended "setting up his own organisation" and suggested that the Officials' leadership wanted to have him killed. (Ibid.)

However, according to others who knew McCann he "hated splits, as they inevitably led to demoralisation, acrimony, and possibly feuds." (Thomas Power, "An historical analysis of the IRSP", *Starry Plough*, December 1987.)

McCann's widow vociferously denied the allegations that her husband had a dispute with the leadership of the Officials. "I know that he had great respect for Cathal Goulding and others whom I will not name. To say that any of his close comrades either in Belfast or Dublin deliberately set him up for murder is a foul lie." (*Irish News*, 12 May 1992.)

The truth about McCann's death is almost certainly more straightforward: bravado made him reckless. He returned to the very area where he was most sought. The allegations about his being deliberately set up seem to have been influenced by the bitterness caused by subsequent splits and feuds.

At any rate, his removal from the scene strengthened the position of those on the Army Council who were growing concerned that the armed campaign would jeopardise their efforts to build a political machine. They were also concerned at the rising tide of loyalist violence, and there were genuine fears that continued republican attacks would rouse a sectarian monster that could not be contained. In April the Republican Clubs had called meetings in the North to condemn the Provos' bombing campaign, which throughout the spring of that year was inflicting increasing suffering on civilians. A clear tendency was emerging in the Official IRA that was trying to dissociate itself from what it defined as "terrorist" violence, and Goulding was its main spokesman. Among the areas where the leadership had most problems was Derry. The city's Official IRA was one of the most active and militant in the North, at times rivalling the Provos in numbers and support. At its peak it had around three hundred volunteers, according to former members. Its OC was Johnny White, a left-winger and a veteran of the civil rights movement. The Army Council feared that there were "ultra-left" elements involved. In early 1972 an attempt was made to bring Derry into line, with a "sound" Goulding supporter being despatched from Belfast to do the job. As subsequent events were to show, the mission was not a success.

Following Bloody Sunday, the Army Council in Dublin had issued instructions that any British soldier, on or off duty, was to be shot. On 21 May the Officials in Derry "arrested" William Best, a young man from the Creggan who was in the British army and at home on leave. He was tried and shot, in keeping with the Army Council's instructions. The killing provoked outrage in the Bogside and Creggan areas, where Best was well known. Two hundred women marched in protest to the Officials' headquarters in the Creggan, calling for the organisation to get out of Derry. A meeting was held in a Creggan school, chaired by a former nationalist councillor, Tom Doherty, and demands were made for peace. Some Official IRA leaders, showed up at the meeting; they were refused permission to speak. The *Derry Journal* refused to continue printing the local Official republican newspaper, the *Starry Plough*. The Derry Provisionals, very conservative and Catholic in outlook, had always regarded the Officials with distrust and dislike, denouncing them in the *Derry Journal* for wanting to set up a "Marxist state ... a one-party state." *Better dead than red* graffiti were to be seen in the Brandywell area of the city, painted by local Provos. The Provisionals jumped on the anti-Official IRA bandwagon, demanding that they leave the Bogside and Creggan.

The day that Best was buried saw another demonstration: this time 1,500 women went to the Provisionals and demanded a cessation of hostilities. Some of the women had met the Northern Ireland Secretary of State, William Whitelaw. Already a group called the Peace Women had been formed in Andersonstown, Belfast, and had also met Whitelaw. It seemed as if the peace movement was gaining momentum.

The killing of Ranger Best, coming as it did after the Aldershot bombing and the failed assassination attempt on Taylor, provided the Army Council with the grounds they needed to call a halt to a violent campaign that some say they were intent on stopping from the beginning. Goulding was the most anxious to end it. On 29 May, six weeks after Goulding's flight of revolutionary rhetoric at McCann's funeral, the Official IRA called a ceasefire. The Army Council claimed that it had done this after being approached by the Executive of the Republican Clubs. "The Army Council of the Irish Republican Army confirms the statement issued by the Executive of Northern Republican Clubs. All units have now been informed of this decision and have been instructed to suspend all military actions, excepting only that we reserve the right of self-defence and the right to defend any who are under direct attack from the British Army or from any sectarian force. We have agreed to this proposal of the Republican Clubs because of our growing concern over the dangers of a sectarian civil war which could only set the cause of socialist revolution back many years. We feel that progress in the situation is dependent on a resumption of political activity, and would call on all Irish men and women to support the five points put forward by the Republican Clubs in their statement." (*United Irishman*, June 1972.)

The demands were listed as: "1) The release of all internees. 2) A general amnesty for all political prisoners in British or Irish jails, for men on the run and for all those against whom charges are pending as a result of their involvement in the civil disobedience campaign or because of resistance to British troops; and a write-off of all debts incurred as a result of the civil disobedience campaign. 3) The withdrawal of troops to barracks pending their ultimate withdrawal from the country, and an immediate end to military repression. 4) The abolition of the Special Powers Act in its entirety. 5) Freedom of political expression must be immediately established; the Republicans Clubs in particular demand their full democratic rights of political existence." (Ibid.)

The *United Irishman* gave this analysis of the ceasefire: "It opens up again the possibilities of political action. The only exception to the general suspension of armed actions is the reservation of the right of self-defence and the right to defend any area under aggressive attack by the British military or by sectarian forces from either side. The oppressed minority in the North who have been able to rely with confidence on the IRA as a defender of the people may still have that confidence.

"The reasons for taking this crucial decision lay in a growing awareness by the leadership of the Republican Movement that we had been drawn into a war that was not of our choosing, and that we were being forced to fight on enemy ground. The IRA has decided to reaffirm its political programme in an effort to avoid sectarian war, to bring about a political confrontation between the Irish people and British Imperialism.

"It is to be expected that the Provisionals may try and sabotage this development. But the onus rests in the main on the British aggressor forces. Obviously, if there were any repeat of the Bloody Sunday episode in Derry the IRA would have to reconsider its position. But for the moment the prospects look good for political progress: already the extreme Unionists and the Provisionals are finding themselves increasingly isolated, as people rally behind the Republican movement's banner."

The Officials spoke of "the beginning of a new phase of civil struggle." (Ibid.) Instead, the truce turned out to be the beginning of a struggle within the Official republican movement that would eventually lead to its disintegration. Many of the Official IRA's northern militants already had deep suspicions about the long-term intentions of the Dublin leadership. They alleged that, beginning in 1971, the Goulding leadership had been attempting to de-escalate the military campaign of the Official IRA, and had tried to use internment to this purpose. "Basically the rank and file wanted to expand the struggle while coming increasingly up against the leadership resolved on stopping it altogether. The introduction of internment was a blessing in disguise for this leadership as it allowed them to gradually wind their involvement in the struggle down as many militants were interned, arms supplies began to dry up etc." (Thomas Power, "An historical analysis of the IRSP".)

Yet whatever the twists and turns of Army Council policy, there remained north of the border a militant, well-organised group of men who by 1972 were veterans of guerrilla conflict. Many of them saw no reason to halt the conflict at that point.

How then did the leadership in Dublin sell them the cease-fire? It was simple: Séamus Costello. Ironically, it was Costello who went around the country reassuring the volunteers that, basically, nothing had changed. "When the Officials went on a ceasefire Séamus had to go out and meet people. People were saying, 'What's this ceasefire thing?' and he'd say, 'Well, generally, it's just to get the internees out' … It was to be a very short-term thing. But it transpired that it was a permanent thing. I'd say Séamus was very much caught out." (Séamus Carraher, "Costello: Scenario for a Nonfiction Film Based on the Life of Séamus Costello".)

The ceasefire terms, allowing the IRA to carry out "defensive and retaliatory" action, meant that the war would go on. According to one former member of the Officials, "many members came away from meetings held to discuss the cease-fire thinking nothing had changed."

The Tupamaros guerrillas of Uruguay had a slogan, "Words are divisive; action unites." (Regis Debray, *The Revolution on Trial*, Penguin Books, 1978.) Following the suspension of regular action by the Officials on 29 May, the organisation's internal divisions began to manifest themselves very rapidly as the internal debate grew more and more bitter.

The two most dangerous areas as far as the leadership was concerned were Derry and Belfast. In both places, local grievances were the same: lack of weapons to enforce the defence and retaliatory clauses of the cease-fire. This was coupled to a certain unease that weapons seemed to be plentiful only when there were disputes with the Provisionals that needed to be settled. The pattern was established within weeks of the cease-fire.

At the end of June 1972 the Provisionals declared their own truce. But, unlike that of the Officials, theirs was a prelude to top-level negotiations with the British government itself. During the two weeks the truce lasted, Provo gunmen manned road-blocks throughout the Catholic ghettos. At one of these, in the Ballymurphy area, James Bryson, Tommy Tolan and John Stone were on guard when a car drove through without stopping. They opened fire, and a man was killed. Jim Sullivan, the hero of the Official IRA during the battle following McCann's death, issued a statement denouncing the Provisionals as "toy soldiers". Angered, Bryson and his men "arrested" Harry Flynn, then a member of the area's Official IRA unit, and took him to "Jim's Castle"—a shop in the Ballymurphy housing estate that Bryson had converted into a makeshift jail; there he held wife-beaters, petty criminals, and drunks who couldn't find their way home. Flynn was furious at Sullivan for issuing the condemnation without warning the local Official unit, whose members had to face the consequences of it.

When the Officials arrived to rescue their imprisoned colleague, there were scuffles. Within hours, weapons flooded into the area for the local Official IRA volunteers who had been complaining uselessly up to now about the scarcity of them. Most of the guns—Ruger rifles and American M16s, known as "grease-guns"—had been moved up from the Lower Falls, which always was the best-armed Official IRA unit in Belfast. It also happened to be the most loyal to the Garland-Goulding leadership. Fortunately, the guns were not required, and confrontation between the two groups was avoided.

It was not long after this that a delegation of Official IRA volunteers from Belfast went to Dublin to protest to Goulding that they lacked the equipment to (a) engage in defence and retaliation against the British and (b) defend themselves against the Provisionals. The delegation laid heavy stress upon the second point. Within a week they had thirty Ruger rifles at their disposal.

From Derry came similar stories. Relations between the Officials and the Provisionals were bad, and grew worse after the truce. Tension reached breaking point when a member of the Provisional IRA took a weapon from an arms dump controlled by the Officials. When Official IRA men went after their gun, the two organisations were on the verge of a shoot-out. The Official IRA leadership in Dublin was contacted and told that the Provos were causing problems. Immediately, Ruger rifles and grease-guns were despatched to the city. Again, as in Belfast, the result was a stand-off. But the Official IRA volunteers who were troubled by the cease-fire began to have even more serious doubts about just who it was their leaders were expecting them to oppose—the Provos or the British. There were efforts, however, to reassure the Northern units that the Official IRA's Army Council was still ready to fight. Over a period of a year after the truce, the Officials claimed to have killed seven British soldiers in retaliatory attacks.

In 1973 the three Belfast battalions were amalgamated into one command structure, with Billy McMillen in charge. McMillen was trusted by many in the movement. He was a veteran of the 1950s, and had spent time—like so many—in the Crumlin jail. He had raised the Tricolour and Starry Plough in Divis Street at the foot of the Falls when the Republican Clubs ran him as candidate in the October 1964 general election, sparking off the first riot in many years in Belfast. He came from the Lower Falls, and his decision to stay with the Goulding leadership in the 1969 split kept many of the volunteers in that area loyal to the Officials. It was there that he had commanded the Officials during the July 1970 shoot-out with the British army. So when, in 1973, he argued that centralisation would ensure greater efficiency, many believed him.

It meant, of course, increasingly tight control from Dublin. However, to dispel any disquiet that might have arisen, the volunteers were told that plans were being laid for a co-ordinated series of mortar attacks against British army bases throughout the North. It would demonstrate the efficiency of the new system and at the same time show that the Officials meant what they said when they talked about "defence and retaliation". Selected volunteers were taken south to a camp in County Tipperary, where they were trained in the use of home-made mortars that were of reasonably good quality. Back across the border, targets were selected. Fort Monagh near Andersonstown, Silver City on the Whiterock Road and bases in Ardoyne and Lurgan were among those to be attacked.

When the day came, the attack on Silver City had to be abandoned. The attack on Fort Monagh was interrupted by the arrival of a foot patrol. One mortar did fire in Ardoyne but caused no casualties. In Lurgan there was a fatality among the security forces, but his death was certainly not as a result of the operational brilliance of his enemies. The mortar jammed in the tube and a volunteer was injured. The equipment was abandoned. A British patrol arrived on the scene, and a soldier unwisely turned the tube upside down. The mortar fell out, exploded, and killed him. According to former Official IRA volunteers, this was the last attempt to put the defence and retaliation option into operation by the command staff. It had proved to be an embarrassing failure.

Discontent found its voice in Séamus Costello, the operations officer for GHQ. As the months passed, he gathered about him others in the movement who shared his unease—people like Mick Plunkett and Gerry Roche from Dún Laoghaire, Tommy McCourt, Johnny White, Séamus O'Kane and Terry Robson from Derry, the Flynns, Vinty Fegan, Frank Gallagher and Ronnie Bunting from Belfast, Stella Makowski from Limerick, and John O'Doherty, Séamus O'Kane and John "Eddy" McNichol from south Derry, where Costello had earned his nickname "the Boy General" in the 1956–62 campaign.

"We came together to try and change Official IRA policy," Terry Robson, who became an IRSP leader in Derry, relates. "We were opposed to the cease-fire, because we felt we were building up support, competing with the Provos." He also felt it was important to offer an alternative to the Provos, who in the mid-1970s remained politically undeveloped, if not downright conservative. According to Seán Flynn, "the INLA/IRSP didn't start on 8 December 1974. It existed within the Officials around Costello from after the cease-fire in 1972."

Costello had decided to fight what turned out to be a rearguard action against Army Council policy: he believed he could change that policy from within. He continued to believe until a week before the formation of the IRSP and INLA that the Official leadership would be defeated and the movement saved from what he saw as "reformism" in the South and betrayal of the armed struggle in the North.

Between 1972 and 1973 the situation within the Officials seemed volatile as the role of the armed struggle was debated. The 1972 Official IRA army convention actually voted in favour of Costello's demands for continued support of the armed struggle in the North. On this topic he had drawn up a document with the collaboration of Seán Garland, the Official IRA's adjutant-general. Garland had formed a revolutionary republican bloc with Costello, the policy of which was laid out in what became known as "document A". It was entitled "A Brief Examination of the Republican Position: an Attempt to Formulate the Correct Demands and Methods of Struggle". It criticised the analysis that held that a three-stage approach was necessary in the North. This envisaged first a campaign for a democratic Northern Ireland state; and then, when the working class had been united on common social and economic goals, a revolutionary situation could be developed.

Costello and Garland wrote: "This position, the demand for a 6 county state, is of course occupied by Conor Cruise O'Brien and those ... who propagate the 2 Nations theory in Ireland. To accept it, even in part, leads one inevitably to the position where, as one foreign observer pointed out recently, we expect and look to the British Army to play a progressive role in Ireland. What a position for republicans!"

Goulding opposed the Costello-Garland document. Eventually he talked

Garland out of supporting Costello. Years later Goulding said: "Seán's big idea at the time was to get back to the high road of the Republic. I felt that meant we were going backwards into the past. I wanted things to move forward in a politically progressive direction. Seán had an idea that we went too fast with the cease-fire. He was deeply affected by the Provo split. He was depressed about things around 1973, when the Provos seemed to be going from strength to strength. He felt another split would be a disaster. But Seán and I never fell out, despite our disagreement about the document. I talked him round. I think that made him change his attitude to Costello, along with seeing our new policies in action: the fish-ins, the housing protests, our involvement in strikes, and so on." (Interview, 8 November 1993.)

Those who backed Costello did not have enough places on the Army Council to carry through the convention's policies. Meanwhile, at the Officals' ardfheiseanna of 1972 and 1973, Costello's position calling for a broad front to fight on the issue of the national question was accepted by the rank and file. However, the party's Ard-Chomhairle succeeded in frustrating the decisions of the delegates, just as the Army Council had done with the policies of the convention. When Garland veered towards the Goulding line, it surprised many of his comrades who had regarded the adjutant-general as still a militant, a physical force man committed to republican ideals. It also made more evident the fact that Costello was being marginalised.

A secret Official IRA document was drawn up in 1973 about "Volunteer Clancy". (Each member of GHQ had a false name. "Clancy" was Costello.) The document made two serious charges against him: that as director of operations he had not done his job, and that he had kept money from operations. In 1974, when Costello's final battle for survival within the movement was looming, this document began to circulate within the organisation. The Ard-Chomhairle was, according to Costello himself, "offering to 'explain' it at meetings throughout the country." Costello asked for the opportunity to attend such meetings in order to "give a balanced account of what actually occurred." His request was refused.

By 1974 the drive against Costello was already well organised. At the end of the previous year there had been a purge of his supporters from the Official republican movement; men like Terry Robson and Seán Flynn were expelled, as was Ronnie Bunting, once used by the Official IRA as proof that it could bridge the sectarian divide and appeal to Northern Protestants.

By early 1974, according to Seán Flynn's brother Harry, "the rumblings against the leadership in Belfast were volcanic." As Costello himself summed it up, "it was undoubtedly during this period of confused leadership as the civilian casualties mounted [in the North] and the strain at local level became unbearable, the National Question came to be abandoned and for the first time many rank and file members began to question the direction in which the whole movement was being led." (Séamus Carraher, "Costello: Scenario for a Nonfiction Film Based on the Life of Séamus Costello".)

The final move against Costello to force him out of Official Sinn Féin began when he was accused of organising block voting at the 1973 ardfheis, during which he had again been successfully elected to the Ard-Chomhairle. On 6 April 1974 the Ard-Chomhairle met and passed a motion setting up a committee of inquiry. It also passed a motion that "Séamus Costello be suspended from membership of Sinn Féin" pending the findings of the committee.

The committee of inquiry met on 20 April to hear the charges against Costello, which included one of "general unsuitability". Two witnesses claimed that Costello had approached them with a list of names that, if elected, would "constitute a good, militant Ard-Chomhairle." A third witness told the committee that Costello had said to him that he did "organise a block vote, but there was nothing could be done about it as it could not be proved, and in any case there was nothing in the rules against it."

However, the report of the committee was "inconclusive and specifically referred to the failure of two witnesses to attend." The full minutes of the proceedings of the committee of inquiry were given to the Ard-Chomhairle, and the decision was left to it. On 6 May the Ard-Chomhairle ruled: "In the light of this … Séamus Costello be suspended from membership of Sinn Féin for a period of six months and that he be debarred from standing as a candidate in the Local Elections."

Under the terms of this suspension, Costello was told that "you will not be entitled to attend Sinn Féin meetings or to participate in any Sinn Féin activity of a public or private nature. Neither will you be entitled to stand as an Independent or to represent any other group in local elections. The meeting also passed a motion instructing you not to attend any further meetings of the two local authorities of which you are a member."

Costello demanded to be allowed to appeal to a special ardfheis. The Ard-Chomhairle began receiving letters from cumainn throughout the country in his support. Among those that backed him in his demand for an extraordinary ardfheis were the Connolly and Wolfe Tone Cumainn in Dublin and the Donegal Comhairle Ceantair, while the North Munster Comhairle Ceantair and the Lalor Cumann in Dublin passed a motion asking the members of the Ard-Chomhairle to discuss the situation. The Official leadership also received letters from two founder-members of the McCaughey Cumann and the Rockfield Park Tenants' Association in Kilmacanogue, County Wicklow. Costello felt that there was a ground-swell of support for him that might still carry him through to victory at the next ardfheis, which was to be held at the beginning of December.

A more immediate problem confronted him, however. He had been barred from attending meetings of either of the two councils on which he held a seat. He ignored this ban, telling the Ard-Chomhairle, "I have consulted local opinion regarding your instructions not to attend any further meetings of the Wicklow County Council and the Bray Urban District Council and I find that representatives of peoples' organisations and working class people in general feel strongly that I should continue to defend their interests by attendance at these meetings."

He further defied the Ard-Chomhairle by standing in the June local election, running as an Independent Sinn Féin candidate for the seat that he had first won in 1967. He topped the poll in Wicklow.

The Ard-Chomhairle met soon afterwards to deal with its truculent member. Costello soon learnt the result: "We wish to inform you that at an Ard-Chomhairle meeting on Saturday July 13th you were dismissed from membership of Sinn Féin on the grounds that your refusal to accept Ard-Chomhairle Directives has rendered you unsuitable for membership."

Costello replied: "I intend to appeal against my totally unjustified suspension and dismissal. I am therefore requesting delegates to the coming Ard Fheis which is the supreme authority of Sinn Féin to forward resolutions requesting that I be allowed to address the Ard Fheis and that the Ard Fheis rejects my suspension and dismissal.

"The issue at stake is basically one of democracy within Sinn Féin itself and I am confident that most rank and file Republicans who have an opportunity to hear both sides of the story will see it in this light and act accordingly."

Costello had been fighting on another front, and there too he had been faced with the growing determination of the Goulding-Garland leadership to get rid of him. In the spring of 1974 he was court-martialled by the Official IRA Army Council on the same grounds that had led to his suspension from the party. The court-martial took place in Mornington, near Drogheda. Costello had summoned witnesses to speak on his behalf, including Ronnie Bunting and the Flynns. But Garland, who acted as prosecuting counsel, refused to allow them to give evidence on his behalf. According to him, what they had to say was irrelevant. Only Stella Makowski from Limerick was allowed to address the court. Her words were not enough to turn back the tide that was clearly running against him. He was dismissed "with ignominy" from the organisation that he had spent the best part of his life serving.

However, while Séamus Costello was being checkmated within the Officials, he was already organising along alternative lines. Beginning in March 1974, he held a series of four or five meetings with those within the movement who were sympathetic to him. They were held in the Railway Bar, Dundalk. Mostly the discussion concerned how to break the cease-fire. At one of them, shortly before his court-martial (from which Costello thought he would emerge victorious), he said to the assembled IRA men: "If I could bring the OCs of the Belfast units and show them a thousand rifles, would they not agree that the cease-fire should be broken?" At this stage, according to a former member of the Official IRA who attended the clandestine meetings, their focus was still on breaking the cease-fire or forcing the Official leadership to break it. However, Costello realised that if this should fail, he already had the makings of an alternative organisation. As it was, planning robberies to finance large-scale weapons purchases without the knowledge of the Official IRA leadership was coming close to setting up such an organisation.

In early 1974, Costello and a handful of his supporters, including several from Belfast, carried out a robbery at Dublin Airport. One of the Belfast men, disguised as a post office worker, stood along the airport road, pretending that his bicycle had a puncture. The target, a post office van, was leaving Dublin Airport when the volunteer posing as a stranded postal worker hailed it down. The driver stopped and offered him a lift into town. When he climbed into the van he pulled out a gun. The van was taken to a quiet spot where Costello and his gang were waiting. They went through its bags, which were found to be carrying around £30,000 in cash and some industrial diamonds, a haul that fell far short of what they had been hoping for. Costello had been talking about a sum in the region of £100,000, which he believed would be needed if they were to enter the arms market in a big way. The money was loaded into the getaway van, which Costello drove himself.

Two months later, in May, another, more ambitious operation was planned: the robbery of a mail train near Mallow, County Cork. Costello knew it to be carrying between £100,000 and £200,000. With a group of Official IRA men from Belfast, including Ronnie Bunting, the plan was to take over a house near the tracks and stop the train close to it. Things went wrong when the would-be train robbers showed up at the house: there was another family there on a visit. As they were being shepherded into a room to be held, one of the sons of the man who lived there produced a shotgun. He was subdued, but in the fracas another son escaped out the back door, where Costello's men had failed to place a guard.

The operation had to be called off, and the would-be robbers left. In the confusion, Ronnie Bunting, who had been waiting for the approach of the mail train, was left behind, having no idea what had occurred at the house, and someone had to return to fetch him. There was a further complication. A pistol was left behind in a ditch, which the Official IRA would soon notice was missing from their arms dump. Costello turned up at the house of one of his young supporters, who had taken part in the robbery. He was driving a white Mercedes car. The two men drove down in the flashy car to the spot where the gun had been dumped and retrieved it. The young volunteer was impressed by Costello's panache.

Smaller, more successful operations were undertaken. Gun shops were raided throughout the 26 Counties and a few weapons obtained. But by the end of 1974 the Costello faction—for that is what it had become—was still poorly equipped. In Belfast, for instance, it had only about two weapons available to it. It was a far cry from the hopes raised by the "thousand rifles" proclamation Costello had made earlier in the year. However, even if such difficulties had caused doubts about the wisdom of the course on which he and his supporters were embarked, the momentum was building; it was too late for them to prevent the coming collision with the Officials' leadership and the splitting, yet again, of the republican movement.

There was an event during the year that might have given Costello and his faction a worrying indication of the steps the Official IRA was prepared to take against those who tried to disrupt the movement. On 2 June, Paul Tinnelly, a friend of Joe McCann and former OC of the Officials in south Down, was shot to death at his doorstep in the village of Rostrevor. Tinnelly's mother, Kathleen, was badly wounded in the attack, which was claimed later by the Official IRA. Tinnelly had been a former hero of the Official IRA who had left the organisation not long after the cease-fire. He had tried to set up his own local group, carrying out bank robberies to finance arms purchases. His local name was "the Scarlet Pimpernel", because he had eluded capture for so long. Yet in the end this was used against him by the Officials, who cited it as proof that "the British forces in south Down had been under instructions to refrain from arresting or otherwise hindering Tinnelly's activities." (*Irish Times*, 11 June 1974.)

In 1974 the ideological demand was to characterise former members of the Official IRA who had broken with the leadership, such as Paul Tinnelly, as "gangsters", "adventurers", or "collaborators". Among the many other parallels that the Tinnelly story has with that of Costello and his faction is that it showed how far the Official IRA was prepared to go not only in eliminating those who opposed it but in destroying their reputations. (This was a tendency that the Officials' off-shoot would inherit as the vituperative denunciations of former comrades during feuds would show.) However, if Tinnelly's fate was a warning, it was not one that Costello noticed at the time.

The fateful ardfheis was scheduled for 1 December. Costello was still hoping, at least partly, that he would have enough clout to sway the rank and file to overturn his dismissal. Nicky Kelly (later arrested and charged with the Sallins train robbery) was to propose a motion to that effect.

Many of Costello's supporters failed to get in to the ardfheis. Of those who did get in, according to the independent TD Tony Gregory, who was briefly involved with the IRSP, most "were not people who would be able to sway a crowd and explain a point and tell them what was happening. Costello would have probably been the only one capable and therefore it was all the easier to isolate him. A lot of his supporters were activists, they were people who went postering, on sit-in campaigns, more militant forms of activists. They weren't orators." (Séamus Carraher, "Costello: Scenario for a Nonfiction Film Based on the Life of Séamus Costello".)

Gerry Roche, a close associate of Costello's who became a leading member of the IRSP, believed that Costello hoped to the last minute that the ardfheis might prevent a split. "He wanted to win out through that structure. The last thing I think he wanted to do was to leave [the Officials] because to splinter weakened your position. I think he was fighting to the last to turn the Officials back, to change the leadership through his popularity in the rank and file but at the same time he was trying to build an alternative structure if all came to all." (Ibid.)

As the ardfheis convened and the fateful moment approached, Costello waited in the Gresham Hotel in O'Connell Street. One of his most active supporters was Tommy McCourt of Derry. McCourt had taken over as chairman of the Wicklow Comhairle Ceantair on Costello's suspension from the party, and his cumann had passed a resolution that Costello should be allowed to speak at the ardfheis. The leadership told him that he had to get his cumann to withdraw their resolution. When he refused, Garland told him to remember that he was in the IRA and under orders.

As McCourt entered the ardfheis, bringing his cumann's resolution with him, his way was blocked. Among those who stood in his path was a hardline supporter of what was now the Garland-Goulding leadership. He told McCourt that he was concerned about Official IRA "stuff" which was in the hands of McCourt's men in Wicklow. When McCourt told him it would be looked after, Garland stepped forward and said, "Remember your orders," whereupon McCourt handed Garland a note declaring that he had resigned from the IRA. On the spot Garland told him he was now suspended from Sinn Féin as well, and therefore barred from going into the hall. Tommy McCourt then left and joined Costello in the Gresham. "You're wasting your time," he said to the former IRA leader. "You're a beaten docket."

Back in the hall, Nicky Kelly put forward the resolution that Costello be allowed to attend the ardfheis and be reinstated. It was defeated by 197 votes to 15. The next step for Costello and his supporters was now almost inevitable. The declaration of the existence of a new socialist republican movement would have to be made.

However, many of the Belfast men had wanted Costello to wait before declaring the formation of the new organisation. They argued that they should win over as many as possible of the Officials' quartermasters, who controlled access to weapons, before showing their hand. They had been hoping that the quartermaster on the Belfast Command Staff would join them, but he was remaining loyal to Goulding. They were worried about the Official IRA's reaction, especially in their native city, the cockpit of the struggle and a place with a capacity for factional violence that could not be underestimated.

Costello, however, did not expect a physical confrontation with his former comrades-in-arms. His judgement was based on the experience he had in 1970 and 1971 during a brief conflict between the Provisionals and Officials, when a serious feud had been avoided through negotiations. Costello was also convinced that his personal prestige and former high standing in the Officials would prevent a serious breakdown in relationships between his group and that of his former comrades.

He was wrong. The coming fragmentation of the IRA and Sinn Féin would prove to be the bloodiest since the Civil War.

NOTES

1. Whatever the people in the Dublin head office might have thought of McCann's famous picture, it remained hanging in the main hall of the Officials' Belfast headquarters in Cyprus Street until 1982.
2. Power was himself murdered in the 1987 feud.

2

A BLOODY BAPTISM

At first it seemed like the least dramatic of splits. Indeed at the beginning it hardly seemed like a split at all, more of a falling away. There were no dramatic walk-outs from the hall where the 1974 Official ardfheis was in progress, no hard-faced men marching off, no small band animated by righteous indignation making its stand against compromise or change. Instead, during the weekend of the ardfheis came announcements of resignations. The first was from the Wicklow Comhairle Ceantair, of which Tommy McCourt of Derry had been chairman since Costello's suspension. On 1 December, after a meeting in Arklow, it announced it was resigning en masse from Sinn Féin. The statement continued: "The Comhairle Ceantair is to remain in existence as a separate political entity, pending the outcome of discussions with republicans throughout Ireland as to how best our political objectives can be achieved." (*Irish Press*, 2 December 1974.)

A few days later came another announcement, this time from the Markievicz Cumann in Dún Laoghaire, saying that the entire cumann was leaving Sinn Féin. The statement accused the leadership of abandoning the national question, of "selling out the internees" by instructing the nine Republican Club councillors in the North to take their seats on the local councils, and of lack of democracy. "We have seen from within the organisation", ran the statement, "the leadership failing to, and indeed stifling, the implementation of policy decisions made at ardfheiseanna over the past few years." (*Irish Times*, 4 December 1974.)

It lamented the falling away of membership, which it alleged had dropped in the Dublin area from three hundred to "a mere 90" within eighteen months. The decline was a malaise caused by the leadership's failure "to implement Sinn Féin policy."

In public, Official Sinn Féin maintained a stiff upper lip and made believe it was business as usual. The incoming Ard-Chomhairle was announced: Malachy McGurran, Cathal Goulding, Seán Garland, Desmond O'Hagan, Éamon Smullen, Francie Donnelly, Billy McMillen, Michael Ryan, Máirín de Búrca, Jim Sullivan, Seán Ó Cionnaith, Donncha Mac Raghnaill,

Tony Heffernan, Michael Montgomery, Brian Brennan, and Andy Smith. They dismissed with contempt talk of splits, the ruin of the old and the birth of a new party. They made a pretence of unconcern. Little did they realise that they were on the threshold of a bloody conflict that would strike at the very heart of the Ard-Chomhairle itself, leaving one of its members dead and another near death.

The erosion continued through the first week of December. On 6 December three cumainn fell away in the north Munster area: the Seán South Cumann (Limerick city), the Joe McCann Cumann (Castleconnell, County Limerick), and the James Connolly Cumann (Shannon). Reports said a hundred members had resigned. The grievances with the leadership were the same: the "deliberate destruction" of the processes of democracy within the movement, its failure to implement the stated policies of the movement, its abandonment of the national question, and the breaking of the promise that its councillors would not take their seats until internment was ended and the last internee released. Among those who signed the statement announcing the latest fragmentation was Stella Makowski, daughter of Brigit Makowski, raised in Philadelphia and destined to play a leading role in the new movement that was even then taking form.

The day after the latest defections were announced, the eighty republicans who had been Costello's faction within the Official republican movement arrived at the Spa Hotel, Lucan, County Dublin. They came from all four corners of the country; they were the nucleus of a new movement and a new party. But by 8 December it was still a movement and a party without a name.

The lack of drama was explained by the fact that the new movement had come together as a result of a gradual process, not, as in the 1969 split, as a by-product of a sudden tremendous shock to the whole republican structure. It only took one day divided into two sessions of a few hours each to formulate basic policy and settle on basic structures. In the morning an open conference was held, chaired by Séamus Costello, to discuss the formation of the new party. Most of the eighty delegates already knew what they wanted the new party to represent: it was to have the policies of Official Sinn Féin before the divisive cease-fire of 29 May 1972. The party must re-establish the link between the national question and revolutionary socialism. National liberation—which meant the ending of partition—was essential to the creation of a socialist state. As Costello said a few days later at the new party's first press conference, their aim would be to "end Imperialist rule in Ireland and establish a 32-county democratic socialist republic, with the working class in control of the means of production, distribution, and exchange. To this end, it was agreed that the party would launch a vigorous campaign of political agitation and education, North and South ..."

Before the morning session was over they had the name of the new organisation: the Irish Republican Socialist Party. A "Temporary National Executive" was chosen. Séamus Costello was made chairman and also represented Wicklow on the executive. The others elected to it were Seán Flynn, Manuel McIlroy, John McAlea and Charlie Craig from Belfast; Séamus O'Kane from Derry; Terry Robson and Joe Sweeney from Derry city; Johnny White from Donegal; Theresa Gallagher, Mick Plunkett and Anne Webb from Dublin; Stella Makowski from Clare; Joe Quinn from Limerick; Tony Quinn from Tipperary; and John Lynch from Cork. Later, Bernadette McAliskey, who did not attend the December meeting, was chosen to represent Tyrone.

The name of the new party was meant to draw those with a knowledge of Irish history back to 1896, when James Connolly formed the Irish Socialist Republican Party. In republican circles, tradition is everything, the establishing of a precedent a necessary basis for making any claim to political legitimacy. To the IRSP, Connolly was a beacon combining Marxist analysis with republican credibility. He was one of the finest revolutionary socialist writers and organisers that Ireland or Britain has produced and perhaps one of their few Marxist revolutionaries. And he died from the bullets of a British firing squad for asserting in arms Ireland's right to national independence. Over the coming years he would be referred to in countless party statements and party propaganda articles, in speeches at gravesides and at Easter commemorations by IRSP spokesmen seeking to reaffirm their claim to be fighting for the kind of Ireland for which Connolly died.

When the morning session had concluded, Costello announced: "For those who are interested, there's an afternoon meeting—other avenues will be explored." There was no need to say more. About two-thirds of the delegates came to the afternoon session, at which the setting up of the armed wing, the cutting edge of the party, was discussed.

Without weapons, it was not much of a cutting edge, of course. That, however, would be sorted out later. Costello was made chief of staff. He selected a temporary GHQ staff. For the early appointments, Costello chose only those men he could manipulate, much to the chagrin of many of his more militant supporters.

There was a dispute about what the new army should be called. One of the delegates from Derry suggested Irish Citizens' Army; no bolder, more direct claim to be the political descendants of James Connolly could be made. Costello objected that a group using that name in Northern Ireland had already carried out several sectarian attacks.[1]

Costello advocated the name National Liberation Army. Though this was rejected by the delegates, it did appear on a few subsequent claims of responsibility made by the new army. But on the afternoon of 8 December it had been denounced by some as too nationalist. Yet shortly afterwards the name Irish National Liberation Army was accepted. The contradiction was not commented upon.[2]

So it was that the INLA came into being—a relatively painless birth for what would turn out to be one of the most destructive and deadly organisations ever to take part in the Irish troubles.

The new movement now had its public and its private aspects, its political and its military wings. As in traditional republican organisations, the overlap was considerable. But in fact the INLA had already broken with traditional republicanism in a profound way: it had abandoned the name and the claim to be the Irish Republican Army, which meant, strictly speaking, it had given up the claim to republican legitimacy. In 1938 the surviving members of the Second Dáil, elected in 1919 and still recognised by purist republicans as the true government of Ireland, had delegated their authority to the IRA's Army Council, which made it, according to republican logic, the real government of Ireland. This made its declaration of war on England, which followed in 1939, legitimate. And, to republicans, it also bestowed a moral legitimacy on the IRA's "right" to wage war against the British in the North. Though the only surviving member of the Second Dáil, Tom Maguire, had in 1969 recognised the Provisional IRA's Army Council, not that of the Officials, the Official IRA still saw itself as the inheritor of that tradition. However, breaking with it does not seem to have been given much thought by most INLA members. Said one, who later became a member of the INLA's Army Council: "We were a different generation—we didn't think much about that high-falutin' republican rhetoric. We were a body of individuals prepared to wage war against the British machine in Ireland." (Interview, 22 May 1993.)

Two organisations had come into existence, but only one of them, the IRSP, had to explain to the public and potential supporters why it existed. This it did five days after the Spa Hotel conference, when it held its first press conference and issued its first press statement. Costello read the three-page statement announcing the aims of the new party.

"Recognising that British Imperialist interference in Ireland constitutes the most immediate obstacle confronting the Irish People in their struggle for

33

democracy, National Liberation, and Socialism, it shall be the policy of the party to seek the formation of a broad front on the basis of the following demands:

"A/ That Britain must immediately renounce all claims to sovereignty over any part of Ireland and its coastal waters, and should immediately specify an early date for the total withdrawal of her military and political presence from Ireland.

"B/ Having specified the date for her total withdrawal from Ireland, Britain must immediately withdraw all troops to barracks, release all internees and sentenced political prisoners, grant a general amnesty for all offences arising from the military campaign against British Forces, or through involvement in the Civil Disobedience Campaign, abolish all repressive legislation, grant a Bill of Rights which will allow complete freedom of political action and outlaw discrimination whether it be on the basis of class, creed, political opinion or sex. Britain must also agree to compensate the Irish People for the exploitation which has already occurred.

"C/ It shall be the policy of the Irish Republican Socialist Party to seek an active working alliance of all radical forces within the context of the Broad Front in order to ensure the ultimate success of the Irish Working Class in their struggle for Socialism.

"D/ It will be an immediate objective of the Party to launch an intensive campaign of opposition to E.E.C membership. We, therefore, intend to play an active part in the E.E.C. referendum in the Six County Area, and through our support groups in Britain.

"E/ Recognising that sectarianism, and the present campaign of sectarian assassinations arises as a direct result of British manipulation of the most reactionary elements of Irish Society, we shall seek to end this campaign on the basis of united action by the Catholic and Protestant working class against British Imperialism in Ireland."

The party's attitude to the 26 Counties followed. Costello declared:

"1/ We will seek to have a United Campaign of all democratic forces against repressive legislation in the South, and against the policy of blatant collaboration with British Imperialism, which is now being pursued by the 26 County Administration.

"2/ The Irish Republican Socialist Party is totally opposed to the exploitation of our natural resources by multi national Corporations. It shall therefore be our policy to give active and sustained support to the present campaign for the nationalisation of the resources.

"3/ Recognising that the rapidly increasing cost of living and rising unemployment are to a large extent a direct result of our E.E.C. membership, it shall be the policy of the Irish Republican Socialist Party to actively support the formation of peoples organisations to combat rising prices and unemployment."

In his statement Costello next explained that the IRSP was "not an abstentionist Party, and will decide its attitude towards the contesting of any particular election, on the basis of a thorough analysis of the conditions prevailing at the time. In keeping with this attitude we have decided in principle to contest the forthcoming Convention Elections in the Six County Area."

The press were then told why it was that the party's members, 90 per cent of whom had belonged to the Officials, had found it necessary to leave that organisation. The reasons were familiar ones, having already been outlined in the statements from the various cumainn that had left the Officials since the beginning of December: lack of democracy within the organisation, failure to carry out policies agreed on at ardfheiseanna, purging of "many dedicated members", and reversal of the decision on the taking of seats in the local councils in the North before internment was ended. The statement also alleged for the first time that the Ard-Chomhairle had tried to "intimidate delegates to the recent ardfheis, when many were threatened with expulsion if they did not vote in accordance with the wishes of the leadership." It condemned the drift towards "almost exclusive participation in reformist activity, and the total abandonment of agitationary political action in pursuit of their objectives ... Under its present Leadership, Sinn Féin has been reduced to a position of almost total irrelevance in the context of the present political situation."

The statement ended with an appeal "to all of those who are genuinely interested in the establishment of a Socialist Republic to re-examine their present position and give their support to the Irish Republican Socialist Party."

Costello claimed, when asked, that the party had a membership of over 300, including 120 in Belfast, over 25 in Derry, and about 40 in Dublin. There was living proof beside him on the platform that the IRSP was pulling in prominent republicans. Next to him sat Bernadette McAliskey.

McAliskey was perhaps *the* most prominent Northern "republican". Though not publicly affiliated to any particular organisation, her successful candidacy in the Westminster general election of April 1969 had been supported by the then still united republican movement. Ironically, for the Officials she had been for a while living proof of what the civil rights movement, their model vehicle for achieving change, could actually deliver: votes, a seat in parliament, and a chance to advance socialist politics that would galvanise the public. She was witty, intelligent, at times scathing, and unafraid of overturning the usual Irish pieties. Some dubbed her "an Irish Castro in a miniskirt". She was a living symbol of the transformation that had come over Northern nationalists, and exuded the confidence that was making itself felt among them as the civil rights movement brought them sympathy and attention from all over the world. But by 1974 that movement had run its course, and McAliskey believed that new vehicles were needed to push the struggle on to a new plane. She had attended a conference in Paris where Costello spoke in the autumn of 1970 but according to her own account had not come to know him personally until 1973. She admired him as an orator, an organiser, and a man "who owed his first allegiance to an ideal—a 32-county socialist republic." (*Séamus Costello, 1939–1977: Irish Republican Socialist.*)

At the 13 December press conference McAliskey said that the IRSP was needed as an alternative to both the Provisionals and Official Sinn Féin. She told reporters: "The Provos are concentrating on getting rid of the British in a military campaign without any policy on the class war. And the Officials now have no policy on the national question. We will agitate on both the national and class issues." (*Irish Times*, 14 December 1974.) The *Irish Times* headlined its report on the press conference: "Mrs McAliskey joins in attack on Official SF"—suggesting that the Officials were being victimised. The reality that was to unfold was somewhat different.

The paper war raged on, with Officials still responding to claims of defections by denying that they had taken place. Though the momentum was gathering, the Officials still tried to bluff it out. A spokesman told the *Irish Times* (10 December 1974) that the reports of mass defections from his party to the IRSP were "a paper war to confuse the general public." He was "not aware of any resignations of Republican Clubs or individuals in Northern Ireland." Up North, at a meeting of the County Antrim Republican Clubs, Jim Sullivan claimed: "Reports in some Irish daily newspapers allege mass defections from Official Sinn Féin. These reports are completely without foundation and are part of an ever-increasing and deliberate campaign to discredit the Official Republican movement and to destroy the growing influence of its progressive policies throughout the 32 counties." (Ibid.)

On 16 December a statement from the "Official Republican Movement" in Newry dismissed claims that some of its members had joined the IRSP. "The fact is that not one member in the South Down-South Armagh area, including Newry, has defected. The attitude of members is that this new fringe group will suffer the fate of many similar groups who, in the past, have tried to set themselves up independently. They will fade into oblivion, and by this time next year will be completely forgotten about." (*Irish News*, 17 December 1974.) The fate that befell Paul Tinnelly, who had been shot dead in June after trying to set himself up independently, was not referred to, but it gave the Newry Officials' statement a certain edge.

The Officials quoted statements from the Wicklow Comhairle Ceantair and the North Munster Comhairle Ceantair repudiating claims made in their names that those bodies had defected from the movement. It was also announced that there would be a meeting between the Ard-Chomhairle and the Officials' nine Northern councillors to discuss "the implementation of the resolution instructing them to take their seats." In the event, it was decided not to implement the resolution right away.

Of course the Officials could not simply ignore what was happening, nor persist in explaining it all as someone's fantasy, particularly as the press kept reporting increasing numbers of their members going over to the new group. The *Irish Press* on 16 December headlined its report: "400 SF defections". Nor did Officials' allegations that there were no prominent Northern republicans linked to the new group look credible when Bernadette McAliskey was seen by all sitting next to Costello on an IRSP platform.

A few days afterwards, evidence emerged that the dispute had reached the imprisoned members of the Official IRA in Long Kesh. On the same day two statements came from the prison on Belfast's outskirts. One announced that a branch of the IRSP had been formed in the prison, because a group of prisoners "had reached the conclusion that neither the apathetic and moderate reformism of the Official Republican movement nor the elite militarism of the Provisional Republican movement" would bring about a 32-county socialist republic (*Irish News*, 20 December 1974.) The second, from the "Co-ordinating Committee of Long Kesh Republican Clubs", said that they "stand by the policies of the Official Republican Movement." The statement went on to say that they had nothing to do with a "Trotskyite organisation known as the Irish Republican Socialist Party." (Ibid.) The term "Trotskyite" was one not commonly used in internecine republican disputes. It came from the communist parties' arsenal of abuse, utilised in the 1930s ideological upheavals within western Marxism as Stalin purged and finally extirpated all his rivals for supreme power in the Soviet Union and eventually in the communist parties linked to him throughout Europe and America. That it had been dusted off and brought into use again in Ireland in 1974 might seem at first rather strange. But it was one indication of the ideological drift of the Official republican movement, which was soon to back up the 1930s-style rhetoric with actions to match.

The "Trotskyite" allegation prompted the IRSP to unfold the green flag and proclaim its indigenous revolutionary credentials. They stated that their position was "based on an Irish Socialist response to the objective material conditions existing in our country." They would not seek to import "alien and mechanical formulas", whether by Lenin, Trotsky or anyone else into their ideas regarding the removal of the imperialist presence: "Connolly, Lalor, Davitt and Pearse are good enough for us in respect of ideology … We suggest the Officials spend less time smearing genuinely anti-Imperialist groups with meaningless and misleading labels and devote some time to the implementation of their own stated position on the national question." (*Irish News*, 4 January 1975.)

Clearly the party was anxious to establish that though it might be red, it was still also green. In Ireland, whether on the left or the right of the political spectrum, being able to prove that one's party's policies are "home-grown" and uninfluenced by "alien" ideas seems essential for the preservation of some notion of ideological purity.

Whatever its ideological pretentious, the new movement was making headway in Belfast. Since the beginning of the current troubles, Belfast has been regarded by the Provisionals, Officials and IRSP as the cockpit of the North: it has to be held at all costs. The Officials were growing anxious about the trend of events in the city as throughout December they lost more members to the new grouping. In several of the areas where the organisation was once strongest, such as the Markets, its membership was halved. Seán Flynn helped start an IRSP branch there and claimed seventeen members by early 1975. In north Belfast, the Ardoyne and the Bone saw desertions from the Officials to the new group, which claimed to have recruited thirty members from both districts, including one whole unit of the Official IRA. In Twinbrook, Bawnmore and Turf Lodge, Costello's supporters gave their numbers as six, four, and nine, respectively. Jim McCorry, former editor of the *Andersonstown News*, was busy in that district, one where the Officials were never very strong. But at the first meeting of the new party there some thirty people came. The Whiterock district off the Falls Road was also very active under Hugh Ferguson and Harry Flynn. It had been a solid Official area before the split, with at one stage 300 houses out of 450 taking copies of the Officials' weekly paper, the *United Irishman*, according to local activists. In contrast, the Beechmount Officials remained one of the units most loyal to the Goulding leadership: out of thirty volunteers only four members resigned, but among them were Vinty Fegan and Frank Gallagher, both of whom were to play leading roles in the new organisation, Gallagher becoming chief of staff of the INLA. Likewise, the Lower Falls, where the

Officials had their headquarters, lost only a few to the new group. But in the Divis Flats it was another matter.

The flats, at the foot of the Falls Road, were one of the toughest "Sticky" strongholds in the city. When it was learnt that the Divis Flats unit was thinking of deserting to Costello, the Officials sent one of their Belfast Command Staff (a man who until recently was prominent in the Workers' Party) to try to dissuade them. The discussion grew heated, and when objections were raised, the Officials' emissary shouted them down. "It was badly handled," admitted a member of the Official IRA who at the time was also on the Belfast Command Staff. "He humiliated them verbally." (Interview, 10 June 1993.) Angered, the entire unit left the Official IRA and—most ominous of all—took its weapons with it, declaring its allegiance to Séamus Costello's organisation.

Those who remained loyal to the Official IRA saw the IRSP as a volatile organisation that could only add to the spiral of sectarian violence then being unleashed in Northern Ireland. One Official IRA volunteer from Turf Lodge said: "I stayed with the leadership because I respected their judgement. You've got to remember the circumstances at the time of the split. The movement was under severe pressure to retaliate not just against Brits but more importantly against loyalists, who were killing Catholics in large numbers.

"The Provos in '74 were bombing bars in the Shankill and getting involved in blatant sectarian actions on the border. There was an element within the army that wanted action on that front. Many of the people that went with the Erps [IRSP] ... were just keen to get into the Brits and the Prods. They were at heart sectarian. They couldn't resist the temptation to hit out at the loyalists.

"I felt this would be a disaster. The last thing the republican movement needed was to get involved in an all-out civil war. And when you look at the way the INLA turned out I think we were proved right in the end ... A lot of volunteers stayed loyal to the Officials because of Billy McMillen. He was respected within the organisation. Goulding was still admired by many. But the central reason for me not joining the IRSP was the belief that if they had seized control of our movement, Costello and his crew would have plunged us into sectarian conflict, which was madness." (Interview, 20 June 1993.)

A lot of those joining the new movement in Belfast were members of Fianna Éireann, the youth wing of the IRA. It had never been very happy with the 1972 cease-fire. "The Fianna was a big problem for the leadership. I was in the Fianna at the time. There was a really militant crowd in the Fianna. I remember one meeting the Fianna was called to in Cyprus Street in

1973. The OIRA quartermaster for Belfast was there. He asked the Fianna members to tell him how many weapons they had. He couldn't believe what he was hearing. Fianna units reported having heavy machine-guns, explosives, rifles, and handguns. He nearly fell off his chair as he took stock of our weapons. Many of those that later went with the Erps came from the ranks of the Fianna. I was like them at the beginning. All we wanted to do was bang away at the Brits. It didn't surprise me that these same people that included the likes of Gerard Steenson[3] joined the IRSP." (Ibid.)

In 1976 the Officials, having learnt their lesson about encouraging overmilitant youths, formally abolished the Fianna, reconstituting it as the Irish Democratic Youth Movement.

As more and more branches of the IRSP were announcing their formation, the Officials backtracked on their resolution, passed at the last ardfheis, instructing councillors to take their seats on local government bodies in the North. Two days before Christmas there were hints that some Officials were unhappy with the rush to political respectability, and there were complaints at a meeting of the County Antrim Republican Clubs about the "lack of time being given to debate." It was also announced that the party would consider fighting the forthcoming Convention elections on an "abstention-until-the-ending-of-internment" basis (*Irish News*, 23 December 1974). The party clearly had been stung by the accusations coming from former members that it had betrayed its pledge to the internees. By the end of February 1975 the councillors still had not taken their seats.

The New Year began on a sinister note. The Provisionals were maintaining a shaky cease-fire as behind-the-scenes contacts with British officials were nervously established in the hope that a more permanent resolution to the violence would be forthcoming. The province was tense, expectant. Loyalists were on edge, suspecting that a nefarious back-room deal was being done at their expense, and stepping up a vicious campaign of sectarian murder that would make 1975 one of the bloodiest years in the history of the troubles.

Accusations began surfacing in the press that the IRSP was out to challenge the Provisional IRA. The suggestion was that the new group was trying to recruit Provos unhappy with the truce. The Provisional leadership in Belfast was concerned that the IRSP might attract defectors; but in fact very few of their men left at the time. One who did was Brendan McNamee, who joined the IRSP after a dispute with the Provo leadership in Long Kesh.

Other allegations tried to link the new movement to the fanatical fringe of republicanism. In a report in the *Sunday News* that was clearly from the pen of an Official sympathiser, it was claimed that the "dissidents" had left the Official IRA because it "had refused to become embroiled in sectarian warfare" (5 January 1975.). It described the IRSP as a "Saor Éire-type organisation".

The original Saor Éire was formed by a group of left-wing IRA men in 1929, led by the republican radical Peadar O'Donnell. But the *Sunday News*, if it knew about this organisation, was definitely not referring to it. Its Saor Éire was a small group that emerged forty years later using that name to carry out a number of bank raids in the North and in the Republic. (During one such raid in Dublin in 1970 a garda was shot dead.) The *Sunday News* described Saor Éire as "a breakaway Republican organisation which loosely allied what have been described as Trotskyite ultra-leftists and down-to-earth bank robbers." (Ibid.) It claimed: "There are reports that the IRSP leadership has talked to the remnants of Saor Éire in Dublin and to some sections of the Provisionals in Belfast."

The Officials had gone from denying that the IRSP was anything other than a "paper" organisation to characterising it as a dangerous coalition of left-wing fanatics, gangsters, and Provo discontents. In other words, they had taken the propaganda offensive; it was as if they were preparing the ground for more drastic action so that when it came, the public would be ready to believe that it was being done to save Northern Ireland from being plunged into further sectarian killings, or something worse.

The slide towards open feuding had begun in Belfast in mid-December. The day before the IRSP's first press conference, a group of former Officials met in the Gem Bar in the New Lodge Road in north Belfast. They were there to discuss the formation of an IRSP branch for their area. According to the IRSP, before the meeting could proceed, members of the Official IRA, led by the local OC, burst in, pistol-whipped two people, and broke up the meeting.

On the weekend of 5 January—the weekend the *Sunday News* report appeared—the IRSP claimed that several of its men were kneecapped by the Official IRA in Belfast. A statement said: "Official Republicans have explicitly assured our members that we will be smashed and prevented from functioning as a political party." (*Irish News*, 10 January 1975.)

The IRSP claimed that two were kneecapped and another was dragged from his house and beaten up by "thugs". After being taken away for questioning by the Officials, they told him, "Hit this party on the head or we'll smash you." Another two party members were shot and wounded by the Officials "for no reason whatever."

At first the Official IRA responded curtly to such accusations with a statement that "the reason for the actions in question was that these people have been engaged in acts of gangsterism." (*Irish Times*, 10 January 1975.) A day later the Belfast Command Staff of the Official IRA issued a longer statement, saying that actions had been taken against "ex-members" of the Officials after they had been found guilty of "various acts of embezzlement of movement funds, and misappropriation of IRA weapons, and other criminal acts." (*Irish Times*, 11 January 1975.). It went on: "At least three of the people dealt with had assaulted and robbed a furniture salesman in the Markets area and a milk roundsman in the Ardoyne district, using the name of the Official IRA while perpetrating these crimes. Such anti-working class activities will not be tolerated. It is evident that these ex-members have now banded themselves together and are seeking a cloak for the continuation of their criminal activities under the guise of a legitimate political grouping ... All means necessary to terminate these anti-social acts and the present scurrilous attempts to denigrate and to subordinate the allegiance of our own members in the Republican movement will be rigorously applied."

The IRSP alleged that the Official IRA Army Council took a decision some time in late 1974 to smash the organisation. The Officials deny that there was ever a formal decision. In fact Cathal Goulding claims he had been opposed all along to attacking the IRSP. "I wanted the IRSP to take the high road and we'd take the low road," he said. He believed, nonetheless, that confrontation between the two groups in Belfast was inevitable but that it was "based on rivalries on the ground." (Interview, June 1993.)

The Official IRA accused the IRSP of provoking the violence themselves. According to a member of the Officials' Turf Lodge unit, "You've got to understand these people were stealing our weapons, raiding our dumps, beating up our members, particularly those that refused to join them. Personally, I couldn't care less if they left the organisation. But there was no way they were going to use our weapons to wage sectarian war." (Interview, 20 June 1993.)

A high-ranking member of the Officials' Belfast Command later admitted that his organisation was taken by surprise at the numbers that went over to the IRSP in late 1974 and early 1975. "I thought it'd be a small, fanatical sect. But it was the ghost of the Provisionals. People overreacted and it was handled badly." (Interview, 10 June 1993.)

Among the Belfast IRSP, anxiety was sharply increasing throughout early 1975. From the start, many of Costello's supporters in the city had cautioned him about declaring the IRSP's existence too soon, before the movement was strong enough. Indeed, some had been of the opinion that the INLA should have been allowed time to consolidate by carrying out a few operations, including bank robberies, which would have provided the party with the necessary funds to launch a newspaper and establish itself.

Costello had gone ahead, confident that there would be no violent confrontation between his supporters and those of Goulding and Garland. By early 1975 it had become clear, however, that he had misjudged the situation, at least in Belfast. The Belfast men knew their own city better. They knew the bitter intensity with which vendettas there are pursued. They were a product of it, after all, as they would soon demonstrate.

In mid-January the Arklow cumann of Official Sinn Féin went over to the IRSP, and shortly after that a branch was set up in the Pomeroy area of County Tyrone. By 22 January the party was claiming thirty-five branches and seven hundred members. Though exact figures are impossible to establish, it would appear that by this stage the Official Republican movement had lost over one-third of its membership to Costello.

The Official IRA reacted to the deteriorating situation by stepping up the pressure. As ever, the situation was most tense in Belfast. Behind the escalation in the city the breakaways saw the hand of Billy McMillen, OC of the Belfast Command. On 15 January, Costello made the most serious allegations yet against the Official IRA, accusing the Belfast Command Staff of drawing up a death list on which were the names of four prominent members "associated" with the IRSP. One of them was Ronnie Bunting, the son of Major Ronald Bunting, once a side-kick of Rev. Ian Paisley and the man who led the attack on the civil rights marchers at Burntollet in January 1969. Bunting Junior was not actually a member of the IRSP (he did not become one until 1979); at the time he was involved in organising the still-secret INLA. Costello said that two masked gunmen had called to Ronnie Bunting's house looking for him, and when they were told he wasn't in they fired two shots into the house, narrowly missing Bunting's wife, Suzanne, and her eighteen-month old daughter, Fiona. Around the same time Vinty Fegan, an ex-Official from Beechmount, was shot in the leg as he walked along Beechmount Pass. When one of the authors went to Belfast shortly afterwards he spoke to a member of the Official IRA in Beechmount and was told that they would not make the mistake they had made with the Provisionals: that is, they intended to wipe out the IRSP.

A statement from the IRSP's National Executive called on "all genuine republicans and socialists who remained within the Official Republican Movement to reject the counter-revolutionary activities of their own national leadership by resigning immediately and applying for membership of the IRSP." (*Irish Press*, 16 January 1975.)

So far the new organisation was portraying itself as purely political; it denied that it had any paramilitary links. "We are not involved in any kind of military activity," Costello insisted, "but are solely a political group." (*Sunday Independent*, 26 January 1975.) The problem for Costello and his organisation was that he could not explain how a purely political group was attracting volunteers away from the Official IRA on the grounds that the Officials were not militant enough. Why would gunmen who had grown restless because of the three-year cease-fire join another organisation that did not offer them some military role? As long as Costello's supporters did not end up in court charged with violent acts, it was just about possible for him to keep up the pretence of being "a solely political group". But given the rapidly deteriorating situation in Belfast, that could not last.

One of the first to allege that the IRSP had a military wing was the Ulster Volunteer Force. In January their magazine *Combat*—which during 1975 was to devote quite a lot of attention to the IRSP—described the new group as "revolutionaries from the same school as Che Guevara, Carlos Franqui and Fidel Castro." It claimed that the IRSP's military wing was called the Irish Citizens' Army, with active service units in Newry, Derry, west Belfast, and part of mid-Ulster. It warned that the IRSP "may well be the movement to unify militant Officials and political Provisionals." The fact that the UVF had given one of the names that the IRSP's military wing had considered but rejected during the first discussions on 8 December would suggest that they were receiving inside information, possibly from the Official IRA.[4]

The article also alleged that British military intelligence had come into possession of letters, confiscated by prison authorities, showing that there had been widespread defections to the IRSP inside Long Kesh. (A few months later, *Combat* would publish similar material in connection with the murder of Michael Adamson, whom the UVF shot dead in March, as proof that he was a member of the IRSP.)

The war of words continued along more conventional lines. The January issue of the *United Irishman* accused the IRSP of seeking to promote confusion with "bogus statements" in the name of dismissed members and lapsed branches of the republican movement. The paper found what became a common formula for describing the new group, calling it an "ultra-left instant revolutionary organisation." It asked—rather prophetically as it turned out—if Costello and McAliskey would be able to "stomach the gangster elements and factionalists who dominate the rank and file."

The jargon of Stalinist abuse was accompanied in the same issue by the first of a series of long articles that were eulogies to the pro-Soviet states of the Eastern Bloc. In January 1975, Hungary was hailed as an economic miracle and the Soviet invasion—or "intervention", as it was called in the *United Irishman*—was defended. The Officials were closer to the target when they derided the IRSP's claims to have six hundred members. They pointed out that "600 people would not be stupid enough to join a party not knowing that party's policy." There had only been one real statement from the IRSP outlining its policies, and that had been almost two months earlier.

At the beginning of February, the IRSP issued a statement praising the Provisionals as a "genuinely anti-imperialist force"—the first clear indication that the sympathies of Costello's new formation lay in that direction; another statement attacked the SDLP and the Officials, who were blaming the Provisionals for a temporary breakdown in the truce. But the majority of IRSP statements had been devoted to accusations about attacks on their members from the Official IRA.

On 12 February the IRSP, as if in answer to criticisms about not having any policies, held a conference in Dublin that, according to reports, attracted five hundred people. Costello and McAliskey spoke to a packed hall, composed mainly of left-wing activists, trade unionists, and curious republicans. The party was going to work to end British interference in Ireland, which, said Costello, was the only way that class politics would develop. And it was only with such a development that the sectarian murder campaign would end. He claimed that the loyalist murder gangs were mainly members of the British army and of the Ulster Defence Regiment, who went out at night, out of uniform, killing innocent people "because they took the anti-imperialist or at least the nationalist viewpoint ... There is a clearly established need for people to defend themselves, and we support any attempt to organise the people's defence." (*Irish Times*, 14 February 1975.)

McAliskey told the audience that the Irish struggle against British imperialism had failed for over eight hundred years because the Irish were doing it the wrong way. "This party is an attempt to create a revolutionary socialist alternative to eight hundred years of failure." (Ibid.)

At the meeting, nothing was said about an armed campaign, or just how the new organisation proposed to oppose British presence in the North. Political education and agitation was mentioned, no more. The way forward, according to Costello, was the creation of a broad front of all anti-imperialist groups. Instead of a broad front, however, the republican movement was about to witness the worst factional blood-letting in many years, one that made Costello's calls for anti-imperialist unity sound like wishful thinking.

Likewise, idealistic sentiments about uniting the Protestant and Catholic working class sounded fine in Dublin. But Belfast, as ever, took its own brutal course.

On 8 February three gunmen sprayed the Princess Bar in the Ormeau Road, seriously wounding a barmaid. Three members of the IRSP were later charged and convicted in connection with the attack.[5] The INLA later claimed that the incident had occurred after a "known loyalist" had been seen near a Catholic pub in the Markets. They thought the UDA was planning an attack, and so struck first at what was a known UDA hang-out. Though the Official IRA condemned the attack and accused Costello's movement of sectarianism, they had fired on the same pub in late 1973, wounding a UDA member. Almost certainly, Costello had not known about the shooting at the Princess Bar, suggesting that already he had little control over what was happening in Belfast. This boded ill for the troubled Northern ghettos, where the flames of sectarian violence were already burning brightly.

In mid-January a young member of the IRSP called Michael Ferguson was crossing the Springfield Road in west Belfast when he was fired upon by a squad of three Official IRA men, one of whom was said to have been Seán Fox, a member of the Belfast Command Staff. They missed but hit a nun's car that was passing at the time. Michael's older brother was Hugh Ferguson, a former OC of the Officials' unit in the Whiterock Road and subsequently in charge of the new IRSP branch there. He was known locally as "King of the Rock". Hugh Ferguson was infuriated when his brother told him what had occurred. He confronted several members of the Officials in a club, threatening that if anything ever happened to his brother he'd sort them out.

A month later, on the afternoon of Thursday 20 February, Hugh Ferguson was working on a building site just off the Whiterock Road, not far from where he lived. A three-year-old-boy, Thomas McDonagh, the son of a Republican Clubs councillor, Bernie McDonagh, was playing nearby. A squad of three Official IRA men arrived. One sat in a car parked not far from the site. Another stood at the corner of Whiterock Crescent and Whiterock Drive to act as look-out while the third, masked, approached Ferguson. When he was close he pulled out a .38 revolver.

What happened next is a matter of dispute. All that is known for definite is that Hugh Ferguson fell under a hail of bullets, shot in the head, leg, and chest. The councillor's son was wounded in the ankle. An ambulance whisked them to hospital, where Ferguson, bleeding from four bullet wounds, died fifteen minutes later.

The IRSP immediately issued a statement claiming that the killing of Ferguson was part of an Official IRA Army Council policy "to smash the IRSP". (*Irish Times*, 21 February 1975.) The Officials' Belfast Command Staff said that preliminary enquiries indicated that none of their members was involved in the shooting but that "further enquiries are in progress." (*Irish*

News, 21 February 1975.) However, though their enquiries purported to find no Official IRA involvement, they now admit that their men were responsible for Ferguson's death, but they claim they did not mean to kill him. A leading member of the Belfast Official IRA who was close to the scene of the shooting at the time said: "He was killed accidentally. He was supposed to be kneecapped: he'd threatened to get revenge on us if anything happened to Michael, his brother. But he put up a fight. Listen, people were shocked. The man involved was badly affected—and still is. I didn't believe Ferguson was dying. People were shouting, 'He's dead, he's dead! He's turning blue on the ground!'" (Interview, 10 June 1993.) Another Official IRA volunteer agreed that the whole thing was a kneecapping gone wrong. "Basically, it was a mistake. He fought back. There was no intention to kill him. After he was killed, they shot Seán Fox and then Paul Crawford. We only hit back proper when Fox was killed." (Interview, 20 June 1993.)

Those who had been friends of Ferguson's and who were involved in the INLA now accept that it was probably not a deliberate killing. But in February 1975, Ferguson's comrades were anxious for revenge, convinced that it was part of an Official IRA plot against them. However, lack of weapons still plagued the new movement. A gun had to be borrowed from the Provisional IRA in order to fire a volley over the young man's coffin as it left his home on the way to the graveyard. Costello came north for the funeral on 24 February. At Ferguson's graveside, before a crowd of about two hundred people, he again accused the Official IRA leadership of deliberately adopting a policy of smashing the IRSP. He described the dead man as "an energetic revolutionary". The Officials, said Costello, had "betrayed the people. They ran away from the struggle."

After the funeral, Costello held a meeting at a house in Andersonstown. His supporters were tense, angry, and anxious. They wanted to hit back; and they needed the weapons with which to do it. But Costello was more concerned to ensure that Ferguson's death would not divert the IRSP. However, he also wanted to use the shooting to gain as much sympathy for his movement as possible: he had asked people to note the number of Officials who had attended the funeral, for instance, to see if later they could be contacted and convinced to join the IRSP. He urged the Belfast men to wait a couple of weeks, and ride it out without retaliation. Though pressed, he vetoed any attacks on Official IRA personnel. However, he did agree to sanction attacks on the property of the Republican Clubs.

Not only were the ghettos tense because of growing fears of a feud, but loyalist murder gangs were stalking the city and the countryside. On 10 February the Provisional IRA cease-fire had been re-established. The same day, loyalist gunmen opened up on worshippers leaving a Catholic church in Derryvolgie Avenue, off the prosperous Malone Road, killing two. Another Catholic was murdered in Belfast the following day, and two more were murdered in Pomeroy. By the time Hugh Ferguson was buried, another five Catholics had been murdered. In Belfast, loyalists bombers struck at Catholic pubs. The day after the funeral, loyalist gunmen entered a factory in Boucher Road where a 37-year-old Catholic named David McConkey worked. The workers were made to line up against the wall. McConkey was singled out, forced to his knees, and shot through the head. The cease-fire had led to an increase in sectarian violence. And because the British government had reduced the number of checkpoints as one of the conditions of the cease-fire, it actually made the movement of gunmen and bombers around Catholic areas easier, so facilitating the movement of loyalist assassins and the conflict between the Officials and their former comrades.

The first act of revenge carried out by Ferguson's comrades occurred within hours of his burial. The Republican Clubs' premises in Turf Lodge—a strong Official area—was set on fire. The Officials identified the arsonists, who had not worn masks, and went hunting for them. Costello's men evaded the gunmen, and decided to take action into their own hands. Ignoring their chief of staff's orders, they sought out a member of the unit that had been looking for them, a man who was also alleged to have been one of the three involved in the killing of Ferguson; when they found him, they shot him in the legs. The INLA had drawn its first blood in the feud.

A former INLA member commented on the deterioration: "Costello wasn't in a position to control Belfast—but then in any feud it's hard to maintain 100 per cent control." (Interview, 4 June 1993.) The Official IRA stepped up its attacks. It machine-gunned the house were Ronnie Bunting and Seán and Harry Flynn were hiding, near the Antrim Road. It launched a propaganda offensive as well, accusing the IRSP of having a military wing, of which it claimed Ferguson had been a member. The military wing had carried out sectarian attacks, the Officials claimed, including the attack on the Princess Bar.

On the day of Ferguson's funeral, his colleagues had applied a touch of macabre humour to the situation. They inserted a death notice in the *Irish News* for Éamon "Hatchet" Kerr, a well-known "enforcer" for the Officials. It read: "Kerr—suddenly. The committee and members of Cyprus Street Social Club wish to express their sympathy to the wife and family of Éamon (Hatchet). All available members please attend the funeral." Éamon "Hatchet" Kerr was alive and well. But on 25 February, the day after the notice appeared, Kerr and Seán Fox, the Official IRA's operations officer for the Belfast Command, along with a third man, were entering the Divis Flats complex when they were spotted by Danny Loughran, one of the local Official IRA unit who had joined Costello's group. Nineteen-year-old Loughran was AWOL from the Irish army, and was a trained shot. From a distance of between eighty and a hundred yards, he opened fire with a carbine rifle. Seven shots were fired at the three Officials. Fox slumped to the ground, fatally wounded in the head. At the time of the shooting the then Secretary of State, Merlyn Rees, was only a few hundred yards away on a visit to a local police station. He had been telling reporters that the "incident centres" recently established to monitor the Provo cease-fire were working well. The visit was cut short and he was whisked out of the danger zone.

Fox's death came on the same day that two other Officials were shot and wounded. Fox had been one of the Belfast Officials whom Costello had hoped to convert. He had met him at an Official IRA training camp in Wicklow. Seán Flynn later spoke to Fox about joining the IRSP and INLA, but Fox had refused. Those members of Costello's group who knew him liked him. One INLA man said that Fox was "game" and recalled him demanding to be allowed to take part in an attack on a security force base in the Whiterock area in 1973. At the time of his death he was thirty-two, and he left behind five children. His widow issued a statement calling for a halt to the escalating feud. But the Official IRA had other ideas. Following the Divis Flats shooting, a spokesman for the Belfast Command told the press: "This is open and vicious war. We have been forced into a position where retaliation is inevitable. Feeling is very high and I am afraid that more people have yet to die." (*Daily Mirror,* 26 February 1975.) He added, in case talk of "open and vicious war" might be misunderstood by the security forces, that there would be no campaign against the army or police. If the Officials had felt any guilt about the shooting of Ferguson, the death of Fox removed it. According to a member of the Official IRA who was active in 1975, "Fox's murder cleared away any guilt feelings. Our attitude then was, let's get the bastards. Fox would be revenged." (Interview, 10 June 1993.)

The leadership of the IRSP were in a dangerous dilemma. Members of the Belfast organisation had defied Costello. By engaging in attacks on the Officials they had exposed the party to charges that it had a military wing— something that Costello had been anxious to keep secret until the INLA was ready and strong enough to conduct proper operations. Yet Costello could not completely dissociate himself from his men's actions without losing the support of what was a vital part of his organisation. He knew the importance of Belfast and had once said, "You'll never win this revolution unless you win in Belfast." At a press conference on 26 February he continued to deny that his party had an armed wing but said that there was a distinction between that and IRSP members having the right to defend themselves. Jim McCorry of the IRSP's Belfast Executive also said that the killing of Fox might have been an attempt by local party members to "defend themselves". The party was to launch its own enquiry into the incident. McCorry claimed, that apart from the killing of Fox, their members in the city had not been involved in any attacks on members of the rival organisation. (*Irish Times*, 27 February 1975.) Bernadette McAliskey was less able to excuse the actions of the movement in Belfast. She regretted the deaths and insisted there was no military wing and that the IRSP was not involved in any violence.

Already, divisions within the movement were showing themselves. The first was between Belfast and Dublin: the Dublin-based leadership was not in control of the actions of its members a hundred miles to the North. This was a fault line that throughout the history of the INLA and IRSP would again and again threaten to pull the movement asunder. The other crack that was opening was between McAliskey on the left wing of the IRSP and the core around Costello in a dispute over the very role of the military wing and the armed campaign. The day before Fox was buried, Costello said he would be willing to talk peace with the Officials at any time. There were also rumours that peace moves had been made by two Belfast priests acting as intermediaries. The Officials denied any knowledge of this.

Fox's funeral was an impressive affair—an opportunity for the Officials to put on a show of strength. The *Irish Times* estimated that there were more than eight hundred men and youths separated into companies of twenty-five marching behind the coffin. The coffin was flanked by a guard of honour of twelve men dressed in black uniforms. There were also fifty youths and twenty-five girls wearing green or black uniforms. Billy McMillen was there and Malachy McGurran, and Goulding gave the graveside oration. It was defiant.

"The thugs of the British Army and the RUC and the Special Branch and the UDR did not stop us. The misguided and cynically led Provisionals did not stop us. The near-fascist loyalist murder gangs did not stop us. And by God, the threats and the assaults of a few power-hungry and confused dissidents will not stop us now." (*Irish Times*, 28 February 1975.)

Among the mourners listening to this were several IRSP members who had attended the funeral. Two hundred death notices were inserted in the *Irish News* for Seán Fox. Among them was one from a branch of the IRSP. It read: "The Andersonstown branch of the IRSP wish to extend their deepest sympathy to the wife and family of Seán Fox. The contradictions between ourselves and the enemy are antagonistic contradictions, the contradictions between the people are non-antagonistic." (*Irish News*, 27 February 1975.) A nice thought, but far from the reality of the developing conflict between the INLA/IRSP and Official IRA. It had already gone well beyond the stage of "non-antagonistic" resolution. Within three days of this rather pious sentiment appearing, the conflict was to take a drastic lurch towards even greater bloodshed.

A group of four INLA men headed south to Dublin carrying with them a handgun and a machine-gun of the type commonly known as a grease-gun; but it was also nicknamed the "spittin' dummy", because it had a silencer on the barrel. When it fired, the only sound heard was the bolt going back and forth. It came from an Official IRA arms dump, part of a haul from eastern Europe. They brought with them also a list. It contained the names of leading Officials that they wanted to murder.

At first the four parked across from the Officials' head office near the corner of Gardiner Place and Mountjoy Square. Their original intention was to kill Dessie O'Hagan, a hardline member of the Official republican movement and one of the names near the top of their list. His car was parked outside the organisation's offices. So the Belfast gunmen waited. Their intended target did not show up; instead, Malachy McGurran got into O'Hagan's car and drove off. McGurran was not on their list. The four Belfast men drove back north, successfully smuggling their "spittin' dummy" through a road check.

They decided to try again. This time they would aim higher, but not at Goulding, the chief of staff: like McGurran, he was regarded as a moderating influence and was not on their hit list. But Seán Garland, adjutant-general of the Official IRA, was. Garland, like Costello, was a 1950s veteran, a man who had been known for most of his life as a dedicated republican. He had taken part in the most famous incident in the 1950s campaign, the bungled attack on the Brookeborough RUC station in County Fermanagh, during which Seán South and Fergal O'Hanlon had been shot dead. In that bloody shambles Garland, badly wounded in the thigh, had volunteered to stay beside his dead and dying comrades with a Thompson submachine-gun and fight off the pursuing police to give his other comrades time to escape into the mountains. This chance to join South and O'Hanlon in republican martyrdom was denied him. He was whisked across the border. Eventually, after returning to active service, he ended up jailed in Crumlin Road prison, where he spent the last few years of the doomed campaign.

Afterwards, Garland took part in the leftward push of the republican movement, developing a southern-oriented political strategy. However, at times he had sided with Costello, with whom he had worked on "document A", analysing the role of the armed campaign in the North. Yet a year later he had acted as prosecutor during Costello's court-martial. Personally as well as politically he was seen as a hard man, lacking in charm or charisma. A former member of the Official IRA who later joined the INLA recounts how after a spell at an Official IRA training camp in Mornington, near Drogheda, some of the Belfast volunteers did not have the money to take a bus back home. They asked Garland what they should do, and he told them to "thumb it". Costello, overhearing the conversation, gave them the money.

The Belfast men believed that Garland, more than anybody apart from McMillen in Belfast, was responsible for the attacks on the IRSP. He was the strong man on the Army Council, a man increasingly Stalinist in his outlook, who was determined to eradicate the new movement.

The hit team of four headed south again. This time—not wanting to risk losing the "spittin' dummy"—they were carrying two handguns, a .38 and a Walther pistol. Instead of going to the centre of Dublin, they went out to Ballymun, where Garland lived. Late on the night of 1 March, after a night out with his wife, Garland parked his car near his flat at Balcurris Road. As he left the car he was shot six times by two of the team wearing hoods. He was seriously injured, but to the amazement of his attackers he survived yet again.

Belfast had taken the feud south on its own initiative. Costello had no idea of the planned attack on his old comrade and was beside himself with anger when he heard the news about it. Costello asked an old friend, a former 1950s IRA man who had joined the IRSP, who he thought had shot Garland.

"I think *we* did," came the reply.

"*We* fuckin' did?" Costello is said to have responded in disbelief. It was not just that the guidelines that he had imposed less than two weeks before had once more been ignored: it was that the whole situation in Belfast was spiralling out of control. The INLA in the Northern capital thought, since it was the one directly under attack, that it should decide how best to defend itself. The pattern was to be repeated throughout the history of the movement; in a way it was the same pattern that had already been established in the original dispute that split the IRA in 1969 and the Official IRA in 1974. The Dublin-based leadership of the new movement, like the Dublin-based leadership of the Officials, found it hard if not impossible to exercise any effective control over the Belfast units. They wanted to fight their own war their own way, and to a large extent they did so.

In Belfast there was a wave of shootings, attempted kidnappings, kneecappings, and beatings. The day after Garland was shot, a hooded gunman burst into a club in Twinbrook and shot Paddy McAllister, a member of the Officials. A man was shot in the leg in the Markets area. The following day, 3 March, there was a shooting incident in Turf Lodge that left a member of the IRSP with a serious head wound and a member of the Official IRA wounded in the wrist. The RUC issued figures showing that the internecine violence had to that date claimed the lives of two men and wounded nineteen others. On 4 March there was a bullet and bomb attack on the Bush Bar, an Official hangout in Leeson Street in the lower Falls area.[6]

Ronnie Bunting was high on the Officials' wanted list. On two occasions they had tried to shoot him. The third time, they were lucky. On 5 March, as Bunting drove out of Turf Lodge along with two others, one of whom was armed, a sniper opened up on their car. One bullet grazed Bunting's neck, narrowly missing the jugular vein. It took a few seconds before Bunting's companion realised he had been shot. Bunting was able to drive straight to the Royal Victoria Hospital. His companion was taken to the Springfield Road police station, where he made a statement about the incident. He entered and left the station with a revolver under his coat. The RUC never bothered to search him.

The next day gunmen fired on two members of the Officials in Beechmount, a hard-core Official area, wounding them. A five-year-old child was seriously injured in the attack. The Officials claimed that the gunmen were from the Divis Flats. Danny Loughran, who had killed Fox, was thought to have been one of the attackers. There was an immediate outcry from the ordinary people of the Catholic areas for a halt to the feuding. A group of women in the Turf Lodge area circulated a petition calling on the two sides to stop. It was revealed that there had already been five attempts to arrange a truce, all of which had failed largely because the Officials' leadership, for various reasons, were unwilling to engage in negotiations.

IRSP leaders from other parts of the country were desperate to bring the violence, which was almost entirely confined to Belfast, to an end. They feared that the city's units were out of control and could precipitate a political disaster for the whole movement. At a meeting of the IRSP's National Executive a motion was proposed calling on the Belfast membership to "stand down" in order to avoid further bloodshed. It was narrowly defeated. Bernadette McAliskey called on those who were retaliating against the Official IRA "to stop it now." She suggested that members of the IRSP in Belfast stay out of the path of the Officials for forty-eight hours.

A few days before, the Officials had refused to meet the IRSP until it ended the violence. Tomás Mac Giolla had responded to suggestions that he act as a mediator by saying, "Sinn Féin had no intention whatsoever of meeting with the IRSP. We simply call on them to stop murdering us. Any talks should be between the IRSP and the IRA." (*Irish Times*, 6 March 1975.) This, of course, was anathema to Costello, who was all along maintaining that the IRSP was a political party without any military affiliations.

Nevertheless, the pressure was growing on the Official leadership to accept IRSP peace moves. It increased after 7 March, when it was announced that the Belfast IRSP had disbanded. Its members were told to reapply for membership individually. The IRSP said that this decision was "the last possible move we could make to defuse the present situation." (*Irish Times*, 8 March 1975.) In response, the Officials could not resist gloating, congratulating the Official IRA, who had "stood firm in the face of a threatened sectarian explosion." They also congratulated the Turf Lodge Peace Women for forcing an "about face" in the IRSP. (Ibid.)

By early March the IRSP was deeply concerned about the effects the blood-letting was having on the growth of the party. Its first ardfheis, scheduled for the end of March, had to be cancelled. Instead of being able to build up to this event, which was supposed to mark the fully fledged appearance of a new and dynamic left-wing republican party, the IRSP was being consumed by the feud, fending off accusations that it was a paramilitary front engaged in acts of gangsterism and sectarianism; its credibility as a political party was being undermined by its supporters in Belfast, over whom it seemed to exercise little or no control. Its leaders were being forced to lie and prevaricate in a hopeless effort to protect the fledgling INLA from being exposed before its time; instead of launching itself upon the world as a challenger of British imperialism it had stumbled into a bloody fratricidal brawl. No wonder the Official IRA were in no hurry to open up peace talks. Why let their rival off the hook on which they were hung? The survival of the infant party was at stake. Said Bernadette McAliskey: "No matter how Sinn Féin emerge from this disaster, unless the IRSP has a chance to put its policies to the people the organisation will be destroyed." (*Irish Times*, 7 March 1975.)

NOTES

1. The name in fact had been used to claim responsibility in 1973 for an attack on a member of the SDLP near Newry. Maverick republicans were

suspected.

2. One of those who came to the afternoon meeting was a farmer from County Fermanagh. He welcomed the formation of the new army but for reasons that had little to do with Connolly-style socialism: he said that he hoped at last someone would deal with the "Protestant problem". He told the startled delegates that no quarter should be given, neither man, woman nor child spared. He was not recruited.

3. Steenson, nicknamed "Dr Death" by the media in 1985, became one of the more notorious gunmen produced by the INLA (see chapters 3, 9, and 12).

4. The Irish Citizens' Army later disclaimed any links to the IRSP in a letter to the *Irish News* of 4 March. Signed "T. Higgins (Adjutant), Northern Command, Irish Citizens' Army", it denounced the "disgraceful bickering" between the Officials and the IRSP. It also said that the ICA was formed in 1967 "to protect and advance the best interests of the Irish people." However, this letter proved to be one of the only public utterances ever made by the organisation.

5. One of them was Karl Hegney, who played a peripheral role in the shooting. On 11 October 1991 he was shot dead by loyalist gunmen while walking down the Ormeau Road, not far from the spot where the Princess Bar used to stand.

6. About two weeks before, a bomb had exploded outside the pub when Cathal Goulding was there after attending the funeral of Seán Fox. Though blamed at the time on Costello supporters, it turned out to be the work of the UVF.

3

THE POLITICS OF FRATRICIDE

Moves were already afoot to find a mediator. By the beginning of March five attempts had been made to find an acceptable go-between to end the blood-letting. Among the names proposed was that of Father Des Wilson—the nearest thing Belfast has to a liberation theologist. Eventually, during the first week of March, Michael Mullen, a personal friend of Costello's, came forward and was accepted by the Officials. Mullen was general secretary of the Irish Transport and General Workers' Union and a senator. Though the Officials were still wary of peace moves, they could not reject overtures from such an impeccable source.

Even as people tried to push the peace process slowly along, the shooting continued in Belfast. The IRSP alleged that on one day, Saturday 8 March, there had been five attacks on their members in Belfast, including the attempted murder of Paul Maguire.

The same day a macabre killing took place that was at first linked to the feud; but though it turned out to have been sectarian, it did accidentally, and rather strangely, reveal something about the loyalists' growing fear of the IRSP.

Michael Adamson, a 23-year old Catholic student, was preparing to go to his brother's wedding. Two men arrived at his front door in Clifton Drive in north Belfast. They were dressed as if they too were attending the wedding, wearing flowers in their lapels. When Adamson's wife opened the door they burst in, and shot her husband in the head. She was also shot and seriously injured. The police said that the gunmen "seem to have vanished into thin air." The bride and groom were kept ignorant of the murder to allow their wedding to go ahead.

Adamson was an arts student at Queen's University whose family came from the Markets area, where he had been involved in community action groups. The Ulster Volunteer Force, in its magazine *Combat*, later claimed that he had been a "finance officer" of the Official IRA unit in the Markets but had joined the IRSP. It also claimed that documents and letters stolen from the dead man's home proved there were links between the Communist

Party of England (Marxist-Leninist) and the IRSP. According to *Combat*, "the letters all express solidarity with the IRSP cause and praise the efforts of the IRSP in being able to persuade many leading Provisionals to defect ..." The UVF concluded ominously: "The documents and letters are regarded by the UVF as significant and go to prove that UVF warnings about IRSP plans to foment revolution in Ulster must be heeded by all who value their Protestant heritage and traditional British way of life." (*Combat*, July 1975.)

According to the IRSP, Adamson was not a member, though he seems to have been involved at some time with the Officials through community groups in the Markets area.

The UVF's warnings about the revolutionary potential of the IRSP echo those of the UDA. The rising loyalist concern was partly fuelled by the fact that the UVF was in possession of material that originated with the Official IRA—though the Officials deny handing it over—that singled out ex-Officials such as Ronnie Bunting as dangerous ultra-leftists who were bent on provoking a sectarian bloodbath. Leading members of the Officials in Belfast, including the city's OC, Billy McMillen, are known to have met the UVF and other loyalists in the Old House, a well-known pub in Leeson Street, to discuss social issues, such as the campaign to stop the demolition of houses to make way for a ring road through west Belfast. It is possible that information about the IRSP might have changed hands at these gatherings. What is certain is that the terms in which the UVF talked about the IRSP are very similar to those adopted by the Officials. In the March issue of *Combat*, for instance, the IRSP is alleged to have set up an armed wing, the Irish Citizens' Army, "to promote sectarian warfare in Belfast and other parts of the province. It is believed that the Official IRA in Belfast has ordered its units to crack down on the sectarian activities of the IRSP—a move which has resulted in the death of an ICA unit commander and an IRA brigade staff officer." The rhetoric comes straight out of the *United Irishman*.

Loyalist naïveté is evident, however, in the way prominence is given to the "Communist Party of England (Marxist-Leninist)", described by the UVF as "the most violent Communist organisation in the United Kingdom." (Ibid.) The Communist Party of England was in fact a fanatical and tiny Maoist organisation, whose revolutionary potential existed only in the minds of the utterly committed or the completely paranoid.

These kinds of accusations and counter-accusations made it extremely difficult to get the peace process started. A new tactic emerged when, on 10 March, the Officials offered an "amnesty" to those IRSP members who would dissociate themselves from the organisation. The offer was dismissed with contempt by the Belfast chairman of the IRSP, Jim McCorry. On 12 March two members of the IRSP were shot and wounded. The next day, twenty-four hours before the Officials' amnesty offer was due to expire, Seán Morrissey, who was on the Executive of the Republican Clubs, was shot by gunmen in the library of St Joseph's teacher training college in west Belfast.

In Dublin on 13 March—the same day as Morrissey was shot and wounded—Michael Mullen wrote to both Costello and the Officials suggesting that they nominate two representatives each from their organisations authorised to speak at a meeting that he would convene. He suggested that as "the root of the problem appears to be in the Six Counties" both representatives should come from there. Costello replied the next day that he agreed and that his representatives would meet Mullen at his earliest convenience. But he added he was agreeing that the two representatives should come from the Six Counties only because the initial discussion would be with Mullen alone. He was insisting that the problem was not merely a product of the North but a result of Official IRA policy.

Mullen met the Officials' representatives in Dundalk the next day. Afterwards he was reported as being "impressed" by their desire for peace. Cathal Goulding was also there to meet members of the Turf Lodge women's peace group, who had undertaken their own peace initiative. He committed himself to ensuring that there would be no more attacks on members of the IRSP. The next day Mullen met the IRSP men from Belfast and emerged from the discussion that took place in Dublin declaring that the two sides had reached a peace agreement. "I'm in the happy position of stating that both parties have agreed to cease hostilities on the understanding that they will engage in meaningful negotiations on their respective points of view. In this connection I have arranged to invite both parties to attend a further meeting next Thursday afternoon." (*Sunday Independent*, 16 March 1975.)

Mullen asked both parties to submit an authorised agenda of matters that they wanted discussed at any future peace negotiations. Costello replied: "On behalf of our National Executive I would suggest the inclusion of the following matters. (A) The series of attacks on our members in Belfast starting on Dec. 12, including kidnappings, beatings, shootings, car burnings, attacks on members' houses and petrol bombing of one house. (B) The shooting of Hugh Ferguson. (C) The wounding of an IRSP member in Newry about 8 weeks ago. (D) The allegation of sectarian murder. (E) The wounding of John Garland. (F) The activities of agent provocateurs. (G) The further attacks which have been carried out against our members since last Friday despite the fact that the Turf Lodge Peace Women received a written guarantee from C. Goulding that no aggressive action would be carried out. (H) The role of the UVF and other loyalist groups in the present dispute. (I)

The role of politically biased 'journalists' in the present dispute. (J) The circulation of private documents to the press and to others by the Officials, in particular documents referring to S. Costello's alleged activities when still a member of Sinn Féin.

"In conclusion, I would like to point out that we were willing to meet the Officials under your chairmanship on the basis of the above suggestions. If, however, agreement cannot be reached on the contents of the agenda we are still prepared to meet them, on the basis of ignoring what has happened in the past and simply discussing ways and means of avoiding a recurrence of the tension and conflict in the future.

"We request that the meeting with the Officials should take place at the earliest possible date, and look forward to your reply." (Letter to Michael Mullen, 19 March 1975.)

For their part, the Officials drew up a list of some forty-five incidents, beginning in early February, "when incident piled upon incident ..." (*Belfast Telegraph*, 19 March 1975.) They alleged that the feud began when the IRSP seized Official IRA weapons, and accused the organisation of bombing the Bush Bar in Leeson Street during a visit by Cathal Goulding, even though the UVF had claimed two days before that it carried out the attack.

In spite of Mullen's confident announcement of 15 March, there remained several obstacles in the path to peace. One was the continued refusal of the Officials to negotiate with Costello himself. In a statement to the magazine *Hibernia* the Officials declared: "We can state that we need no 'talks' with Mr. Costello for the simple reason that we have talked with him for two years now at Sinn Féin Ard Comhairle level while he argued for a political formula which would swing the Movement in support of the Provisional campaign and which would have us support a policy of tit-for-tat sectarian assassinations." (21 March 1975.)[1] Costello wrote to Mullen: "We have discussed the problem of my presence at any peace discussions with the Officials and we are of the opinion that my presence would be essential, even if we were to occupy separate rooms during the discussions." (Letter to Michael Mullen, undated.)

Another obstacle was the Officials' demand that the IRSP acknowledge that it had a paramilitary wing. In their *Hibernia* statement the Officials had declared that before a solution to the "IRSP-created problem" could be found, "it is necessary to gain a clear admission from the IRSP that they have engaged in military violence against our members. How can you begin to 'talk' to a group which does not even admit it is attacking your members?" (*Hibernia*, 21 March 1975.)

This Costello still refused to concede. He replied: "We are not prepared to publicly announce the existence of a military wing of the IRSP as it does not exist, however we would like to draw your attention to the contents of the enclosed press statement issued by the Belfast Regional Executive of the IRSP. In accordance with that press statement, we are prepared to publicly accept that there are groups outside of the IRSP who have taken action against the Officials and that they have done so following their offers of protection to our Belfast Regional Executive." (Letter to Michael Mullen, undated.)

The groups referred to had emerged some two weeks after the peace talks started. On 28 March the IRSP issued a statement announcing that twenty-nine of its Belfast members who had been "stood down" because of the feud with the Official IRA were returning to assume their normal political activities. The statement went on: "During the last number of months we have been approached by various groups offering their services in defence of our right to organise. On each occasion we have rejected these approaches and asked that they take no action which would further escalate the situation, or be seen as in any way provocative.

"However, because of the continuation of attacks by the Officials against our members and supporters we now have no option but to accept these offers of protection." (*Belfast Telegraph*, 29 March 1975.) When Jim McCorry was asked who these groups were he refused to name them, saying they were merely people who were "militantly sympathetic" to the IRSP. (Ibid.)

The unnamed groups referred to were, of course, a fiction, an attempt to conceal the fact that the IRSP did have an armed wing—the Irish National Liberation Army—whose members had carried out attacks on the Officials. That the IRSP was now pretending that unnamed groups of "militantly sympathetic" individuals were ready to protect it was an attempt to put pressure on the Officials to come to the conference table. Costello's insistence that the INLA name should not be used to claim responsibility for any attacks on fellow-republicans meant that the IRSP had to engage in what were increasingly transparent prevarications.[2]

Meanwhile, the usual allegations and counter-allegations were building up again. The IRSP had accused the Officials of further attacks. The Officials countered with a claim that the IRSP had attempted to murder Séamus Lynch in a flats complex in the New Lodge Road. Fears grew that the feud would erupt on a serious scale just in time for Easter, one of the two most sacred occasions in the republican calendar. For the most part, however, the violence was verbal. It was the week before the IRSP's first ardfheis, and the party held Easter commemoration ceremonies in Limerick, Killaloe, Dublin, and Bray. Jim McCorry gave the oration at Glasnevin, which began, strangely enough, with a quotation from Glenn Barr, one of the UDA leaders behind the Ulster Workers' Council strike that had brought down the power-sharing government the year before. Said McCorry: "Glenn Barr had a statement which said, build your dream and then show it to us. That is what we are going to do. We are going to build our dream." (*Starry Plough*, April 1975.)

The speech continued, sounding sometimes like that of a 1960s radical: "For many of us our socialism is simple. It starts with concern, compassion, and love … It will come to fruition because we are the embryo of the new society." Sometimes it was more like that of a hard man from Belfast: "Well, for the past few weeks we have taken whatever was thrown at us. But this weekend we decided: no more. If we have to fight those who should be with us before we can get at the real enemy, then that will be the case." What the new party's contribution to republican and socialist politics would be was hard to discern from McCorry's oration, which mixed wishy-washy good-will socialism with paramilitary menace. He announced that party members would be returning to Belfast the next day. They were now under the protection of unnamed groups.

A hundred miles to the north, in Belfast City Cemetery, Mick Ryan of the Official Ard-Chomhairle gave no sign in his speech of any likely compromise with the IRSP in the search for peace between the two groups. Instead he made the usual accusations. The IRSP had launched "murderous attacks" on the Officials and fomented civil war. He was followed by Billy McMillen, the Belfast OC, who read a statement from the Official IRA Army Council. It too attacked the IRSP, laying the charge of agent provocateur against the party. The Officials, it seemed, had resumed their hard-line stance against their former comrades in arms.

Yet within a few days of this tough talking, the Officials had agreed to a meeting with the IRSP. Mullen contacted Costello with an outline agenda, which Costello accepted at once, replying to Mullen on 3 April. The nationalist ghettos heaved a sigh of relief, and the members of the new party thought that at last they could concentrate on the coming ardfheis, for the first weekend in April. But on the very day Costello was penning his acceptance of the new talks agenda, word came from Belfast that Hugh Madden, a member of the party's Belfast executive, had been shot four times and was seriously ill. The Officials accepted responsibility for the shooting, alleging that Madden had drawn a gun on two of their volunteers during a dispute. This was vociferously denied by the IRSP. Once more it looked as if the intractable nature of the Belfast organisations was going to frustrate the hoped-for talks. Mullen called it a "terrible blow". (*Belfast Telegraph*, 3 April 1975.)

It was feared that the IRSP's so-called "protectors" would be as good as their word. The party's armed wing did in fact contemplate a whole series of counter-measures, which were outlined in a long statement that, as far as is known, was never published. It demanded that breweries and wholesale drink suppliers stop supplying clubs and pubs run by the Officials; among those to be boycotted were the Cyprus Street Social Club, the Turf Lodge Social and Recreation Centre, the Mellows-McCann Club, the Bush Bar, and the Victoria Bar. The statement also said that "all drinking clubs run by the official Republican movement are to be handed over to community-based organisations by Saturday night. Where they are running shebeens the necessary action is to be taken by our units to see that they are closed." In the event, the IRSP's "protectors" did not carry out these threats. But the statement ended with this warning: "They will find we fight a different kind of war where the values of socialism play as large a part as the cynical tactics of Stalinists. They have begun the war. We will finish it." In this, at least, they would be as good as their word.

To add to the tension, reports came in of two further shootings in the city. A leading Belfast member of the IRSP, Anthony Doran, had been wounded, as had Robert Elliman, an Official IRA man. It seemed as if the feared tit-for-tat shoot-out had begun again. It was not quite that simple, however. As it turned out, rather confusingly, both men had been having a friendly drink together in Mooney's pub in the Markets when a member of the Provisionals came in and fired an Armalite rifle at Elliman, seriously wounding him and injuring his companion.[3]

Meanwhile, the first ardfheis of the IRSP convened in the Country Club in Dublin on Saturday 6 April. Over a hundred delegates arrived—a somewhat smaller number than might have been expected given the claims by Costello that the party had around eight hundred members.

In his opening address Costello launched into a scathing and bitter attack on the Officials. "At one of the most critical periods in our history, when practically every Irishman and woman instinctively recognised that a courageous change in strategy was called for in 1969, we found ourselves led by people whose most ambitious demands were for the democratisation of Stormont, and for a Bill of Rights as a defence against the murder and terror of the Imperialist troops and their native allies, the loyalist murder gangs. Almost overnight the sectarian murderers of the UVF and UDA became potential allies in the struggle for a Socialist Republic. All that was needed for this miraculous transformation was that they should display some slight interest in co-operation on the question of the re-development of the Shankill or the proposed route of the new Ring Road ... The Rent and Rates strike has been betrayed by the secret payment of arrears on the Republican Clubs premises in Cyprus Street. The RUC were given a safe conduct into the Lower Falls in order to inspect the Cyprus Street drinking club cum torture centre, so that they would support the granting of a liquor licence when the application came before the courts. The RUC kept their part of the bargain with the result that the Officials now have the unenviable distinction of being the only organisation with a fully licensed torture centre and knee-capping factory in full swing. The principal targets for the Officials' vicious campaign of murder, torture and felon setting, are the Belfast members of the Party." (*Starry Plough*, May 1975.)

Referring to the peace talks, Costello said that the "only obstacle in the way of a solution is the absolute refusal of the Officials to even indicate a possible date for discussion ..."

While policy was being hammered out in Dublin, the Official IRA struck again in Belfast. Eighteen-year-old Danny Loughran was leaving a club near the Divis Flats late on the night of 5 April when he was machine-gunned to death by two Official IRA gunmen. Loughran was one of those who had been involved in the shooting of Seán Fox in February, and was blamed for his death. When the news reached the delegates at the ardfheis in Dublin, the Belfast members left immediately and headed home. Within hours two Official IRA men were shot and wounded at a social club after being lined up against a wall. A caller to the Belfast office of the *Irish Times* claimed responsibility for the attack on behalf of an organisation whose name had not been heard before—at least not in Ireland: the People's Liberation Army (PLA). The IRSP claimed that the PLA was one of several groups that had offered to protect it from the Official IRA. The Officials mocked this claim, alleging that the PLA was in fact the armed wing of Costello's party. Another victim of retaliation was Dessie O'Hagan, a member of the Officials' Ard-Chomhairle, who was shot and wounded on 6 April.

Jim McCorry continued to deny the existence of such a wing. As for the PLA, he told the press, "They offered assistance and we accepted it ... We have no control over its activities." (*Belfast Telegraph*, 8 April 1975.) At least in this last assertion McCorry was being more truthful than perhaps he realised. However, the truth about the PLA was rather different from the story put out at that press conference. The name "People's Liberation Army" had come about after a discussion on the need to claim responsibility for the attacks on the Officials while at the same time avoiding involving the INLA, which Costello was adamant must not be sullied by being linked to a republican feud. PLA sounded good. After all, at that time, in the spring of 1975, the Vietnamese PLA was marching towards Saigon and final victory over the US army.

Two of the death notices that appeared for Danny Loughran in the *Irish News* were from the PLA. One identified Loughran as a member of "G Cell". It read: "The People's Liberation Army extend deepest sympathy to his family circle. Those who support peaceful coexistence with Imperialism while it is slaughtering the people are not revolutionaries regardless of what they call themselves. They belong to a sinister form of Mafia whose ultimate goal is to serve a new form of Bourgeoisie." (*Irish News*, 8 April 1975.)

At Loughran's funeral the PLA emerged in public to give him a full paramilitary send-off. The hearse was flanked by eight men dressed in black clothing, with black berets and wearing dark glasses. Gunmen fired three volleys of shots over his coffin. McCorry gave the graveside oration, bitterly predicting that the deaths of Ferguson and Loughran would mean that the Officials would be "cast into the rubbish bin of history." (*Belfast Telegraph*, 9 April 1975.) A cross marks Loughran's grave in Belfast City Cemetery. There is something oddly poignant about the inscription, which describes him as a "staff officer" of the PLA, an organisation that never existed. What people were witnessing that day, as the black-clad men marched alongside Loughran's coffin, was the first appearance in public of the Irish National Liberation Army.

On the day of the funeral the IRSP issued a statement saying that it had been informed by the PLA that it had been responsible for a series of actions against the Officials, which it listed. There were five (see chronology, p. 358), and they included the shooting of Des O'Hagan, which was, said the PLA, "in direct retaliation to the murder of Danny Loughran." (*Irish News*, 9 April 1975.) It seemed as if the feud was ready to sink to bloodier depths.

Michael Mullen was anxious and angry. The day after Loughran was shot, he wrote to both the Officials and Costello, threatening to withdraw his services as mediator because of the delays in convening talks between the two groups. "I am concerned and disappointed at the delay which I have experienced, and which I continue to experience, in having agreement on a positive date and time upon which the representatives of your Organisation and the Opposite Side would meet, under my Chairmanship, for the purpose of endeavouring to satisfactorily reconcile all outstanding points of difference. I am particularly disappointed having regard to the fact that the representatives of both organisations have already informed me (when I met them separately) that they were agreeable to accept my Chairmanship and were interested in bringing about a peaceful solution to the matters at issue. Indeed, my frustration as an agreed Mediator is quite understandable when one has regard to recent Radio, Television and Newspaper reports, all of which indicate that hostilities are still continuing between both organisations.

"I now find it necessary to state that if I do not receive a clear indication, in writing, from both Organisations by 6 p.m. on Wednesday, 9 April, 1975, to the effect that the Organisation concerned is immediately prepared to meet to discuss the Agenda which I have already submitted to them at a time and date to be specified by me following the deadline and date which I have found it necessary to mention above, I shall have no option but to make a public statement simply stating 'That I have decided to withdraw my offer of Mediator.' In the event of having to make any such statement, it is my intention not to make any further comment by way of clarification etc., to any newspapers, radio or television.

"Trusting I will have your Organisation's affirmation that its representatives will attend the 'Peace Talks' meeting which I have offered to convene."

As before, Costello, on behalf of the IRSP, accepted at once. "Our representatives will be available at 24 hours notice to attended meeting under your Chairmanship," he replied. (Letter to Michael Mullen, 8 April 1975.) But he also expressed his surprise at "the general tone of your letter, particularly in view of the fact that we have repeatedly informed you, yourself, both verbally and in writing, of our willingness and indeed urgent desire to engage in discussion with a view to ending the present conflict."

The Turf Lodge Peace Women were also getting impatient. They threatened to march from Turf Lodge—an Official IRA stronghold—to the Divis Flats, which had become almost synonymous with the IRSP and was referred to as "the Planet of the Erps" (as the party was known in the city). The women were going to call on both sides to halt the internecine killing. Unfortunately, the moves came too late to halt the bloodshed.

The Officials had a book and newspaper stall outside Beacon's pub at the corner of the Springfield Road and Falls Road. (A photograph of the stall appeared on the back page of the January edition of the *United Irishman* to mark its opening.) On the afternoon of Saturday 12 April, Paul "Cheesy" Crawford, a postman by trade, was standing at the stall with two other members of the movement, selling papers, when a car drove by. Gunmen in the car opened fire, killing Crawford and wounding one of the men beside him, who was the real target.

Crawford was the first fatality the Officials had suffered since Fox had been killed in February. But, unlike Fox and most of the others targeted by the INLA, he had no significant role in the organisation—he was cut down merely because he was in the wrong place at the wrong time.

Four men were now dead and over forty injured. The peace initiative seemed to have stalled for good. The mood in the Belfast Catholic ghettos was one of growing frustration, anger, and fear. They were already under assault from a vicious sectarian assassination campaign being carried out by the UDA and UVF—the worst since 1972. In the midst of this the sight of republicans killing each other was greeted with incomprehension.

At this point the Turf Lodge Peace Women rounded on the Official IRA. They had asked both the Officials and the IRSP to send a woman representative to a meeting. When the IRSP responded and the Officials did not, the women issued a statement saying that "the Officials were not interested in talks for peace and were hell-bent on continuing their campaign of murder, assault and raiding of homes in our districts." (*Irish News*, 14 April 1975.) The women said they were "determined to expose the Officials' callous indifference to the sufferings of the working-class people."

They had called off their planned march down the Falls Road, because the area was too tense. But they were demanding that the Officials sit down at once to negotiate an end to the feud with the IRSP. The Officials rejected their call, saying that as long as the IRSP continued to attack them they would not talk. They also accused the women of being a front for organisations that were opposed to the Convention elections and were trying to undermine the Officials' election campaign. Giving the graveside oration at the funeral of Crawford, Des O'Hagan attacked the "so-called Peace Group in Turf Lodge", calling it "wanton" and "malevolent". (*United Irishman*, May 1975.) A month before, Cathal Goulding had been singing its praises.

The Peace Women answered by saying they were not a front for anyone, nor did they take sides in the dispute: they merely wanted it ended. They said that "we fervently believe that the last two deaths could have been avoided if the Official IRA had sat down and talked." (*Irish News*, 17 April 1975.)

At the same time the IRSP announced that it had asked its "support groups" to cease offensive action against the Officials in order to give the peace talks another chance. The PLA had agreed to suspend actions until 20 April, giving both sides some four days to get peace moves started. The Officials said they treated the statement with caution. Within hours of the expiry of the PLA truce Jim McCorry offered himself as a hostage to the Officials. This dramatic gesture did little to affect the Officials' thinking. They stubbornly refused to be drawn into the talks process, and responded by scorning McCorry's offer, alleging that further attacks on their members had taken place.

The feud, almost entirely confined to Belfast, now threatened to break out in Derry. There were allegations that two Official IRA gunmen from Belfast had threatened IRSP members in the Shantallow area of the city. The IRSP also claimed that the Official IRA was planning a nationwide purge of the party after the Convention elections in May. According to a statement from the party's National Executive, "this decision was made in the belief that the IRSP could not be smashed in Belfast alone and that other areas outside of Belfast would have to be attacked. It is also felt by the Sinn Féin Ard Comhairle and the Official IRA Army Council that the political damage caused to the Official Republican Movement by the campaign is so serious that they have nothing further to lose by escalating the terror." (*Irish Times*, 22 April 1975.)

Towards the end of April, in spite of the bitter rhetoric flying between the two groups, the number of incidents showed signs of diminishing. Between 22 and 28 April there were some eight incidents involving attacks or allegations of attacks from one side or the other, including the Derry incident, which the Officials denied ever occurred. All were of a relatively minor nature. However, Costello believed that when the forthcoming elections for the Northern Ireland Convention were out of the way, the Officials would renew their campaign with increased ferocity. On 28 April he wrote to Mullen again to try to reactivate the peace process. He put some suggestions to the trade union leader that he thought "may help to overcome the difficulties arising from the dispute between ourselves and the Officials." Costello wrote: "I would suggest that the only means now available to secure an end to the conflict is through publication of an open letter to the press and media in general. The letter could be in your name with other people who may be agreeable also signing it." He advocated that the letter should contain a list of proposals for ending the conflict, such as an immediate agreement from both the IRSP and the Officials, and supporters of both, to end attacks on each other, and that the signatories of the letter should form a peace committee to adjudicate on alleged breaches of the cease-fire. Among those Costello thought Mullen should contact with a view to signing the letter were Father Des Wilson, Matt Merrigan of the ATGWU, Pádraig Ó Snodaigh of the National Museum—who, according to Costello, was a personal friend of Tomás Mac Giolla's—and Con Lehane, a solicitor.

Costello concluded: "It is absolutely essential that the open letter should be published immediately as there are indications of a serious escalation in the conflict immediately after the Convention elections. In my view it is important also that neither organisation should receive any prior notice of your intentions in this regard, as it is likely that the Officials would discourage any such attempt at mediation. As far as the IRSP is concerned I have not discussed the idea with them and the suggestions contained in this letter are from myself alone." (Letter to Michael Mullen, 28 April 1975.)

That afternoon, as Costello sent off his latest peace appeal to Mullen, the Officials' Belfast commander, Billy McMillen, was attending a meeting in the Republican Clubs' election headquarters in Cyprus Street, near the Falls Road. He was with his wife, Mary, a woman much younger than himself whom he had married less than two months before. Shortly before three o'clock that afternoon the couple left the meeting. Getting into McMillen's van, they drove up Leeson Street to the Falls Road, where they stopped outside Harden's hardware shop at the corner of Spinner Street. Both went into the shop, and McMillen bought 66p worth of nails, according to the shop assistant. McMillen probably did not notice the black taxi that had pulled up on the other side of the road near the corner of Dunlewy Street. Inside were Gerard Steenson, an ex-member of the Official Fianna and now at sixteen a member of the INLA, and Brendan McNamee, a former member of the Provisional IRA who had left after a dispute with the leadership in Long Kesh. Steenson was from Dunlewy Street, but if his intention had been to go home that afternoon, it quickly changed when he saw McMillen go into the hardware shop. McNamee pulled a gun and pointed it at the taxi driver while Steenson walked across the Falls Road, a revolver behind his back. McMillen and his wife came out of the shop. As they climbed back into the van, Steenson fired four shots at McMillen. He was hit in the neck. As he struggled to get out he was struck again, and slumped forward onto the pavement.

The young woman who had served him in Harden's heard the shots. According to her account, "immediately after they went out I heard three or four shots. But I was unable to go into the street for a few minutes. He was lying on the pavement with his feet in his van. There was a hole the size of a 2p piece in his neck. I saw him trying to breathe and as he breathed his neck caved in. He died on the pavement. There didn't seem to be anybody about.

"A few minutes later a woman came into the shop and said: 'I'll have six rolls of that purple wallpaper, please.' I felt sick. I felt like smashing her face in and throwing her out of the shop. He was still lying out there on the pavement outside.

"A crowd had gathered round and it seemed that everyone believed it was Billy McMillen. The girl who had been with him was standing on the pavement with her fists clenched, just screaming. I was so sorry for her. She was only a young girl. I thought at first that she was his daughter but someone said: 'It's his wife, they have only been married two months.'"

(*Daily Telegraph*, 29 April 1975.)

Steenson strolled back across the road and got into the taxi with McNamee. They then drove off towards the Divis Flats, into which the two escaped. The cool brutality of Gerard Steenson as he gunned down McMillen laid the foundation for the reputation that would follow him to his grave and earn him the nickname "Dr Death".

When the news of McMillen's murder reached Costello that afternoon, he was furious. On one level it was a personal reaction. McMillen in earlier and happier days had often stayed with Costello when in Dublin. Costello, who was not much of a drinker himself, always had a bottle of whiskey in the house when McMillen was expected. At another, political level he had as much cause for anger. The death of a man so close to the Dublin leadership and so well liked by the Officials in Belfast might destroy any hope of a settlement between the two organisations. Costello immediately put out a statement:

"The National Executive of the IRSP condemns without reservation the shooting of Billy McMillen in Belfast to-day. Despite the fact that Billy McMillen was known to be the commanding officer of the Official IRA in Belfast, and therefore responsible for the violence against IRSP members and supporters, the IRSP was in no way involved in his death. His death is particularly sinister when viewed against recent developments in the dispute between our organisation and the Official IRA. Despite the fact that the Official IRA had refused to engage in peace discussions with the IRSP the dispute between our organisations was in the process of being brought to an end, as a result of informal discussions between both organisations at local level in Belfast.

"During the past 48 hours members of the Belfast Regional Executive of the IRSP had been informed through intermediaries that the Official IRA intended to issue a public statement on Tuesday or Wednesday which would bring an end to the conflict. As a result of the general relaxation of tension the Belfast Regional Executive of the IRSP have held a series of public meetings in Belfast during the past 48 hours, and were in the process of selecting delegates to attend the final session of the IRSP National Conference.

"We are aware that the possibility of an end to the dispute was also known to British Intelligence Services and possibly to other sources with a vested interest in a continuation of the conflict. In these circumstances, the death of Billy McMillen must be seen as a deliberate and well-timed attempt to prevent a solution to the conflict. The only beneficiaries of his death are the British Imperialists and their allies in Ireland.

"The dangerous confusion surrounding the dispute is an open invitation to agents provocateur, and makes it all the more urgent that a peaceful solution emerges without further delay. We therefore make an urgent appeal to the Official IRA to engage in peace discussions and prevent a further tragic escalation in the conflict."

Costello's statement—more or less a repeat of what he had said after the attempted assassination of Seán Garland—was at complete variance with the letter he had written earlier in the day to Mullen in which he had shown no hint that there was any sign of an end to the dispute with the Officials. Certainly there was no indication that he believed the feud was on the verge of a settlement. It is likely that the statement's assertions about the coming resolution of the conflict were an attempt to make his allegations about an agent provocateur being responsible for McMillen's death sound plausible. The Officials, however, had no doubt who was responsible. Within a day of the assassination they had issued a detailed account of what had happened. They said that the killers were "well known members of the IRSP and are among the organisation's leading gunmen." (*Belfast Telegraph*, 29 April 1975.) Witnesses told them that the killer had "fired four shots at McMillen and then casually walked back to the taxi."

While their leader was angry over the shooting, the reaction in Belfast among his supporters was undisguised glee. In Long Kesh, where a few members of the IRSP/INLA were being held in cage 14, they shouted across to cage 21, where the Official prisoners were kept, "What about Billy? What about Billy?"

The Officials admit that the killing of McMillen was a bad blow to the organisation, from which it was never to recover in Belfast. He was largely responsible for holding the Official IRA together in the Northern capital during the 1969 split and the dispute with the IRSP five years later. Many volunteers had stayed with the Dublin leadership and rejected Costello's overtures because of his influence.

As might have been expected, the immediate reaction of the Official IRA in Belfast was to swear a terrible revenge. "We know the men who did it," a statement proclaimed, "and we won't rest until they are dead. They're in hiding but we will track them down to the ends of the earth. There is no hiding place." (*Daily Mirror*, 30 April 1975.) As it turned out, the two men involved in the murder of McMillen were to die at the hands of others.

The first attempt to get revenge proved somewhat less than determined. An Official IRA gunman burst into the home of Jim McCorry but was repelled by his mother-in-law. She recognised the gunman, who panicked and fled.

The Official IRA did not, as many feared it would, launch a series of bloody reprisals. The Army Council had decided who was to be held responsible for the deaths of its men in Belfast: Séamus Costello. Before the killing of Fox, the Official IRA had warned: "The responsibility for any deaths that should occur lies squarely on the shoulders of the people who organise and lead such individuals." (*Belfast Telegraph*, 24 February 1975.) This warning actually appeared the day before Fox was shot dead in the Divis Flats. It was repeated by Des O'Hagan at the graveside of Paul Crawford. "The people who organise these killer squads cannot expect to be permitted to continue with their crimes," he said. (*United Irishman*, May 1975.)

When Goulding came north to give the graveside oration at McMillen's funeral he did not issue any threats. But the vituperative rhetoric he directed at the IRSP made all too plain the depth of hatred felt for his former comrades. He described the IRSP as "a small, mad band of fanatical malcontents ... the sewer rats of Costello and McAliskey ..." Yet within weeks of McMillen's murder, mediation had begun again, involving Mullen, Con Lehane, and Father Wilson. This time it would succeed in patching up a peace of sorts between the two organisations, one that was monitored by a mediation committee. However, though tension between the Officials and the IRSP/INLA remained, especially in the North, and there would be frequent accusations of violations of the peace agreement as well as occasional outbreaks of violence, for all intents and purposes there was no more serious violence between the two groups—with one exception. After the killing of McMillen, the Official IRA Army Council had sentenced Séamus Costello to death. The vote was carried by a narrow margin.

At the beginning of May, Costello and Bernadette McAliskey took part in a whirlwind series of public meetings around Ireland to try to bring the party's politics to a wider public. On 7 May, Costello and Séamus O'Kane, a member of the Ard-Chomhairle from Derry, were returning from a meeting in the Granville Hotel, Waterford. They noticed that a motorbike was following their car. As it drew alongside, Costello saw the pillion passenger raising a machine-gun. He accelerated as the gunman raked his car. No-one was injured. This time the IRSP leader had escaped. But one thing was clear: though the feud was finished, for Costello the danger had not passed. As far as the Official IRA was concerned, there was still an outstanding score to settle, and Séamus Costello knew it.

When he had heard the news of Billy McMillen's death, he turned to a close friend and supporter, Tony Hayde, and said, "That's my death warrant."

The Irish Republican Socialist Party was registered as a political party on 22

May 1975 in Leinster House. The party put out a statement saying that "this decision should convince all that we are a genuine political party and will refute the allegations made in the past that we were a splinter group from the Official Republican movement." The statement claimed that the IRSP had a membership of 400 in the 26 Counties and 390 in Northern Ireland, with branches in Dublin, Wicklow, Carlow, Donegal, Limerick, Clare, Kerry, Cork, Monaghan, Wexford, Tipperary, Derry, Belfast and County Antrim, Tyrone, Armagh, and Newry in south Down. Its sixteen-member National Executive had been elected during the ardfheis six weeks earlier; the members were Séamus Costello (Wicklow), Mick Plunkett (Dublin), Tommy McCourt (Dublin), Gerry Jones (Dublin), Joe Quinn (Limerick), Stella Makowski (Clare), Jim McCorry (Belfast), Seán Flynn (Belfast), Vincent Fegan (Belfast), Terry Robson (Derry), Kitty O'Kane (Derry), J. Quigley (Derry), Johnny White (Donegal), Peter Pringle (Donegal), Séamus O'Kane (Donegal), and Bernadette McAliskey (Tyrone). Costello was also party chairman. Plunkett was made general secretary and White organising secretary.

The party ardfheis had been held in the middle of the feud, during which it had been subjected not only to physical attacks from the Official IRA but also to a propaganda assault that set out to characterise it as a band of sectarian gangsters bent on creating civil war in the North. The actual policies that emerged from the ardfheis received little attention in the media. They were for the most part unremarkable enough.

In Costello's address to the delegates he had not spent long on general policy. He congratulated the Vietnamese on the continuing success of their struggle against American imperialism, spoke of supporting the small farmer and the unemployed, and committed the IRSP to oppose the EEC and all national wage agreements.

The most important point to emerge from the speech was Costello's commitment to the creation of a "broad front". "On a National level, it shall be our task to organise the maximum possible degree of popular support for our demands for National Liberation. To do this we will seek the formation of a broad front composed of all organisations and individuals at home and abroad who are prepared to assert the right of the Irish people to full control of their own destiny." (*Starry Plough*, May 1975.)

The "broad front" had been a principle that Costello had tried to get the Officials to adopt between 1972 and 1974, but they suspected it was simply a device for swinging their support behind the Provisionals. It became the principal policy plank of the IRSP. But unfortunately the party had found itself calling for a broad front in the middle of a vicious feud with another republican organisation. To call for such a policy against British imperialism when republicans were shooting each other was a touch unrealistic, if not grimly ironic. Unrealistic too was the party's attitude towards Northern Ireland Protestants. Costello told the delegates that the IRSP would "explain" its policies to the Protestant working class "on the basis of our social and economic programme and the need to defeat British imperialism in Ireland …" (Ibid.) Like all republican organisations, the IRSP ignored the fact that the Protestant working class strongly identified with "British imperialism"—or at least with Britain's presence in Ireland, from which it had benefited enormously. As usual, the hatred loyalists felt for republicanism in any shape or form, left-wing or right-wing, was conveniently forgotten about.

However, the IRSP's programme was notable for its emphasis on women's issues. At the first ardfheis three hours were spent debating these questions—quite a novelty in a republican group in 1975. A detailed resolution was passed demanding social, economic and sexual rights for women, including the right to abortion, though Costello himself was outspokenly "pro-life". Of the sixteen members on the National Executive three were women. As a movement the IRSP would remain notable for the role women would play in its history.

The main emphasis of the party was on the relationship between socialism and national liberation. According to the account in the *Starry Plough* (May 1975), "the delegates unanimously accepted that the struggle against foreign imperialism and native capitalism is one struggle and that it would be ludicrous to attempt to suggest the possibility of establishing socialism in Ireland while ignoring the struggle for National Liberation."

The party did not debate, at least not in public, how the struggle to drive British imperialism out of the north-east of Ireland was going to be conducted. Clearly, Britain was not going to be forced out by political means alone. The IRSP as a registered political party had to maintain a political front. But by the early summer of 1975, about six months after it had come into existence, some forty of its members were already in jail in the North on various paramilitary offences, including possession of weapons and explosives, murder, attempted murder, and robbery. The feud had forced the IRSP's armed wing into the open before it was ready, exposing its members to the security forces; it had stemmed the flow of recruits and irredeemably linked the party's name with fratricidal violence, crippling its growth, regardless of how progressive its policies were.

Among those who were already behind bars was Vinty Fegan, a former member of the Official IRA's Beechmount unit, which specialised in bank robberies. Fegan was on the IRSP's National Executive. He had been arrested along with Harry Flynn, Billy Basset and Hen Doherty and charged with attempting to rob a bank in central Belfast a few days after the ardfheis had concluded its first sessions. Flynn was the brother of Seán Flynn, an Ard-Chomhairle member and former OC of the Officials' Whiterock unit. He had been involved with the Costello faction within the Officials since early 1974 and would play a crucial role in the history of the movement until 1986. At least one member of the new group, Jake McManus, was in jail charged with an attempted sectarian murder. The shooting had occurred during an attempt to find and kill an RUC man. When the intended target could not be found, a passer-by was shot instead. Four other members of the new movement had been charged with shooting up the loyalist Princess Bar in the Ormeau Road at the beginning of February. These sectarian attacks would seem to justify the Officials' allegations that the IRSP was basically anti-Protestant. In fact its contribution to the sectarian bloodshed that made 1975 one of the most violent years in the history of Northern Ireland was, while vicious, comparatively small. Costello's group can be definitely linked to two major sectarian attacks, one in Derry and one in Gilford, towards the end of the year (see chapter 4). The vast majority of the killings of Protestants were carried out by the Provisionals.

A more serious threat to the integrity of the organisation than sectarianism was the issue of the relationship between the armed wing and the party, which had become critical before anyone in the movement had had the time to think it out. The gunmen in Belfast had broken loose from political control and, against the wishes of Costello and his closest Dublin supporters, had taken action into their own hands. The killing of McMillen, carried out on the spur of the moment, without any sanction, was simply the most blatant example of how Belfast was not answerable to the Dublin-based leadership. It was a fatal flaw that would run through the INLA during its entire history, creating the conditions for dangerous internal disputes that too frequently ended in bloodshed.

Such a division would probably have occurred anyway—but what is certain is that the feud with the Officials exposed it right at the start. Said Seán Flynn, one of the National Executive members from Belfast: "The Stickies didn't know the damage they did. They upset a good organisation."

NOTES

1. The statement was in reply to an article written by one of the authors about the feud. After it appeared he received a telephone call from a then prominent member of Official Sinn Féin, who threatened that if he continued to criticise the Officials his career as a journalist in Dublin would be ended.

2. There was much press speculation at the time that the IRSP's protectors were members of the Provisional IRA. This was vehemently denied by Séamus Loughran, the Belfast Sinn Féin leader and the Provisionals' OC in the city. "We don't want to get our heads stuck between these two dissident groups," he told the *Sunday News* on 30 March. However, the speculation was encouraged by a case then before the courts in Belfast involving Patrick Smith and James Kearney, who were charged with firing on the security forces and possession of weapons. Smith was said to be in the IRSP and Kearney a sympathiser with the Provisionals. In another case, Seán Gray, Francis McCann and Edward McCann were charged with possession of a sawn-off shotgun and ammunition in the Divis Flats. Francis McCann was identified as a Provisional IRA man and Gray as a member of the IRSP. It was clear from these instances and from others that would emerge later that whatever the stated policy of the Provisional leadership towards the IRSP, there was frequent sympathy and co-operation at ground level between the two groups. Francis McCann went on to become a local councillor for Sinn Féin in Belfast. His brother Paul was an INLA gunman killed in an incident with the police in 1984 (see chapter 12).

3. The Provisionals were determined to kill Elliman, it seemed. They shot him dead just over six months later during a subsequent feud with the Officials.

4

OF ARMS, AND SPLITS, AND TRAINS

South Derry lies between the bleak slopes of the Sperrin Mountains in the west and the low, featureless shores of Lough Neagh to the south-east. It is a maze of narrow, twisting roads and desolate countryside, with a scattering of small towns and villages, remote farms, and derelict buildings. South Derry was the area where between 1956 and 1962 Séamus Costello commanded an active service unit, earning himself the nickname "the Boy General" because of his youth and exploits. Nineteen years later, in 1975, it was still an ideal place for low-intensity guerrilla operations, booby traps, and ambushes.

Costello's reputation from the last campaign still carried weight in south Derry, and his new organisation had no difficulty in winning recruits from the Officials. The second issue of the IRSP's monthly newspaper, the *Starry Plough*, proclaimed in May 1975: "Party zooms ahead in south Derry." The report said that party branches were being formed in Glenullen, Dungiven, Slaughtneill, Maghera, Desertmartin, Bellaghy, Ballymena, and Ballycastle. Among those who became active members of Costello's group were John "Eddy" McNichol and Séamus O'Kane from Glenullen and John O'Doherty from Swatragh. O'Doherty, however, was arrested within weeks of the formation of the IRSP, and then interned. But by the late spring of 1975 Costello's new organisation was strong enough militarily to begin operations. And where more appropriate to launch its military campaign than in the area where he had won republican glory all those years ago?

On 24 May 1975, two days after the IRSP was registered as a political party, a 22-year-old member of the RUC named Noel Davis tried to move a car that had been abandoned outside a gun club near Maghera. The movement detonated a landmine, which killed the policeman instantly, leaving his wife of two months a widow. The car had been stolen at gunpoint two days earlier by three masked men. The Provisional IRA—still engaged in secret meetings with the British—immediately denied responsibility (though in fact their agreed truce with the security forces excluded the police from its terms).

Constable Davis was the first member of the security forces to die at the hands of the Irish National Liberation Army. Costello did not want the INLA to claim responsibility for any operations until it had carried out a sufficient number to give it some credibility. He had estimated that it needed to do at least two operations a month to keep in the public eye. Davis's killing was therefore not claimed until January 1976, by which time the INLA's chief of staff had judged that his organisation had done enough jobs—claiming the lives of two other members of the security forces and seriously wounding fourteen—for it to make its formal appearance on the paramilitary stage. Until the INLA became active in south Derry not one member of the security forces had been killed in the area in six years.

Within two months of the killing of Constable Davis, a second policeman was to die at the INLA's hands. On 26 July the RUC in Dungiven were called out to examine a car said to have a bomb in it. As they approached it, two INLA volunteers opened fire on them. Constable McPherson was shot dead and his colleague was seriously wounded. Other security forces were quickly on the scene. With some difficulty, the INLA unit managed to extricate itself from encirclement, taking the dead RUC man's gun with them. The same month the INLA carried out two operations of a different sort. In Dungiven they held up an RUC man and a soldier and forced them to hand over their weapons, uniforms, and documents. Shortly afterwards, in Limavady, during a brawl in a dance hall two policemen who had been summoned to restore order were also disarmed. Some within the organisation were not too happy that the south Derry men had freed their prisoners: the Belfast INLA thought they should have been "executed".

The police eventually arrested Eddy McNichol and Séamus O'Kane; by the beginning of 1976 they were being held in Long Kesh on murder charges. But not for long: both escaped along with seven other members of the organisation in May 1976.. The attacks in south Derry did not stop. Between May 1975 and the beginning of 1977 one member of the security forces was murdered every month in the area, and many more narrowly escaped death, as both the Provisional IRA and the INLA kept up the pressure. In one of the INLA's most daring attacks, on 3 August 1976, two of its men ambushed an army foot patrol in Dungiven. One of the gunmen was armed only with a shotgun. He opened up on the patrol as it walked passed the broken window of a derelict house, killing Private Alan Watkins, who was hit at almost point-blank range.

With the collapse of the Provisional IRA cease-fire during the late summer of 1975, that organisation had become active in south Derry. Among its most prominent gunmen were Francis Hughes, who had begun his paramilitary career in the Officials; later he would come to prominence as the second man to die on the 1981 hunger strike. Dominic McGlinchey was also operating in the area. He would later abandon the Provisionals to join the INLA, eventually becoming its chief of staff, earning as he did so a reputation as one of its most notorious gunmen. By the spring of 1977 the South Derry INLA was being hit hard by arrests. During those eighteen months of violence in south Derry the Provisionals and the INLA had worked together, with volunteers from both organisations carrying out joint operations.

In Derry city no such co-operation was forthcoming from the Provisional leadership. Martin McGuinness, conservative in his views and a strict Catholic, was fiercely opposed to the new organisation. Shortly after the INLA was formed in the city he had one of its leaders tarred and feathered, accusing his organisation of carrying out criminal acts. The INLA countered by saying that they were engaged in "finance-raising" operations, i.e. robberies that were needed not for criminal purposes but for "the struggle". Such was the tension between the two groups that at one time leading Provisionals, afraid that a feud was going to erupt, moved across the border. Costello had to go to Derry to repair relations. Almost the entire Official republican movement in Derry had gone over to Costello. Among the chief Derry organisers were Terry Robson, Johnny White—formerly prominent members of the Official movement—and, a little later, Tommy McCourt, who returned from Dublin, where he had been based during the formation of the IRSP. Their strongest areas of support were Shantallow, the Creggan, Rosemount, the Bogside, and Brandywell. By December 1975 the Derry INLA numbered over a hundred members.

The Official IRA in Derry had been noted for its militancy, which had got it into trouble with the Dublin leadership. Its successor, the INLA, wanted to carry on that tradition. Its aim was to outgun the Provos, according to one of its founding members, who said: "The INLA had to compete with the Provos. We had to out-shoot them." (Interview, 2 April 1993.) Perhaps he was remembering the days when the Officials were the dominant organisation in Derry and was hoping that the INLA could achieve that position. During the time when the Provisionals were maintaining their truce it might have seemed possible. Between the summer and winter of 1975 the INLA were carrying out more operations in Derry than the Provisionals. Old animosities between the Provisionals and those they regarded rather contemptuously as ex-Stickies had been heightened when two members of the Provisionals joined the new organisation because they had become disgruntled with the IRA cease-fire.

The INLA in Derry from the start seems to have been better armed than it was in Belfast. It possessed a couple of carbine rifles taken from the Officials, a few Garrand semi-automatic rifles, a .22 high-velocity hunting rifle, and a Walther pistol, which was the first weapon it acquired in Derry. It had established training camps near Mamor Gap in Inishowen and Fintown in central Donegal.

The first attack for which the new group claimed responsibility was carried out on 18 June 1975. INLA gunmen wounded an RUC man on mobile patrol in Hamilton Street in the Brandywell district of Derry. Three months later, on 6 September, the INLA attacked Rosemount RUC station. According to the INLA the attack lasted for fifteen minutes, and one RUC man was seriously wounded by high-velocity fire from the hunting rifle. A week later two soldiers were seriously wounded when the INLA ambushed their patrol in Drumleck Drive in the Shantallow area of the city.

On 26 September the INLA inflicted its first fatality in the city. Private David Wray of the Prince of Wales's Own Regiment was shot in the chest as his patrol passed the corner of Lingsfort Drive and Iniscarn Road in the Creggan area. He subsequently died from his injuries, which were inflicted by the high-velocity hunting rifle.

The next month the Derry INLA struck again. This time, however, its victims were not members of the security forces. A Derry Catholic named Thomas McGlinchey had been injured in a booby-trap car bomb. The UDA was responsible. Soon afterwards the INLA shot two Protestant garage workers, alleging they were UDA men. The allegation seems to have been based on the fact that both victims had been before the courts on arms charges. The Provisional IRA immediately condemned the shooting, saying that the organisation involved had no right to act on behalf of the nationalists of Derry, since it had never been engaged in an "anti-imperialist war". The Provisional leadership strongly resented any attempt being made by the INLA to present itself as the "protector" of the Catholics in Derry.

However, this did not deter the INLA from striking again. On this occasion the organisation made one of its first "mistakes". On 2 December, Charles McNaul, aged fifty-five, and Alexander Mitchell, aged forty-six, were in a café near the Strand Road when gunmen shot them dead. Both men were Protestant businessmen, involved in a wood importing company. Within twenty-four hours of the attack the Provisional IRA had denied responsibility for the killing, expressing outrage at it. Then came a statement from the People's Liberation Army—which name the Costello group still used occasionally in Derry—condemning the killing and disclaiming any responsibility for it.

However, a former INLA leader has since acknowledged that his organisation killed the men, thinking they belonged to the UDA. The killings inspired a wave of protests. A meeting was called by the Derry Trades Council and a one-hour work stoppage was organised. Workers gathered in Guild Hall Square to hear a local SDLP man condemn the killings as sectarian and hint that republicans had carried out the shooting. (Ironically, the only organisation to oppose the stoppage was the loyalist Ulster Workers' Council.) It looked as if the INLA had produced a situation similar to that confronting the Officials after they shot Ranger Best in May 1972. But, unlike the Officials, the new group did not present an easy target for protests, since there was still so little known about it that was definite. Anyway, other, political events would soon overtake the Derry INLA: in the same month that the Protestant businessmen were murdered, Bernadette McAliskey resigned from the IRSP, and most of the movement's leaders in Derry resigned with her.

Costello regarded Belfast as the key to the Northern situation. He maintained that a republican organisation had to have a base in Belfast, otherwise it would become irrelevant. By the time the feud had ended, Costello's movement was in bad shape in the Northern capital. Two of its men had been shot dead, dozens had been wounded, and many more were in jail, including a few key men such as Vinty Fegan, Phil McDonnell, and Harry Flynn, as was Gerard Steenson, who had been picked up on arms charges. Ronnie Bunting, one of the leaders of the Belfast INLA, had fled to Wales with his family after a third attempt on his life during the feud. Though he was back in Ireland by July 1975, he based himself in Dublin and would not return to Belfast again until late 1976, when he would become OC of the INLA in the city. In the meantime Belfast had had two OCs. The first was Kevin Holland, who left after a short time to become an intelligence officer for the Provisionals. He was succeeded by a former quartermaster for the Official IRA in north Belfast.

The Belfast INLA had some access to explosives, thanks to a Costello supporter who worked in Tara silver mines at Nenagh, County Tipperary. He smuggled gelignite out in small amounts in his lunch box. Early in 1975, Costello sent about 40 pounds of it into Belfast, packed into acetylene cylinders. However, two members of the organisation in the Markets area, Phil McDonnell and Billy Basset, were arrested while moving it from one safe spot to another. The INLA had been hoping to make up several small bombs, including some blast bombs, to attack the security forces. "It wasn't for anything sectarian," a former Belfast INLA OC told one of the authors. "We were socialists."

Badly armed, mauled from the feud, hit hard by arrests, the Belfast organisation was in no position to begin a military campaign against the security forces. The city remained tense as talks with the Officials dragged on, and the possibility of another feud always seemed on the horizon, even after a formal peace agreement was reached between the two groups on 13 June. There was also considerable bitterness towards the leadership in Dublin. The Belfast men had felt abandoned, left to act on their own during the feud when they had little with which to defend themselves. Suspicions and doubts were planted about Costello's leadership, which were to grow over the next year.

However, at the beginning of May the organisation enjoyed something of a morale boost. Harry Flynn, Vinty Fegan, Phil McDonnell, Billy Basset and Henry Doherty were in Crumlin Road courthouse waiting to appear on various charges, including attempted bank robbery and possession of explosives. There was a skylight in the room in which they were being held before going before the court. Flynn noticed that it was not closed properly; within minutes all five had scrambled onto the courthouse roof and escaped. They made their way across the border and reached Dublin.

However, on 5 June it looked as if Belfast was going to suffer another outbreak of feuding. Brendan McNamee had just left a pub in the Stewardstown Road near Andersonstown, accompanied by his girl-friend. They were waiting at a mobile fish-and-chip shop when a gunman wielding an Armalite rifle shot him in the chest. McNamee managed to run some distance after being hit, pulling his girl-friend with him. He was followed and shot again several times.

Brendan McNamee had been involved in the murder of Billy McMillen. It was assumed at first that the Official IRA had been as good as their word and taken their revenge. However, the Officials issued a strong denial and—unusually—blamed the Provisionals, who also said they had nothing to do with it. In any case the IRSP did not break off the peace talks with the Officials, which were continuing, and the feud did not erupt again. The Officials' information was correct. McNamee, a former member of the Provisional IRA and twice interned, had been murdered by his erstwhile comrades. His death came about partly as a result of a dispute he had had with the IRA leadership in Long Kesh the year before. He had been one of a group of Provo detainees in cage 8 who had appeared before the Long Kesh tribunal to have their cases reviewed, though this was against Provisional IRA policy. To punish them, the Provisionals told them they could no longer have visitors. In their turn, McNamee and the others destroyed the transcripts of their hearings, which they had been ordered to produce.

When McNamee left Long Kesh he joined Costello's group. This, it is suspected, may have sealed his fate. The Provos, as well as wanting to punish him for his disobedience in prison, were keen to discourage any of their volunteers who might be thinking of abandoning them for the new organisation, and decided to use McNamee as an example.

McNamee was claimed as a member of the People's Liberation Army. His death notice was a strange mixture of left-wing revolutionary rhetoric and Catholic piety. "Wherever death may surround us, it will be welcome, provided that this our battle cry reaches some receptive ear, that another hand stretch out to take our weapons, and that other men come forward to intone our funeral dirge with the staccato of machine guns and new cries of battle and victory. Ever onward. Mary, Queen of the Gael, pray for him." (*Irish News*, 9 June 1975.) The contrast between the rhetoric of the obituary and the reality of McNamee's death could not be greater. He had not died in a heroic struggle against imperialism but had been mercilessly gunned down by another republican in an obscure dispute.

"The staccato of machine guns and new cries of battle" were not to be heard from the Belfast INLA for another two months, when they carried out their first attack on the security forces. On 9 August, the fourth anniversary of the introduction of internment without trial, an INLA sniper shot a British soldier in the neck in the Ballymurphy area of west Belfast. The same day another unit of the organisation ambushed a British army patrol in Waterford Street in the Lower Falls district, wounding a soldier in the head. INLA units were also active in the Divis Flats, but claimed no hits.

A month later, on 12 September, the INLA struck again in Belfast. This time using some of the explosives taken from an Official IRA dump, they planted a bomb in Corrigan Park, near the Whiterock Road. The bomb was set off by a command wire that led from the playing field to the spectator stands, wounding Major Ian Sheppard and a private of the Royal Highland Fusiliers.

However, it was not until the following year that the Belfast INLA managed to kill a member of the security forces. It happened in the west Belfast housing estate of Turf Lodge. A series of incidents involving the British army, including the deaths of two local youths, had led to a sharp deterioration in the relationship between it and the local population. Leo Norney had been shot dead by soldiers on 13 September 1975; Brian Stewart, who was only thirteen, was killed by a rubber bullet in September the following year. In both cases the youths were unarmed and were not involved in paramilitary organisations. Tension between the army and the people of the estate was such that foot patrols could not enter the area without being attacked by mobs. The King's Own Borderers regiment stationed there at the time of Stewart's death was strongly disliked, being frequently accused of anti-Catholic bigotry. According to the INLA, local women met them and the Provisional IRA in the autumn of 1976 to demand action. By the time it was taken, the King's Own Borderers had been withdrawn and a new regiment, the Royal Welsh Fusiliers, was in place. It had to pay the price for the actions of its predecessor. On 24 November 1976 a patrol entered the estate and was attacked by a mob. As it tried to extricate itself, a sniper opened fire; Corporal Andrew Crocker was hit in the neck and killed. At first the Provisionals said they had carried out the attack; but a telephone call to the BBC in Belfast from a "Captain Green" claimed responsibility on behalf of the INLA. He said the corporal had been hit by a soft-nosed bullet from a .303 rifle. (A soft-nosed bullet fragments on entering the body, causing terrible lacerations.)

"Captain Green" was Ronnie Bunting, who had returned to Belfast from Dublin to reorganise the INLA. He was deliberately mimicking the Ulster Freedom Fighters (UFF), one of whom used to claim responsibility for UDA murders using the name "Captain Black". Not long afterwards, the British army arrested and charged three young members of the INLA, who were subsequently convicted of Crocker's murder.

Outside Derry city, south Derry, and Belfast, the only area to report INLA activity in 1975 was County Armagh. In the September issue of the *Starry Plough* there was a short report proclaiming the setting up of an IRSP cumann in Armagh. It said that two members of the IRSP had managed to sell a hundred copies of the paper in less than one hour. The military organisation was under the control of Tommy Trainor, battalion OC for County Armagh, and Dessie Grew, OC in the town of Armagh, though his brother Séamus was said to have been "the main man" when it came to operations.

The earliest operations that the INLA claimed responsibility for in the area came on 9 August 1975, when it launched three attacks on British patrols in Armagh town, wounding two soldiers. There was no further action until the following October, when on the tenth a garage outside Armagh was blown up because, it was alleged by the INLA, it had serviced RUC vehicles. A few days later INLA snipers fired on an army patrol at the junction of Emania Terrace and Navan Terrace in Armagh, seriously wounding one soldier.

The Armagh-Portadown area was notorious for the activities of loyalist death squads. Early on they began claiming the lives of IRSP and INLA members and their families. In April 1975 loyalists had murdered Tommy

Trainor's mother as she walked home with her husband after a night out at the local British Legion hall. His fifteen-year-old brother, Ronnie, who had joined the IRSP, was killed when the UVF threw a bomb into his house on 15 December 1975. He was the first IRSP member to die at the hands of the Protestant death squads.

Sixteen days later a bomb left in a duffel bag killed three people in the Central Bar in the mainly Protestant town of Gilford, near Portadown. The explosion that killed Richard Beattie, Sylvia McCullough and William Scott was claimed by the Armagh People's Republican Army. Between 1974 and 1976 several such bogus organisations had sprung up as a cover for purely sectarian attacks carried out by the Provisional IRA. Sectarian killings were claimed under such names as the South Armagh Republican Action Force, the Red Flag Avengers, and the Young Militants of Ireland, to name a few. However, in this case an INLA man, Francis Corry, was eventually charged and convicted of the Gilford killings. The pub attack seems to have been a direct retaliation for the killing of Ronnie Trainor. Corry was also convicted of the murder of Thomas Rafferty, a schoolboy who accidentally set off a booby-trap bomb meant for the security forces in February 1976.

Corry was jailed in late 1979. Though there was a debate in the Ard-Chomhairle of the IRSP about whether or not he should be "recognised" as a political prisoner, he was accepted into the IRSP prison structure, in spite of the fact that according to INLA sources he had been expelled from the organisation earlier for shooting someone during a post office robbery.

The Gilford bombing was one of the worst sectarian incidents ever attributed to the INLA. It was part of a local vendetta, in which north County Armagh INLA members were involved for family and personal reasons. It would not be the last: the Darkley massacre eight years later would show the vindictive power possessed by such disputes, in which the ugliest face of local sectarian hatreds displayed itself and the republican cause became submerged in a far older, purely vengeful tradition of rural gang warfare.

By the summer of 1975 the IRSP was a registered political party, with a head office in Dublin at 1A Essex Gate, just off Parliament Street and within a stone's throw, ironically enough, of Dublin Castle, then headquarters of the Special Branch. It had held its first ardfheis, issued an Easter statement, and paraded out to Bodenstown to Wolfe Tone's graveside. The mediation between it and the Officials was moving slowly along, not without its hitches. A few weeks after the shooting of McNamee had brought renewed fears of another outbreak of internecine violence there was an attempt to bomb the train taking the Officials to Bodenstown. A local man was stabbed to death in the attempt, which took place near Sallins, County Kildare. Immediately press speculation pointed towards the IRSP, and the Gardaí swooped, arresting eleven members of the party, who were questioned about the incident. However, as in the case of the bombing attack on the Bush Bar in Belfast three months before, the UVF were in fact responsible.[1]

At the party's own Wolfe Tone commemoration ceremony, its first, held at Bodenstown on 8 June, a reported eight hundred members turned up to listen to Costello appeal to the rank-and-file members of the Officials to "join us in the struggle against imperialism." He rounded on Goulding and Garland: "To your leaders who are responsible for the promotion of this murder campaign, we say: 'Go back to your drinking dens and sheebeens, get off our backs, so that we may get on with the struggle against imperialism.'"[2] Yet, even as his organisation was launching its first armed attacks against the British army and police north of the border, the contradictions within were beginning to manifest themselves.

After a trip to Boston to take part in a conference on Northern Ireland, at which, by all accounts, he made the strongest impression of any of the contributors (see chapter 5), Costello returned to face a deepening political and organisational crisis within the IRSP, which he never succeeded in resolving.

The feud had confronted the party with two interlinked issues. There was the Belfast organisation's constant pressure on Costello for weapons. Then there was the debate within the party on the role of the armed wing and its relation to the political structure. Throughout 1975 and the following year Costello was under tremendous pressure, mainly from Belfast, to live up to the promises he had made in the spring of 1974, when he had rhetorically asked, "If I could bring the OCs of the Belfast units and show them a thousand rifles, would they agree the cease-fire should be broken?" He was also confronted by a left-wing political bloc, mainly centred on the Derry Ard-Chomhairle members but supported by McCorry from Belfast and led by Bernadette McAliskey, which was pushing for party control over what was termed in the Ard-Chomhairle notes "Section B". According to a former Derry INLA leader, the left bloc wanted a "Bolshevik-type structure with the armed sections subordinate to the central committee." (Interview, 3 April 1993.) Costello denounced this position as "naïve". He argued that the armed struggle was crucial to the future of the whole organisation. His experience with what had happened in the Officials made him concerned about the party having too much say over "Section B". He feared that the armed campaign would eventually be undermined by the politicos.

This debate took place at the ardfheis when it reconvened for its second session on 3 and 4 May. The left block had secured a majority on the Ard-Chomhairle, but their resolution concerning the relationship between the IRSP and "Section B" was defeated by the delegates. Those who supported Costello on the Ard-Chomhairle were Seán Flynn (Belfast), Mick Plunkett (Dublin), and Stella Makowski (Clare)—all prominent members of the INLA's Army Council but still a minority of the Ard-Chomhairle.

Costello was caught between Derry and Belfast. The two disputes were of course linked. It had been the feud in Belfast that had forced a crisis in the relationship between the IRSP and the INLA. The Belfast organisation had acted on its own. Without orders it had assassinated McMillen and attempted to assassinate Seán Garland; it represented to the left-wing bloc its worst fears come true. This was what would happen if the armed wing was given priority: its actions would simply undermine the political development of the party and make ordinary politics impossible.

Underlying this there was, of course, a fundamental dispute about what form the IRSP, as a self-declared republican-socialist organisation, was supposed to take. At the end of October 1975, a few months before the dispute broke out into the open, McAliskey wrote an essay, "Revolutionary republicanism?" in which she drew distinctions between republicanism and socialism and how those differences express themselves organisationally. She observed: "The building of a working-class movement requires mass organisation on an open basis, with decisions being reached by rational argument and full discussion, policy coming from the rank and file and being reflected by the leadership. Because of its clandestine and militaristic nature, participation in 'the Movement' demanded the exact opposite. Since the survival of the organisation, the safety, at times, of its members, depended on personal loyalty, secrecy, unquestioning acceptance of directives from above, it was virtually impossible to envisage the development of a democratic mass organisation from within." (*Hibernia*, 31 October 1975.) This is a fair outline of the nature of the problems she and her supporters were facing within the IRSP. As a republican organisation it was dedicated to military action, which by its very nature meant the organisation of a conspiratorial, secret, underground army. For socialists this had to be subordinated to the party if the party was to engage in mass agitation, link up with the trade unions and fight for its policies on the factory floor as well as in local councils and parliament, if necessary.

The defeat of the left bloc's arguments over the armed wing was the second it had suffered at the ardfheis. After the IRSP's formation it had been stated that it would probably fight the coming Convention elections in Northern Ireland. At the ardfheis on 6 April, McAliskey had put forward the motion that the IRSP should contest the elections. A counter-motion was tabled by Donegal delegates that, "realising the inevitable downfall of the Convention," it was a waste of time. Theirs was passed and McAliskey's rejected, by a "small majority". (*Irish Press*, 7 April 1975.) It was a personal setback for her, as she would have made the ideal candidate. Many thought the election contest would have given the party an important opportunity to establish its political identity.

On this issue Costello had sided with McAliskey. He had attacked the Officials for taking part in the 1973 Assembly elections; but in an interview that appeared in the first issue of the *Starry Plough* he explained why the Convention was different from the Assembly. "A large section of the population of the North had rejected the existence of the Stormont Assembly. In the context of that situation, we felt that it was a totally unrevolutionary and a very reactionary decision by the Official Republicans to agree to contest these elections. We felt that they were lending validity and credence to Britain's claim to govern any part of this country, despite their repudiation of this claim. The Convention, on the other hand, has no powers. It is not an Assembly. It is not a parliament. The only task of the Convention will be to discuss constitutional arrangements for the future government of Northern Ireland."

Other disputes followed. The left bloc wanted the IRSP's concept of a broad front to include links with the People's Democracy and Trotskyist groups such as the Revolutionary Marxist Group and the International Socialists. Costello firmly rejected such connections, fearing that the IRSP would become identified with the politically irrelevant far left. The Derry socialist and journalist Éamonn McCann, who had attended Hugh Ferguson's funeral, had applied to join the IRSP during the summer. He was a friend of Bernadette McAliskey's, but Costello and other republicans on the Ard-Chomhairle suspected him and his left-wing supporters of trying to use the party for their own ends. McCann, a prominent member of the International Socialists, was told that he had to resign from that group. He was also told that he had to submit any articles he wrote to the Ard-Chomhairle for vetting before publication, and that the *Starry Plough* would have the first option on them. McCann objected, asking that his contributions to the Dublin tabloid *Sunday World* be excused since they were not political in nature. Though this was agreed, he finally withdrew his application for membership after several months' wrangling with the Ard-Chomhairle. According to one report, this further "soured" relations between the McAliskey and Costello tendencies. (*Sunday Independent*, 7 December 1975.)

The crisis came to a head in late 1975 when, at a meeting in Monaghan,

Costello proposed that McAliskey join the Army Council as a means of satisfying the left bloc's demands that the party should control "Section B". She refused this option and led her supporters out of the party. Eleven members resigned, ten of whom were on the Ard-Chomhairle. Along with McAliskey went Johnny White, Terry Robson, Kitty O'Kane, Tommy McCourt and Joe Quigley from Derry, Jimmy McCorry from Belfast, Peter Pringle and Séamus O'Kane from Donegal, and Gerry Jones from Dublin. Of these ten, however, Robson did not leave because he sympathised with McAliskey politically but because he simply did not want to be involved in another split. (Along with Tommy McCourt and Séamus O'Kane, he would rejoin the organisation later.) McAliskey issued a stinging statement, accusing the IRSP of "being objectively indistinguishable from either wing of the republican movement and possibly combining the worst elements of both." (Quoted by Derek Dunne and Gene Kerrigan in *Round Up the Usual Suspects*, Magill Publications, 1984.)

On 1 December the IRSP issued its version of the events that led to the resignations. It said the eleven had resigned "as a result of their failure to accept and implement the democratically decided policies of the party. Since our Ard Fheis last May the members concerned have consistently attempted at almost every meeting of the Ard-Chomhairle to divert the party from its policies and to introduce policies which were clearly rejected by our members.

"Having failed to convince the majority to depart from existing policies they have now resigned. The policy differences which gave rise to their resignations were as follows:

"A/ The refusal of the resigned members to accept the vital link between the National Liberation struggle and the struggle for Socialism in Ireland. The disagreement centred around the party's policy on the National Question which the people who defected refused to accept and led to their accusation that 'the IRSP have retreated to traditional republicanism'. On this point we wish to state that the IRSP sees the solving of the National Question as an integral part of the struggle for socialism, and we do not view the struggle for national liberation as a mere means of gaining support for the economic struggle of the working class. Specific resolutions on this question were put forward by these people at our Ard Fheis and defeated. Since that time the internal democratic processes of the party were not availed of by these people. The political dishonesty of the people who resigned is reflected in their denouncements of the party's programme as 'objectively indistinguishable from either wing of the republican movement'. This statement is proof to us that these people joined the IRSP on a politically dishonest basis.

"B/ The refusal of the resigned members to accept party policy on the building of a genuine broad front based on the party's demands on the National question and repression. This led to repeated efforts on their behalf to have the IRSP publicly identify itself with a certain bloc of the Irish 'left', the results of which would have been a total failure in our attempts to establish a genuine broad front.

"We reject allegations that 'sections' of the leadership were engaged in internal manipulation, unless of course these people view the adherence by the majority of the Ard Comhairle to party policy as 'manipulation'.

"C/ Refusal to implement and work on the party programme. On this point the IRSP is accused of having downgraded the struggle for class politics and having reverted to the so-called sterile nationalism of traditional republicanism. This statement relates to their almost complete economist approach to the Irish struggle, an approach which is completely hostile to the progressive aspects of the republican tradition. It has become obvious that these people, while giving support to the struggle in the north see that struggle as irrelevant to the building of socialism in Ireland.

"In conclusion the IRSP views these resignations as an attempt to destroy the credibility of our organisation and to sow confusion within our ranks. The fact that these people joined the party, secretly opposed to the party policy, and having failed to subvert the party leadership, then resigned, and made known their hostility to the party programme will result in a situation where the overall structure of the party, in terms of membership, will not be adversely affected."

The dispute referred to in paragraph A as being concerned with "the vital link between the National Liberation struggle and the struggle for Socialism" was in fact a euphemistic way of referring to the disagreement over the role of the IRSP's armed wing. The party was still maintaining in public that it had not got an armed wing, so all references to it had to be indirect. But it remained at the heart of the split with McAliskey. A few weeks afterwards, in an interview, she returned to the subject of republicanism and its flaws as she saw them. "Republicanism is also a conspiracy—with a secret conspiratorial armed wing. While that may have had its place in the development of the national struggle—before urbanisation of great sections of the Irish working class—you can no longer approach the question and attempt to build a mass organisation of workers on a conspiratorial basis; it is completely alien to the organising of the working class. I think that is one of the major stumbling blocks which republicans have got to get away from—the idea that we can build the political organisation and then the leadership will fish in that organisation for people who are capable of carrying guns, so that even within the organisation our comrades will not know which of us is carrying the gun. This breeds dishonesty, deception and distrust inside the revolutionary organisation; there can't be a full discussion of issues, because you don't know from what basis other comrades are talking. It separates the role of armed struggle from the role of political struggle." (*Red Weekly*, 18 December 1975.)

Within a year of its formation, the IRSP was in tatters. Ten members of the Ard-Chomhairle had resigned. The organisation in Derry was in a state of collapse. Belfast was alienated from the leadership in Dublin. Overall recruitment had been stunted by the disastrous feud with the Official IRA. Funds were desperately needed to provide for the welfare of the forty or so imprisoned members who were already behind bars.

An indication of the IRSP's economic difficulties was given in the December edition of the *Starry Plough*. It was an announcement that "the *Starry Plough* had opened a prisoners' Welfare Fund to support the families of IRSP internees and political prisoners. We have set a target of £200." To date, the paper reported, the party had raised £8. Shortage of money would be a problem that would dog the organisation throughout its years of existence. It did not have the solid support network of the Provisionals nor the chain of drinking clubs and building site scams of the Officials, which meant that it was constantly in need of money. This in turn meant that a lot of time, energy and ingenuity was exhausted in carrying out "finance-raising" operations, such as had led to the arrest of the Ard-Chomhairle members Vinty Fegan and Harry Flynn in April.

The year ended with the rearrest of Flynn in Belfast, where he was picked up at his mother's house along with two others who had escaped from the courthouse, Phil McDonnell and Henry Doherty. The Belfast men had found living in Dublin uncongenial. They had been squatting for most of the time in a small block of flats in Pembroke Lane, near Baggot Street, where Ronnie Bunting had found an apartment in July 1975 (see chapter 5). They had decided, against Bunting's advice, to return north, preferring the risk of imprisonment in Belfast to the inconveniences of life in Dublin, which they thoroughly disliked. Their whole experience since they had escaped had been one of deep disillusionment. "We had escaped because we wanted to fight," said one. "We didn't escape to starve in Dublin." They complained that not enough operations were being carried out or even planned. Nor, from what they could tell, was Costello showing himself able to provide the arms they needed to carry out operations in the future.

Between Belfast and Dublin the basis was already laid for a confrontation with Costello that would have a profound impact on the organisation and on the fortunes of its leader. As if this was not enough for Costello to worry about, at around the same time the southern authorities decided on a massive move against the IRSP, one that produced a human rights scandal that still dogs the Republic.

The authorities had already launched a probing operation against the new party in June 1975, when eleven members were rounded up for questioning after the attempt to blow up the train taking the Officials to Bodenstown. As well, there had been allegations from the IRSP in Cork of constant harassment from the Special Branch. The party claimed that over a period of six weeks the chairman of the Cork cumann was arrested nineteen times. Complaints were also made that people selling the *Starry Plough* were frequently stopped and threatened by gardaí.

The IRSP was still known only as a political party. The only action that its armed wing had carried out in the South after its formation was the attempted assassination of Garland. But the Gardaí had reasons to suspect that Costello was involved in train robberies. There had been the Dublin Airport robbery of early 1974, which was carried out by Costello and his supporters while they were still technically part of the Official IRA. Whether or not the Gardaí suspected that his men were involved in that, they had evidence to link the attempted train robbery of May 1974 in Mallow to Costello. One of the gang was stopped and questioned as he made his way back to Dublin. A second was arrested and held at the Bridewell for several days before being released on 17 May.

As yet, however, the IRSP's links with illegal actions were based on the past history of its leader and its members. These, regardless of how suspicious they were, did not constitute proof that the IRSP had links to an organised, armed paramilitary group. Then in the January 1976 issue of the *Starry Plough* came the first announcement from the "National Liberation Army" (It did not use its real name, for reasons that emerged the following month). Under the heading "New army announced", the report carried claims of responsibility for "military operations carried out by active service units of the National Liberation Army." Listed were fifteen violent attacks, including three murders (those of Constables Davis and McPherson and Private Wray). A month later came another announcement. It was a press statement, dated 16 February 1976, emanating from "Irish National Liberation Army, Department of General Headquarters". It began: "We wish to announce that a series of discussions have recently taken place between representatives of the Army Council of the National Liberation Army and representatives of the People's Liberation Army. The purpose of these discussions was to ascertain to what degree a unified approach could be agreed on in the struggle for National Liberation and Socialism in Ireland. As a result of these discussions it was agreed by both organisations that they should unite in the struggle against Imperialism." (*Hibernia*, 26 March 1976.)

The whole "merger" was, of course, a fraud: anyone who claimed to have been a representative of the National Liberation Army engaged in negotiations with a representative of the People's Liberation Army would most probably have been talking to himself. It was a convoluted and rather outlandish attempt to disguise the fact that the INLA had been in existence from early 1975 and that both the National Liberation Army and the People's Liberation Army were figments of the imagination. The use of NLA—Costello's preferred name—for the first claim of responsibility in January was merely meant to further cover the tracks that led back to the group that had followed Costello in the split from the Officials in late 1974.

Not many people in the press paid attention. However, the emergence of an armed organisation clearly linked to the IRSP would have registered with the authorities in Dublin, who had been monitoring the activities of Costello's party since June the previous year.

The Coalition Government, led by Liam Cosgrave, had been in power since 1973. Paddy Cooney was the Minister for Justice. Though he had the reputation of being something of a liberal when he came into power, his period in office had shown that he was thoroughly committed to implementing the Government's tough law-and-order programme. The Labour-Fine Gael coalition was determined to smash any attempts that republican groups might make to assert themselves in the 26 Counties. This was partly through fear of being dragged into the Northern paramilitary morass. Already, by 1976, loyalist paramilitaries had targeted the South in a series of bomb attacks that killed dozens of people. The last one had been in November 1975, when the UDA planted a bomb in Dublin Airport that killed a worker. The Government's attitude was that if they were seen to be clamping down on republican organisations, then the loyalists would stay at home.

There had also been a series of incidents involving republicans: the escape from Mountjoy jail in 1973, the murder of Senator Billy Fox in 1974, and numerous robberies and attempted robberies. Increasing numbers were being arrested under section 30 of the Offences Against the State Act (1939), which allows any garda to arrest a suspect and hold him or her for twenty-four hours; a chief superintendent may then extend the period for forty-eight hours. All that is required legally for such detention is that there exist in the mind of the garda a suspicion that the person is about to commit or has just committed a crime.

The Coalition's law and order stance had not been altogether successful, with the Provisionals scoring some embarrassing successes, such as the Mountjoy helicopter escape. So the Government was determined to prove its mettle.

On 12 March three armed men attempted to rob the Dublin–Wexford train as it passed through County Wicklow. On the train were armed members of the Special Branch. After a shoot-out, in which no-one was injured, the three would-be robbers escaped. No-one was ever charged with the attempt, though the Gardaí suspected that Costello was behind it. They were right: the attempt had been organised by the INLA, according to a former high-ranking member of that organisation.

Almost three weeks later, and just five days after the *Hibernia* story on the emergence of the INLA, the Cork–Dublin mail train was stopped at Hazelhatch, near Sallins, County Kildare, and robbed in a paramilitary-style operation. Around £200,000 was taken (the exact sum was never established). Within hours, Special Branch detectives had raided the flat of Nuala Dillon, the girl-friend of IRSP man Nicky Kelly, and the home of Brian McNally, a former member of the party. The detectives asked for Kelly; Ms Dillon told them he wasn't there. They returned later to find that he still had not returned. Brian McNally was briefly questioned at his home. (Kelly had actually stayed that night at the McNallys' and was sleeping upstairs at the time.) The gardaí also went to the home of Tony Gregory, the future TD, who was a friend of Costello's and was for a brief time a member of his party. On the afternoon of the robbery, 31 March, Special Branch men arrested Osgur Breatnach as he arrived at the IRSP's new head office at 34 Upper Gardiner Street. Breatnach was the editor of the *Starry Plough*, and he was held under section 30 of the Offences Against the State Act. After being held for just over forty-seven hours, Breatnach was released without charge.

At the beginning of April, Paddy Cooney, the Minister for Justice, warned in a speech at St Ann's Church in Dublin: "The Government's first duty when faced with violent attacks on its institutions is to strengthen its laws. As a consequence, there may have to be a derogation from laws protecting the freedom of the individual, but it should be temporary, publicly enacted and subject to review." (*Hibernia*, 7 May 1976.)

Within days of this speech the Gardaí claimed to have received "confidential information" that Costello's organisation had carried out the

Great Train Robbery. They never disclosed of what their information consisted. They already had evidence linking Costello's men to the attempted train robbery near Mallow in 1974, and the abortive robbery in Wicklow just three weeks before. Perhaps those were enough to point the finger at the IRSP.

A major swoop was planned. Seventeen members of the IRSP were to be arrested. In fact, between 5 and 9 April some forty were arrested under section 30, including Séamus Costello, Mick Plunkett, Gerry Roche, Ronnie Bunting, Nicky Kelly, Osgur Breatnach, Mick Barret, Brian McNally, and John Fitzpatrick. Half the arrests took place in Dublin. It was intended to be a massive blow against the IRSP. According to Dunne and Kerrigan, "the scale of this mass arrest is better understood if it is remembered that on the last occasion when internment was introduced in the South, in 1957, just over 60 people were lifted initially and about 100 in all over two years."

Within a few days of their arrest, fifteen of the IRSP men reported being beaten, and nine of them alleged grievous assault. Bunting, on his release, reported that detectives had beaten him and told him that he was "Northern scum" and had no legal rights. One Special Branch interrogator with particularly massive hands would hold them out and ask Bunting if he thought that hands like those could play the piano. If Bunting was slow to answer he would suddenly clap him on both ears at once so hard that the Belfast man's head would ring. Similar stories were told by the others who alleged mistreatment. Soon the gardaí involved were being called the Heavy Gang. Eighteen months later Amnesty International substantiated many of the allegations made by those who had been arrested during the swoop and found evidence that there had been widespread use of brutality by the gardaí.

Kelly, McNally, Fitzpatrick and Breatnach signed statements admitting their involvement in the train robbery. Plunkett and Barret were also charged, though neither had signed statements. The only evidence against Plunkett was a dubious identification made by the couple whom the robbers had held hostage while the operation was being carried out. The identification was based on one of a series of photographs the Gardaí had taken of people at demonstrations. The couple alleged that a man in one of the photographs led the gang. This man, the Gardaí alleged, was Plunkett. However, they could not produce the photographer to identify the person photographed, nor could they produce the negatives. As for Barret, the evidence against him was, if anything, even flimsier. According to Dunne and Kerrigan, Barret had been staying at the home of a friend, a member of the Provisional IRA, who was also arrested. Barret's friend's car was searched, and pieces of sheet were found that were linked by scientific tests to a piece of sheet found at the scene of the crime. Though the Provisional was released, Barret was held.

The subsequent story of those charged and tried belongs more to the history of civil rights than to the story of the IRSP. The case against Kelly, Breatnach, McNally, Plunkett, Fitzpatrick and Barret was dismissed by Justice Ó hUadhaigh on 9 December 1976, because of the failure of the Director of Public Prosecutions to produce the book of evidence. On 17 December, Kelly, Breatnach, McNally and Plunkett were rearrested, but not Barret and Fitzpatrick. The case against them was dropped without explanation.

The remaining four accused were brought before the Special Criminal Court, which had been established in 1972 by the Jack Lynch Government. It sat without a jury, the cases being heard by three judges. Their trial did not begin until 19 January 1978, almost two years after the robbery. By that date the trial had undergone a dramatic development. After a series of adjournments, Mick Plunkett stood up on 5 May and said that the delays were being caused by the fact that Judge O'Connor was sleeping on the bench—something to which, though everyone had noticed it, no-one in court had dared draw attention. A month later O'Connor was dead, and the trial was stopped. When it resumed, on 10 October 1978, Plunkett was asked how he pleaded. He replied that "the Heavy Gang are guilty, I'm not. The dogs in the street know I'm not guilty and I'm not." (Dunne and Kerrigan, *Round Up the Usual Suspects.*) The next day, 11 October—Mick Plunkett's birthday—the gardaí told the court they could not substantiate his alleged identification. The court told him he was discharged. He went home to celebrate.

Kelly jumped bail before the judgement was handed down on 14 December 1978. In his absence he was found guilty and sentenced to twelve years' imprisonment, as was Breatnach. McNally received a nine-year sentence. Kelly found his way to the United States, where he stayed until June 1980. In April that year the Provisional IRA had said that it had carried out the 1976 robbery (something that had been suspected from a very early date); in May, both Breatnach and McNally were freed on appeal. It was safe to assume, then, that Kelly would finally receive the justice he had long been denied. He returned to Ireland on 4 June 1980, and was imprisoned. When his appeal was finally heard in April 1982—six years after the robbery—his conviction was upheld, to the outrage and shock of those who had been campaigning on his behalf.

Nicky Kelly was finally released without warning on 17 July 1984. Eight years later he received a pardon from President Mary Robinson, who at the time of the Train Robbery case had been a young lawyer highly critical of the proceedings of the Special Criminal Court. Kelly, Breatnach, McNally and Fitzpatrick all eventually received compensation. Kelly commented about the whole extraordinary case: "Seventeen years of my life have been dominated completely by this. To an extent I'm probably obsessed by it. I try not to be." (*Irish Times*, 9 April 1993.) The whole long, complex case had subjected the Irish justice system to the most embarrassing exposure it ever experienced. Instead of disabling the IRSP, the case had damaged the Coalition Government and compromised its whole "law and order" stance.

The episode was a public triumph for the IRSP in one sense, for it showed the party in the role of victim of injustice. And it vindicated Costello—though he did not live to witness its final outcome. He had seen the trial as a chance to attack the state's repressive legislation. According to Osgur Breatnach, Costello "had used the case to discredit the State and its institutions, particularly its judiciary and the Gardaí." ("Fighting a frame-up", from *Séamus Costello, 1939–1977: Irish Republican Socialist.*) Mary Reid, a former editor of the *Starry Plough*, who was active in publicising the issues around the case, also credits the IRSP chairman. She says that Costello realised that the train robbery controversy was "not just a minor human rights issue: it was a chink in the Irish Government's armour. Costello was the first person to challenge the Special Courts. The Provos had never done it." (Interview, 3 April 1993.)

Ireland stood condemned by Amnesty International. The human rights organisation had criticised the Special Criminal Court for having "failed to scrutinise such allegations according to the principles of law." (Ibid.) Amnesty had demanded that an impartial enquiry be set up, in accordance with article 9 of the UN Declaration Against Torture. But even after a change of Government, with a Jack Lynch-led Fianna Fáil having ousted the Fine Gael-Labour Coalition in June 1977, the new regime was just as reluctant as its predecessor to risk exposing the truth of what had happened between 5 and 9 April 1976. A committee was appointed, but when it reported back to the Government in June 1978 its recommendations were ignored.

Nicky Kelly became the focus of a widespread human rights campaign, which enlisted support from the Birmingham Six and the Guildford Four, as well as Judith Ward, all of whom had been convicted wrongly under British law and whose cases had been taken up—eventually—by the Irish Government. However, in the Train Robbery case the Government refused to deal with the implications of a human rights scandal of its own making. In 1993 an Amnesty International booklet listed Ireland as one of those countries that engages in "torture and other cruel treatment of prisoners," because of succeeding Governments' failure to investigate the allegations against the police. A spokesman for Amnesty was quoted as saying: "It's the only appearance Ireland ever makes in the Amnesty International report. We are still calling for a proper investigation." (*Irish Times*, 9 September 1993.)

To date, the serious questions about Garda conduct remain unanswered.

NOTES

1. One of the UVF men involved died later that summer in the attack on the Miami Showband. He was also believed to have been part of the team that bombed Dublin and Monaghan on 17 May 1974.

2. A few weeks later, after Goulding gave his oration at the same venue, Costello sent a copy of it to the mediator, Michael Mullen, claiming that Goulding had violated the terms of the peace agreement reached on 13 June between the two organisations, one of which forbade them to publicly comment on their dispute. Costello said that Goulding's accusations that the IRSP was sectarian in origin, had murdered Seán Fox, Paul Crawford and Billy McMillen and was seeking to divide the working class violated that understanding.

5

THE LOST LEADER

The beginning of the end for Séamus Costello was a tunnel under Long Kesh.

In November 1975 the INLA leadership in compound 5, Long Kesh, set up an escape committee. They had not chosen a propitious date. One year before, a group of Provisional IRA men had tunnelled their way out of the internment camp. On emerging, they had run into a British army patrol. It opened fire on them, killing Hugh Coney. All the other escapers were eventually arrested and brought back.

No-one had led a successful mass break-out from what was called the "escape-proof" prison. A few individuals had managed to get out, but the elaborate system of security developed since the camp was opened in 1971 had defied the repeated efforts of the more ambitious. Between them and freedom lay a fifteen-foot steel wire fence. After that there was a zone twenty yards wide, lit by enormous arc lamps. Then there was the wall— twenty feet high, built of breeze blocks, with watch-towers manned by sentries at regular intervals. In the air a helicopter did a circle of the camp once every two days, taking x-ray pictures of the ground beneath to detect tunnels. In the ground itself—which was sandy, and easy to dig—was buried sensory equipment meant to detect unusual movement such as might be made by tunnellers. The ground around the camp was full of tunnels plugged by cement, testimony to the failed efforts of the prisoners and the efficiency of the technology at the disposal of their jailers.[1]

However, the sixty prisoners who occupied the two huts in compound 5 were undeterred. They thought of themselves as political prisoners and were treated as such. Like prisoners of war, they were held in long Nissen huts, were free to wear their own clothes, and lived under the command structure of their own organisation. They had an OC, with whom the prison authorities dealt. As an organised group their resolve was strengthened, their morale was kept up, and the whole regime helped give them a sense of purpose. They were not like "ordinary" criminals. In particular, like other prisoners of war, they regarded it as their duty to escape.

These privileges had been extended to sentenced prisoners following a hunger strike in June 1972. Beginning on 1 March 1976, the British government was to undertake a complete dismantling of the whole system of special privileges, little realising the crisis into which Northern Ireland would be plunged as a result. But by March 1976 the inmates of compound 5 had their minds on other things. Their intention was to organise a mass break-out, involving at least thirty prisoners.

In late November they had begun smuggling in the tools they would need for the escape attempt. It was a difficult and exacting process. One of the first items brought in was a pair of wire-cutters. This would be required in the event that the escapers found that the projected tunnel had left them on the inside of the wire fence. The Belfast INLA had cut the blades into small sections; alternate sections had threads bored into them in which to fit screws; the screws were in turn fixed into other sections. Each section was then smuggled into the camp, and the whole implement reassembled when the time was ripe. Handles were constructed from the tubular frames of chairs, and were made long enough to give whoever was using the cutters the maximum amount of leverage on the blades. The prisoners realised that if they did miscalculate and have the misfortune to come up inside the wire fence, they would have to face the daunting task of cutting through a barrier of steel.

Among the other pieces of equipment smuggled in were several chisels, needed to chip away the concrete floor of the hut under which lay the soft, malleable sand. Meanwhile, various items were stolen from the camp workshop, including the material required to fashion a rough grappling-hook, which would be required to scale the breeze-block wall, and scraps of iron from which shovels were wrought. A blow-heater was acquired from the Long Kesh authorities and adapted to provide the prisoners with a crude but effective system of ventilation while working underground. In the meantime, on the outside, the Belfast organisation was busy having false identifications made up, and getting compasses and maps, all of which were slowly but surely smuggled into Long Kesh. As well, each of the escapers was to be provided with a small sum of money to help them survive for a few days after the break-out—assuming, that is, it went well. Under the circumstances, that was a large assumption to make.

Between February and March 1976, compound 5's huts received a batch of new prisoners. Among them were the Belfast men Harry Flynn and Hen Doherty, both of whom had escaped from the Crumlin Road courthouse in May 1975. As well, there were three INLA members from south Derry: John "Eddy" McNichol, Séamus O'Kane, and Joe Kelly.

Shortly after they arrived, the digging began. The work was carried on in relays of two, in two-hour shifts, working day and night, for three weeks. The tunnel was kept no more than eighteen inches wide, to avoid having to use too many support beams. A trap-door was needed to cover the entrance to the tunnel, which lay under a bed. It was constructed out of four floor tiles from the hut, glued to a thick block of wood that, under foot, felt as firm as the floor itself. The sand and soil that was removed during the three weeks of digging was stored in the men's lockers and between the corrugated walls of the Nissen hut. During the dig there were three searches of the hut by prison staff, who failed to detect any evidence of the tunnel.

The men adapted the blow-heater to provide ventilation by using empty bean cans. The tops and bottoms of the cans were removed and the cans laid end to end, with a plastic shower-curtain wrapped around them. The heater blew the air through this improvised tube, which collected it and funnelled it to the tunnel's face.

The tunnel could not go deeper than about six-and-a-half feet. Below this the ground was waterlogged. The men needed good weather. Because the tunnel was close to the surface, persistent rain could seep through and bring the whole thing crashing down. Until the end of April, things went well; the weather was dry and warm. But then it began to rain. Conditions in the tunnel were already bad: it was partially flooded, cramped, and stifling. They began to realise that the prospect of getting thirty men through the tunnel without it collapsing completely were very dim.

Underground, the escapers had also been running into obstacles. Their tunnel had come up against a seam of solid concrete. It was an old Provo tunnel that had been discovered and filled in by the British. They had to go under the concrete plug. This could only be done by sloping the tunnel gradually, which meant that a longer distance had to be covered and at a slower rate. Then, after two days of digging under the first obstacle, they ran up against another. As with the first, it had been blocked by a seam of concrete. Once again the tunnellers were forced to make a diversion under the plug. Altogether they encountered five filled-in tunnels. Each one meant that their escape route was being lengthened by more and more gruelling yards of digging in near-suffocating conditions. It was not for nothing that compound 5 was known as the "Mole Hill" to camp inmates.

Because of the numerous diversions they were forced to make, it was difficult to judge how much progress they had made or the distance travelled. But when almost three weeks had gone by, the prisoners estimated that they were at least as far as the outer side of the steel fence. However, something happened that made such considerations academic. On

3 May a prisoner who was lounging outside his hut noticed about ten yards in front of him a crack in the ground. A quick check showed that the crack was undoubtedly directly above the tunnel, and that it was widening by the hour.

The immediate concern was to hide the evidence of their handiwork. A mattress was brought from one of the huts and thrown over the tell-tale signs, on the pretence that it was drying in the sun. Several times during the day a patrol of prison officers doing a circuit of the compound came dangerously close to stepping on it. Had this happened, the whole tunnel might have collapsed.

The prisoners' escape committee decided that the break-out had to take place that evening. Because of the conditions underground it had been decided that only ten men would make the break.

The decision about who was to be selected was based on a number of factors. The most important one was length of sentence: those prisoners facing a long sentence or (if not yet convicted) likely to face a long sentence were given first choice. The next factor was usefulness: those prisoners regarded by the organisation as being the most useful should be offered the opportunity to escape. The ten men picked were Eddy McNichol, Séamus O'Kane, Cahir O'Doherty, Harry Flynn, Hen Doherty, Jake McManus, Gerard Steenson, Dessie Grew, Joe Kelly, and Gerry Clancy. McNichol and O'Kane were both facing the prospect of long spells in jail, having been charged with murder and attempted murder of members of the security forces, as was Joe Kelly, also from the south Derry area. Jake McManus was also in on an attempted murder charge. Flynn and Doherty had both already proved their resourcefulness in a tight situation the year before, and both were valued in Belfast. Gerard Steenson had won his stripes during the feud by killing McMillen. Though Grew was facing the prospect of a short sentence, he was OC of the Armagh area and a key activist.

As the hour approached for the selected men to go, other prisoners in the huts became restless. A few could not resist the temptations of freedom and tried to get into the tunnel, and had to be held back. At around nine in the evening Harry Flynn and Eddy McNichol opened the trap-door. Before they descended, however, there was a little ceremony to go through. A Polaroid camera had been smuggled into the prison. It was produced, and photographs were taken of the escapers. (These later appeared, blurred and difficult to discern, in the *Starry Plough*.) The plan was to pair a country man with a man from the city, to cover all eventualities. Carrying a change of clothing, wire-cutters, the improvised grappling-hook and a length of string to enable them to signal their position to the two who would be following them, Flynn and McNichol squeezed into the narrow mouth of the tunnel.

When the first pair emerged at the far end they found themselves staring up at the towering steel-wire fence. They had miscalculated. The five diversions forced on them by the filled-in tunnels had confused them, causing them to misjudge the distance dug. There was nothing for it but to cut their way through. They tugged on the string to signal to the next two to begin the dangerous journey. Then, in the shadow of the enormous arc lamps lying between the fence and the wall, grimly they began the laborious task of cutting through the steel.

The last pair to come through were Jake McManus and Dessie Grew. By the time they had squeezed up through the ground, the steel fence had been breached. They crawled through the ragged gap. On the way through, lying between the rolls of cut wire, the escapers came across a plank of wood about eighteen feet in length. They decided to drag it along with them. They thought it was probably not strong enough to use as a gangplank but that it might still prove useful.

It was now around four in the morning. At half past seven the prison authorities would have roll-call, and the news of the escape would be out. A massive cordon would be thrown around the area near the camp. They had roughly three-and-a-half hours to complete their escape and get clear.

Between them and the wall stretched twenty potentially deadly yards. It was lit day and night by the arc lamps, which bathed everything in an eerie amber light. Opposite them rose two watch-towers. From where they were crouching it was impossible to see what was happening at the top of the towers: a sentry could be staring in their direction and they could not tell. The only way to find out was to run across the open space. If there was a soldier looking in their direction, it is doubtful if they would make it across to the wall.

With a sudden dash, Flynn and McNichol darted across the space. Luck was with them: there was no reaction from the watch-towers. The others followed until all were across and crouching under the wall. A new problem arose. The grappling-hook would not catch on top of the wall, no matter how many times it was thrown. Flynn put the plank against the wall and made his way up. Though it was short of the top by a few feet, it enabled him to attach the grappling-hook. While the others scrambled up, he hoisted the plank over the wall and used it as a gangway down to the field below. As Joe Kelly, the last but one, made his way down, the plank broke, throwing him to the ground. It made such a loud cracking noise that the men froze, sure that the sirens would start to blare at any second. Nothing happened.

Dessie Grew was still on the inside of the wall. He had been paired with Jake McManus, who was waiting for him to come over. Grew, however, did not appear. McManus asked him what was wrong. He said he'd hurt his legs trying to scale the wall and he couldn't make it; he was going to go back to the hut. It is probable that he had decided that since he was facing a short sentence it wasn't worth the risk to continue.[2]

The remaining nine found themselves in a disused RAF airfield. Aware that they had less than three hours to go before their absence would be discovered, they began running hard towards the dark fields beyond. After about twenty minutes Steenson was having difficulties keeping up with the others, as was his partner, Cahir O'Doherty, who was much older than his companions. They decided that their best hope was to turn back towards the M1 motorway and try to hijack a car. Originally it had been planned that the organisation in Belfast would provide cars. In fact several INLA cars were cruising in the vicinity of the escape but for security reasons decided to return to Belfast.

Other aspects of the plan were now abandoned. It had been worked out that they would go in their allotted pairs, but the only two to execute this part of the scheme were McNichol and Flynn. Being the first over the wall, they had already disappeared into the darkness. The remaining five decided to find a farm and, with luck, a car. It proved surprisingly easy, and soon they were driving towards Lurgan.

Meanwhile, eight miles from Long Kesh, police spotted Steenson and O'Doherty. Though at that point the escape had yet to be discovered, the police thought the two were acting suspiciously. Steenson got away but was later arrested near the motorway. He was not, as was reported at the time, thumbing a lift: he had been trying to make contact with the Belfast organisation but after six phone calls had failed to reach anybody. He was walking along the edge of a road when arrested.

When the five in the stolen car reached Lurgan they spotted a police checkpoint and had to abandon the car. They found themselves in a loyalist housing estate and quickly hijacked another vehicle, heading west. Eventually they arrived at the shores of Lough Neagh, where they took a barge across the lough. Then they set out towards south Armagh. There they made contact with sympathisers, one of whom put up three of the men—O'Kane, Kelly, and Clancy—in a hotel he owned. They stayed there for three days. McManus and Doherty crossed over into Monaghan. McManus was arrested under section 30 of the Offences Against the State Act; Doherty was picked up by the gardaí the next day. They were transferred to Port Laoise and held for almost two months on a provisional extradition warrant from the British.

Flynn and McNichol had kept walking. They walked for three nights, sleeping during the day and travelling after dark, until by a circuitous route they reached the mountains of south Derry. Supporters then arranged for them to cross the border.

Meanwhile, hot on the heels of the escapers had come a squad of eight plain-clothes soldiers. Travelling in a van and armed with automatic shotguns, they were arrested on the southern side of the border by the gardaí. The soldiers claimed they had strayed over by accident; but republicans alleged that they had gone over quite deliberately in the hope of either kidnapping or ambushing the wanted men. The IRSP protested when, within hours of their arrest on 7 May, the plain-clothes soldiers were granted bail by the Special Court and flown by helicopter from Baldonnell back to their base in Northern Ireland. A party statement contrasted the way in which McManus was being treated.

The IRSP had, of course, welcomed the escapers with the usual republican fanfare. It helped establish the party's republican credentials—after all, nothing could have been more in keeping with republican tradition than a daring jail-break against the odds. In the celebrations that followed, it is doubtful if anyone considered that the IRSP's identification with jail-breaking paramilitaries would make its pretence that it was no more than an ordinary political party (registered as such a year before) harder to sustain. But at the time this was hardly an issue: the party, reeling from the Train Robbery swoops, needed a morale booster. And to the rank and file the fact that the first successful mass escape from Long Kesh had been carried out by their organisation was just that.

For Séamus Costello, however, the break-out could not have happened at a worse time. His leadership of the INLA was being challenged, and the organisation was in crisis. This time it was not a dispute with the left but a confrontation with Belfast. In Dublin, Flynn and his companions found themselves in a similar state to that they had experienced after the 1975 break-out. They were squatting in a small block of four one-bedroomed flats in Pembroke Lane, just off the fashionable Baggot Street. By the summer of 1976, INLA men from the North were occupying two of the flats. Ronnie Bunting had returned from Wales in July 1975 and was in one with his wife and daughter; next door was another member of the Belfast INLA, Tom McCartan, and his wife. His father, Jack "Fingers" McCartan, was a leading member of the Provisionals in Andersonstown, where he ran one of their main drinking clubs.[3] Tom had graduated from the Officials to the Costello group. He brought with him the reputation of being quick-tempered and violent—character traits that in later years would be given unfortunate scope in his role as the man who tortured suspect informers for Dominic McGlinchey.

The conditions in Pembroke Lane were squalid. There was little or no money. Rent was not paid, and the landlord soon became too afraid to attempt to collect it. People slept in bunches on Bunting's floor. There were drunken fights. Pembroke Lane had become another Planet of the Erps in the heart of trendy south Dublin. Costello christened the laneway Bash Street, after Harry Flynn, whose nickname was Basher. When the IRSP leader drove up in his car his arrival was often greeted with beer cans and empty bottles flung over the wall. It was one of the less serious—and certainly less harmful—ways the residents of "Bash Street" had of expressing their displeasure at their leader's continued failure to deliver the gear and give them some meaningful form of action. Later they would squat in the IRSP's offices in protest, much to the disgust of many of Costello's Dublin supporters, who looked on their attitude as uncouth and thuggish. The Belfast activists' argument was straightforward: "You cannot have a war unless you have equipment." Over eighteen months had gone by since the formation of the INLA, and Costello had yet to deliver any equipment. Now, after a second escape, his supporters from Belfast felt they had earned the right to confront him. One of them commented: "The escape was the noose around Costello's neck."

There had already been a move from Belfast to challenge Costello's leadership of the INLA. Now, following the escape, there were several heated meetings in the Pembroke Lane flats, one of which almost came to blows. There was a final confrontation at an Army Council meeting in Cootehill, County Cavan, in July, when a vote was called challenging his position as chief of staff. The Belfast delegates expressed to Costello their position with brutal simplicity: "There's no dispute over strategy or politics. The fact is we're in Belfast and we need the guns." Costello tried to swing the meeting in his favour by hinting that Gaddafi was interested in supplying the INLA with weapons. His Dublin supporters on the Army Council, men such as Mick Plunkett and Gerry Roche, stuck with him; but the Belfast delegates, including Bunting, who had the casting vote, were not impressed. Costello was forced to resign, and one of the escapers, Eddy McNichol from south Derry, became the INLA's second chief of staff.

The new chief of staff was a respected "operator" on his home ground, but out of his depth as the leader of the organisation. In the end, during the few months he was chief of staff he was more of a figurehead. Costello still gave the orders. Nor did the change-over help assuage the complaints coming from Belfast. At one point, McNichol was so anxious to avoid confronting the Belfast men, who were, as ever, pressing him for weaponry, that he hid in a wardrobe. By early 1977 he too had been replaced. A Belfast man, Frank Gallagher, took over. Gallagher had been an effective leader of the IRSP in Long Kesh. He had led eighteen members of the Officials into the new group, which he had then built up in prison until it was about seventy strong. However, like McNichol, he did not have the experience or authority to make an effective chief of staff. The instability and demoralisation that characterised the IRSP/INLA's crisis at this period was set to continue and deepen.

The IRSP had been unable to hold an ardfheis in 1976. By then only four of the original sixteen Ard-Chomhairle members still remained. Vinty Fegan was in jail, Joe Quinn had been expelled for failing to attend three consecutive meetings, and the other ten had resigned with McAliskey in December 1975. By October 1976 the Ard-Chomhairle consisted mainly of regional delegates and those who had been co-opted. These setbacks did not prevent Costello from presenting a very different picture of the IRSP. At a Troops Out Movement conference held in the Mansion House, Dublin, on 18 September he told delegates that "our party is organised on an all-Ireland basis with approximately eight hundred members."

The true state of the IRSP was revealed just five weeks later when the general secretary, Mick Plunkett, drew up an internal report that starkly outlined the situation facing the organisation. It was presented at a conference held in the party's head office between 23 and 24 October. It revealed that the IRSP's registered membership was not eight hundred but forty. It was financially crippled, politically confused, its members so lacking in enthusiasm that there had not been one collection taken up for its imprisoned members.

The document begins: "Since the inception of the IRSP in December '74 and our first and only Ard Fheis in May-June '75 the party has not enjoyed any major successes in the intervention of the political life of this country. Party membership has remained static and in fact show signs of decreasing in recent times ... Our problem is that we have not been able to carry out the implementation of policy. At present this is due to the existing state of the organisation and does not stem from any internal political divisions and hence this meeting which is convened solely to discuss the past and present internal organisation difficulties."

Almost two years after it began, the feud was still casting its shadow over the IRSP. It was, according to Plunkett's gloomy report, "the major single event which was most responsible for stunting the development of the organisation. The net result was from our point of view three lives lost,[4] many woundings and injuries sustained by our comrades in the Belfast area ... For the duration of the conflict the major portion of the energies of the leadership were taken up with this issue. In practical terms the Officials' onslaught halted potential recruits from leaving the Officials and joining our organisation and in the public mind ourselves and the Officials were seen as rival factions engaged in a gangland war ... In the South the state and the media sided with the Officials who were seen as the lesser of two evils. Because we lost out in the propaganda war on a national level we are still suspect in the eyes of the general public. The conflict is also an indirect factor in the difficulties in establishing an active political party organisation in local areas in Belfast."

It goes on to deal with the dispute between Costello and the McAliskey bloc, the effect of the Kildare train robbery frame-up, and the confusion over the "broad front" policy.

Under the heading "Finance" the document spells out a dire situation. "This above all is the major factor in the disorganisation of the party. As is known the major source of income is donations. The party has received no more than £6000. Less than £1000 was received this year. The following are our most urgent debts:

telephone—£150
premises—£17,000
electricity—£60."

The main donations came from money received from robberies, as the document implies: "As finance has been the problem effecting the organisation of the party a lot of members wrongly blame Group B for this. That we have received little money from Group B does not mean that there has been an unwillingness on their part to make donations. In stating this, however, it is my opinion that after the resignations last year Group B have totally ignored the whole question of the political development of the party. We should ensure that this does not continue."

"Group B" was the INLA, which at that point had still not managed to pull off the major robbery that Costello had wanted and that was needed to set the political party on its feet and provide the finance necessary for serious arms purchases.

The most telling section is the breakdown of party organisation throughout the country.

"*Cork*. Until recently we had a very active membership of approx. 20 members in Cork and west Cork. The organisation seems to have collapsed in recent months.

"*Carlow.* Initially we had three active cumainn. The activities of an informer wrecked the organisation. Transport is a big problem and papers are being sold.

"*Limerick.* No sign of any organisation in the city. West Limerick are selling papers and need co-ordination. It must be pointed out that the lack of organisation in the city effects the situation re. the whole of North Munster.

"*Clare/Shannon.* The Ennis cumainn seem to be very active, sell a large amount of papers and are engaged in local activities. Shannon suffers from a lack of members but are active on many external issues.

"*Nenagh.* Papers sold but meetings are not regular. Cumainn effected as a leading member had to leave the area.

"*Wicklow.* Scattered and transport is a problem. Papers are sold in most areas.

"*Derry City.* No organisation, but good potential if we had an organiser.

"*Dublin.* 4 Cumainn. Comhairle ceanntair has not met in a long time. A lot of demoralisation among members. Have worked hard over the past 2 years.

"*Donegal.* One member, sells paper.

"*Co. Derry.* No information as delegate has not attended recent meetings.

"*Newry.* Isolated but very active selling papers. This cumann was set up after the collapse of a previous cumann who were intimidated by the Officials who are strong in that area.

"*Portadown.* Recently sold papers for the first time and are doubling order.

"*Belfast.* Until recently, no organisation. A comhairle ceantair has been set up and papers are being sold.

"*Armagh, S. Down, Monaghan.* No idea of these areas."

The IRSP was a mere skeleton of a political party. It had ceased to exist in places such as Belfast and Derry where it once claimed to be strongest. The difference between what Costello was saying about the state of the IRSP and its real, seemingly terminal condition can be partly explained by defections caused by the feud, and partly by the fact that the chairman was certainly exaggerating from 1975 onwards when he was claiming it had almost eight hundred members. But there is another factor that will help explain the difference between what Costello claimed was the strength of the IRSP and its actual weakness.

Many of those whom Costello was claiming as members of the IRSP in fact belonged to the INLA. Former INLA leaders from both Belfast and Derry have said that in both cities right from the beginning the military wing was far stronger than the political wing. According to a former OC of Belfast, there were three times the number of people in the military wing as there were in the IRSP in the city around 1975. This is an ironic reversal of the perceived relationship between the IRSP and the INLA. The IRSP always said that it had not got a military wing. However, it would be more accurate to say that by 1976 in Belfast and Derry, and throughout much of the North, the reverse was the case: the INLA had not got a political wing.

Even in County Wicklow, where Costello was a well-known and extremely well-liked councillor, the IRSP was weak, with only "scattered" support. It is no wonder that Plunkett concluded by saying that the party was "in its worst ever state." He went on: "The coming year will be the hardest yet for republicans and socialists in both parts of Ireland. It is vital that the present membership do not become the victims of demoralisation."

Plunkett's words were to prove prophetic. 1977 would confront the party with an even worse crisis than anything experienced in 1976, one that would stretch morale to breaking-point. The INLA began 1977 with a fatal attack on a British army patrol in Belfast (see chapter 6), the second within a few months. Showing its military muscle may have helped the movement's morale, but another, more ambitious scheme shortly afterwards proved a fiasco. A plan was hatched to kidnap the West German consul from his home in Ballymena. It was a South Derry job. The idea was to hold him and demand that IRSP prisoners be freed in return for his release. The would-be kidnappers entered his house but were forced to abandon the attempt, said one, because of "lack of communications". However, the operation signified that the INLA was ready to depart from more traditional republican methods if it thought something might be gained. The attempt was never reported, and it is doubtful if Costello knew anything about it. The rest of the year would be dominated by other, more pressing concerns.

The party's policy of trying to establish a "broad front" of anti-imperialist groups was to dominate much of 1977. In Plunkett's document, the concept of the broad front was said to have "caused much confusion in our ranks. The confusion lies in the definition of a Broad Front. To a small degree the question of working with other groups was clarified by the resignations last year. Within the party immediate clarification is necessary on the following:

"1/ Political conditions necessary to bring about a broad front.

"2/ Types of organisations that would comprise such a front.

"3/ Role of the left and more particularly the IRSP in such a front."

Costello had been promoting the broad front concept since the early 1970s. In the eighteen months following the formation of the IRSP there were meetings with the People's Democracy and its offshoot, the Red

Republican Party, as well as the minuscule Trotskyist organisations such as the League for a Workers' Republic and the Socialist Workers' Movement—though Costello had ruled out joint action with these because of their insignificance.

In October 1976, a month after the Troops Out conference in Dublin, the IRSP became involved in a series of meetings in Derry under the aegis of the Irish Front, which was described as "an experiment in anti-imperialist unity" (*Starry Plough*, May 1977.) Participants included the Provisionals, the Nationalist Party, the Magilligan Prisoners' Welfare Committee, the Prisoners' Dependants' Fund and the Political Prisoners' Action Committee. The Irish Front was organised around four demands: (1) An end to harassment, torture and intimidation. (2) Full support for political status and an eventual unconditional amnesty for all political prisoners. (3) The repatriation of all Irish political prisoners. (4) The withdrawal of British troops and an end to "British interference in the political, cultural and economic life of the nation." (Ibid.)

The front organised a few marches, rallies and pickets in Derry, where, by the beginning of 1977, the IRSP was becoming active again. A former Republican Clubs councillor, Micky Montgomery, had resigned from the Officials and joined the party. However, the IRSP's hopes that the Irish Front would become a mass movement were to be disappointed.

An anti-imperialist conference was sponsored by the IRSP on 12 March at the Spa Hotel in Lucan, County Dublin, where the party had been formed two years earlier. Costello prepared a document on the concept of the broad front that was presented for discussion between the various groups. It was also put before the IRSP Ard-Chomhairle. It listed seven key demands on which to organise anti-imperialist unity. Basically they were the same as those elaborated by the Derry Irish Front. Britain must "renounce all claims to sovereignty over any part of Ireland." The RUC and the UDR must be disbanded. All political prisoners were to be released. Britain must pay compensation to "all who have suffered as a result of imperialist violence and exploitation in Ireland." The Irish Anti-imperialist Front was pledged to oppose "all forms of imperialist control over our wealth and resources." It rejected a federal solution to the Irish crisis, which in the mid-1970s had been adopted by the Provisional leadership. The final demand was for the convening of "an all-Ireland Constitutional Conference representative of all shades of political opinion in Ireland for the purposes of discussing a democratic and secular Constitution which would become effective immediately following a total British military and political withdrawal from Ireland."

The broad front meetings failed to achieve the unity between the major republican and socialist organisations that Costello desired. Yet the programme he outlined was a precursor of policies and ideas later taken up by Sinn Féin when it was developing into a serious political party after the hunger strikes. In his 1977 document Costello had written, referring to a constitutional solution that would allow the development of normal politics in Ireland: "In our view the first step in securing a constitutional solution which meets this requirement must be for Britain to concede the right of the Irish people to exercise total sovereignty over their own affairs." A similar demand would form the core of the Hume-Adams peace initiative, a report on which was presented to the Government in October 1993. In this, as in much else, the IRSP was certainly ahead of its time. However, for Séamus Costello time was running out. In June, with Plunkett as his election agent, he had stood as the IRSP's candidate in the general election that saw the defeat of the Coalition "law and order" Government. He won only 955 first-preference votes. According to Plunkett, Costello was "devastated" by the result. When he had last run for the Officials, in 1973, he had taken 1,966 votes. The party's only other candidate, another Ard-Chomhairle member, Íte Ní Chionnaith, had also fared badly.

The following month a Waterford court awarded Costello £300 for malicious damage to his car, inflicted by an Official IRA gunman in May 1975 when an attempt was made to assassinate him.

On 20 August 1977, Costello attended what would be his last Ard-Chomhairle meeting. It seems to have been a depressing occasion. The party's head office in Dublin had stopped functioning after its occupation by the Belfast members, Mick Plunkett had offered his resignation as general secretary, and the only good news was a "donation" from "friends of the party" of £1,682. This undoubtedly refers to proceeds from robberies carried out by the INLA. It was used to pay off debts totalling £970.82, which left the IRSP with £711.18.

Costello reported on the progress—or lack of it—of the broad front talks with the Provisionals, the Communist Party of Ireland, the Irish Front, the Irish Sovereignty Movement, and the Belfast Anti-Imperialist Group. He had to report that, because of differences among some of the organisations in their attitudes to the use of violence to achieve unity, "a broad front did not seem possible at the moment but that another meeting of the organisations involved would be called to discuss joint action on specific issues such as prisoners, repression, etc." (Minutes of the Ard-Chomhairle meeting, 20 August 1977.) The Communist Party, it seems, was the main obstacle. As a result of its difficulties over the physical force issue, the document drawn up to cement the alliance between the organisations was left unsigned. Though the Provisionals and the IRSP were prepared to sign it, Costello felt that such an alliance would not constitute a broad front, and he outlined the reasons why he thought it was important for the Communist Party to be involved.

Jim Daly, a recent arrival on the Ard-Chomhairle, disagreed with Costello's refusal to sign the broad front document because of the Communist Party's refusal to sign it. Daly, an academic who taught at Queen's University, had joined the IRSP earlier in the year. Both he and his wife, Miriam, were former members of Provisional Sinn Féin. She also taught at Queen's and, like her husband, had strong antipathies to the Ó Brádaigh-Ó Conaill line on federalism. She had been brought into the party by Costello and was co-opted onto the Ard-Chomhairle at that meeting. The Dalys were to play leading roles in the organisation over the next couple of years.

Costello had other things on his mind besides the broad front. His failure to provide weapons for the organisation still haunted him. According to a former INLA leader, "at that time he was only interested in getting guns and money." (Interview, 22 April 1993.) It was this that led him in September 1977 to regular meetings with the late Will Stacey, then head of the Seamen's Union, in the hope of getting his help in moving a small arms shipment—consisting of about twenty-two rifles—from the New York docks to Dublin. The rifles are said to have come from a New York policeman.

Costello would park under a bridge at the junction of Northbrook Avenue and the North Circular Road, Dublin, not far from the union's offices. He would arrive there around noon and sit reading a newspaper in his car. Not far from where he waited is a pub that was then frequented by members of the Official IRA, among whom was Jim Flynn from south Armagh. Flynn was on the Official IRA's Headquarters Staff. He was known as a good "bag man": in four or five robberies he had taken roughly a million pounds for the Officials. The Official IRA's former director of operations for the South said of Flynn: "He was as game as Joe McCann. He was afraid of no-one." (Interview, 28 September 1993.) Some time around the middle of September, Flynn noticed Costello parked under the bridge at Northbrook Avenue.

Mary Reid joined the IRSP in late 1977. She became education officer for the IRSP and editor of the *Starry Plough*. In October 1977 she was a young mother looking after her son, Cathal Goulding, grandson of the Official IRA's chief of staff. The boy was attending a nursery school not far from Northbrook Avenue. Every day, shortly after noon, Reid went to collect him. Over the weeks she had noticed several members of the Official IRA in the area. "I sort of wondered what they were going to do. There was a credit union up the road and a bank, and I thought, 'They must be going to do something here.'" (Interview, 3 April 1993.) Costello was so secretive that nobody in his organisation at the time knew about his contacts with Stacey.

On Tuesday 4 October, Costello attended a meeting of Wicklow County Committee of Agriculture. He was as active as ever in local politics, and put forward proposals "for the immediate introduction of an upper acreage limit on land ownership," arguing that "unless radical steps are taken over acquiring and dividing land, small farmers would be doomed." (*Irish Times*, 6 October 1977.) That evening he did something uncharacteristic. He called on a former member of the party from Derry, who was living in Dublin at the time. To the man's surprise, Costello, normally consumed by politics, spent the evening playing with his children and watching television.[5]

Next day, Wednesday 5 October, just before noon Costello met Osgur Breatnach at the party's premises in Gardiner Street. There he picked up two hundred copies of the *Starry Plough*, which he intended to deliver. According to Breatnach, Costello had an appointment back at Gardiner Street at 1.30 p.m. After loading the papers, he drove to the North Circular Road and parked under the railway bridge at the corner of Northbrook Avenue. There he began reading a newspaper.

Jim Flynn had now been watching Costello's movements for three weeks. He knew his routine and was expecting him that day. Flynn, wearing a full-length navy-blue coat, walked up to Costello's car. Perhaps it was because Costello recognised him that he rolled down his window.[6] Flynn pulled a sawn-off shotgun from under his coat and fired into the car. The first shell struck Costello in the head and face. Flynn reloaded and fired again. This time two shells struck his victim in the back as he lay slumped between the seats. Flynn escaped on foot after trying unsuccessfully to break into a nearby Morris Minor. Soon afterwards he caught a bus to a supporter's house in the north of the city.

Costello lay dying from three wounds. According to the pathologist who carried out the post-mortem, his right lung was so badly lacerated that death would have been almost immediate. (*Belfast Telegraph*, 19 October 1978.)

In the nursery school across the road, Cathal Goulding's grandson had heard the fatal shots. Though Costello had been under sentence of death by the Official IRA Army Council since 1975, the news of his murder apparently came as a surprise to Cathal Goulding himself. Mary called Goulding with the news. When told that the man for whom he had been best man, and for whom he had once acted as an inspiration, had been murdered, Goulding replied, "Jesus Christ, I'm sorry to hear that."

As might be expected, people's views on Séamus Costello largely depend on their politics. He was adored by a close group of followers, many of whom, like Tony Hayde, had been through the republican movement with him; others who had no republican background, such as Mick Plunkett and Gerry Roche, were attracted by his socialism.

He was reviled by his former colleagues in the Officials. In the republican movement, personal animosities always run deep and are often the explanation for what on the surface appear to be ideological disputes. Even to this day Cathal Goulding has bitter words for his former friend and comrade. "Costello was quite sectarian. He wanted to drive [Protestants] out. Look at what happened to the INLA. They turned into a ruthless sectarian organisation." (Interview, 25 May 1993.) Goulding also accused him of being arrogant and of antagonising IRA members in 1969. According to Goulding, Costello left a meeting called in Louth to discuss the future of the movement to watch Bernadette McAliskey on television.

One prominent member of the Officials was once heard to remark of Costello: "We should have shot him in 1967."

The Official IRA's former director of operations for the South and a friend of the man who murdered Costello called him "an incurable romantic, but at times totally irrational." (Interview, 17 September 1993.) Billy McMillen, OC of Belfast until Steenson gunned him down, once referred to Costello at a command staff meeting as a "waster". Ronnie Bunting regarded this as such a slur that he wanted to bring it up at Costello's court-martial in May 1974, but Seán Garland had prevented him from speaking. Later, as the feud raged and former colleagues gunned each other down on the streets of Belfast, the Officials knew who to blame. Costello had to pay for what his men did. As one Official IRA man put it, "he was the man responsible for creating these people." (Interview, 17 September 1993.) Principally, in the eyes of the Belfast Official IRA, he was the man responsible for the death of Billy McMillen. The loss of McMillen was every bit as traumatic for the Official IRA as Costello's loss proved for the IRSP and INLA. Both losses were watersheds for the organisations involved.

Even those within the organisation Costello founded said bitter things about him when he was alive. In 1976 he and some of the INLA men from Belfast then holed up in Pembroke Lane almost came to blows. It was always about guns, guns, guns. Sixteen years later, many of those fortunate to have survived the feuds and faction fights have changed their minds about Costello. "Only a head case would have sent guns into Belfast then," said one who spoke with the experience of the Official IRA, the INLA and the IPLO behind him. "Now you know what he was saying then was more or less right." (Interview, 4 September 1993.)

Enemies and allies alike, and those who belonged to neither group, agree on one thing: Costello was charismatic. Among the Official IRA men who spoke about him the word kept reoccuring. He had the power to impress.

From 28 August to 3 September 1975, Costello and his adjutant, Johnny White, took part in a forum devoted to Ireland held in the University of Massachusetts in Amherst, near Boston. Andy Tryie of the UDA also attended, as did Tomás Mac Giolla, representing the Officials. Visas were refused to the Provisional delegates, preventing them from taking part. Also there was the former Labour TD and Government minister Noel Browne. Later, Browne wrote: "Séamus Costello spoke for the IRSP and gave a scintillating display of good humour, history, politics and hard facts. No-one who listened to his three hours in the afternoon, and, by unanimous demand two hours additional repeat in the evening, now doubts but that they will have to shoot him or jail him, or get out of his way, but they certainly won't stop him. Costello, the revolutionary Marxist socialist, whose ambition is a secular, pluralist united socialist republic, won't go away until he gets it.

"I've never heard his brand of republicanism before. He has his own socialist republican following. As well as that, he has gathered around him a considerable block of support from the militant 'Officials', now tiring of their own seeming tiring leadership.

"Is it not a triumph of our radio, TV and newspapers, and of the venomous Dublin political denigration machine, that none of us has ever read, heard or seen this man's remarkable dialectical skill and political ability?" (*Séamus Costello, 1939–1977: Irish Republican Socialist.*)

The UDA leader was also impressed—but in a rather different way. Costello and Tyrie reached an agreement that their two organisations would co-operate to end sectarian killings. But in reality Tyrie came away from Amherst convinced that the IRSP was a greater danger to loyalism and Northern Ireland than the Provisional IRA.[7]

After being acclaimed by Browne in Amherst, Costello had returned to Ireland that autumn to find his organisation in a crisis that would lead to the breaking away of the McAliskey bloc. Two years later, after his death, when the dust of their political dispute had settled, Bernadette McAliskey gave this view of the man with whom she had disagreed so vehemently: "Much is said of his single-mindedness, his ruthlessness and organisational ability. At his hardest, Séamus Costello was never hateful, nor was there a fibre of his being that was petty or personally malicious, and despite the slanders of his enemies, he was neither politically nor religiously sectarian ... His single greatest attribute was, however, his ability to relate to the mass of the people. His potential as a leader of mass struggle is not easily replaced." (Ibid.)

Mary Reid, another woman who rose to prominence in the IRSP, was in the unusual position of being married to Cathal Goulding's son but of having powerful political links to Costello and his party. She is a witness to both the personal and political entanglements that shaped relationships between the two groups and is convinced that very personal jealousies contributed to the Officials' hatred of Costello. Of Costello himself she says: "He was the only person with a genuine North and South perspective that dovetailed. He had more authority as a contemporary figure than, say, Goulding or Garland, who were still at the end of the day 1950s men." She is convinced that he would have made a republican-left TD without compromising his beliefs. "He was good at constitutional politics, extremely good at it, and had actually touched that sort of grass-roots politics in the South—populist, republican, that Fianna Fáil base. Costello could touch it directly." (Interview, 3 April 1993.)

Tony Gregory, the independent TD who was for a time close to Costello, had followed the usual route from the Officials to the IRSP, though his stay there was very brief.[8] But the impression Costello made on him was permanent, and he credits him with inspiring his own brand of community-oriented activism. In Gregory's assessment, "Costello had huge leadership qualities. In a way he epitomised everything that the [republican] leadership wanted in a republican activist. But you always heard about Costello before you knew him. He very rarely spoke to the members [of the Officials] in Dublin—Garland kept him from being a figure of influence." (Interview, 29 July 1993.) Gregory gave this estimate of Costello the local politician: "As a councillor, his achievement was to show clearly at local level how activists could organise politically to build a mass movement which people would support—or, in a word, to accomplish what he had set out to achieve, to point the way forward for all those who seek the republic of Pearse, Connolly, and Costello." (*Séamus Costello, 1939–1977: Irish Republican Socialist.*)

Costello's potential as a political leader was, however, forever compromised by the fact that he was engaged in an underground conspiratorial organisation that robbed banks, supermarkets and trains and that bombed and shot people. That is, he was a very Irish phenomenon: nowhere else, at least in western Europe, would one find a man of his obvious political abilities driving the getaway vehicle after robbing a post office van. He was an outstanding example—perhaps the outstanding example in recent times—of how men and women of ability are still drawn to violent republicanism.

Costello's role as a leader of the republican movement and then of the IRSP was fairly consistent. The vision he had of the republican movement was that of a radical, popular left-wing organisation, rooted in the poor and the working class, and linked to the armed struggle with its prime focus on removing the British presence in Northern Ireland. It was very much what Provisional Sinn Féin became from the mid-1980s onwards. Indeed the kind of popular activism espoused by Costello and developed by him in the council chambers of Bray was a forerunner of Provisional Sinn Féin's own brand of nationalist working-class advocacy that sprang up after the hunger strikes.[9]

His failures as an organiser, however, were what mattered in the end, for ultimately they cost him his life. His experience as a guerrilla leader was derived from the limited rural campaigns of the late 1950s. He was not prepared for the sectarian and bloody factionalism of the Belfast back streets. He once told Harry Flynn, who went on to become one of the INLA's leaders: "You'll never win this revolution unless you win Belfast." (Interview, 29 July 1993.) That maxim could be adapted to describe Costello's own plight: "You'll never control this organisation unless you control Belfast." Costello lost control of Belfast early on, and never regained it. But even if he had it would have been too late: once McMillen was killed, the Belfast Official IRA wanted Costello to pay. A member of the 1975 brigade staff said that Costello had to be killed so that "anyone who attacked us in the future would know they'd pay the ultimate price." (Interview, 10 June 1993.)

The feud, though long over, had created the conditions that led to Costello's death. It weakened the IRSP to such an extent that by the summer of 1977 Costello was at the lowest political ebb he had ever reached. The Officials were aware of this, and must have noticed his poor performance at the June 1977 general election. By crippling the IRSP, they had made him vulnerable.

However, the Official IRA's former director of operations for the South, who was a close friend of Jim Flynn's, maintains that Flynn carried out the 1975 death sentence on his own initiative. "There was no formal order to kill Costello in 1977," he asserts. "In other words, there was no big meeting and the execution order was made." (Interview, 28 September 1993.) As proof he cites the fact that Flynn did not tell anyone in advance of the assassination. "We only heard about it in Belfast hours later. No-one was prepared for it. Everyone was working openly across the city. We didn't know and we were quite vulnerable. The Erps weren't the only ones to be confused. The majority of Sticks had no idea it was going to happen that day."

The IRSP was confused about the political identity of the gunman. It seems that right from the start the name "Flynn" was linked to the assassination. Relations between Belfast and the Dublin leadership were so bad at that time that it was briefly assumed that the INLA units in the North's capital might be responsible. Miriam Daly was despatched to Belfast, where she went to the Divis Flats to speak to Seán Flynn and his brother Harry, who had surreptitiously returned to his home city at the beginning of 1977. The Flynns assured them that neither they nor any INLA member from Belfast was involved in the killing.

The Officials denied killing Costello, and the IRSP refrained from accusing them of being responsible. The INLA had a good idea who was responsible but decided to bide its time. The reason was that in late 1977 the organisation was too weak to do anything else. It was in fact split, with the Belfast INLA running its own show outside the orbit of Dublin. Under such circumstances it could not risk a renewed outbreak of feuding so soon after the last disastrous confrontation.

The postscript to Costello's murder had still to be written. On a June afternoon some four-and-a-half years later Jim Flynn had just finished lunch with Cathal Goulding at Cusack's pub in the North Strand. A few weeks before, Flynn had carried out a £500,000 robbery for the Officials, from a Securicor van in—ironically enough—south Derry, Séamus Costello's old stamping-ground. Flynn, one of the few militants still active on the Officials' GHQ, was apparently pushing for the Officials to launch a "people's war" in the North. On 4 June 1982, after leaving the pub where he regularly had lunch with Goulding, Flynn was walking along North Strand when an INLA gunman shot him dead. He fell just a few yards from the spot where, on 5 October 1977, he had ended the life of the man whom some regard as the greatest republican of his generation.[10]

NOTES

1. As far as is known, the Provisional IRA's tunnels were not detected as a result of this technology but through careful inspections and searches by the prison staff. This had led some former inmates to suggest that the sensors and x-ray photography said to be at the disposal of the authorities never actually existed but were merely invented to discourage prisoners from attempting to escape.

2. Grew was also wanted in the Republic, which meant he had little prospect

of staying free for long south of the border.

3. "Fingers" McCartan was shot dead in disputed circumstances in August 1977. His death occurred during a purge by the Provisionals of those suspected of corruption. Though the Provisionals blamed the British army, it is believed he was killed by his own colleagues. A similar fate awaited his son, Tommy McCartan.

4. In fact the IRSP/INLA lost only two men. Plunkett was undoubtedly including Brendan McNamee among the victims. However, he was not shot as part of the feud but by the Provisionals (see chapter 4).

5. Terry Robson also reported that a week or so before this incident he had met Costello in a hotel in Monaghan. Robson's family was with him, and he was surprised at how much time Costello spent playing with his children.

6. The scorching and powder burns on the skin show that he had been shot at close range. The pathologist was reported to have found "large numbers of leaden shot and shotgun cartridge wads in the tissue of the face, chest cavity and lung," but no trace of broken glass, which would surely have been present if the gunman had fired through the car window, as reported in the press.

7. In Amherst a photographer took an interesting shot of Tyrie holding a fake Thompson submachine-gun, pointing it at someone who was not in the picture. That someone was Séamus Costello.

8. Though several accounts have Gregory at the Spa Hotel meeting in Lucan on 8 December 1974 at which the IRSP was formed, he was not there; nor was Bernadette McAliskey.

9. In contrast, Official Sinn Féin/the Workers' Party took another route, one that led them towards political respectability. The party for a while filled the political vacuum to the left of the Irish Labour Party.

10. Jim Flynn has been portrayed by J Bowyer Bell in *The Troubles* and in *IRA: Tactics and Strategies* as a drunk and thug who was an embarrassment to the Officials. In fact he was highly thought of, as he was regarded as a key operator by most members of the Officials who knew him. Cathal Goulding also believe that the gunmen were after him as well, and claims they went in search of him earlier. However, the INLA denies that the Official IRA's former chief of staff was ever a target.

6

TERROR IN THE CATHEDRAL, MURDER IN THE PALACE

Following the murder of Séamus Costello, neither the IRSP nor the INLA looked like they were destined to survive. Yet in less than a year the IRSP had recovered something of its early pre-feud momentum and the INLA was in a position to hatch a series of extraordinary plots to assassinate high-ranking British diplomatic and political figures. One would come to bloody fruition and claim the life of Airey Neave in the Palace of Westminster itself.

After Costello's death, Bernadette McAliskey was moved to quote the words of a Black American revolutionary on the death of Malcom X: "Without him, we feel suddenly vulnerable, small and weak, somewhat frightened, not by the prospect of death, but of life and struggle without his contribution, his strength and inspiration." (*Séamus Costello, 1939–1977: Irish Republican Socialist.*)

The feeling of being "suddenly vulnerable, small and weak" struck the IRSP with full force, threatening it with collapse. In fact within a few days of Costello's death, moves were made to dissolve the party. According to Terry Robson, who had left during the McAliskey crisis but rejoined, "the organisation went into a state of shock after the Costello shooting." (Interview, 2 April 1993.) Back in a leadership position, he proposed that the IRSP/INLA should be wound up.

At a meeting of the Ard-Chomhairle on 9 October a caretaker committee of six people was established, combining the functions of the leadership of the party and of the INLA. Among its members were Terry Robson, Miriam Daly, and Mick Plunkett. The Ard-Chomhairle proposed that the caretaker committee "get possession of and administer the movement's assets, that it carry out the administrative and executive business of the movement, that it control all publicity in connection with the movement, that it summon within 4 weeks a general meeting of the movement to which delegates will be sent by the committee. This general meeting will be charged with charting the progress of the movement towards a 32 county democratic socialist republic." (Ard-Chomhairle minutes, 9 October 1977.)

In the meantime Costello's funeral had taken place on 8 October.

According to the *Starry Plough*, almost six thousand people attended, including some leading members of the Provisionals. Jim Daly gave the oration; Nora Connolly O'Brien, daughter of James Connolly, also spoke, as did Bernadette McAliskey. The Wicklow Comhairle Ceantair of Sinn Féin the Workers' Party was among the thousands of organisations and individuals that sent a wreath, a telegram, or a Mass card.[1]

A breakdown of the IRSP's finances after Costello's death showed that it had exactly £393.91 in the kitty. Its other major assets were listed as the party's premises in Bray and Dublin (both technically owned by Costello's heirs), the *Starry Plough*, a Volkswagen car, and Costello's Cortina. The Ard-Chomhairle voted unanimously to give the Cortina to Costello's widow, Maelíosa. The Bray premises were also to be left to be disposed of by Wicklow Comhairle Ceantair. The party was in debt over the mortgage for the new headquarters at 34 Upper Gardiner Street. The Ard-Chomhairle minutes for 7 October note: "Belfast had a copying machine, three projectors (slide) and a camera which might be in dispute. Derry's slide projector might also be in question. It was decided to contact Finnigan and Colgan Solicitors to discover the exact position."

During 1977 the INLA in Belfast had continued to function almost as a separate organisation. Ronnie Bunting had returned to the city in late 1976 and taken over command. The city had had two previous OCs, Kevin Holland and a former quartermaster for the Official IRA in north Belfast, both of whose reigns were comparatively brief. But Bunting was to remain as OC for four years. He set up home with his family in a house in Sevastopol Street, off the Falls Road. Bunting maintained a façade of normality, raising his family (he now had two children) and looking for work, which he eventually found in the nearby Royal Victoria Hospital.

Harry Flynn also came back to the city after the Gardaí began seeking him in connection with a bank robbery. (He was later acquitted of this charge.) As one of the North's ten most wanted men, he was forced to lead a very different kind of existence from that of Bunting. Moving continually from house to house, but using the Divis Flats—the traditional fortress of the organisation—as his base, he managed to evade arrest for some two years before returning south.[2]

The INLA, like the Provisional IRA, was confronted with a harsher regime than it had experienced before in Northern Ireland. In September 1976, Roy Mason had become the Secretary of State. He was a very different man from his predecessor, Merlyn Rees. Mason was a hard man, devoted to hounding terrorists, disdainful of the political manoeuvres of Rees. He boasted that he would smash the IRA. It was during Mason's rule as Secretary of State for Northern Ireland that Castlereagh interrogation centre was to gain notoriety as a "conveyor belt" for sending suspected paramilitaries to jail. Between 1976 and 1978, 2,293 people would be charged in Belfast courts with terrorist-type offences; the vast majority of the charges were based on confessions. The INLA took a strong dislike to Mason and resented his continual bragging about "squeezing the terrorists like rolling up a toothpaste tube." (Quoted by J. Bowyer Bell, *The Troubles.*)

On 23 January an INLA sniper operating in the Markets area shot dead a British soldier, Gunner George Muncaster. Bunting rang up the BBC, as he had done in November after the INLA shot a soldier in Turf Lodge, and claimed the killing on behalf of "Captain Green". Four months later, on 26 May, an INLA gunman seriously wounded a British soldier on duty in the Royal Victoria Hospital. The Provisionals had earlier warned that the British were using the hospital for "counter-insurgency surveillance". The INLA was to use the Royal as a base for several operations over the years.

During 1977 the Belfast organisation had turned to methods other than bank robbery to "raise finance". On 28 April it kidnapped the son of a Belfast banker who lived in Whitehead, a small seaside town just north of the city. The original plan had been to rob the bank in the Springfield Road for which the man worked. However, this fell through, and the kidnap was carried out instead. The RUC believed that the organisation involved was loyalist, because the phone calls asking for the ransom and arranging for it to be picked up were all made from Protestant areas. The police were surprised when they learnt that the drop-off house for the money was in Turf Lodge. A police car gave chase, but though it cornered the men, they shot their way out, wounding two RUC detectives as they made their escape. As a result the INLA netted £25,000. Once more it had shown that it was willing to depart from standard republican practices to carry out operations more in keeping with the left-wing terror groups of Europe or the Drangheta in the south of Italy.

When Ronnie Bunting learnt that the RUC wanted him for questioning about the kidnap, he went along to the nearest police station, together with SDLP man Paddy Devlin, and handed himself in. The police were not used to dealing with such a self-assured republican; but Bunting's Protestant middle-class background gave him a certain confidence when dealing with the authorities that working-class Catholics did not possess.

Bunting was taken to Castlereagh interrogation centre. He claims he was abused and beaten and had the initials *UVF* scratched on his arm. On being released, he lodged a complaint against the RUC, who in turn charged him with "wasting police time". He was convicted and fined a year later.

Not long after the INLA shot dead Private Muncaster in the Markets, it emerged in public for the first time to give an interview. Jeremy Paxman, then working for the BBC Northern Ireland current affairs weekly programme "Spotlight", was taken to a house near the Turf Lodge housing estate. In the back room he met the chief of staff of the INLA. John "Eddy" McNichol had resigned (he was soon to give up all involvement in the republican movement); the post was now in the hands of Frank Gallagher, formerly a member of the Beechmount unit of the Official IRA.

It was not, as it turned out, a very enlightening interview. The INLA's chief of staff, who spoke with his back to the camera, told Paxman that the INLA "was formed in 1974, December. Its objectives is [sic] for national liberation and socialism in Ireland."

"What's your connection with the IRSP?" Paxman asked.

"Our connection with the Irish Republican Socialist Party, in so far as a physical connection or intercourse of membership ... is very restricted indeed."

"It's surprising that you were formed at the same time as the IRSP was formed, then," Paxman commented, sceptical of the INLA leader's rather muddled answer.

While agreeing that both were formed at the same time, the INLA's chief of staff explained: "The Irish National Liberation Army seen the need for armed struggle. We are an independent organisation and an army. We are not a political party."

"You are not the armed wing of the Irish Republican Socialist Party?"

"We are not the armed wing of the Irish Republican Socialist Party."

"Under what auspices, then, do those members of the INLA who are arrested and charged and convicted—under whose auspices are they looked after inside Long Kesh?"

"They find themselves in a Republican Socialist Party compound in Long Kesh. Ah, because of several security positions of the INLA we have refused to bring ... the beacon of light on us. This has proved a successful tactic. There is a command of the Irish National Liberation Army within Long Kesh, that is correct. It's in cage 14."

Paxman commented: "Compound 14 of the Maze Prison is in fact made up of self-proclaimed members of the IRSP ... which has maintained all along since its inception that it has no military wing."

The interview was broadcast on 17 February, at a time when some in the security forces were still sceptical that such an organisation as the INLA existed at all.[3]

Meanwhile, throughout 1977, the INLA's armed campaign was coming up against fresh difficulties and experiencing losses. One of the hallmarks of Mason's rule in the North was an increasing reliance on undercover operations against republicans. On Holy Thursday an INLA unit moving through the fields of the south Derry countryside near Bellaghy was ambushed by men of the Grenadier Guards. Gerry Dowdall, originally from Belfast, was badly wounded but somehow kept the soldiers pinned down long enough for the other members of his unit to escape. Dowdall was hit several times in the front of his body. He was so badly injured that when the troops got to him it was at first thought he was dead. The troops were later accused of delaying calling for an ambulance in the hope that he would bleed to death. However, local people arrived on the scene, and Dowdall was rushed to hospital. He lost a kidney and half his stomach and bowels, but somehow managed to survive.[4]

With Eddy McNichol and Séamus O'Kane on the run in the Republic, Dowdall's arrest was a further blow to the INLA's campaign in south Derry, which was soon after brought to an end. Dowdall was later sentenced to twenty years on a variety of charges, including involvement in the gun battle in Dungiven in July 1975 during which a policeman was killed and another seriously injured.

Eight months later, the Derry INLA lost its first volunteer. On 12 December, Colm McNutt was sent out to hijack a car. Though he was carrying a gun, it was not loaded. He approached a vehicle in the car park in William Street, near the city centre. It was occupied by two SAS men, who shot him dead.

Politically, the IRSP had recovered its nerve sufficiently to plan an ardfheis. Only one ardfheis had ever been convened, and that was in the spring of 1975. In the following two years the IRSP was too weak or in too much disarray to hold another. The party had to wait until 1978 for its second ardfheis, which took place on 18 and 19 February. It attracted about eighty delegates from Belfast, south Derry, Armagh, Portadown, Newry, Monaghan, Wicklow, Dún Laoghaire, Dublin, Limerick, Shannon, Clare, Nenagh, Cork, Carlow, and Donegal. The biggest turn-out was from Belfast, with twenty delegates. Wicklow and Dún Laoghaire—Costello's old power base—sent fifteen each, as did Dublin.

The struggle to regain political status figured prominently in the ardfheis deliberations, as did the campaign inspired by the train robbery controversy; both issues had given the party momentum, causes around which to rally. On the streets the IRSP was regularly picketing the courts where the trial of their four members was being held. One of the accused, Mick Plunkett, who was out on bail, and other party members held meetings outside the GPO to publicise the case. By March that year the party had distributed over twelve thousand leaflets and put up four thousand posters attacking the whole apparatus of the Special Courts. They were also were campaigning about the plight of the "blanket men" in the H-blocks—prisoners who, resisting the criminalisation policy, were refusing to wear prison uniforms and were left with only a blanket or towel to cover themselves.

A new set of officers to fill Ard-Chomhairle posts was elected. Miriam Daly became the IRSP's chairperson; Mick Plunkett and Gerry Roche were made joint secretaries; Jim O'Doherty, the brother of John O'Doherty, one of the founding members from south Derry, was made finance officer; James Daly became PRO and also assistant editor of the *Starry Plough*, which was still under the editorship of Osgur Breatnach. A young man from Belfast named Jimmy Brown had appeared on the Ard-Chomhairle in late December; after the ardfheis he was made the party's Northern organiser, and Roche was put in charge of Munster. Patsy O'Hara was another new member on the party's ruling body. A Derry man, O'Hara had fled across the border after he was arrested and charged with breaking into a gun-shop. The gun-shop was owned by a party sympathiser, who had been known to supply the occasional weapon; O'Hara's break-in was something of a blunder. Among the men charged with him was Micky Devine.

A week after the ardfheis the IRSP addressed a large protest meeting in Belfast, attended by several thousand people, in support of the blanket men. The march and rally marked the second anniversary of the abolition of political status. The issue was fast developing into a political crisis for the Mason administration in Northern Ireland.

The train robbery prosecutions and the H-blocks issue had galvanised the IRSP and shaken it out of its political torpor. The authorities had forced the party to go on the political offensive, thus, ironically, saving it from the collapse that had threatened it in the wake of Costello's murder. It is no coincidence that the issues that enabled the IRSP to rally its forces were the treatment of its members in the courts and in prison. It is often the case with republicans that the more the system tries to grind them down, the stronger they grow.

Political agitation on the streets was complemented by the armed struggle. On 26 February, the day the second anniversary of the abolition of political status was marked, the INLA struck in Belfast. That evening after the rally an INLA unit ambushed a Saracen armoured car in the Springfield Road after slowing it down with a makeshift barricade. A soldier was wounded in the attack. At the same time a hand grenade was thrown at the RUC station on the same road, damaging security netting. An INLA gunman armed only with a handgun fired at point blank range into an armoured car. A BBC camera team who happened to film the incident had their film removed at gunpoint by the INLA and destroyed.

However, shortly after this attack the INLA was to suffer its third serious loss in five months. This time it was the County Armagh organisation that was hit.

The year before, on 1 March 1977, the INLA in Portadown had shot Walker Whitten, who was from a family of leading local unionists. The 73-year-old man was the brother of Herbert Whitten, a well-known Orangeman and former member of the Northern Ireland Assembly. He died on 19 June. In revenge, the UVF targeted members of the Trainor family, whom it knew were deeply involved in the new republican group. (Mrs Trainor had been murdered in April 1975, and Ronnie, one of her sons, in December the same year.) The INLA's OC for Armagh was Tommy Trainor. On 8 March 1978, along with his older brother, Frankie, and a friend, Denis Kelly, Trainor was walking home after signing on at the local employment exchange in Portadown. It was a year and a day after the attack on Whitten. A Suzuki motorcycle approached them carrying a pillion passenger. The bike passed Frankie Trainor, who was walking a little in front of them. When it reached the two men the passenger dismounted and levelled a Stirling submachine-gun at them. Tommy Trainor and Denis Kelly died under a hail of fire. The killings were later claimed by the UVF.

The IRSP accused the RUC of collaborating with loyalist gunmen and setting up Trainor. According to the *Starry Plough* (April 1978), the murders "coincided with the hysteria that followed the La Mon bombing and Roy Mason's promise of more SAS surveillance units." (In the La Mon bombing, carried out by the Provisionals, twelve people had been burned to death at a hotel reception.) The party rarely missed an opportunity to attack Mason, for whom it was developing a particularly strong distaste.

Trainor, like McNutt, was given the full panoply of the republican funeral. Miriam Daly gave the oration—the first time she had performed such a function. The Queen's University academic, who taught economics, showed something of the influence of her discipline when at the beginning of her speech she said: "Portadown is a new Irish town, owing its importance to its situation on the railway. Its population grew because work was to be had in factories and as labourers for the past hundred years or so." (*Starry Plough*, April 1978.) However, her speech quickly turned into a species of left-wing diatribe against capitalism mixed with traditional republican rhetoric about "Orange fascist thuggery" and "the tyrannical

British enemy" that became the hallmark of IRSP oratory. "Portadown", she said "is in the forefront of the struggle for rationality and decency in Irish political life." To an outside observer, appeals to rationality might have seemed rather anomalous in the presence of the hooded men with dark glasses, their pistols raised over the victim's coffin.

However, though Tommy Trainor's funeral drew a large turn-out—the *Starry Plough* claimed three thousand were there—it was not a complete success in propaganda terms. Miriam Daly later complained that nobody from Derry or Dublin had attended. Nor did the Provisionals send a representative. Relationships between the two organisations had declined since the arrest of Gerry Adams, who was charged with membership of the IRA after the La Mon hotel bombing. No members of the IRSP had been invited to attend the funeral of the Provo volunteer Paul Duffy, shot dead earlier by the SAS, and Jim Daly had been refused the use of the Provisional Sinn Féin telex to send out a statement about an IRSP member, Joe Heaney, who had been shot and wounded by the Official IRA in Belfast.

Shortly after Tommy Trainor's murder there was a revenge attack on the loyalist Queen's Bar in Portadown. Kevin Trainor, Tommy Trainor's 22-year-old-brother, was arrested and charged with the shooting. He was also charged and convicted in connection with the shooting attack on Whitten, and was sentenced to twenty years' imprisonment.

Yet another loss occurred on 28 March when the RUC intercepted a three-man INLA bomb team in Finaghy Road North. The police shot and wounded one of the men, Tom McAllister; his leg was broken and he was paralysed from the waist down. Eventually he was sentenced to fourteen years' imprisonment. This temporarily removed one the organisation's most active members in Belfast.[5]

By the spring of 1978 the south Derry man John O'Doherty was chief of staff of the INLA. O'Doherty had been interned soon after the movement was formed in December 1974; it was his second period of internment. After he was arrested the *Starry Plough* reported: "John's revolutionary example has been an example to many young and old throughout the county for almost a decade ... Locally, the IRSP has not suffered unduly by John's early removal from the scene. The fact that he had left behind a dedicated hard core of genuine radicals has resulted in steady growth." That "hard core" had launched the INLA's armed campaign and for almost two years made south Derry one of the most dangerous areas of Northern Ireland.

According to a man who was on the INLA GHQ, O'Doherty was a "military genius". But he was volatile, given to bouts of depression, and he drank heavily. While he was in jail his brother Jim had become Costello's lieutenant. On his release O'Doherty based himself in Dublin as the movement set about planning a series of robberies to finance the INLA's escalating campaign. The first operation was a bank robbery in Listowel, County Kerry, in the spring of 1978, from which the INLA netted £30,000. Another, more ambitious robbery was planned for May in Mallow, County Cork. Two banks were to be hit at once. Involved was Ronnie Bunting, who went to Mallow and took a room in a hotel next to one of the banks, posing as an English tourist. (Bunting's English accent made him sound at times like Basil Fawlty, according to his former colleagues.)

The scheme was to break into one of the banks that night, then wait for the staff to arrive in the morning. However, things went badly wrong when one of the gang set off the alarm. They then had difficulty getting out through the car park at the back of the bank, but managed to do so. Bunting returned to his hotel, and his accomplices fled. However, the operation was not a total waste of time. One of the INLA robbers noticed a Brinks-Mat security van heading into town. It had already stopped at several banks in Killarney and Tralee. "We made a quick calculation," said one of the gang. "We estimated the number of banks it had stopped at and then multiplied by ten thousand. We knew there'd be more money there during the summer months." (Interview, July 1993.)

The robbery was planned for the week before the June holiday weekend. The Brinks-Mat security van was to be stopped at Barna Gap, County Limerick. Two vans were stolen in Belfast, to be painted in the colours of Limerick County Council. But on the way down from the North gardaí stopped them for questioning. Though no arrests were made, the gardaí were suspicious, and the operation was aborted and rescheduled for the following week.

At that time the original plan went ahead. Twelve men were involved, including Ronnie Bunting and Patsy O'Hara. They were to pose as council workers who were doing road repairs. Traffic diversion signs were put up, directing the security van and the Garda escort behind it onto a by-road. The INLA brought along a metal-cutting device, but in the end it was not needed. When the van was stopped along with its escort it was found that the gardaí were not armed and that the Brinks-Mat men were offering no resistance. The security van was quickly opened. The money was transferred in two large black bags to the robbers' second van, which was to be used as a getaway vehicle. It amounted to £460,000.

So far everything had gone smoothly—better than could have been expected. Then the men piled into the getaway vehicle to find that the ignition had burnt out. They were dismayed: they were stranded on a by-road without much hope of any traffic coming their way, sitting on almost half a million pounds of stolen money. Suddenly a Land Rover turned the corner. It was full of German tourists, diverted onto the by-road by the road signs. They were stopped, their vehicle was seized, and the twelve-strong unit crowded into it with the money. The £460,000 and the weapons were hidden in a forest twenty-five miles from the scene of the robbery.

The robbery—the largest the INLA had ever carried out—served two purposes. The first, obviously, was to supply it with much-needed funds; the second was organisational. "It brought together all the main strands of the organisation. It was a unifying act," said a former Army Council member. (Interview, July 1993.) Belfast was involved, as were Dublin and Derry. The INLA proved it could work together on a "spectacular". Now the money would enable it to enter the arms business in a serious way and plan more ambitious operations. According to a former leading member of the INLA, "after Barna Gap, people slept in flats on layers of banknotes."

The IRSP's fortunes too were transformed. At an Ard-Chomhairle meeting on 7 June, Vinty Fegan, the party's finance officer, reported that it had only £136.66 in hand. Terry Robson complained that Derry needed its public address system back from Dublin. Two meetings later, Derry's delegate felt confident enough to put forward a "list of desired finance for Derry". The Ard-Chomhairle agreed to give the Derry IRSP £1,090. At the same meeting the possibility of setting up a Belfast office was discussed. "It was agreed that this would be an asset and would help firmly establish the organisation." By October, within a year of Costello's murder, not only had the Belfast IRSP its own premises in a handsome house at 292 Falls Road but the money owed on the party's head office in Upper Gardiner Street, Dublin, was paid.

However, the Barna Gap money was mainly intended for weapons. Some three years earlier, members of the Belfast organisation had established a vital connection, one that would give the INLA a steady supply of arms for years to come. In the very first issue of the *Starry Plough*, in April 1975, an announcement appeared from the "West German Ireland Solidarity Committee", which said it had withdrawn its support from the Officials and was now "in complete agreement with the policies and objectives of the IRSP." The committee, said the statement, had been formed four years earlier and was "one of the major support groups in Europe for Civil Rights and National Liberation in Ireland. During the course of the past few years, they have arranged numerous speaking tours in Western Europe for members of the Sinn Féin Ard Comhairle and have given significant financial support to that organisation."[6]

The West German Ireland Solidarity Committee was the first overseas group to swing behind the IRSP after the split. Rudolf Raab was a member of the committee and also an activist in the Revolutionary Cells. Unlike the Red Army Faction, which was a split from the Baader-Meinhof gang, the Revolutionary Cells did not agree with attacks on civilians, and confined its activities to actions against NATO, British army bases, and financial institutions. Raab provided the INLA with links to Palestinian members of F18, the intelligence section of Yasir Arafat's Fatah wing of the PLO.

In 1977 the Palestinians agreed to supply weapons and explosives to the INLA. Using the money acquired from the kidnapping of the banker's son, the first shipment was brought to Ireland with the help of the INLA's German supporters, one of whom took care of the transport: he employed his father's white Mercedes car. The shipment consisted of ten rifles and three cases of Russian and Chinese grenades, which came into Ireland in the back of the Mercedes driven by the German sympathiser. Though there was an accident, with the car being badly dented, the small shipment got through. Some six shipments were brought in like this, piecemeal, from Lebanon and across Europe over a period of about three years. In later years the PLO source would provide the INLA with hundreds of Czechoslovak VZOR pistols as well as Chinese-made SKS rifles, Browning pistols and Rhodesian submachine-guns, which were modelled on the Israeli Uzi. From other Arab sources much more was actually available to the INLA, but the organisation lacked the facilities to fully exploit their offers (see chapter 11).

After the Barna Gap robbery, the INLA could afford to make its own transport arrangements. In the summer of 1978, INLA members Phelim Lally and Séamus Ruddy, a 25-year old language teacher from Newry, set out on the first of two arms purchasing expeditions to Beirut. Among the weapons they brought back were thirteen AK47 automatic rifles. However, the most important materiel acquired from the PLO in 1978 was an explosive, which Ruddy transported packed behind the door panels of the van the INLA had bought. It was Soviet-made, pinkish in colour, composed of a mixture of penthrite and tolite. It was extremely rare and hard to find in western Europe. It came in two separate consignments. The first consisted of eighty small blocks, each the size of a bar of soap, wrapped in cellophane and packed round with newspapers. The blocks weighed about eight ounces each and had holes already in place for detonators. A second consignment consisted of two five-pound blocks; this was a slightly harder material than that of the soap-sized bars.

The explosive would prove to be devastatingly effective when used for under-car booby-trap bombs. It caused an upward explosion that was very easy to direct—easier than other explosives, such as Semtex. The blast could be directed by simply packing newspapers around the explosives; this meant that the force of the bomb was not dissipated, so not much explosive was needed for any one bomb. Also—most usefully for the INLA's purposes—it could not be detected by ordinary security scanners such as those then in use at airports in Ireland and Britain.

The September 1978 issue of the *Starry Plough* carried a front-page story headlined: "Republicans, Socialists Launch OFFENSIVE". Next to it was a picture of three INLA members "in training in the 6 cos." armed with rifles (one of them was Ronnie Bunting). Inside were more pictures. One showed a masked man getting ready to throw a hand grenade—one of those just brought back from the INLA's PLO contacts in the Middle East. Underneath, an article about the situation of the Palestinians described Israel as "the Jewish Ulster". The article concludes: "The IRSP fully support the Palestinian struggle and believe that it is important to expose Israel as a racist colonial state."

The same issue reported a speech by the party's chairperson, Miriam Daly, in which she said: "Airey Neave built his career on his escape from Colditz Prisoner of War Camp yet Brendan [Jake] McManus who successfully escaped from Long Kesh Concentration Camp in 1976 has been sentenced to two further years imprisonment and is protesting on the Blanket in H3 Block that successful escape from a Special Category Compound is not a crime." Neave, the Conservative Party spokesman on Northern Ireland, was coming increasingly to the attention of the movement with his hard-line rhetoric in favour of tougher security measures.

August saw a series of INLA sniping attacks on the security forces in Belfast using the AK47s. But the new rifles were proving difficult to use, and the gunmen succeeded only in sending "bullets bouncing all over the place," as one put it later. As a result, the INLA only succeeded in wounding four soldiers in the ambushes in the Markets and Whiterock areas. The movement wanted a "spectacular" that would establish the name of the INLA as a real threat to Britain.

"The campaign was just stumbling on. We needed an exceptional operation that would create enough confidence in the leadership to continue." (Interview with former Army Council member, May 1993.) The first plan they hatched to meet these goals was an attack on Horse Guards Parade, London. Options considered included planting a bomb under a manhole cover, or riding into the parade on a motorbike and tossing some of the new hand grenades at the cavalry troop.[7] However, this target was abandoned in favour of another: the British Ambassador to Ireland, Sir

Robert Haydon, and his military attaché.

On 21 July 1976, following the Provisional IRA's murder of the British Ambassador, Christopher Ewart-Biggs, Séamus Costello drove to Pembroke Lane to warn Bunting, Flynn and the others that internment was imminent and that they should take precautions. He was convinced that the Government would crack down on republicans as hard as it could. The Cosgrave-led coalition did introduce some sweeping changes: it gave the army powers of search, arrest, and detention; it increased the length of time a suspect could be detained from forty-eight hours to seven days; and it increased the sentences imposed for membership of illegal organisations. But Costello's fears did not prove justified: the Government did not bring in internment.

However, the idea of inducing a major crisis within the state was one that appealed to the INLA Army Council. A former member of that body reasoned in this way: "It would have generated support for the IRSP and raised a challenge to the state. We believed it would have created an environment where people would have supported the IRSP. We could have lived off the land and survived." (Interview, September 1993.) In other words, the INLA were convinced that in a showdown with the state, people's sympathy would swing behind the movement. But the means they chose to bring that about were hardly conducive to creating sympathy; rather, it seemed certain they would provoke outrage and disgust.

Sir Robert "Robin" Haydon, aged fifty-six, was appointed as a replacement to Ewart-Biggs within hours of the assassination. He and Ewart-Biggs had served together at the Foreign Office in the 1960s. His experience in Britain's diplomatic service was extensive: he had served in embassies from Sofia to Washington over a period of twenty years; he had been High Commissioner to Malawi from 1971 to 1973; in 1973 he became chief press secretary to the Prime Minister, Edward Heath, and was a member of the British government's team at the Sunningdale Conference, which had led to the setting up of Northern Ireland's only power-sharing executive. He had taken part in the weekly briefing sessions with officials from the Northern Ireland Office, so he was no stranger to the Irish situation, though he had visited the country only once, when on holiday in 1971. His hobbies were listed in *Who's Who* as walking, swimming, and collecting English watercolours. On coming to Ireland he said that he would have to give up the walking, for security reasons.

Haydon arrived with his wife, Elizabeth, to take up his appointment in November 1976. He told reporters: "I'm not scared of coming to Ireland. I would have been happier if I had taken the appointment in different circumstances and not following the death of a colleague. But I myself have no apprehensions." (*Sunday Independent*, 13 April 1980.)

Ewart-Biggs had not been impressed by the Garda's security arrangements, and called it "the department of keeping your fingers crossed." (Quoted by Dunne and Kerrigan, *Round Up the Usual Suspects*.) But the Government were not going to risk another embarrassing failure on that front, and security measures were intensified around Haydon. In November 1977 Mrs Haydon told the press: "Your marvellous Special Branch men ... have been really wonderful since we got here a year ago. We go around with a large entourage at all times, and have got to know them, especially the regulars, very well. They are all so tactful, conscientious and extremely kind. This seems to be a characteristic of you Irish—being adaptable, and having a talent for humanising a situation." (*Irish Press*, 18 November 1977.)

Adaptability might also be cited as a characteristic of Irish republican organisations. After briefly considering an attack on the military attaché's car as it turned the corner coming out of the ambassador's residence at Sandyford, County Dublin—the same one from where Ewart-Biggs began his last journey—the INLA decided on a more unexpected course. On Remembrance Sunday, 1978, the English ambassador, along with his wife and the military attaché, would be present at the ceremonies in St Patrick's Cathedral in Dublin. It had been noted that while the security presence was strong outside the cathedral, inside there were almost no precautions. After all, St Patrick's Cathedral was a sacred monument, situated on one of the oldest Christian sites in Dublin, a beautiful historical edifice and a part of Ireland's literary history because of its associations with Jonathan Swift, who became dean in 1713. No-one conceived of the possibility of murder in the cathedral. Except, that is, the GHQ of the INLA. They decided that the ambassador should be blown up with a remote-controlled bomb as he prayed in the cathedral.

On the Saturday before the ceremonies were to take place, an INLA volunteer broke into the cathedral and removed the prie-dieu from the Lady Plunket pew on the cathedral's south side, where Haydon, flanked by his wife and the military attaché, would be kneeling. The cover of the prayer stool was opened and a soap-sized block of the pinkish Soviet explosive, detonator in place, was inserted inside the lining, which was then sewn up. The block weighed about eight ounces. It was easily enough to sever both of Haydon's legs; he would die of shock and blood loss. The bomb would also almost certainly injure or kill the military attaché and Mrs Haydon.

The INLA had rigged up a remote control device that was operated from the aerial of a car, powered by a 2-volt battery. Shortly before the planned assassination, the device (without explosives) had been left next to an electric drill and the drill turned on to make sure it would not be activated by static electricity and detonate the bomb prematurely. On the Saturday afternoon before Remembrance Day, the prayer stool was replaced.

A German woman posing as a tourist was in St Patrick's Cathedral when Haydon, his wife and the military attaché took their places in the Lady Plunket pew. When the ambassador knelt on the stool, she got up and left, signalling to the waiting car outside. The car drove slowly down St Patrick's Close, and passed the cathedral's entrance and southern flank. The remote control device was pressed. Inside the cathedral, nothing happened. The ceremonies continued peacefully. The car drove on around the building, on to Upper Kevin Street then left into Bride Street. It turned into Bull Alley, down St Patrick's Street and back into St Patrick's Close, where the INLA volunteer pressed the remote control device again. Once more the expected explosion did not occur. A third turn around the cathedral produced the same result. According to a former INLA member, "we thought we'd done it. But the remote control battery needed a booster: the signal wasn't strong enough to penetrate the cathedral walls."

The attempt was abandoned. Mediaeval stonework had defeated modern terrorist technology.

The problem now was what do about the bomb in the prie-dieu. GHQ held a discussion. Some, including Bunting, suggested that it be left there and the media informed of the attempt; that way, he argued, the INLA would at least get some publicity from the failed plot. But this was opposed by those who advocated that the bomb be retrieved and the explosives used later. After a brief debate, the second course was adopted. A member of GHQ then had to go into the cathedral and get the bomb. There were few volunteers. Then one man agreed to do the dangerous job.

Late that same night the bomb was taken out and defused in the back of a car not far from the cathedral. The whole extraordinary episode had come to an end with no-one being injured, nor the intended victim even knowing what had happened. Two-and-a-half years later, Haydon announced his retirement with the words: "My wife and I will be extremely sorry to be leaving Ireland. We have made a lot of very good friends and have had some wonderful times." (*Sunday Independent*, 13 April 1980.)

Ireland had been close to experiencing a killing that would probably have ranked in shock and outrage with the Phoenix Park murders of 1890. Had the signal been strong enough to detonate the bomb, the British ambassador would have been blown to pieces inside one of the nation's most renowned churches. Ireland would have experienced a Remembrance Day massacre nine years earlier than it did. The Government's horror can easily be imagined; its reaction can only be surmised. To have two British ambassadors murdered within two years would probably have precipitated an unprecedented crackdown that could well have included the introduction of internment without trial. The INLA would have succeeded in provoking a crisis. It is doubtful, however, if such measures would have brought sympathy to its political wing. Its scenario that envisaged the Irish people springing to the party's defence seemed unlikely, to say the least.

The INLA turned its attentions elsewhere: to the hated figure of the Northern Ireland Secretary of State, Roy Mason. Squat and bull-like, he gloried in his background as a miner. He had been the Labour Party's spokesman on defence, and then Minister of Defence in Harold Wilson's government and Secretary for Defence in that of James Callaghan. From the moment he came to Stormont in September 1976, he was determined to smash the republican movement. His predecessor, Merlyn Rees, had been interested in finding a political solution of some sort. Rees had attempted to bring the Provisionals into the political process; but Mason thought of them mainly as a security problem that had to be dealt with firmly before there was any hope of finding a settlement.

By early 1977, the British Government's "conveyor belt" system of obtaining convictions through relying on confessions was in full throttle. In May he faced down the UDA-Paisley coalition that had attempted to bring about another "general strike" in support of the return of majority rule. In August he could celebrate the success of the Queen's visit to Northern Ireland, which the Provisionals had threatened but failed to disrupt. He increased the numbers of SAS-type units operating in the North; on 2 May 1977 he revealed that their numbers had been doubled. Between December 1977 and December 1978 eleven people were shot dead in disputed circumstances by the security forces, including an INLA man, Colm McNutt. And Mason forced through the government's prison policies in spite of the growing protests both inside and outside the jails and the increasing unease in the nationalist community. By the summer of 1978 there were 250 republican prisoners "on the blanket"—twenty-seven of them INLA members—refusing to wear prison garb, living in ghastly squalor, smearing their cell walls with their own excrement rather than conform to the authorities' demands. Mason blamed the prisoners themselves. To him they were criminals, and terrorism was a disease that had to be eradicated.

After undercover troops shot dead an innocent teenager, John Boyle, near an arms dump in Dunloy, County Antrim, on 11 July 1978, the IRSP accused Mason of running a "murder on sight" policy (what would later be termed "shoot-to-kill") in which suspected republican paramilitaries were given no chance to surrender. (*Starry Plough*, August 1978.) The party accused Mason of instituting this policy as a concession to the demands of extreme loyalists.

At the beginning of January 1979, Miriam Daly accused Mason of trying to "smash" the IRSP. (*Sunday Press*, 21 January 1979.) A few weeks later the party issued a statement alleging that the Secretary of State was involved in a "dictatorial attempt to crush all political opposition in the Six Counties," claiming that the Emergency Powers Act was being used to detain and interrogate IRSP members "as a means of harassment and intimidation." (*Irish News*, 8 February 1979.) More ominously, the *Starry Plough* carried a New Year statement from the INLA "Department of General Headquarters" on its front page that warned: "In the coming year the strategy of the INLA will be geared to ensure that Imperialism and its agents will see the futility of its policy of inflicting large scale human misery on the people." Underneath was a photograph of an AK47.

In March 1979 the organisation's GHQ decided to assassinate Mason in his home constituency of Barnsley in Yorkshire. An elaborate plan was worked out to enable the INLA to catch their well-protected target off guard. The plan was to stab to death Mason's election agent, Trevor Lindley, as he left his favourite pub in Barnsley. It would be made to look like a purely criminal act, with no political motives involved. Mason would, of course, be prominent at the murdered man's funeral; he would be shot by a sniper at or near the cemetery.

Volunteers were despatched to Barnsley. The pub where Lindley drank was watched, and he was even followed after he left the pub. The cemetery was cased, and a good sniping position chosen. The getaway route was also established.

By then, however, the Labour government had begun to look more and more vulnerable, and the prospect of a general election loomed. There were problems with the assassination plan: Lindley had temporarily vanished. Then a dispute arose within the INLA leadership, some of whom were increasingly unhappy with O'Doherty, the chief of staff. The plot against Mason was abandoned. However, shortly thereafter another target suddenly and unexpectedly presented itself: Airey Neave.

Much of the information that follows is based on an interview with Ronnie Bunting that one of the authors conducted in August 1979, the year before he was assassinated.[8]

Neave had masterminded Margaret Thatcher's take-over of the Tory leadership in 1975 and had been her spokesman on Northern Ireland for four years. He also headed her private office. He came from a military background: he was the first British officer to escape from Colditz prisoner-of-war camp in Germany in 1942, and after the war he was attached to the War Crimes Executive and brought indictments against leading Nazis at Nürnberg. His views on Northern Ireland were, like those of Mason, based on what he saw as the primary need to defeat the IRA. He singled out the Official IRA in particular. In a speech at Eaton Delaval in Northumbria in September 1976 he said: "Both wings of the IRA, but especially the Officials, have increasingly Marxist aims. The first is the creation of a socialist republic in Ireland for which Cuba is the model. They also work to end the links between the UK and Northern Ireland and the overthrow of the Irish Government in Dublin." (Quoted by Paul Foot, *Who Framed Colin Wallace?*)

Though at first the Unionists had problems with him—mainly because he had been critical of their support for Callaghan's government, which had kept it in power—they soon warmed to him as it became clear that his attitudes to security coincided with their own. On 26 May 1977, the same day that the INLA wounded a soldier in the Royal Victoria Hospital, he hinted that he would reintroduce internment if ever in a position to do so. A few weeks later, he called for stricter anti-terrorism laws. Like Roy Mason—whom he frequently praised—he wanted more SAS operations. But he went further than Mason and advocated the death penalty for terrorist offences. He constantly attacked the media for undermining the security forces by being too critical of their procedures and "magnifying" their "lapses".

As for politics, Neave declared that "power-sharing" was "no longer practical politics". (W. D. Flackes and Sydney Elliott, *Northern Ireland: a Political Directory, 1989.*) He thought such politically ambitious schemes were dangerous. The Conservative Party's 1979 manifesto instead suggested a series of regional councils to run the province. It was a policy that was never enacted. By the time Thatcher had become Prime Minister the INLA had intervened violently in the British democratic process.

"Neave was the only one, apart from Mayhew, who sought to be Secretary of State," a former INLA GHQ member said. "He was coming in on the heels of Mason—to settle the Northern problem and make Mason look like a lamb. He wanted to bring in more SAS and take the war to the enemy." (Interview, May 1993.)

On 28 March, Callaghan's Labour government fell after being defeated on a vote of no confidence by 311 to 310, precipitating a general election, which was called for the beginning of May. As the government fell, important information unexpectedly came to the INLA from a political source in England. The information concerned Airey Neave. The source feared that Neave was preparing a right-wing backlash, with Thatcher as his chosen "front". Thanks to this source, the INLA had the access and the information necessary to launch one of the most daring assassinations in British political history.

There was little time to plot the assassination—a matter of two days. Information they received indicated that in the Palace of Westminster a situation existed rather similar to that in St Patrick's Cathedral earlier: while security around and outside the House of Commons was tight, inside the security guards took for granted the bona fides of the individual and did not challenge him or her.

The INLA was told that access to the underground car park of the Houses of Parliament was possible. The attempt on Neave could take place there, but it had to be arranged so that when it occurred, the operators would be elsewhere. A booby-trap car-bomb was needed, but one that would allow the bombers to get a safe distance away from the scene of the attack. And since they did not know exactly at what moment Neave would leave the chamber, it could not be a bomb set to go off at a certain time. GHQ decided to use a bomb employing a mercury-tilt switch; the timer was equipped with only a one-hour battery.

The device had been used before, in the wounding of a prison officer in Lisburn in December 1978, and in Portadown on 6 March when the INLA planted one under the car of Robert McNally, a UDR man. The blast injured him seriously, and he died seven days later after having a leg amputated. (Though this was later described as a trial run for the Neave operation, it was not. The attack on Neave was a matter of seizing a sudden opportunity.)

Another advantage of the mercury-tilt switch was that, because the switch itself was only a few inches in size, the device was extremely small and portable. A sixteen-ounce chunk of the pink Soviet explosive—twice the amount that had been used in the attempt on the ambassador—was cut from one of the five-pound blocks, made of slightly harder material than the smaller bars that had arrived with them from the PLO contacts in Lebanon. It was then smuggled into England via a third country in a chocolate-box.

In the early afternoon of Friday 30 March the INLA unit penetrated the House of Commons underground car park posing as workers, carrying the device in a tool kit. Their informant had not exaggerated: it was remarkably easy to gain access to the Palace of Westminster. The security cameras inside the car park, the INLA also knew, were not monitored very strictly. Neave's blue Vauxhall Cavalier was found.

It was then that there occurred a hitch. The INLA unit realised that the timing device for the bomb was not functioning properly. They had to improvise—and quickly. They replaced the original timer with a wristwatch. Watches would not normally be used by experienced bomb-makers, as they are often inaccurate. Also, the hands of a watch are frequently coated with plastic, which would break any current, so the bomb would not detonate. A member of the unit scraped the hands of the watch with sandpaper to ensure that there was no plastic coating on them to break the circuit.

The INLA unit attached the bomb to the floor panel under the driver's seat. The device was then armed. It was set to remain lethal until the one-hour battery expired. But it would not explode until the bubble of mercury within the mercury-tilt switch surged towards two electrical contacts that complete the circuit. This usually happens when a movement tilts the bomb.

Shortly before three o'clock Neave left the chamber of the House of Commons as the Parliament broke up and politicians left to prepare for the coming election. He made his way to the car park, a matter of a few minutes' walk. He got into his car and began the drive up the ramp that led out of the car park. As the car went up, the mercury surged, completing the circuit and detonating the sixteen ounces of explosives. The force of the blast, directed upwards, severed his legs, mutilated his face, and trapped him in the devastated car.

David Healy, who worked for the Press Association, was on the scene within thirty seconds of the explosion. He found Neave still in his seat but thrust forward, almost as if he was standing up, his face bloody and blackened. "His grey pin-stripe trousers and black jacket were torn and ragged. I thought he looked dead, but a policeman who felt his pulse shouted, 'He's still alive.'" (*News Letter*, 31 March 1979.) Blood was running from the car and down the ramp, meandering among the broken glass and mangled metal fragments. A doctor and a nurse arrived and fought desperately to save Neave's life. It took half an hour to cut him from the gutted car. Their efforts were useless. He died eight minutes after arriving in hospital.

The INLA estimated that the cost of the explosives involved in the bomb that robbed Airey Neave of his life was £5.12.

In the immediate aftermath, the Provisional IRA claimed responsibility for the killing. From Dublin, an INLA member tried to claim responsibility on behalf of his organisation in a call to Ulster Television in Belfast, but when he began to make the claim, the person at UTV told him to "fuck off," and hung up. In Belfast, however, there was one man who had no doubts about what had happened. When the news came through, Ronnie Bunting was on his way to attend a fund-raising social on behalf of the movement's prisoners that was being held at the IRSP's new offices in the Falls Road. The party had started by the time Bunting reached the premises. He announced that Neave had been killed. "We did it!" he shouted, throwing his arms around Seán Flynn. The idea of raising funds for their prisoners was abandoned. Drinks were on the house. "Everybody was elated," recalls one of the party members who was there.

The INLA described the assassination as the "operation of the decade" (*Starry Plough*, April 1979.) And yet the removal of Airey Neave had surprisingly little political impact on the incoming Thatcher government's policies towards Northern Ireland. Humphrey Atkins became Secretary of State, and the province slid down the agenda of the new Prime Minister. His rule there was characterised by half-hearted attempts at uninspired political reform. Thatcher herself was uncompromising when faced with the prison and hunger strike crisis between 1979 and 1981. It is possible that personal bitterness at the loss of such a close friend and colleague played a part in her unflinching resolve to face down the protesters.

A massive investigation, staffed by three hundred detectives, turned up very little information about the perpetrators of the assassination. Contrary to several fanciful accounts of the crime, none of those involved ever fell victim to the SAS or loyalist death squads. In April 1987, eight years after the assassination, the Home Office Minister, Douglas Hogg, told MPs: "I very much regret to say that nobody has been charged in connection with this matter, and I think it would be misleading for me to say that a charge is likely now or in the immediate future." (*Irish News*, 10 April 1987.) In 1994, the assassins are still alive and at liberty.

NOTES

1. The list of those who contributed their condolences in one form or another gives an idea of the breadth of Costello's contacts. The names include the Fine Gael TD Oliver J. Flanagan, the American Trotskyist George Novack, and the senator and trade union leader Michael Mullen. The organisations ranged from the Army Council of the Provisional IRA to the Queen of Peace Youth Club, Bray.
2. Flynn continued to live up to the reputation gained because of his two escapes. On one occasion two INLA leaders from Derry were meeting him in the Divis Flats when a British army patrol raided the building. Flynn was last seen abseiling down the side of the block of flats using bed sheets as an improvised rope.
3. The RUC later questioned Paxman, asking him to name the man he

interviewed, the source who had set up the interview, and the technicians who had recorded it. He refused. The BBC's management, however, gave the names of the camera operator and sound recordist to the police. Both were then questioned by the RUC. This provoked a dispute between the BBC and the Association of Broadcasting Staff, which blacked the programme, putting it temporarily off the air.

4. The incident occurred two fields away from where Francis Hughes was wounded in a gun battle with the SAS in 1978. The loss of Hughes and the arrest of McGlinchey in the Republic brought the Provos' south Derry operation to a close by late 1978.

5. Neither his injuries nor his sentence, however, deterred him from involvement in the INLA. He would briefly become Belfast OC in 1986.

6. In July 1975 the group invited IRSP Ard-Chomhairle member Peter Pringle on a tour, along with Séamus Loughran of the Provisionals and Fintan Vallely of the People's Democracy. The three not only toured West Germany but spoke at venues in the Netherlands, Belgium, Austria, and Switzerland. This was the IRSP's first venture abroad. The burgomaster of Osnabrück in northern Germany received the trio in the town hall and, after a ceremony at which some fine wines were served, presented them with LPs of the Osnabrück Symphony Orchestra. Apparently he only realised what their politics were when they presented him in turn with a copy of the book *The Battle of the Bogside*. He was extremely embarrassed, as Osnabrück was a garrison town with some eight thousand British troops. (Pringle eventually left the IRSP. In November 1980 he was sentenced to death for the murder of Garda Henry Byrne during a robbery. The sentence was later commuted to forty years' imprisonment.)

7. Once more the INLA anticipated the Provisionals, who four years later did launch a bombing attack on Horse Guards Parade, which killed two soldiers and injured many others.

8. Contrary to what has been claimed, Bunting himself took no part in the murder of Neave. But he was one of the few people who knew most of the details of the assassination plot.

7

FROM BOOM TO BUST

With the assassination of Airey Neave, the INLA had finally made the big time. Journalists were queuing up to interview the organisation's spokesmen. Interviews appeared in *Magill* and *Paris Match* and on the BBC's "Panorama" —the latter causing much annoyance to the new Conservative Government of Margaret Thatcher.

Yet while the organisation strutted on the stage of international terrorist notoriety, behind the scenes there were fresh signs of instability, both in the political and military wings. The crisis in the INLA, which would come to fruition within months of Neave's death to undermine the new-found unity, was preceded by political upheaval in the IRSP.

The party's problems dated back to late the previous year, when the IRSP's chairperson, Miriam Daly, had threatened to resign. She complained that it had been impossible for her to carry out agreed policy, that the H-block campaign had not gone as planned, and no new cumainn had been formed. As well, she was unhappy because of communication problems between the general secretary and herself. Jim Daly also implied that another organisation—meaning the INLA—was undermining his wife's position on the Ard-Chomhairle.

Plunkett had pleaded with her to withdraw her resignation, saying it would be "disastrous" if she did so. He blamed the organisational problems on the officer board, which ran the party organisation from day to day. Daly agreed to remain in the post "when it became clear that the officer board was reconstituted to meet the wishes of the Ard Comhairle and that she had the confidence of members of the Ard Comhairle ..." (Ard-Chomhairle minutes, 30 September 1978.)

However, there were further disputes at the Ard-Chomhairle meeting of 6 October about "federalism", to which both Dalys were fiercely opposed in any shape or form, this being the reason they had resigned from Provisional Sinn Féin. There was a feeling among other Ard-Chomhairle members that it was being overemphasised, particularly at a time when relationships with Provisional Sinn Féin were sensitive and attempts were being made to build a united front on the H-block issue. Another dispute followed in November about money, with Miriam Daly complaining that it was being allocated "outside of the due process"—the treasurer had borrowed £700. "The discussion developed into many personal allegations," according to the minutes of the meeting.

Miriam Daly finally resigned as party chairperson in March 1979 after a dispute about the powers of the Ard-Chomhairle and the Coiste Seasta, or officer board, which met every week. She was replaced by the general secretary, Mick Plunkett, just weeks before the INLA assassinated Airey Neave. However, there were further disputes about the party's failure to contest the local elections in the south and the European parliamentary election in June 1979. Many felt that the IRSP had become too like Sinn Féin and was going down the abstentionist road.

The recent turmoil within the party was not apparent, of course, in the aftermath of 30 March. There was a considerable amount of gloating about the operation, as was apparent from the statement that appeared in the August issue of the *Starry Plough*. "In March, retired terrorist and supporter of capital punishment, Airey Neave, got a taste of his own medicine when an INLA unit pulled off the operation of the decade and blew him to bits inside the 'impregnable' Palace of Westminster. The nauseous Margaret Thatcher snivelled on television that he was an 'incalculable loss'—and so he was—to the British ruling class."

The INLA was at pains to stress that while the Neave killing might have brought "recognition", the organisation that carried it out had been there all along, fighting in the North. In the *Irish Times* an INLA spokesman claimed that they "had probably the best armoury of any Republican paramilitary group, including modern Kalashnikof rifles manufactured both in the Soviet Union and China." (*Irish Times*, 9 April 1979.) He told the paper that the organisation was responsible for weekly operations in Northern Ireland. At the end of 1978 in Derry the INLA had carried out a series of bomb attacks on banks. Then, beginning on 23 January, there had been gun attacks in Belfast against the RUC and British army that left one policeman seriously injured. Several banks in Belfast had been bombed on 9 March; and INLA snipers had fired on troops and policemen in separate incidents on 10 and 22 March, again in Belfast, in which one RUC man was hit in the thigh and the side. As for the Neave killing, the spokesman warned, "this was not a one-off job. We hope to be carrying out other attacks."

He was as good as his word. A spectacular—and brutal—attack came within a few weeks of the Neave bombing. On 19 April four women prison officers were leaving Armagh prison at lunch hour when Dessie Grew and his unit opened fire on them. As they lay wounded and moaning on the ground, one of their attackers threw a Russian hand-grenade into their midst. Agnes Jane Wallace was killed. She was forty years old and the mother of six children. Her husband explained that normally she took a packed lunch to work but that Thursday had decided to go out "with the girls". The INLA's statement claiming responsibility made no apologies for killing women: "If the British Government wish to place women in the front line of their repression and torture machine they must accept full responsibility for the consequences." (*Irish Press*, 21 April 1979.)[1]

Disgust at the attack on the women was widespread. The IRSP decided it had to be countered. The May issue of the *Starry Plough* published a letter from "the PRO, Women Against Imperialism, Belfast", complaining about the "amount of propaganda the Brit media has given to the death of a female screw." Implying that it was rather sexist to shed tears over the fact that it was a woman killed, she wrote: "Women should be seen for the people they are, and as such seen as equals not only in life but in death."[2]

Three months later the INLA's Armagh unit struck again outside a state institution. On 31 July they opened fire on policemen outside the Armagh courthouse, killing Constable George Walsh.

The kind of recognition that came with the "operation of the decade" had its drawbacks. On 3 July the INLA was declared an illegal organisation in Britain and Northern Ireland.

In the Republic, meanwhile, it had come under further scrutiny from the authorities. Within days of Neave's assassination, the Gardaí swooped on Mick Plunkett's flat in Cabra, Dublin. Plunkett was not in at the time. The police searched the place and found walkie-talkie radios, and switch and timing devices of the sort used in making bombs. Five men were arrested as they arrived at the house. Plunkett was picked up later. Immediately the English press began to speculate that the raid had been inspired by a tip-off from Scotland Yard and that the bomb-making equipment might be linked to the Neave killing. This was strongly denied by the Gardaí, who said that the arrests had come as a result of a routine investigation and the finds had nothing to do with Neave's assassination. But they did find material in the flat relating to England: some sixty photographs of Horse Guards Parade, including a series of a manhole cover in the street.

All but Plunkett were released without charge. He was charged with "possession and control of explosives". Freed on £5,000 bail, he was remanded to the court on 14 May. On 5 May he attended the party's Ard-Chomhairle meeting. He discussed the situation in Port Laoise prison, where over fifty republican prisoners were protesting about the lack of facilities in the recreation area, and listened to Miriam Daly's account of her recent tour of the United States, where she had spoken at various universities. A few days after the meeting, the date of his next court appearance fast approaching, Plunkett jumped bail and vanished. Years later he would resurface in Paris; but the man who had been acquitted in the Great Train Robbery case was to find that his sojourn in the French capital was not without controversy.

The IRSP was without a chairperson yet again. The loss of Plunkett was a bad blow to the whole organisation. He had been close both to Costello and the Belfast activists; indeed, they regarded him as one of the only members in the Dublin leadership who understood them; thus, he had acted as a stabilising force. Without him, the movement began to lurch about in frighteningly familiar ways. A Wicklow man, Gerry Roche, was elected to replace Plunkett, becoming the party's third chairperson since the death of Costello.

Plunkett's disappearance meant the loss of £5,000 in bail money, a loss that the organisation could ill afford. Less than one year after the Barna Gap robbery had put almost half a million pounds into the coffers, money had run out for both the IRSP and INLA.

The party's third ardfheis, held on 16 and 17 June, was not the post-Neave triumph that party activists would have liked it to be. The instability at the top of the party meant that the 1979 ardfheis was mostly devoted to organisational problems. The new Ard-Chomhairle that was elected included Harry Flynn, the Long Kesh escaper, and another Belfast man who had recently served a prison sentence and was soon to disappear to the United States. This meant that more than a third of the Ard-Chomhairle's sixteen members were now from Belfast.

An attempt was made to galvanise the weak party structure in the North by appointing Liam Ó Comáin of Derry to the new post of Northern organiser. Ó Comáin, a graduate in psychology and philosophy with a postgraduate degree in continuing education, was a lecturer in psychology—the third academic on the Ard-Chomhairle.

The lack of money was the dominant issue, affecting the movement at all levels. By the summer of 1979 the IRSP was almost broke. By July the party had only £315 in the kitty and was facing a £442 printing bill from the *Irish News*, £220 of which had to be paid immediately. As a result, the INLA was under increasing pressure from the political leadership to provide funds. At an Ard-Chomhairle meeting on 14 July, Vinty Fegan said that "Group B could accept half of this" bill. However, two months later the situation had worsened. Bills for electricity, telephone, insurance and from the *Irish News* "were urgent. Jim Daly said he had to pay £500 by Thursday." The matter would again be raised with "Group B". As for the *Starry Plough*, "a massive amount of money was owed and the paper couldn't continue indefinitely." (Ard-Chomhairle minutes, 1 September 1979.)

At the Ard-Chomhairle meeting of 28 October it was noted in the minutes: "Financial situation very bad—G[roup] B had not been in a position to give money. Situation regarding Green Cross [the oganisation that took care of INLA prisoners' welfare] very serious—no good will left." Under "Finance" was written: "None." The IRSP did not have enough money to provide for its own prisoners, of whom there were then about ninety. Neither the party nor the INLA ever succeeded in satisfactorily solving the problem of funding; unlike the Provisionals, they never developed a funding network and had constantly to resort to robberies or other risky measures.

Much more serious, however, was the impact the financial crisis had on the armed wing of the movement. It was this that provoked a showdown with the chief of staff, John O'Doherty.

At the beginning of July, Séamus Ruddy was returning from Beirut with his second shipment of weapons and explosives from the PLO when he and his companion, Phelim Lally, were stopped at the Greek-Turkish border. The Greek police were searching the vehicle when the door on the driver's side, which was open, broke off its hinges. Suspicious, the police scrutinised the door; they quickly discovered the false panelling, behind which they found a pinkish substance. At first they thought it was drugs. Lally and Ruddy were dragged out and flung on the ground: suspected drug-dealers were not treated with consideration.

The police also uncovered several dozen hand grenades and a mini-arsenal of AK47s, which made them suspect that they were not dealing with run-of-the-mill drug dealers. When the substance that had been stuffed in large amounts behind the door panelling turned out to be explosives, the attitude of the authorities changed drastically. Their prisoners were Irish and "freedom fighters". They were treated accordingly. The governor of the prison where they were held after their trial proudly posed for a photograph with Ruddy and Lally before they were freed.

But the failure of this shipment to get through meant that another arms run had to be made. In September another deal was arranged, and six INLA members set off for Lebanon. However, when they reached the Lebanese border they found that, because of a mix-up, their PLO contact was not there to meet them. They were hustled onto various planes to different destinations, one of the would-be gun-runners ending up in Baghdad. Eventually they reassembled in Paris, and contact was re-established with the

PLO. Another run was set up. But by this time the operation had exhausted the money set aside for it. A message was sent back to Dublin to the chief of staff that another £5,000 was needed. A few days later the word came back from Dublin that the money was not there. The whole operation collapsed.

It was the third arms shipment fiasco in a row. There was anger and frustration, a lot of it directed at O'Doherty. This intensified when later that year the prospect of another arms haul, involving a hundred Uzi submachine-guns, came up from a tried and trusted source. The Israeli-made Uzi was a powerful weapon, according to some one of the most deadly guns ever developed and perfect for urban guerrilla warfare. £25,000 was needed to clinch the deal. A GHQ meeting was called to discuss financing the operation. In the middle of the discussion the chief of staff, to everyone's amazement, burst out: "We'll never beat them. We may as well give up now." At this, some members of the GHQ walked out in disgust. Apart from everything else, it had become clear that O'Doherty had a severe drinking problem and was subject to fits of intense despondency. They assumed his admission of defeat was a product of such a depressive state. At any rate, it did not inspire confidence in his ability to continue as chief of staff.

An Army Council meeting was called and a vote of confidence was taken on O'Doherty's leadership. He lost by one vote. O'Doherty, along with Vinty Fegan, Dessie Grew, and a handful of other supporters, walked out of the meeting and refused to accept the majority vote. They claimed that the Belfast organisation—meaning mainly Ronnie Bunting and the Flynn brothers —was attempting a take-over.

Bunting had always distrusted O'Doherty. This partly stemmed from the fact that Bunting suspected that O'Doherty's other brother, Anthony, who had links with the Provisional IRA, was an informer. On one occasion the INLA gave Tony O'Doherty explosives in order to carry out an operation against a UDR man in Ballymena. However, nothing but the UDR man's car was destroyed, making Bunting, who had personally delivered the explosives himself, even more convinced that the chief of staff's brother was secretly at work for the security forces. But Tony O'Doherty used this operation to convince the Provos that he meant business. It was later revealed in court that Anthony O'Doherty was in fact an informer and had formed a bizarre relationship with a Special Branch man from Ballymena.[3]

Things took an ugly turn when one of O'Doherty's supporters intercepted a message meant for one of the Belfast men who had voted against him. The message came from an important arms contact in Prague, and it related to the possibility of another arms shipment. O'Doherty's man went off to Prague himself in the hope of bluffing his way into an arms deal.

At this stage the out-voted leadership of the INLA was considering the possibility of eliminating their opponents in the organisation. They needed weapons, since the Belfast men had control of their own supplies. However, the chief of staff's backer was disappointed when he reached the Czech capital. The deal would only be done with the established contact. He returned empty-handed.

A plot was then hatched, at the instigation of Dessie Grew, to lure the leader of the anti-O'Doherty group to Paris and have him murdered there. That too did not get beyond the discussion stage. The INLA was not yet ready for such internal blood-letting.

In the meantime the Grew-O'Doherty-Fegan axis had become in effect a separate organisation. The other "wing" had not gone ahead and appointed a new chief of staff: they feared that if they took that step it would precipitate a feud, which they had to avoid at all costs. O'Doherty was still a much-respected republican, and there were many who could not understand what lay behind this latest organisational crisis and would not support anything resembling a split.

Before the crisis there were attempts to bring Seán Mac Stiofáin into the INLA as chief of staff. It was reasoned that Mac Stiofáin, who had been chief of staff of the Provisionals until 1972, possessed the much-needed maturity that in turn would help stabilise the movement. He expressed interest and met the Army Council representatives on six or seven occasions between 1978 and 1979 to explore how it might be arranged, but the move had come to nothing.

Now the organisation was effectively split, with a deposed chief of staff commanding his own band and acting in the name of the INLA. The crisis came to a head in January 1980.

The family of Tom Scully, a Dublin bank manager, was kidnapped on 9 January. The kidnappers took his wife, Noreen Scully, and their two children from their home in Rathfarnham, Dublin. A ransom of £30,000 was paid for their return. The Gardaí claimed to have recognised the man who picked up the money from a telephone kiosk in Bray as a leading member of the IRSP.

The party's head office in Gardiner Street was raided and turned upside down, and thirty members of the party were arrested under the Offences Against the State Act while attending a meeting. The party offered its "sincere sympathy" to the Scully family and said that it knew nothing about the kidnapping (*Sunday World*, 13 January 1980): the arrests were "black propaganda". (*Irish Independent*, 14 January 1980.) Said a spokesman: "The Offences Against the State Act is being used to prevent people from organising themselves and the right of political assembly. This right has been denied to the IRSP from its foundation." (*Irish Press*, 14 January 1980.)

Gerry Roche was among those held and questioned, as was Tom McCartan from Belfast and Henry Doherty, who had escaped with Harry Flynn back in 1976, together with Brendan O'Sullivan, from Killorglin, County Kerry. O'Sullivan had just joined the IRSP in November 1979, after being proposed for membership by John O'Doherty. O'Doherty was arrested on 16 January, as were Ard-Chomhairle members Vinty Fegan and John Dunne. O'Doherty was eventually charged with kidnapping one of the Scully children. Fegan was also charged in connection with the incident.

O'Doherty and Fegan got bail of £15,000 each; Fegan absconded to the United States. Between 1979 and 1980 five IRSP members jumped bail, costing the organisation thousands of pounds. O'Doherty, however, stood trial, and was acquitted.

The kidnapping caused confusion and anger within the movement. It had been an unauthorised action, and it spelt the doom of the old leadership, which anyway by now was broken and scattered. Thus it was that in the spring of 1980 a new chief of staff took over—a man who had been a close friend of Costello's. He was a prominent member of the IRSP and came from the Dublin area. Some of those who had supported O'Doherty were invited to rejoin. A few did; others, including O'Doherty himself, gradually became inactive.

In an attempt to consolidate the anti-O'Doherty group and galvanise the organisation generally, an ambitious attack was planned in England. Information came to the INLA from a British army source that indicated that a training camp on Salisbury Plain was vulnerable to attack. Netheravon was an artillery training school, where soldiers were taught how to fire wire-guided anti-tank missiles. After reconnaissance, facilitated by the inside information, it was decided to target the officers' sleeping quarters.

In March 1980 twenty pounds of black commercial explosive was smuggled through Wales into England. Two INLA volunteers carried out the actual attack, involving two ten-pound bombs, which caused severe damage to buildings but did not result in any army casualties. The INLA team then left for France before returning to Ireland. It would prove to be the last INLA operation to enjoy any success in England for twelve years. However, its effect on the INLA's internal problems was positive: it helped to convince waverers that those who had been opposed to O'Doherty's leadership were capable of carrying on the war.

However, there followed a series of "mistakes" that claimed the lives of three civilians and demonstrated the hazards of fighting such a campaign. The first victim was James McCarran, shot dead by the INLA in Andersonstown,

Belfast, on 19 August during an attack on the security forces. Ten days later, in Carnagh, County Armagh, Frank McGrory was walking along a path when he glimpsed a 50p coin lying on a pornographic picture. He bent down to pick up the coin. It was glued to the photograph, which in turn was attached by catgut to a landmine. It exploded, killing him. It had been meant for the security forces. The INLA issued a statement and expressed "deep regret" for his death. The man who made the bomb was Paddy "Tweesy" McDonald, who when he was not practising his trade as a hairdresser was highly regarded in the INLA for his engineering skills and was involved in many bombing attacks in the Armagh area. (McDonald was to die eleven years later in a gangland shooting in Dublin, where he ran his own hairdressing salon.)

Three months later Thomas Orr was gunned down in Boucher Road in south Belfast, near the Ulster Bank, where he worked as an assistant bank manager. Mr Orr had been mistaken for a police officer from whom he had just purchased a car.

The crisis within the INLA had a severe impact on the IRSP. The party, in deep financial trouble, had endured another leadership change in October 1979, when Gerry Roche resigned as chairman after just a few months. Now its members were being rounded up yet again, and its spokesman, Niall Leonach, was having to fend off embarrassing accusations about the involvement of party members in serious crimes. On 19 January a special Ard-Chomhairle meeting was called to discuss the coming ardfheis, which had been scheduled for 19 April. But instead it was dominated by anxious questions raised because of the deteriorating situation. Half the Ard-Chomhairle was missing: many of them were being held for questioning about the Scully kidnapping. The meeting was also told that Miriam and Jim Daly had resigned from the party.

After some two-and-a-half years of political activity the Dalys had become demoralised by the almost constant state of crisis and uncertainty in which the IRSP found itself. Their decision was the culmination of months of frustration. During the 6 October meeting at which Roche had announced his resignation, Jim Daly had lamented that this was "the fourth Chair-leadership crisis". (Ard-Chomhairle notes, 6 October 1979.) The party's constitution was being "set aside" and members of "Group B" were being recruited directly in order to bolster up numbers. The IRSP, meanwhile, after a surge in 1978, had made no headway in the North. Belfast was particularly weak. The party organisation there was called a "joke" at the Ard-Chomhairle meeting of 28 October. It was proposed that "Group B" members be allowed to attend Belfast Comhairle Ceantair meetings and vote.

At the same meeting it was proposed that Ronnie Bunting be accepted into the party. The Dalys and he did not see eye to eye. Bunting had been involved only in the military side of things; giving him a role in the IRSP meant that the party would be increasingly indistinguishable from the INLA.

However, there were also intensely personal reasons why Miriam and Jim Daly were disaffected. Miriam Daly had complained about being sexually molested by a member from Belfast. Nothing was done about her complaints. Bunting refused to act against the man accused; instead he allegedly made a disparaging remark about Miriam Daly. "Had it been a Dublin man who'd been accused, he would have been taken up the mountain," commented an IRSP member, a former comrade of Costello's, who felt that the Belfast men were forming a clique. This fed into the O'Doherty dispute, and deepened the feeling of division within the whole movement.

The party newspaper, the *Starry Plough*, took on an increasingly shoddy look as its rhetoric became more grandiose. Like the party, the paper was suffering from a lack of stability. Mary Reid, who had resigned as education officer the year before, was asked to become editor in December 1979, but her influence was not felt for a few issues. In the meantime the *Starry Plough* looked more and more like the newspaper of the INLA, not the IRSP. The February issue pictured an INLA volunteer on the front page with the headline: "On to liberation". The report went on to celebrate the success of liberation struggles from all around the world, with the notable exception of Ireland's. It declared, however, that the Irish freedom struggle had "taught oppressed people all over the world that freedom is meaningless if the working class are not the masters of their own destiny." These fantastic assertions were contradicted two issues later when the paper admitted that the Irish working class are "confused" about "the war of national liberation".

That war had fallen to a lower rate of intensity, thanks partly to the confusion and near-split within the INLA leadership. But Belfast claimed a few attacks in the early part of 1980, including the wounding of a UDR man in a booby-trap car-bomb attack on 8 March. Derry too was showing flashes of activity. However, their most spectacular attack turned out to have more to do with the movement's financial needs than the "war of liberation". At the end of March the party had outstanding bills that amounted to £5,393.10, of which £3,027 was due to legal fees. No doubt pressed partly by the need to alleviate this debt, the Derry INLA agreed to bomb a restaurant in the city, the Gate Inn, in return for a cut from the insurance payments. The bombing succeeded, and the restaurant was destroyed. The *Starry Plough* dutifully carried a statement from the INLA that claimed that "the premises were frequented by the RUC Special Branch ... The owners had previously inserted an advert about their property in the RUC 'Beat' magazine. We intend to hit all commercial property which serves anyone associated with the Brit war machine in our country."

Five years later a court heard that the owner of the Gate Inn, who had received £91,674 in compensation, had paid the INLA £20,000 for bombing his premises. A former INLA leader from Derry later admitted that it was "quite common" for the INLA to raise money by this means. (Interview, 2 April 1993.) It had destroyed at least four pubs in the city between 1978 and 1981 in return for pay-offs from their owners.

The party's fourth ardfheis went ahead on 19 April. Not surprisingly, the chairperson's report to the meeting was a gloomy one. Niall Leonach had been elected to the chair in January. He had been a member of the IRSP's UCD cumann in 1976, when he had taken part along with Miriam Daly and Séamus Costello in a 1916 commemoration meeting at the university. At the 1980 ardfheis he told the delegates that if they looked back over the last nine months "despite progress in a few areas it has to be said that the party has largely stood still and in some respects even gone backwards." He said it was time for the party to honestly look at its role. It had also to admit that a lot of its problems "stem from our own lack of talent and inefficiency." The party had been badly damaged right at the start by the attacks of the Official IRA and the subsequent feud, which had "damaged our image and completely disillusioned many potential supporters from taking any further part in republican politics." The party had made mistakes in 1979 in failing to contest the local elections in the 26 Counties and the EEC election; this meant that it had lost a lot of its base in Bray to Sinn Féin the Workers' Party and missed "an opportunity to build a political base in the six counties." The loss of experienced members such as Mick Plunkett was another blow.

Organisational failures were damaging. "In the fifteen-month period from February 1978 to the ardfheis of June 1979 we produced no basic policy pamphlet, no education programme and not even a basic recruiting leaflet. Because of lack of political debate at Ard-Chomhairle level the political differences tended to appear as personality clashes." The party was still bedevilled by lack of money, apathy and "indiscipline which run through the organisation from Ard-Chomhairle to cumann level."

Leonach also pointed out a more general problem for the party: the left-wing shift within Sinn Féin and the growth of the Officials in the south. "Whatever way we analyse it," he said, "the Provos have definitely shifted significantly to the left in the five years since our formation. Today's

Republican News puts forward a brand of left-wing republican politics which is a far cry from *An Phoblacht* of 1975. On the other hand the Sticks have built a strong electoral base in most of the major population centres and Trade Unions in the 26 counties and have won some credibility as a radical party."

In between the two the IRSP was being squeezed. By 1980 it was becoming apparent that the party had failed to find its own political identity. The more left-wing Provisional Sinn Féin became, the less reason there was for the IRSP to exist in the North; the more political success Sinn Féin the Workers' Party enjoyed, the more difficult it was organisationally for the IRSP to find room to grow in the South.

There was also a fundamental North-South tension, which kept showing itself in different ways. Though Leonach did not say it in his address, those who most opposed the party becoming involved in local elections and backing a candidate for the European Parliament had been the Belfast members. They were the most fiercely opposed to "reformism", to anything that might lead down the road that the Officials had taken. The Dublin leadership, on the other hand, inspired by the example of their founder, Séamus Costello, realised the importance of building up a political base in the South. This North-South tension had become greater after the disappearance of Plunkett and with the resignation of Miriam Daly and her husband.

The one issue that had enabled the party to make progress was the prison dispute in the North. But its dramatic escalation during late 1980 and 1981 would throw the party's plans and good intentions into disarray. And by then, also, the movement had suffered further blows that led to a drastic increase in its fundamental instability. Miriam Daly and her husband, Jim, had been strongly identified with the prison dispute. Jim had spoken at the big Belfast rally in February 1978. Miriam Daly had addressed a meeting outside the GPO in Dublin and at the 23 August 1978 Relatives' Action Committee (RAC) rally in Dungannon, which attracted thousands of supporters (the *Starry Plough* claimed that twenty thousand were there). At this rally Miriam Daly went out of her way to attack loyalism, declaring that "Republicans can never recognise the rights of any section of Irishmen to opt out of loyalty to the Irish nation, and any arrangements that are made to accommodate such people can only be at the expense of the full sovereignty of the Irish people and as such be unacceptable to Republicans." (*Starry Plough*, September 1978.) She had spoken again at a H-block rally in Armagh in November 1978, and at other venues the following year.

By 1980, though no longer members of the IRSP, Miriam and Jim Daly were strongly identified in the minds of loyalists with the party, the H-block issue and a strain of militant nationalism that seemed particularly unsympathetic to the Protestant position.

On 26 June, in the early afternoon, Miriam Daly went to a bakery shop opposite to where she lived on the Andersonstown Road in west Belfast. Because she was unable to have children, the couple had adopted twins, named Dónal and Marie. A woman who worked in the bread shop said that Mrs Daly came in at roughly the same time most afternoons, shortly before Dónal and Marie returned from school, to buy something for them for tea. She left with her purchase and went home to await the arrival of the children. The bakery shop attendant was one of the last people to see her alive.

The Daly home was a large semi-detached house on the front of the road along which live the middle-class section of west Belfast's Catholics. It is a busy stretch of road, with plenty of shops and a constant flow of traffic.

Unknown gunmen, believed to have come into the grounds through the small back garden, gained entrance to the house. Once inside, they cut the telephone wires and tied Miriam Daly hand and foot. They were waiting for Jim Daly to come back. He was their prime target; but that day he was in Dublin. The gunmen grew impatient. Putting a cushion to Miriam Daly's head, they shot her five times with a 9 mm semi-automatic pistol. The cushion deadened the sound of the shots. A short time later, her ten-year-old daughter, back from school, found her mother lying dead in the hallway of their home, the bloodstained cushion not far from her body.

At the inquest, held on 29 October, a detective said that no organisation had claimed responsibility for her murder. He told the coroner that in his experience no loyalist group had ever gone into the completely Catholic area to carry out such a shooting. In the years since, no group has ever come forward to claim responsibility for Miriam Daly's murder. But a member of the UDA's Inner Council has claimed that his organisation carried out the killing. He called the Daly's "cheer-leaders for violent republicans" and accused them of being "anti-Protestant".

Miriam Daly was given a republican funeral. Four masked men fired shots over her coffin as it was being carried from her Andersonstown home. Though she had left the IRSP four months earlier, mainly because of bitter disputes with elements of its Belfast leadership, it was they who insisted on the paramilitary display. Ironically, the woman who had been concerned about the growing influence over the party of Belfast's military wing was claimed as a "volunteer" on the headstone erected to her memory in Milltown Cemetery. However, according to a former INLA leader, though occasionally she would move equipment for the group, she was never a member of it. Her body was taken to St Agnes's Oratory, where her many friends, including the SDLP councillor Pascal O'Hare and Father Denis Faul, the human rights campaigner, crowded into the chapel. Later her remains were taken across the border to be buried in the family plot at Swords, County Dublin.

The turn-out there came from a cross-section of Irish society unusually broad for a republican funeral. It reflected as well as her republican links her middle-class origins and academic standing—an uncommon combination in contemporary republican organisations. As well as IRSP and INLA representatives it included the former Provisional IRA chief of staff Seán Mac Stiofáin, and Ruairí Ó Brádaigh, the leader of Provisional Sinn Féin, Dónal Barrington, a High Court judge, Rev. F. X. Martin, a professor of history at UCD, and Rev. James McEvoy, professor of scholastic philosophy at Queen's University.

Among those at the Belfast rites was Ronnie Bunting. He had followed her coffin as far as St Agnes's Chapel. Someone who saw him that day said he looked haggard and uneasy. Bunting had long been regarded as a prime target for loyalist paramilitaries, who once described him as a "renegade Protestant" (*Combat*, vol. 2, no. 6). But throughout his life as a political and paramilitary activist he had made enemies in just about every camp.

His father, Major Ronald Bunting, a teacher and former British army officer, had become a familiar presence on television screens in the late 1960s as he led his loyalist "troops" into action against civil rights marchers. A flamboyant figure, Major Bunting had begun his involvement in politics working to help elect Gerry Fitt, the Catholic politician who was one of the founder-members of the Social Democratic and Labour Party and represented West Belfast until 1983. In 1968, following a cross-over almost as extreme as that his son made, Major Bunting was to be found in the ranks of the Paisleyites. In those days Paisley was a frequent visitor to the Bunting home. When Ronnie Bunting became involved in student politics in Queen's University, he took the side of the people that his father loved to attack. Suzanne Bunting, whom Ronnie married in 1969 while still a student, remembers being terrified when invited to his home. But the major turned out to be not as fearsome as his reputation. In spite of his political differences with his son they got on extremely well together. "I loved Ronnie's father," she says. "He always stood by his son." At the same time, however, it is acknowledged that Major Bunting did not realise his son's paramilitary connections, imagining that he was merely a political organiser for the IRSP.

Having a Protestant with such family associations actively campaigning under the civil rights banner was something of a novelty. It was even more so when Bunting joined the Official republican movement. From that point onwards, the trajectory of his life took an increasingly dangerous course, quite different from that which might have been expected of someone who came from a middle-class Protestant background. For Bunting, the appeal of the Officials lay in their socialism, the fact that they stressed that they were a non-sectarian, revolutionary organisation. (At the time the Provisionals were still very much the "Rosary-bead brigade", as a former IRSP member put it.) By 1971 he was actively involved in the Official IRA's Markets unit. However, he never had much of a reputation as an operator. On his first job he was back-up to a sniping attack on a British army patrol. He was armed with a grenade and a pistol, which were only to be used in an emergency. However, when the gunmen opened up on the patrol as it neared Cromac Square, Ronnie panicked and threw the grenade into the street, where it exploded. Fortunately there no people around.

Even among the Officials, where he was used as living proof that their movement was non-sectarian, he aroused hostility. Robert Elliman, an Official IRA gunman who was shot dead by the Provisionals in late 1975, once remarked about him: "I don't trust that fucker—that's Major Bunting's son." He was interned between 1971 and 1972.

In 1973 the Officials moved Bunting into Ballymurphy, a tough housing estate where relations between the Officials and the Provisionals were at that time very bad. The top Provo in the area was Jim Bryson, whose habit was to drive around the streets with his rifle sticking out the window of his car. There had been disputes between Bryson and the Officials in Ballymurphy in 1972. Another one arose in 1973, and Bunting called a meeting with Bryson to sort it out. Shortly after Bryson left, he was ambushed and shot dead by British soldiers hiding nearby. The Provisionals blamed Bunting. Some accused him of having set up Bryson, and threatened revenge.

When the split came and the IRSP and INLA were formed, Ronnie Bunting had to add the Official IRA to the list of organisations that were out to get him. The Officials tried to kill him three times, without success. But it was enough to bring Suzanne Bunting to the verge of a nervous breakdown. She demanded of her husband that he leave Belfast. They moved to Wales, where he took up teaching for a short time. By the summer of 1975 he was back in Dublin, a resident of "Bash Street". Less than eighteen months later he was back in Belfast, in spite of warnings that his life would be in real danger. "He had no street sense," commented Seán Flynn.

Bunting was a hate figure for both the UVF and the UDA, who had him near the top of their hit list. A story that appeared in *Combat*, the UVF magazine, in early 1975 was headlined "Bunting behind killings" (vol. 2, no. 6). Echoing Official IRA propaganda, it alleged that he was part of an IRSP conspiracy to foment sectarian civil war. The story correctly names the area in which Bunting, along with the Flynn brothers, had gone to ground in north Belfast, in a house that was raked with gunfire by the Official IRA. This, along with the tone of the *Combat* report, would suggest that information about him was being exchanged between the two organisations at that time.

Two years later the UDA's boss, Andy Tyrie, was known to be keenly interested in Bunting's whereabouts. Bunting was frequently taken in for questioning by the police; it would have been very surprising if over the years information had not leaked out about where he lived.

Though he was constantly referred to in newspaper reports as a "founder" of the IRSP, Bunting had only joined the party in October 1979, after being proposed as a member by Vinty Fegan, supported by another Belfast man. Until then his role had been restricted to activities in the INLA. He was involved at some level (usually intelligence gathering) in several of the organisation's biggest operations, including the Barna Gap robbery. And he was one of the few aware of the plans behind the assassination of Airey Neave. From late 1976, he was OC of Belfast.

By June 1980, Bunting was attending Ard-Chomhairle meetings as the party's Belfast regional delegate. On 5 July the Ard-Chomhairle heard plans for Bunting and Seán Flynn to hold a press conference on the release of Tommy McGinn, one of the movement's "blanket-men", who was being released. On 6 September he was one of only seven members to show up for an Ard-Chomhairle meeting that had to be abandoned because they were not enough to form a quorum. He was in Dublin again on 4 October. Bunting reported to the meeting about the situation in Belfast. He said that the party's offices were being re-organised. There were now two local papers, one in the Markets and one in Divis Flats, and there was a new cumann formed in the Whiterock district.

The last time Bunting was arrested was on 8 August 1980. Along with Seán Flynn and Francis Barry of the Troops Out Movement, he was taken to Castlereagh interrogation centre for questioning. Bunting was held for several days, and for most of the time refused to answer questions, giving only his name and address. After he was released he gave a statement to the Association for Legal Justice. In it he alleged that a detective "asked me how it would go for me on the Shankill ... It could be arranged that I would get three slugs in the head, and then these people could inspect me on the slab in the morgue … The older cop said, 'Look at my face. This is the face you'll see before I kill you.' I broke my silence and asked these cops their name. They refused to give me their names."

On the weekend of 11 October another IRSP member was arrested. He was Noel Lyttle, and he was held in Castlereagh for questioning. Lyttle, an ex-member of the tiny Red Republican Party, had joined the IRSP just a week before. The Ard-Chomhairle meeting of 4 October had formally ratified his membership, and he had been made PRO of the Belfast Comhairle Ceantair. Like Bunting, Lyttle was a Protestant, and extremely left-wing in his views. And, like Bunting and Miriam Daly, he had been very active on the H-block campaign.

Shortly after Lyttle was released from Castlereagh, he came to spend the night with the Buntings. He showed up unexpectedly at eleven o'clock on the night of 14 October.

Since moving back to Belfast in the autumn of 1976, the Buntings had set up home deep in the nationalist area of west Belfast, first just off of the Falls Road and then at 7 Downfine Gardens, a quiet cul-de-sac, where the couple lived with their three children, Fiona, aged seven, Deirdre, aged three, and Ronan, aged eighteen months. Close by is the Turf Lodge housing estate, a republican stronghold. These were areas that were usually regarded as immune from loyalist assassination gangs.

Though the UDA and UVF had carried out hit-and-run attacks over the years on the Falls Road itself, it was regarded as most unlikely that any loyalist paramilitary group would venture into the maze of back streets of the Catholic ghetto, if for no other reason than that they are among the most heavily patrolled of any zone in Northern Ireland. Though the assassination of Miriam Day had shown that nationalists were vulnerable even deep in west Belfast, it was partly explained by the fact that the killers had easy access to her home, which was on a main road. Downfine Gardens, on the other hand, was hard to find, deep in the ghetto, close to Turf Lodge. However, it lay not far from the Monagh by-pass, a major link road for the M1 motorway in one direction and the Upper Springfield Road in the other.

According to Suzanne Bunting, on the night of the fourteenth Lyttle and her husband sat up to about one o'clock. Their guest went to sleep in the room occupied by their baby son, Ronan, who was in a cot next to the bed. At around half past three Ronnie and Suzanne were awakened by the sound of banging downstairs. Men with sledgehammers were smashing the front door off its hinges. Within seconds, two gunmen were running up the stairs to the bedrooms. Though there were seven doors at the top of the stairs, they went directly to the Buntings' bedroom.

"We both jumped out of bed, but by the time we got up the men were already pushing in the bedroom door," Suzanne Bunting told the *Irish News* in November. The Buntings tried to force the door closed. They had almost succeeded when one of the gunmen managed to reach through the gap with his gun. "Then", she said, "the shooting started and I fell back on the bed." She had been wounded in the hand. "The next moment two men were in the room and started shooting Ronnie ... They wore those green, ribbed pullovers with suede patches on the shoulders and ski-type masks which covered their whole faces with only holes for the eyes ... They knew which rooms to find Noel and Ronnie in. They were cool and calm—like animals, without fear—they had no smell of fear about them." (Ibid.) They kept shooting at him for what seemed to her like eternity. Ronnie Bunting fell on the landing.

One of the gunmen was now backing down the stairs very calmly, covering the other who had kept firing at Bunting. Suzanne jumped on his back and began strangling him to try to get him to stop shooting. "While I still struggled with one of the men, the other left, casual like, without a care, and as he walked downstairs he called, 'Come on, Geordie'—or 'Georgie'." From downstairs the first gunman saw that the distraught woman was still clinging to his colleague. Though his accomplice was blocking his aim, he raised his gun. With only Suzanne Bunting's shoulder and arm visible, he managed to hit her with two well-aimed shots. One struck her on the left shoulder, the other under the right arm, making her lose her grip. She slumped against the wall, next to the body of her husband. "I turned and saw Ronnie. I knew he was dead: his eyes were wide and staring." (Ibid.) It was then that the second gunman, who also by now was walking coolly backwards down the stairs, paused and shot her in the mouth. She was seriously wounded, and for forty-eight hours was on the danger list.

Noel Lyttle had also been shot and lay draped across the bed. When neighbours rushed to the house, they found him near death. The two young girls ran crying into the street, and their baby brother was screaming upstairs in his cot next to the dying man.

Suzanne Bunting survived, and from her hospital bed she blamed the security forces for the double killing. She said the police "know, as I do, that the people who killed Ronnie and Noel knew where they could be found, in what rooms, and how best to break down the doors. I told the police what I believe and know in all my heart, that it was the SAS." (Ibid.)

As with the case of Miriam Daly, no organisation publicly claimed responsibility for the murders of Lyttle and Bunting. Unusually for such attacks, the killers' car was never found. (Witnesses say they saw men wearing balaclavas escape in a light-blue car.) However, within days of Suzanne Bunting's interview being published, the UDA issued a statement warning Catholics that it would "eliminate those who pose a threat to the state of Ulster and all its people." The threat was addressed to those involved in the H-block campaign; but it can be read as an indirect claim that the UDA was involved in the murders of 15 October.

Three months later a gang of UDA men was arrested after they had attempted to murder another prominent H-block campaigner, Bernadette McAliskey, and her husband at their home near Coalisland in County Tyrone.

Though the Buntings' home was in the heart of a nationalist ghetto, the killers had an easy escape route. Within a few seconds' drive of Downfine Gardens was Monagh Link, which connects to the Monagh by-pass. This major thoroughfare would have taken them via the Upper Springfield Road into a loyalist area.

However, it should be noted that there are some extremely unusual features in the murders of Daly, Bunting, and Lyttle. The fact that no organisation made a direct claim of responsibility and that the getaway cars were never found already makes the killings stand out from the pattern of sectarian assassination characteristic of Northern Ireland. What is also striking about them is the extremely disciplined behaviour of the two assassins who murdered Bunting and Lyttle. With military-like order they carried out their task, one providing cover for the other, confidently walking backwards down the stairs, for instance. The gunman who calmly shot Suzanne Bunting as she clung to the back of his accomplice must have been something of a marksman. They never displayed any trace of panic or nervousness, though they were in the heart of a well-patrolled nationalist area. At the very least, the circumstances of the deaths of Bunting and Lyttle suggest some form of collusion, if only because the gunmen knew which of the seven doors to go to when they reached the top of the Buntings' staircase. According to Suzanne Bunting, the only people who would have been able to provide them with that information would have been the police, who regularly raided their home. Though one of them called his colleague by name, his accent was impossible to distinguish, because his mouth was muffled by the ski-mask.

Suzanne Bunting recalls that when Airey Neave was assassinated the year before, Ronnie came to her and said, in reference to Margaret Thatcher, "She'll want her pound of flesh." Suzanne Bunting remains convinced that the murders of Daly, Lyttle and her husband involved the security forces at some level. She thinks that Miriam Daly and Ronnie Bunting were targeted because the British assumed that, being middle-class and university-educated, they were the "brains" of the IRSP and INLA and that their removal would cripple both groups. In fact the removal of Bunting did have a profound effect on the INLA.

The attempt on Bernadette McAliskey, which came three months later and led to the arrest of a group of UDA men, stands in contrast to these murders. According to McAliskey's own account, the would-be assassins were "whooping like cowboys" when they burst into her home: they bore little resemblance to the disciplined assassins who struck on 15 October. The question of who it was that carried out those assassinations remains unanswered.

Major Bunting was badly affected by the death of his son. Already suffering from a heart complaint, when he heard the news he took ill and had to be detained in hospital. On the first anniversary of his son's murder he again took ill, and two days later suffered a massive stroke, from which he never recovered; he died in 1984. In spite of their profound political differences, they had maintained cordial relations. When his son lived in Dublin, Major Bunting would telephone him often, ever concerned about his welfare. The two used to meet outside the school where Major Bunting taught near the centre of Belfast.

There were still a few ironies left for Ronnie Bunting after death. His body was kept in a funeral parlour in the Newtownards Road in east Belfast, opposite the headquarters of the UDA. As his coffin was removed on the day of the funeral, UDA men waved flags and jeered from the windows of their building. The IRSP had wanted a republican funeral, of course; but with Major Bunting in charge of the arrangements, that was ruled out. He was buried in the family grave in a Church of Ireland cemetery near Donaghadee, County Down. The man who had devoted so much of his life and energy to the republican cause was denied the final recognition given to all its martyrs. In death, he had been reclaimed by his own.

The murder of Ronnie Bunting was a bad blow for the INLA, and not only because it deprived the organisation of a valuable and experienced man. It was a "watershed" according to one veteran of the INLA and IPLO. After Bunting, friction between younger INLA members and the older leadership would increase drastically, eventually provoking an outbreak of internecine bloodshed that heralded the disasters to come.

However, in late 1980 the attention of the IRSP and INLA, along with that of the whole nationalist community, was riveted elsewhere. The situation in the Maze Prison was approaching breaking-point as seven republicans prepared to launch the first of two hunger strikes that would transform the political map of Ireland. It was the final stage of a long protest in which from the beginning the IRSP had been deeply involved.

NOTES

1. As with the Airey Neave killing, the Provisional IRA were the first to claim responsibility for Mrs Wallace's death. They later withdrew the claim.

2. A few months later, women were again at the centre of a dispute involving both the INLA and the IRSP after the INLA kneecapped a young woman in Turf Lodge, accusing her of stealing weapons from them. In Derry a group called Women's Aid picketed the IRSP's headquarters in Connolly House. They carried placards calling for liberation from male violence. One slogan proclaimed: *Women unfree shall never be at peace.* Women IRSP supporters heckled them and accused them of being "in the pay of the British army and anti-working class." (*Sunday News*, 9 September 1979.)

3. Tony O'Doherty testified that the Special Branch man, Charlie McCormick, had been involved with him in bank robberies and other crimes. The Special Branch man was convicted, but acquitted on appeal; O'Doherty was jailed for twenty years.

8

FROM BEHIND BARS

In the December 1975 issue of the *Starry Plough* in an article headlined "Political prisoners status must stay", the IRSP declared its complete opposition to any attempts by the British government to remove "special category" status for paramilitary prisoners. The article appeared some four months before the removal of that status was due to come into effect, on 1 March 1976, as part of an overall government "criminalisation" programme, designed to put the Northern Ireland legal system for dealing with paramilitary violence on a more acceptable footing.

At a very early stage the IRSP had defined the battleground of what would prove to be one of the North's most important conflicts: "The British Government intends to end the special category status of Prisoners next March," warned the *Starry Plough*. "This follows continuous attempts to put a more legal and just face on oppression in the North, where there are over 1,500 special category prisoners, i.e. political prisoners. The attempt to do away with their special category is intended to portray all political prisoners as common criminals, psychopaths, thieves, intimidators, whose actions for personal gain are devoid of any politics. This is of course rubbish and forecasts a hard struggle in and out of the North's four main prisons and concentration camps."

Defending those demands would lead republican prisoners through a series of escalating protests that climaxed with the hunger strikes of 1981. Right from the beginning the IRSP and INLA, both from behind prison bars and outside on the streets, pushed the issue when others, including the Provisional movement, seemed at times reluctant to do so.

Almost from the day the IRSP and the INLA were formed their members had become involved in prison protests. John O'Doherty, the party's south Derry organiser and future chief of staff of the INLA, was interned in December 1974. Seven months later he launched a hunger strike in protest at his detention. By the summer of 1975 there were about forty members of the movement—described variously in the *Starry Plough* as IRSP members or "their supporters"—held in prisons in the North.

Because the prison authorities refused to recognise them as political prisoners, since they did not belong to either of the other two republican organisations, they were immediately forced into confrontations with prison regimes. In the summer of 1975 a group of IRSP prisoners were denied political status by the Long Kesh authorities. This meant that certain privileges were not granted, such as the right of the prisoner to wear his or her own clothes, to associate freely, to refuse to do prison work, and to elect their own spokesmen. (These would later become the core of the demands over which the bitter H-block protest and hunger strike was fought.) Twenty of them went on hunger strike in protest. William Truesdale, the governor of Long Kesh, conceded the demands, and the hunger strike was abandoned.

At around the same time fifteen members of the IRSP appeared in court naked in protest at what they claimed was mistreatment in the Crumlin Road jail, where they were being held awaiting trial.

In late 1975 the British opened contacts with the paramilitaries to try to sell them the idea of the removal of special category status in return for other concessions, including a 50 per cent remission of sentences. The British made approaches through the prison authorities, who brought the proposals before the camp council at Long Kesh. This consisted of representatives of all the paramilitary groups held inside: the UVF, UDA, Official IRA, Provisional IRA, and IRSP. It was chaired by Gusty Spence, the founding member of the UVF, who was serving life for the murder of a Catholic barman, Peter Ward. Frank Gallagher, who later became INLA chief of staff, spoke for the "IRSP" prisoners. As part of the programme of convincing the paramilitaries to co-operate, an official from the Northern Ireland Office met a representative from each group and took them on a tour of the facilities at the new prison, to be called the Maze, with its soon-to-be-notorious H-block configuration, then still under construction. The NIO man told Gallagher that life in the Maze would be more like "Nirvana" than "Nissen".

The NIO organised meetings in early 1976 with representatives of the organisations from outside the jails. Chosen to represent the IRSP was Mick Plunkett, its general secretary, and Joe Heaney from Belfast. Heaney had been a founder-member of the movement. As well as a generous remittance of sentences, the men were being offered a rehabilitation office in Royal Avenue, Belfast, to help released men readjust, where each organisation would have its own field worker, who would be on a salary of £3,500 a year plus expenses.

From the start, Gallagher and his organisation opposed the offer. The article on political status that appeared in the December 1975 issue of the

Starry Plough declared unambiguously that "the demand for political status is an important demand and must be defended."

However, as the count-down approached for the formal ending of political status on 1 March 1976, the sounding-out continued. Mick Plunkett, as the party's welfare officer, was brought into Long Kesh to meet officials and the prisoners' Camp Council. The NIO officials talked about arriving at a "workable compromise" with the paramilitaries; according to Plunkett, this meant a permanent cessation of violence. Those in favour of this were the Officials, the UDA, and the UVF. Even the Provisionals were at least toying with the idea of accepting the concessions in return for giving up political status. But the IRSP said no.

On one occasion, after a session with the NIO and the Camp Council in Long Kesh had ended, Plunkett left the jail to find that the car that was supposed to have been supplied by Jimmy Brown to transport him to Belfast was nowhere to be seen. It was late, and there were only two cars left in the prison car park: one occupied by UDA men and the other by members of the Official IRA, with whom Plunkett's organisation had recently had a bloody feud. He felt distinctly uncomfortable. After much trying, he finally persuaded the officer in charge of the soldiers on guard duty to allow him back into the prison. Following discussion, a prison officer was found who was finishing his shift and returning home to Lisburn, a few miles away. He reluctantly agreed to give Plunkett a lift to the town, from where he caught a train for the city. Plunkett recalls the journey with the prison officer through the dark countryside surrounding Long Kesh as being rather strained.

About a month later the Provisional IRA killed their first prison officer. Negotiations with the authorities were broken off, and the scene was set for a prolonged and bitter struggle. Like the Provos, the INLA carried out the prison campaign on two fronts. Between September and December 1976 the INLA claimed to have carried out six attacks against "property and individuals associated with the prison service" in Belfast, Armagh, and Derry. (*Starry Plough*, May 1977.) They then halted their campaign, "awaiting the outcome of a British Government reassessment of their policy of phasing out political status." (Ibid.) By November, the first member of their movement had gone on the blanket protest: James Connolly Brady of Derry. Brady had been sentenced to six years' imprisonment for possession of a shotgun. He went on the blanket on 14 November. The INLA alleged he was being singled out for particular ill-treatment by the prison authorities.

One of the earliest testimonies about the conditions of the protesting prisoners came in a letter written by Patsy O'Hara, describing a visit to his brother Tony, who was in the H-block. It said: "On Tuesday 1/11/77 I visited my brother Tony O'Hara who is serving a five year sentence in H-Block. This was the first visit he had taken in seven months as he is one of the very many republican socialist prisoners on the blanket protesting in the H-Block.

"When I walked into the cubicle at first I did not recognise my brother for he had changed beyond recognition from the last time I saw him. He has lost at least two stone in weight, his eyesight has deteriorated and all his skin has broken out in sores. His lips are full of hacks. In fact, his general physical condition was very weak, this being due to the total lack of fresh air and normal diet.

"While I am deeply worried about my brother's physical state I am even more worried by his state of mind as he was shaking all through the half-visit and, at times, stared at me as if dazed.

"I should point out that the only reason that my brother took the visit was to let people know some of the facts about the treatment the Republican socialist prisoners are being subjected to in H-Block, and also to reiterate that he and his comrades are more determined than ever to keep protesting at the British Government's attempts to criminalise Irish Republican Prisoners of War."

Less than four years later, Patsy O'Hara would become the first INLA prisoner to die on hunger strike.

The INLA threatened to intensify its campaign against prison officers. However, unlike the Provisionals' political wing, the IRSP saw the importance of agitating on the streets. By late 1977, when the movement had twenty-two members on the blanket, the party was holding anti-H-block demonstrations outside the GPO in Dublin. By this time Relatives' Action Committees were forming all over Northern Ireland to try to step up the campaign. A series of Christmas protests was held. The Belfast RAC thanked the IRSP for its support, while noting the lack of a Provisional Sinn Féin presence. In early 1978 the party distributed over eight hundred H-block posters in Belfast, Cork, Derry, Shannon, Dublin, and Dún Laoghaire. It took part in a conference in Coalisland in January organised by the local relatives' action committee that attempted to broaden the base of the dispute to include the SDLP, the People's Democracy, the Communist Party, and the Northern Ireland Civil Rights Association, as well as Sinn Féin.

But the attempt to build a "broad front" on the H-block issue was rendered ineffective by the IRSP and the Provisionals themselves. They wanted to use the conference to try to win support for a wider republican programme. The IRSP's motion to the conference declared the "right of the Irish people to self-determination and sovereignty ... the withdrawal of British Forces of occupation, disarming and disbanding of UDR, RUC and

RUC reserve." It also called for an amnesty for all republican and socialist prisoners "detained for their part in the war for national liberation." Clearly, the more moderate groups could not become involved in a movement that was seen to endorse all the demands of militant republicanism. By going for too much, the IRSP and Sinn Féin undermined their own efforts.

The following month, some indication of the growing strength of the H-block campaign was evident at a march in Belfast to mark the second anniversary of the removal of political status. It was attended by several thousand people. Jim Daly spoke for the IRSP, portraying the prison struggle as essential to the whole "national liberation struggle"—saying that they were, in fact, one and the same thing. The prisoners, he claimed, were "in the front line of the resistance to British imperialism and the war for independence and sovereignty of their country. And that war must be won—because there will always be torture, imprisonment, brutality and arrogance from Mason and his troops until we get our country free. Today we know that we are winning ... We are showing by this tremendous turn-out that Irish liberation is going to be won and won shortly."

This rhetoric was for public consumption only. Behind the scenes, at Ard-Chomhairle meetings, there was no such optimism—quite the reverse. Fear of the Provisionals' lack of commitment to the H-block campaign was growing. In March, Jim Daly reported to the IRSP that there were "big problems with H-Block and there was a possibility of the collapse of the Provo protest." (Ard-Chomhairle minutes, 11 March 1978.) Sinn Féin's Ard-Chomhairle had put a complete ban on any co-operation with the IRSP in protest activities in the South.

The Provisionals' apparent lack of interest in the protest campaign was felt by some members of the IRSP to indicate that they were secretly holding talks with the British to resolve the dispute. This was confirmed when in June the protests stopped, and the IRSP learnt that the Provisionals were in secret negotiation with mediators. Though these contacts came to nothing, the IRSP was angry that it had not been informed. There were now twenty-three INLA men involved in the prison protest. It had been going on for almost two years without any movement from the British, and the pressure in the prison was building. There was talk of a hunger strike. By August 1978 there were unconfirmed reports coming out of Long Kesh that one had started.

At a special Ard-Chomhairle meeting it was stated: "If there is a hunger strike they are to be given the full support of the movement." (Ard-Chomhairle minutes, 5 August 1978.) The *Starry Plough* had been running regular communications or "coms" that had been smuggled out of the prison, detailing the conditions in the H-blocks. One, published in the June 1978 issue, related a never-ending series of complaints, both trivial and otherwise: "James Connolly Brady ... has now been naked in these sub-human conditions for 19 months. He has bad skin rash and he will no longer take his monthly visit as he refuses to appear in this appalling state. Micky Devine doing a 12 year sentence, a Derryman, had the contents of a slop pail thrown over him and another prisoner, Tommy McGinn from Ardoyne, Belfast, has a serious weight loss and is suffering from fever ... the prison establishment have refused to provide chairs or any other seating for the men attending mass. The stress and strain of having to stand up for an hour has caused a number of men to faint. (Two men collapsed today. Micky Ferguson recovered after resting, and the other, Brendan McCaughey, had to be taken to hospital. His condition is not yet known but before he was taken out he looked very grave.) They made us wear towels going to mass but after a number of complaints from Fr. Faul about prisoners attending mass indecently dressed they returned to provide us with trousers. But they gave out ones which are too big or too small for the men who have to wear them. This resulted in 12 men being unable to attend mass. They continue to put disinfectant which burn eyes and nose in the cells, usually followed by the hose. One cell which has a broken window gets water logged everyday. As each day progresses it is imminent that some serious disease will break out. So far the most widespread problem is worms which 26 men in H-5 have contracted alone. One man (Tony O'Hara) took a mild heart attack on Saturday night, this was his second in 2 months." One blanket man, Paul Duddy, was bitten by rats. "He refused a visit on Wednesday because he did not want his relatives to see the sores that have developed as a result of the rat attacks," claimed a statement issued by the IRSP in Derry. (*Irish News*, 18 August 1978.)

The litany of suffering was accompanied by rousing proclamations that victory was on its way. The front page of August 1978 issue of the *Starry Plough* was headlined: "POWs winning!" Said the report: "The prisoners' relatives are justly proud of their men, the finest men in Ireland today, the true spearhead of human progress in their lonely campaign against the inhumanity in its ruthless path." It was a truly Swiftian idea that a battle for human progress was being fought by men smearing their own excrement on their cell walls.

As conditions inside the H-block deteriorated, so did relations outside between the IRSP and the Provisionals. The Sinn Féin Ard-Chomhairle put out a directive in September banning any IRSP speaker from sharing a Provisional platform. During October, at a meeting held in Liberty Hall in

Dublin to discuss the prison crisis, all the Provisionals walked out when Mick Plunkett stood up to speak. In March 1979 the INLA representative at the IRSP's Ard-Chomhairle meeting told the party that they had evidence of fresh contacts between the Provisionals and the Northern Ireland Office on the H-block issue. Miriam Daly, ever suspicious of the IRA leadership, had earlier suggested that the Provisionals were actually trying to negotiate a new cease-fire.

The Provisionals still regarded the anti-H-block campaign as a distraction from the main emphasis, which was on the armed campaign. As one indication of the IRA's lack of interest in the prison dispute, in an interview with an IRA spokesman that appeared in the August 1978 issue of *Magill*, the H-block was not referred to once. As a rule, the Provisionals have always shown themselves to be wary about getting involved in any protest movement unless they can control it completely. The H-block issue involved too many unpredictable groups, such as the IRSP and the People's Democracy; the RACs were also too independent for the Provos' liking.

The H-block issue, however, was taking on a new dimension. The Archbishop of Armagh, Tomás Ó Fiaich, visited the H-blocks twice in 1978, and his outrage at the conditions he found there drew international attention to the situation. Support for the campaign was growing both at home and abroad. At the beginning of the New Year, Mick Plunkett, along with a delegation from Sinn Féin, took part in an international conference held in Frankfurt organised by the West German Ireland Solidarity Committee, the main theme of which was the H-block and the Irish crisis. At one meeting, in the University of Frankfurt, over a thousand people attended to hear Plunkett speak. He then went to Paris, where on 27 January he spoke at a meeting of several hundred organised by the Ligue Communiste, a French Trotskyist group. That same month a delegation from Comité Irlande—the IRSP's main French support group—accompanied by a reporter from *Libération*, the left-wing daily, delivered a petition to the British embassy in Paris containing eight hundred signatures demanding the restoration of political status.

Later that year an opportunity arose to further publicise the prison crisis before a wider audience. Bernadette McAliskey, who had been actively involved in the H-block campaign since 1977, decided to run as a candidate in the election for the European Parliament, making the prison dispute the only issue of her campaign. There was a heated debate within republican ranks about how to respond to her initiative. The Provisionals had decided to boycott the election, and Sinn Féin actually campaigned against her. The IRSP also decided to boycott the election. But at a meeting of the Ard-

Chomhairle on 19 May, Dessie Grew, who attended the meeting as a representative of "Group B"—the INLA—told them that all the prisoners' relatives in his area, Armagh, were supporting McAliskey. He said that the party would have to "get out of the straightjacket of tailending the Provos" (Ard-Chomhairle minutes, 19 May 1979.) When an organised boycott was advocated, John O'Doherty warned that "it would be political suicide to give out boycott leaflets in South Derry." In the end, with the Dalys, Seán Flynn, Vinty Fegan and other leaders forcefully opposing any involvement in McAliskey's campaign, the party stuck with its abstentionist policy. The following year its new chairman, Liam Ó Comáin, admitted at the party's ardfheis that it had been a grave mistake to have opted out of the election, though he had been one of those supporting that course of action. McAliskey received almost 34,000 first-preference votes, a good showing for a single-issue candidate, and this in spite of the opposition of both the Provisionals and the IRSP.

The dispute over whether or not to support her campaign had proved divisive to the anti-H-block movement. According to Liam Clarke, "the casualties were the Relatives' Action Committees, morale amongst the prisoners and to a lesser extent Sinn Féin which, with whatever justice, was felt by some of its own supporters to have campaigned against the blanketmen." (*Broadening the Battlefield: the H-Blocks and the Rise of Sinn Féin*, Gill and Macmillan, 1987.) At any rate, the McAliskey vote gave a hint of the electoral potential of the prison issue, but one that would not be realised for some years to come.

The escalation of the dispute inside the jails led to increasing bitterness without. In December 1978 the INLA had for the first time tested its new under-car bomb with a mercury-tilt switch on a prison officer in Lisburn, wounding him. A more ruthless plan was now hatched. Information came from the Derry INLA concerning a bus that carried prison officers from Magilligan prison in County Derry. It was decided to ambush it. Two members of the INLA's GHQ came up from Dublin, one of them a former chief of staff of the organisation. Armed with AK47 automatic rifles, they waited, but had to abandon the operation when the Derry unit did not show up with the getaway vehicles. Both men were left wandering around the mainly Protestant countryside carrying the rifles. They were eventually found by the Derry INLA's OC and driven to safety.

A graphic indication of the bitterness republicans felt about the whole issue was given on 21 April 1979 at a European Political Prisoners' Conference held in Liberty Hall. Mary Reid of the IRSP spoke, as did Claire Delany, an ex-prisoner from Armagh jail. When Claire Delany was asked how she felt about the murder of Agnes Wallace, the prison officer and mother of six children killed by the INLA two days before, she replied that she was "sorry there had not been more shot." (*Starry Plough*, May 1979.)

During the summer of 1979, increasing pressure came from the prisoners, now in their third year of protest, to further escalate the dispute by undertaking a hunger strike. The Provisional leadership were less keen than that of the IRSP to support such a measure. The prisoners were told to hold off while a new initiative was given time. This was the National H-Block-Armagh Committee, which had been originally mooted as a possibility in talks between Sinn Féin, the RACs and the IRSP on 24 June. It was finally launched at a meeting in Andersonstown towards the end of October 1979.

The IRSP Ard-Chomhairle met on 1 September and discussed the forthcoming initiative. According to the minutes, "it was agreed to put forward our own demands but accept others if necessary. These were: the right of the prisoners not to wear prison clothing; not to do prison work; the right to full free association; and the right to elect their own spokesman."

It was agreed that "if there cannot be broader unity the committee should confine itself to H-Block because of the gravity of the situation ..." That is, there was to be no attempt to turn the prison issue into a referendum on militant republicanism, though the IRSP did hope later on to have a future conference at which "the broader issues of self-determination and British withdrawal" would be pushed. The first three of the four demands were at the core of the prison struggle. With the addition of the right to a weekly visit and parcel, and full remission of sentences, which had been withdrawn from those prisoners involved in the protests, these would become the five demands of the 1981 hunger strikers. (The right to elect spokesmen did not become an issue: it was actually contained in the demands for free association, which gave prisoners the right to organise according to paramilitary allegiance.)

The H-Block Conference elected a seventeen-member committee chaired by a Dublin priest, Father Piaras Ó Dúill. Niall Leonach of the IRSP's Ard-Chomhairle was made secretary of the committee, and Miriam Daly was also elected to it; but the National H-Block Committee was dominated by the Provisionals. However, in spite of the fact that the Provos were so closely involved in the new initiative, they were still playing a double game, as the IRSP had all along suspected. Provo negotiators were talking to Ó Fiaich, hoping that he would use the influence of the Catholic Church to persuade the British government to relent and restore political status. "In essence the committee was being used as backup and held in reserve in case the Ó Fiaich negotiations failed. It was not entirely trusted." (Liam Clarke,

Broadening the Battlefield.)

In contrast to the uncertainties lying behind the organisation of the H-Block Committee, the propaganda put out by the IRSP portrayed complete unity, determination, and confidence of victory. "Our confidence is also boosted in the knowledge that the Republican Movement and our own movement are increasingly co-operating in the struggle against British imperialism," proclaimed a statement from the IRSP in April 1980. "Long may this continue for such unity is impregnated with success and victory." (*Derry Journal*, 11 April 1980.)

A big demonstration was called for in Dublin on 7 June. It was to be followed by a second National H-Block Conference on 15 June in Andersonstown. The IRSP hoped to have five people elected to the committee, which would be attended by delegates from all over the North. In the event, the Dublin march was judged only a "partial success but turn out very poor." Out of ninety copies of the *Starry Plough* brought to the march, only twenty were sold. (Coiste Seasta minutes, 10 June 1980.) The party's performance at the conference was also not all it might have been. A bus to take people to the Belfast meeting from Dublin had to be cancelled because of the poor response. In the event, only two IRSP members, Osgur Breatnach and Niall Leonach, were elected to the committee—the same number as before and far short of that for which the party had hoped. "Results show the need for much organising to be done for future events. Had we mobilised for H-Block Conference we could have ensured 2 more members on Committee." (Coiste Seasta minutes, 17 June 1980.) This failure of the rank and file to turn out for the party at the conference was all the more disheartening given the fact that the leadership had declared, "Our attendance at the conference is our most important tactic—all areas to send maximum representation." (Coiste Seasta minutes, 3 June 1980.)

The leadership was now beginning to have doubts about the efficacy of a strategy based on marching. The IRSP's new chairman, Liam Ó Comáin, gave the Bodenstown address at the Wolfe Tone commemoration on 29 June. He warned that "although marches are of some importance, a glut of them can have a negative effect by breeding apathy and generating a sense of futility. Therefore a clinical approach to the campaign on behalf of the prisoners will have to be adopted. Otherwise the National Smash H-Block Committee may unknowingly be counteracting their own objective."

The protesting prisoners' impatience was growing. Some were pressing hard for a hunger strike. Since the beginning of 1980 there had been rumours that one was imminent. In late September the rumours increased. The National Smash H-Block Committee had been given a year, and there was still no progress. At the Ard-Chomhairle meeting of 4 October the prospect of the prisoners' taking the ultimate step in the protest was discussed. "We must support the hunger striker with the full involvement of all Party members. Belfast Comhairle Ceantair have had discussions with the RAC on the need for unity on the issue. They will see Sinn Féin later this week to discuss activities. Agreed that Special Edition of the *Starry Plough* will be brought out and that finance must be got to ensure we can carry out a good campaign ... Belfast to get all background information on our prisoners within the next week. Also to get photos. Many of our prisoners are against the hunger strike but will probably take part in it." (Ard-Chomhairle minutes, 4 October 1980.)

Six days later the prisoners announced that seven men were going on hunger strike on 27 October. The five demands were not mentioned; instead the prisoners said they were campaigning for "political recognition and that we be accorded the status of political prisoners." (Quoted by Liam Clarke, *Broadening the Battlefield.*) One of the seven was John Nixon, OC of the INLA/IRSP prisoners in the Maze. By October 1980 there were fifty, of whom thirty-four were on the blanket. Nixon was twenty-five years old and from Armagh. He had been sentenced to fourteen years' imprisonment in September 1977 after being convicted on the basis of a confession of robbing a post office. He was described as being extremely powerfully built, a man who had kept himself fit by frequent exercising in spite of the deprivations of the blanket protest. He was also highly thought of as an OC. His companions were six Provisionals: Brendan "the Dark" Hughes—a former OC of the Belfast Brigade—Thomas McKearney, Seán McKenna, Leo Green, Raymond McCartney, and Thomas McFeely. Patsy O'Hara, who had been rearrested on his return to the North the year before, took over from Nixon as OC.

Originally the plan envisaged a second wave of seven hunger strikers coming on, and then a third. Patsy O'Hara, Micky Devine and S. Cassidy were to form part of the second wave, and Jake McManus of the third.[1]

Within two weeks of the hunger strike beginning, Seán McKenna was already being described as "ill". With the situation worsening, John Hume offered to act as an intermediary. The IRSP issued a statement on 9 December firmly rejecting any such outside intervention. "It was obvious that he is not acceptable to the blanket prisoners as a mediator ... The IRSP blanket prisoners have informed us that the only person who can negotiate on their behalf is their spokesman, Patsy O'Hara." (*Irish Press*, 10 December 1980.)

To preserve some continuity in the leadership within the prison, Patsy

O'Hara decided not to go ahead and join a second wave, which in any case never had the chance to materialise. Nixon sent out a "com" that appeared in the December edition of the *Starry Plough*. "All week there has been no sensation but the hunger pangs. I can hear and feel my stomach collapsing within me. My reflexes are stagnated, my speech and thought are slowed up. The constant dizziness, like a floating sensation, develops into severe pains in my head … I am well aware that the worst agony still awaits me. I have resigned myself to the fact that death may be inevitable."

By mid-December the IRSP believed that the Provisionals had instructed their prisoners to do a deal on securing just two of the demands—the prisoners' right not to work and to wear their own clothes—and "not to worry about other concessions." (Ard-Chomhairle minutes, 16 December 1980.) A com was sent in to Nixon saying that "whatever the Provos decide … he must make his own decision." (Ibid.)

As McKenna neared death, the British seemed to be offering immediate concessions on the clothing demand, with the promise that others would follow if the protest ended. Hughes decided that the concessions were sufficient and that McKenna's life should be saved. The hunger strike was ended just a week before Christmas.

Within a short time it was obvious that the prisoners had been misled. A letter from the hospitalised John Nixon declared that the "Brits reneged on agreement with prisoners." First, the authorities asked for a delay before the concessions were implemented; then they told the prisoners that they had to wear a convict's uniform and do prison work while waiting for their own clothes. The prisoners rejected this.

In addition, the militancy of the INLA blanket men, who were reluctant to withdraw from the protest, was creating problems in the prison. According to a report to the Ard-Chomhairle meeting of 1 January 1981, IRSP visits were being blocked, and there were attempts to "confuse and isolate" IRSP/INLA prisoners. The new Provisional OC in the prison, Bobby Sands, had access to the prisoners, but Patsy O'Hara was not allowed by the authorities to see his own men. The INLA prisoners threatened further action. On 27 January the prisoners rioted in the Maze, causing thousands of pounds worth of damage. The situation was set for another confrontation. The IRSP got ready for one more propaganda assault to accompany the struggle in the jails.

By the end of February the H-block committees were "back in full swing". (Ard-Chomhairle minutes, 22 February 1981.) On 1 March, five years to the day after political status had been abolished, Bobby Sands began his hunger strike. The INLA had twenty-nine men on the blanket protest in the

Maze. Patsy O'Hara, who had been the INLA prisoners' OC and spokesman during the last hunger strike, joined Sands on 22 March. Rab Collins, a Belfast man serving eight years, took over from O'Hara as the prisoners' OC. Seán Flynn and Séamus Ruddy, the Newry schoolteacher and former gun-runner, were to act as the main liaison between the INLA hunger strikers, their families, and the movement.[2]

The H-block issue was already having a dramatic effect on support for the party. The minutes of Ard-Chomhairle meetings from January 1981 onwards note an influx of new members. In south Derry twenty people applied to join in January; the same month, new cumainn were being set up in County Limerick. Eight people in Strabane approached the party to join—four of them Provisionals who were apparently disgruntled with their organisation's handling of the H-block issue. It was also reported that people were interested in joining in Ballyshannon, and Derry city had formed three new cumainn by April. Newry and Dundalk became more active: sales of the *Starry Plough* picked up, as they did all over the country.[3] Three hundred papers were sold in Ennis in March and 150 in Limerick, which recruited seven new members. In March the IRSP printed and distributed three thousand copies of its theoretical magazine, *Saoirse*, in Turf Lodge, the Markets, and Lower Falls. By April two new cumainn were established in west Belfast.

These numbers are far from astronomical, but to a party that had been moribund for years they looked like heralding the long-awaited breakthrough.

The IRSP leadership discussed the dangers of being swamped by the Provisionals. They were concerned about having to accept statements from the Provos on behalf of INLA prisoners. Seán Flynn, Gerry Roche and Osgur Breatnach arranged a meeting with the INLA's bigger brother to straighten out such issues. It was agreed that the PRO of the blanket men and hunger strikers—Bik McFarlane—could deal only with issues of harassment of the prisoners, and that he could not make any deals as a result of negotiations unless the INLA's representative had taken part in them.

Patsy O'Hara did not come from a traditional republican background. He had joined the Official Fianna in Derry in 1970, when he was thirteen, as a result of the social and political agitation that had been shaking the city since 1968. A British soldier shot and wounded him as he manned a barricade late in 1971. Three years later he was interned, and on his release in April 1975 he joined Costello's new movement. Eighteen months later he was arrested again and charged with possession, along with Micky Devine. Both had been involved in the robbery of an arms store in Donegal; they were stopped at the border by the RUC. Though O'Hara did not have any weapons on him, he was held for four months and then released, and he fled to Dublin. There his activities were fairly low-level: he acted as chauffeur for prominent members of the INLA such as Ronnie Bunting, and took part in IRSP pickets. On 10 May 1978 he was arrested with Stephen King in O'Connell Street while postering. He was held under section 30 of the Offences Against the State Act for eighteen hours and released. In June he was part of the team that carried out the Barna Gap robbery. By then O'Hara was a member of the Ard-Chomhairle, though he did not attend many of the meetings. He continued on the party's ruling body for a year, becoming joint treasurer along with Vinty Fegan in February 1979. He was rearrested in Derry in May of that year, and charged with possession of a grenade. Convicted, he was sentenced to eight years.

As an INLA volunteer the only major operation that O'Hara took part in was Barna Gap. However, one long-time INLA member recalls attending bomb-making classes in which O'Hara was the instructor. He remembers one occasion when O'Hara taught him how to build a mercury-tilt bomb like the device that killed Airey Neave.

O'Hara's older brother, Tony, was also serving time in the Maze. The IRSP wanted to use another family member, Patsy O'Hara's sister Liz, in the campaign, but as usual the Provisionals lodged objections to her speaking on H-block platforms. However, their objections were overcome. Though never a member of the IRSP, Liz O'Hara became actively involved in the H-blocks issue on the party's behalf, meeting Charles Haughey just after Sands died to demand Government intervention. She reported that Haughey had assured her that no more hunger strikers would die. Her dark-haired good looks, vivacity and articulateness were definite assets, particularly when she undertook a tour of the United States in the summer.

Bobby Sands's victory on 10 April in the by-election for the Westminster constituency of Fermanagh-South Tyrone sent an electric current through the IRSP. The party, though never abstentionist on principle, had been prevented from fighting in any elections since 1977 mainly because of opposition from the Belfast organisation. One of the results of this was that it had seen the electoral base that Séamus Costello had so assiduously build up in County Wicklow collapse. Sands's victory inspired a new boldness in those who had been convinced that the IRSP should have used the European election of 1979, for instance, to push the H-block issue. At an Ard-Chomhairle meeting a week after Sands's election, Gerry Roche proposed a resolution, seconded by Terry Robson, that advocated that the National H-Block Committee put forward candidates in the coming local elections in the North, with the proviso that if successful a candidate should not take his or her seat until the hunger strike was resolved. It was passed unanimously.

It was accompanied by a second resolution, also passed without opposition. It declared: "We recommend to the various C.C.'s [comhairlí ceantair] in the 6 counties that they stand IRSP candidates in the forthcoming local council elections. This assumes a negative answer to our proposal on elections to the National H-Block/Armagh Committee."

"We saw what had happened in Fermanagh-South Tyrone," said a former IRSP Ard-Chomhairle member. "But the republican movement was against it, except for Gerry Adams and a small group around him. We tried to put pressure on them through the H-Block Committee to stand candidates." However, the Provisionals opposed running candidates and left the nationalist field to the IRSP, the People's Democracy, and the Irish Independence Party—a decision they later regretted.[4]

Seán Flynn believed the party could win in Belfast and set about campaigning for the Lower Falls ward. He was an old hand at electioneering and had stood for the Republican Clubs in various contests in the early 1970s. But the Belfast organisation objected so strongly to fighting the election that Flynn found it impossible to convince any party member to stand with him. Eventually Gerry Kelly, a well-known GAA figure, and Billy Browning agreed to stand with him. Though both were running on the IRSP ticket, neither was in fact a member of the party. Flynn topped the poll, and Kelly won in the Andersonstown ward. Browning came close to making it a trio.

A month later the IRSP stood prisoner-candidates in the general election that brought about the defeat of the Haughey Government. The IRSP put up Kevin Lynch in Waterford, where the party had been approached to set up a new cumann. A hundred activists went to work on his campaign, with Roche as his election agent. Lynch came within three hundred votes of winning a seat.

Whatever electoral success the IRSP had north and south came without the assistance of the Provisionals, who refused to support the party's candidates. Even at a time when the nationalist community was under extreme political pressure, it was proving impossible to forge a united political front with the other main republican force.

Sands died on 5 May, Francis Hughes on 12 May. Day by day Patsy O'Hara weakened. A small camera had been smuggled into the prison, concealed in a visitor's anus (one of the most common ways of bringing banned items into the jail). A blurred photograph of the dying man gives an appropriately ghostly aspect to the scene, showing the hunger striker, wearing striped pyjamas, slumped in a wheelchair, his head on his hand, his arms skeletal.[5]

In spite of the rhetoric used to celebrate the death of a volunteer, republican organisations have a very matter-of-fact approach to the event itself. On 16 May the Ard-Chomhairle of the IRSP considered the mundane steps that would have to be taken when, as it seemed likely, O'Hara would die. "Preparations for events around Patsy's death. Colour party prepared. Republican Socialist Plot acquired in Creggan. Route for March arranged. Furled flags will be carried. 3 tri-colours and two Starry Ploughs. Derry will order wreaths and organise insertions in papers.

"Speaking equipment organised. Statement to be read by National H-Block Committee. B. McAliskey to be asked. Proposed that Liam Ó Comáin chair meeting. Proposed that Maelíosa Costello give oration. In the event of M.C. not willing, Naomi Brennan to do it. Proposed Séamus Ruddy seconded Gerry Roche." (Ard-Chomhairle minutes, 16 May 1981.)

When he was within a few days of death, Patsy O'Hara's mother threatened to intervene. On 19 May she had told her son: "I don't care about Ireland or the whole world, you are the only thing that matters to me—everything else has failed and now I am the only one who can save you and I am going to do it." Her son's succinct reply was: "Let the fight go on." (Quoted by Liam Clarke, *Broadening the Battlefield*.) Two days later, Patsy O'Hara died.

The turn-out for his funeral in Derry was immense—equalling, it was reported, that for the victims of Bloody Sunday. It took over two hours to wind its way through the Brandywell, Bogside and Creggan areas, flanked by a 34-strong INLA guard, six of whom were armed, to the cemetery. After the funeral rites, James Daly chaired the proceedings. He began by introducing a spokesman from the INLA. Rarely, if ever, had the organisation such a huge audience. "Our response will not be a wild emotional one—but a highly disciplined one," he told the mourners. "In the future we intend to better the deeds we have done in the past." (*Starry Plough*, June 1981.)

The plan to have Séamus Costello's widow give the oration had fallen through, and it was Gerry Roche, former chairman of the IRSP, who spoke, celebrating the dead volunteer as an "outstanding revolutionary". Republican funerals are myth-making occasions, and this was no exception. Their triumph is to turn the ordinary into the extraordinary. Like nearly all of the hunger strikers, there was nothing remarkable about Patsy O'Hara except his mode of dying. (Francis Hughes was the exception: his renown as a gunman had already made him stand out.) That briefly allowed O'Hara's name to be mentioned by Roche in the same breath as those of James Connolly and Séamus Costello.

O'Hara was replaced by INLA man Kevin Lynch, and a month later Micky Devine began refusing food.

The Provisionals not only lacked the will to co-operate on a united front basis but the IRSP suspected them of being engaged in secret negotiations with the British. Shortly before Joe McDonnell's death, Councillor Flynn received a telephone call from a man from the Northern Ireland Office, who told him to go to Long Kesh. "There are developments," was all he said. Even though it was late at night, Flynn went, accompanied by Séamus Ruddy. The NIO official, who refused to give his name, met him, and revealed that there had been discussions between Sinn Féin and the government and that it looked like they might settle. Flynn was given permission to go into the jail and speak to Lynch and Devine, who corroborated the NIO man's assertion but said that the five demands were not being met, so whatever Provisionals did, the INLA hunger strikers would not budge. Flynn could not get the official to reveal what was being offered. Later, when he confronted the Provisionals, they denied that they were engaged in any secret talks with the NIO.

In fact the problems of creating a united front were coming not only from the Provisionals. As usual, the young hotheads in the Belfast INLA were not happy about the amount of time and money spent on the elections, just as they were unhappy about money being spent on such things as a printing press for the Belfast headquarters—they thought it would have been better spent on weapons. The men who emerged as their leaders were Gerard Steenson, released from jail in April 1980 and once more active in the INLA, and Seán Mackin. Both had opposed the IRSP's decision to fight the local elections and had tried to obstruct IRSP candidates, which held back the party's vote. Steenson changed his mind after the results had come in, declaring that more candidates should have been run. But the dispute had exposed some old fault lines that were emerging even as the movement seemed to surge ahead politically.

During that highly charged summer the INLA successfully recruited hundreds of young nationalists to its ranks. A new three-letter message appeared on gable walls: *UTE*—Up the Erps. The organisation's fortunes appeared to be on the up. In the Markets area of Belfast the INLA seemed to have won over almost every teenager to their side. Fashion reflected the INLA's newly found prowess among the young in the inner city area: teenage recruits copied the older INLA volunteers by wearing green combat jackets, sprouting bum-fluff and sticking Connolly and Starry Plough badges on their lapels. This new urban guerrilla look became the uniform of the young Erps in such areas.

In the middle of the hunger strike the INLA could call on the support of up to fifty young men from the Markets, Lower Ormeau and Short Strand who had joined the Patsy O'Hara Youth Movement. It portrayed itself as a political youth group. The movement did distribute a news-sheet that summer, called *Venceremos* (the Latin American equivalent of "Tiocfaidh ár lá"). The news-sheet contained poorly written poems and articles on Patsy O'Hara's contribution to the struggle. It also included reports on ultra-left European organisations such as the German Red Army Faction. But distributing *Venceremos* was about the height of the Patsy O'Hara Movement's political work in the Markets. In reality the group was regarded as the INLA's equivalent of the IRA's Fianna Éireann. Like the Fianna, the new youth organisation carried out military-style operations, including concerted petrol bomb attacks on RUC patrols. It also became a teenage police force, threatening and at times viciously beating other young people who crossed them.

In one incident in September twenty members of the junior INLA attacked a young man from the Lower Ormeau area inside the Markets Community Centre. The victim was beaten with hurley sticks and iron bars during his engagement party. He was left unconscious on the disco floor and then taken to hospital. His "crime" had been to beat up a member of the Patsy O'Hara Youth Movement. Their revenge had been brutal and vindictive. The incident did, however, illuminate just how much the INLA's ranks were swelled during the hunger strike.

There was a Wild West feel to the Markets during that period. Even though the redeveloped red-brick estate had been designed, on security grounds, with only one way in and one way out, INLA volunteers brazenly displayed their weapons on foot patrols through the area's narrow streets and entries. Under the glare of British army observation posts on high buildings overlooking the Markets, the INLA unit were quite open about their activities. Weapons and ammunition were hidden under small slate roofs and drains. INLA volunteers, including John O'Reilly and "Ta" Power, posed with guns for American newspapers and the IRSP magazine *Saoirse*.

The Markets unit comprised a new breed of INLA volunteer who had graduated through the ranks of the Official IRA Fianna towards the breakaway group, including Power and O'Reilly. Power came from a strong republican family. He resembled a Che Guevara figure with his flowing red beard and army jacket. Power was respected by his friends and enemies alike in the Markets as a thinker as well as a military activist.

On 6 May, one day after Bobby Sands's death, Power's younger brother, Jim, blew himself up making a bomb in an entry off the inappropriately named Friendly Street. So delighted were the RUC about Jim Power's death that they were heard singing sick songs about the explosion: "Jim Power's dead—He's only got half a head."

The most revealing operation carried out by the Markets unit during the hunger strike period was an attempt to kill the DUP leader, Ian Paisley, on Friday 3 June. As Paisley's car passed along East Bridge Street on his way to east Belfast, John O'Reilly opened fire from a house overlooking the route. He missed.

Provisional leaders had always regarded Paisley as one of their greatest recruiting sergeants. Every time he thundered on, republicans hoped more nationalists would join up. To many republicans Paisley was a propaganda asset. The INLA was not concerned with such subtlety. The spectacular hit was all that mattered.

The Markets unit contained some of the most ruthless operators in the North. During 1981 they carried out several murders in the city. One in particular, at Cromac Street on 27 March, stands out for its careful planning and ruthless execution.

John Smith, a 25-year-old part-time UDR man, was not very security-conscious. He had been working for some time in a garage in Ormeau Avenue. Every morning he came from east Belfast through the Markets, walking along Cromac Street, sometimes calling in to a local confectionery shop for the morning paper. On the morning of his death a crowd of schoolchildren gathered at the bus stop in Cromac Street. They noticed two local INLA volunteers passing by. The INLA volunteers were dressed in white painters' coats, carrying a tin of paint. They crossed Cromac Street and followed John Smith. As he reached the pavement outside the local chemist, the INLA members drew their guns and fired into the back of his head at point-blank range. The gunmen then ran across the road towards the maze of streets into the Markets, leaving John Smith lying dead on the pavement.

The killing outraged one of the local parish priests. On the Sunday after the shooting Father Kerr challenged those in the congregation of St Malachy's church who supported the killers to leave the chapel. No-one budged from their seats.

The activities of the Markets unit during 1981 attracted the attention of loyalist paramilitaries. On Thursday 15 October a UDA hit team entered the area. Their intended target was the local IRSP activist Seán Hanna, who lived in Stanfield Row.

Hanna and his wife, Kathleen, were awakened by hammering at their front door. Fearing the worst, they banged ferociously on the wall beside their neighbours' house. As the UDA hit team tried to get inside, Hanna's banging managed to waken the occupants next door, who switched on their lights, scaring off the would-be assassins. But before getting into their getaway car a gunman saw a silhouetted figure in the window of an upstairs flat. Baying for blood, the UDA man kicked in the door and ran upstairs. He opened fire on the figure at the window, a 68-year-old woman called Mary McKay killing her.

In the aftermath of Mrs McKay's murder the INLA and local PIRA members set up vigilante patrols, as residents feared that loyalists might strike again. The patrols eventually petered out, but the fear remained. Mrs McKay's murder would not be the last time loyalists entered the area to kill.

By the middle of 1981 the IRSP had peaked politically. The slow collapse of the hunger strike consumed the rest of the summer. Two more hunger strikers, IRA men Joe McDonnell and Martin Hurson, died during the first two weeks of July. On 18 July there were serious riots outside the British embassy in Dublin, the worst that the capital had yet seen. Twenty men were arrested, among them IRSP and INLA veterans Harry Flynn and Gerry Roche. The riots, in which 120 gardaí and 80 protesters were injured, had a detrimental effect on support for the prison protest in the Republic, where public opinion was beginning to grow concerned about the dangers of the Northern troubles coming south. Only four hundred people had turned up for a Dublin demonstration after McDonnell's death.

By the end of July the number of deaths in the prison had reached six. The INLA had two hunger strikers well into their fast. The IRSP feared that the family of one of them, Kevin Lynch from Dungiven in south Derry, would intervene after he went into a coma. The family had strongly opposed their son joining the protest. "The Lynches need care," the IRSP leadership had been told on 20 June. However, Kevin Lynch, like Patsy O'Hara before him, fought off his family's doubts, and died a martyr on 1 August. Seán Flynn believes that the hunger strikers' resolve was reinforced by the fact that they were together, in the hospital ward. Before one died, the others would shout to him, promising that they would not let him down.

Almost three weeks later, Micky Devine followed. Shortly before he had died, Bernadette McAliskey had visited him. A month earlier she had walked out of a funeral service for Martin Hurson when the priest had condemned the hunger strike. Devine said to her: "If you walk out of mine, wheel me out along with you."

A note of desperation crept into some of the IRSP's statements. Five days

Séamus Costello in April 1975.

(Courtesy of Victor Patterson)

Former Official IRA chief of staff, Cathal Goulding, at Bodenstown.

(Courtesy of The Irish News)

INLA and IRSP inmates of Compound 14, Long Kesh, pictured outside the study hut, shortly before the "great escape" of 4 May 1976. Three of those pictured here took part in that escape: Harry Flynn (bearded, third from left in the second row from the back), Henry Doherty (dark glasses, front row) and Dessie Grew (bearded, on extreme right, second row from the back). Grew, however, was unable to scale the perimeter wall.

Jackie Goodman, who briefly turned supergrass in 1982, is on the extreme left, second row from the back, arms folded. Among the other prominent members are Phil McDonnell (extreme left, second row from the front), Billy Basset (third from left, front row) and Hugh Torney (extreme right, second row from the front, long-haired).

Immediately above McDonnell is Bernard Dorrian, and to the right of him, Karl Hegney. Directly behind Hegney is John Nixon (balding) who took part in the 1980 hunger strike. Directly under Hegney is Seán Hanna.

Hegney was shot dead by loyalists in October 1991. Grew later joined the IRA and was killed by the SAS in October 1990. The photograph was taken by Gerard "Sparky" Barkley who was shot dead on the orders of Dominic McGlinchey in October 1983.

(Private Collection)

October 1980: Former loyalist leader, Major Ronald Bunting, weeps at the graveside of his murdered son, Ronnie, an INLA leader.

The funeral of Jim Power, killed by his own bomb, May 1981. In the left-hand corner, Harry Kirkpatrick, "Sparky" Barkley and Gerard Steenson can be seen talking.

(Private Collection)

Hunger striker Patsy O'Hara had been active in the INLA and was on the Ard-Chomhairle of the IRSP before his death on 21 May 1981. *(Courtesy of The Irish News)*

May 1981: Harry Flynn speaking at the funeral of Patsy O'Hara. Behind him,
Jim Daly looks on. *(Private Collection)*

May 1981: Jim Daly on the platform along with Belfast IRSP councillor Seán Flynn.
Beneath the platform, immediately to the rear of Daly, is Harry Kirkpatrick.
Nine months later he would begin his career as a supergrass. *(Private Collection)*

INLA hunger striker Mickey Devine. Died 20 August 1981. *(Courtesy of The Irish News)*

Supergrass Harry Kirkpatrick and wife Liz. They were married in September 1981. Among the guests were Gerard Steenson and "Sparky" Barkley, both of whom were to die violently. *(Courtesy of The Irish News)*

July 1984: Volley of shots for INLA member "Bonanza" McCann at St Peter's Cathedral. *(Courtesy of The Irish News)*

Summer 1984, Paris: (L–R) Séamus Ruddy, Mick Plunkett and Harry Flynn. A year later, Ruddy was beaten and murdered by INLA members, including John O'Reilly.

Gerard Steenson, a Belfast INLA leader, pictured shortly before he was shot dead on 14 March 1987.

December 1986: Former INLA man and IPLO leader Jimmy Brown walks from Crumlin Road Jail after serving three and a half years. *(Courtesy of The Irish News)*

1986: The PLO villa in the Middle East where the INLA's main link to the Arab world often stayed when engaged in arms deals. *(Private Collection)*

IRSP men Kevin McQuillan and Terry Harkin carry the coffin of Frank Kearney, 23 February 1987. *(Courtesy of The Irish News)*

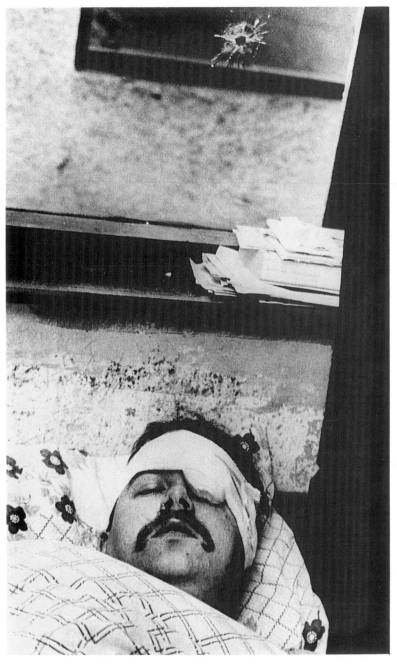

IRSP vice-chairperson Kevin McQuillan was shot twice at his Springfield Road
home, 10 March 1987. *(Courtesy of The Irish News)*

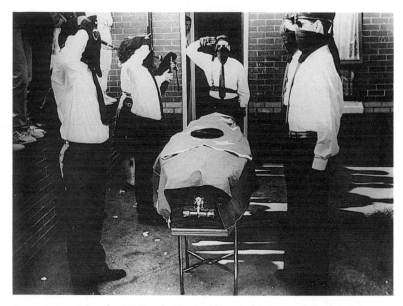

August 1991: Salute for IPLO man Martin O'Prey at his Leeson Street home, Belfast. *(Courtesy of The Irish News)*

Dominic McGlinchey, INLA chief of staff from July 1983 to March 1984, who was murdered by gunmen on 10 February 1994. *(Courtesy of The Irish Times)*

after Devine's death, Seán Flynn issued an appeal saying, "With 10 hunger strikers already dead, and massive support at home and abroad, for the prisoners' five demands, Margaret Thatcher has got more than her pound of flesh for Airey Neave and we again call on her to grant the prisoners' five demands in order to avoid more deaths in Long Kesh prison." (*Irish News*, 25 August 1981.)

Tensions began to surface about the wisdom of continuing the protest. The IRSP leadership was convinced that the Thatcher government would not relent. The INLA had agreed initially that the ratio of hunger strikers would be one of their men for every three Provos. Liam McCloskey had joined the fast after the death of Lynch, but no-one had replaced Devine. The *Irish Times* reported that the INLA was refusing to put any more of its prisoners on the doomed protest. The IRSP vociferously denied this in public, but in private it was concerned that members of the press had gained access to prisoners' coms, in which doubts were expressed about continuing the hunger strike. Some within the movement distrusted the Provisionals and believed that they were interested in prolonging the hunger strike in order to win support for the electoral campaign of Owen Carron, Bobby Sands's election agent, who was standing in the Fermanagh-South Tyrone by-election.

Outside, moves were also being undertaken by Father Faul to end the protest. All earlier attempts had failed; but several factors were now in Father Faul's favour. The relatives of the remaining hunger strikers were growing ever more desperate, and by September Jim Prior had taken over the Northern Ireland Office as Secretary of State. Prior, a leading liberal in the Thatcher cabinet, believed that she had mishandled the situation badly. (He later accused her of having no understanding of what was happening.) He was determined to bring the crisis to an end. The day Mickey Devine died, polling opened in the Fermanagh-South Tyrone by-election, which the Provisionals won. Carron actually increased Sands's majority by more than seven hundred votes. Two Provisional hunger strikers came off the protest shortly afterwards. On 26 September, Liam McCloskey, who had replaced Kevin Lynch, was on the verge of lapsing into a coma when his mother told him she would intervene once he became unconscious: she was not going to let him die. According to McCloskey, "the writing was on the wall at that stage anyway. A lot of men had come off in the few weeks before that, and the whole hunger strike was beginning to crack. I knew deep down that it was beaten. I think that most of us knew that. We were caught in our own trap where there were ten men dead and we felt we had to keep going and look for a way out of it." (Quoted by Liam Clarke, *Broadening the*

Battlefield.)

McCloskey agreed to take vitamin shots; within a week the hunger strike was officially ended. Prior had made it known that he would be prepared to make concessions if the prisoners came off the protest. On 6 October it was announced that the prisoners would be allowed to wear their own clothes. Other concessions followed, until before long the substance of the demand for political status had been completely restored. So it has remained to this day.

For the IRSP and INLA, however, the struggle was not yet finished. The hunger strike had proved the futility of their attempts to build a broad front with the Provisionals, who at almost every turn had tried to block their influence and diminish their role. The Provos had refused to back IRSP candidates at elections; they had refused even to share platforms with them at various times. The most bitter clash, however, came over the IRSP's share of the financial cake that had been the result of the American fund-raising tour undertaken by three of the hunger strikers' relatives, Liz O'Hara, Malachy McCreesh, and Seán Sands. The tour had been organised by the Irish Northern Aid Committee or Noraid, the Provisionals' main support group in the United States. Noraid had objected to O'Hara being on the tour, because her brother Patsy was a "communist" and sullied the emerald-green image that republicans had in the United States. However, Sands and McCreesh had refused to go unless she was allowed to accompany them. The tour was a financial success: O'Hara remembers fund-raising dinners at which Noraid supporters stuffed fistfuls of dollars into large buckets. (Jack Holland, *The American Connection: US Guns, Money and Influence in Northern Ireland.*)

According to the IRSP, $350,000 was collected. Noraid denied this and claimed that no more than $200,00 was taken up for all of 1981, a remarkably modest sum and actually less than what the committee would expect to raise in a normal year. However, one thing is undisputed: the INLA prisoners did not get a cent of it. At a meeting of the Ard-Chomhairle after O'Hara's tour it was noted that "Derry prisoners relatives got nothing from money collected by NORAID. Collections were to go to all prisoners' relatives. We should exert more pressure here." (Ard-Chomhairle minutes, 25 July 1981.) In September, Seán Flynn set off to New York, where he met Martin Galvin, one of Noraid's leading spokesmen. Galvin said he knew nothing about giving money to the IRSP. The meeting turned into a shouting match, and Galvin denounced Flynn as a communist and had him thrown out of his house. Noraid and the Provisionals hogged the whole financial cake that had been won as a result of the hunger strike.

Flynn, who was in the United States as a representative of the H-Block Committee, had just as little luck raising funds as he toured the country. Noraid was told to stay away from any meeting at which he was speaking. A rich Noraid supporter who did turn up was so disgusted by Flynn's evident sympathy for Native Americans and Blacks that he tore up a previously promised cheque for $10,000. He told Flynn: "I don't like niggers." (Holland, *The American Connection.*)

However, the IRSP did benefit in a small way from the American tour. Contacts were made with sympathisers in California, who set up a support group—one of the very few American contacts the party ever made.

The hunger strike had produced more support for the IRSP and the INLA than they had enjoyed since the heady days following their formation. But it had also exacerbated an internal crisis that would have lasting consequences for the whole republican socialist movement.

NOTES

1. However, there was another prisoner connected with the IRSP/INLA who was already well into a hunger strike and who caused some complications. Séamus Mullan, a County Derry man, had undertaken a 72-day hunger strike earlier in the year, protesting his innocence of the blackmailing charge on which he had been convicted. When the authorities refused to allow him an appeal he embarked on another hunger strike on 18 September, in spite of pleas from the IRSP. A woman prisoner in Armagh jail, 23-year-old Pauline McLoughlin, was also seriously ill, suffering from a severe case of bulimia. Though it was feared that either could die before any of the seven official hunger strikers, thus confusing the campaign, neither did. Mullan ended his hunger strike in November, and McLoughlin was eventually released.

2. Flynn contradicts other accounts of the hunger strikes in which it is alleged that the party did not discuss with the families of the hunger strikers beforehand what was happening. He says Ruddy went to the family of each proposed hunger striker to talk it over with them. According to Flynn, he always approached them in a sensitive manner.

3. The Ard-Chomhairle meeting of 4 April 1981 noted that the newly recruited Newry and Dundalk members wanted to have pins on their Easter lilies rather than adhesive. Pins were associated with the Provisionals and adhesive with the Officials (from which they got the nickname "Stickies" in 1970). Ard-Chomhairle member Séamus Ruddy agreed to get the pins on the lilies.

4. According to a former Sinn Féin councillor, "definitely it was a major

chance missed for us. It might have made a difference today—the vote we would have taken would have been well in advance of anything since, and Sinn Féin might have been taken more seriously. Fair enough, the effects of the hunger strike have made Sinn Féin what it is today, but we lost out to a certain extent." (Quoted by Fionnuala O'Connor, *In Search of a State: Catholics in Northern Ireland.*)

5. It appeared in *Too Long a Sacrifice: Life and Death in Northern Ireland since 1969* by Jack Holland, Penguin Books, 1982.

9

THE TOUTS' TALE

1980 was a turning-point for the Irish National Liberation Army, though why would not become obvious immediately.

In April of that year, four months before his twenty-third birthday, Gerard Steenson walked through the gates of the Maze Prison a free man, having served his time on a weapons charge and for an attempted escape. He was known in republican circles for having killed Billy McMillen five years earlier, and for not much else. Some older members of the INLA distrusted him because of that killing, which took place during a time when the Officials and the INLA were trying to patch up a cease-fire. In particular Jackie Goodman, the Belfast brigade operations officer, and Seán Flynn, brigade adjutant, regarded Steenson with some concern. Being a cautious person, Goodman was especially anxious because, as he put it, "If you give Steenson a job he'll end up running the whole show."

On the face of it, it was hard to see why Gerard Steenson provoked such strong reactions in people. He was slight of build, physically not very strong, with a rather "small, weak voice," as Terry Robson of Derry described it. Said Robson: "He was a plausible young man, extremely articulate, not without a sense of politics—he had enough of the rhetoric to pass himself. He was the kind of person that if he wore jeans they'd have been creased. His hair was always neat and tidy. But he was dangerous—perhaps more dangerous than a lot of others." (Interview, 2 April 1993.) All who knew him, both friends and enemies, agreed that he could lead men. And he was ruthless.

When, after a month of freedom, Steenson asked to rejoin the INLA, he was called to Dublin to meet the Army Council. His application was blocked by Seán Flynn and Jackie Goodman, who both spoke against him. But Ronnie Bunting, the Belfast OC, told Flynn and Goodman that he could control Steenson, arguing that it was tactically better to have him in the movement than outside of it. The fact that Bunting also had a particular hatred of McMillen and was unreservedly delighted when he heard the news of his death probably helped sway his decision in favour of the young man who had pulled the trigger. Steenson was readmitted into the ranks of the INLA.

Some five months later, Bunting was assassinated along with Noel Lyttle.

On 17 October, just two days after Bunting's death, the gates of the Maze opened to release another young man, an acquaintance of Steenson's. His name was Henry Kirkpatrick, known to his friends as "Harry O" or "Harry". Unlike Steenson, however, Kirkpatrick had no reputation as a gunman, however earned, nor as anything else for that matter, other than that of a low-ranking volunteer with a petty criminal past. He had been arrested and jailed, like Steenson, in 1975. He was convicted of possession of a shotgun and of robbing the Northern Bank of £2,107.92 along with his childhood pal Gerard "Sparky" Barkley and a third man, G. P. McIntyre. The second offence had occurred while Kirkpatrick had been out on bail from the first. Before the 1975 offences, which had taken place while Kirkpatrick was a member of the so-called "People's Liberation Army" (the cover name for the INLA), he had been up on two minor theft-related charges. With Sparky, Kirkpatrick had spent most of his young life joy-riding around west Belfast, playing truant from St Thomas's Secondary Intermediate School on the Whiterock Road, and doing odd jobs such as barman, labourer and laundry worker at the Initial Towel Laundry, where his main task was cleaning British army socks and pullovers.

His family situation had not been a happy one. In January 1969 his mother, Eileen, had gone off to live with an Englishman named Richard Hill. The following August he and his three sisters, Donna, Michele, and Andrea, along with their father, Ronald, fled in terror before Protestant gangs who set fire to their home on the Crumlin Road. The Kirkpatricks moved from place to place, eventually settling in Ballymurphy in 1971.

According to his father, "when he went into prison he was a person of very little education. When he came out he was using big words, and talking about political theories—Marxism and the like." Whether Kirkpatrick understood these big words was questioned by Thomas "Ta" Power, who gave lectures on Marxism in the IRSP compound in Long Kesh. What Power recalled most about "Harry O" was his habit of catching and cutting up flies, bees and wasps and feeding them to spiders.

Kirkpatrick had been in compound 13 along with Steenson. Like many others, he fell under the Lower Falls man's influence. Kirkpatrick joined others such as John O'Reilly and Jimmy Brown in seeming to adulate him. Robson, recalling the time he spent in jail with Steenson, commented: "They seemed to follow Steenson around like dogs."

When Kirkpatrick was released he applied to rejoin the INLA. By now there had been a change at the top in Belfast. With Bunting dead, Seán Flynn was in charge and was named in court as OC of the Belfast Brigade. Under him on the brigade staff were William Browning, Jackie Goodman, Bernard Dorrian—who married Kirkpatrick's sister Michele—and Seán Mackin. Kirkpatrick met Goodman in the IRSP's headquarters on the Falls Road to discuss resuming his activities in the INLA. Goodman refused him. The older man simply did not trust him.

Goodman had been in the INLA from the beginning. He was an ex-Official IRA man, a member of the "Dirty Dozen" unit, which had specialised in "raising finance"—i.e. bank robberies—for the Officials. In 1970 he had been wounded along with Hugh Torney during an attack on the Henry Taggart army base in Ballymurphy. He left the Officials in 1973 and became involved in the IRSP and INLA when serving a prison sentence in 1975.

Rebuffed by Goodman, "Harry O" approached his old friend Steenson, who was now on the brigade staff. Steenson not only got him into the INLA but made him his "assistant". In Kirkpatrick's train came his childhood pal Sparky Barkley. Sparky by then had a job in the Royal Victoria Hospital as a porter, a lowly post but one that the INLA would put to good use when it carried out robberies there and even stored weapons on the hospital grounds.

The older INLA men continued to look on Barkley and Kirkpatrick as no more than "a couple of rogues". The resistance of Flynn, Goodman and Dorrian to Steenson and then Kirkpatrick created resentment. "Bunting had kept them in line," according to a former INLA leader, "and diluted the antagonism. But his assassination meant there was no buffer between Flynn, Goodman, and them." (Interview, 22 May 1993.) Another ex-member agrees. "Bunting's death was near enough a watershed for the INLA in Belfast." (Interview, 8 July 1993.)

In the meantime Steenson set about proving his mettle. Armed mainly with VZOR pistols that had come from Czechoslovakia via Paris, he carried out a series of attacks. Colin Quinn, an off-duty UDR man, was shot dead as he left his job near the Grosvenor Road on 10 December. Kirkpatrick acted as the getaway driver, according to his own account in court. Eighteen days later Steenson and Kirkpatrick went to Armagh to see Roddy Carroll, OC of the local INLA. Carroll opposed a plan to shot a local RUC man, because he was a Catholic and, according to Kirkpatrick's testimony, "it would go down very badly with the local community." Instead Kirkpatrick, Steenson and Carroll murdered Hugh McGinn, an off-duty member of the Territorial Army at his home.

On 9 January 1981, at a meeting in Friendly Street in the Markets area,

Jimmy Brown as intelligence officer for the Belfast Brigade put forward a plan to shoot policemen in Botanic Avenue. This fell through, but as the gunmen were about to abandon their operation they found Reserve Constable Lindsay McDougall with a colleague walking up Great Victoria Street near the centre of Belfast. Steenson and a second gunman opened fire on the two policemen from behind. However, the second gunman only let off one round, as the magazine of his Browning pistol fell out. But Steenson, using the VZOR, shot Constable McDougall in the back of the head. The policeman died five days later. His colleague escaped injury.

A month later another reserve policeman (this time off duty) died at the hand of Steenson's men—Alexander Scott, who was shot in front of his daughter as he left his shop in My Lady's Road in east Belfast. Among those allegedly involved in this killing was Jim Power, Ta Power's younger brother.

The attacks continued throughout the spring. Steenson as operations officer showed that he liked to vary his targets. A new and important departure for the INLA occurred when for the first time it targeted local loyalist leaders. In January 1981 the INLA in Craigavon attempted to murder a DUP councillor, David Calvert. Frank Millar, a UDA man and member of Belfast City Council, was next. The INLA shot and seriously wounded him as he sat watching television. There followed an opportunist attempt on Rev. Ian Paisley himself on 3 July (see chapter 8). Later, in April, the INLA tried to murder Kenneth Schimeld, a civil servant, with a mercury-tilt bomb attached to his car, but the device was spotted. On the twenty-seventh of that month the INLA booby-trapped a lorry in Andersonstown; when the RUC patrol opened the cab door, an explosion killed one policeman instantly. Three others were seriously injured, one of whom died later.

A bombing attack was carried out against the Howard Street army base on the Falls Road; an RUC patrol was ambushed in the Clonard area by a unit that included Barkley, using a Chinese-made SKS semi-automatic rifle; and there was an attempt to ambush an army patrol using a landmine in the gardens at the back of Friendly Street. When the opportunity passed, Jim Power was killed trying to defuse it—the only member of the INLA to die while handling explosives.

The INLA was stepping up attacks as the hunger strike crisis in Long Kesh galvanised the Catholic community. On 12 May, five days after Power blew himself up, Matt McClarnon, an INLA sniper in the Divis Flats who had just fired on troops, was himself shot in the back by an army sniper, and died on the way to the hospital. (According to one of the first aid men who attended him, the ambulance was held up at an army checkpoint for three minutes, even though there was a dying man inside.) McClarnon had gone out to operate after learning of the death of the hunger striker Francis Hughes, whom he had met in prison.

As the hunger strike crisis deepened there were rumblings of discontent among Steenson's men about the Belfast leadership. There were also the usual suspicions that Dublin wasn't doing all it might to help the struggle in the North. Early in 1981 a Dublin Sunday newspaper had published a front-page story alleging that the INLA had just received tons of weapons from Libya. Included with the supposed shipment were, according to the story, RPG7 rockets. A Steenson supporter went south to speak to Harry Flynn; he told Flynn that Belfast wanted the rockets. Flynn said that the story was a myth and that the INLA had never received tons of weapons from Libya. "We're going to shoot someone," he is alleged to have told Flynn. "Then shoot me," Flynn replied.

Several months later, at the funeral of Jim Power on 9 May, Steenson got his revenge for the INLA old guard's earlier objections to his rejoining. Seán Flynn, OC of the Belfast INLA, was asked to attend a brigade staff meeting in the Divis Flats. When he showed up, he was taken to another house where Steenson, Ta Power, Seán Mackin and Kirkpatrick informed him that he was no longer commanding officer. He was informed that volunteers were unhappy with his leadership because he was not authorising enough operations. Flynn was angry, and warned that the Dublin HQ would not accept it. "He pointed out that myself and Gerard Steenson would definitely not be accepted by Dublin," according to Kirkpatrick's court statement. Later, Steenson's coup was ratified by the whole Belfast brigade staff, though some units in the Beechmount and St James's Road areas stayed loyal to the old leadership. But the way it had been orchestrated boded ill for the future of the organisation. According to Kirkpatrick, the younger men had struck when Goodman, Flynn's old ally, had been taken in for questioning by the police. The OC of the new-model Belfast INLA was Seán Mackin, one of Steenson's supporters. Ironically for a man whose entourage included several petty criminals, Steenson had accused Seán Flynn of corruption: taking a hundred pounds a week for himself from a building site fraud in the Markets. The site was indeed providing a hundred pounds a week, but Flynn's supporters maintain that it went into the IRSP coffers and was used to pay the wages of two women, his sister-in-law, Eilish Flynn, and Margaret Tumelty, who worked in the party's offices in the Falls Road.

The building site was run by a former Official IRA man who had formed a lucrative partnership with another racketeer with Official IRA links. Both men are notorious throughout Belfast for every form of racketeering, including the running of "massage parlours" in the early 1970s, and both were driven out of the Officials in 1980 after a dispute about money. They were accused of creaming off substantial sums, which they used to buy a pub near the city centre.

The two racketeers linked up with the INLA for protection against their former colleagues in the Officials. There have never been any allegations of financial corruption against Steenson, but he was not averse to using such contacts to provide money for the Belfast organisation. Much of it came from a big development site then under way in the Bone area of north Belfast and run by the former Official IRA man. However, these latest additions to Steenson's growing empire of influence brought with them more than money. Both men also had connections with loyalist paramilitaries, among the most prominent of whom was the UDA leader Jim Craig, also a notorious racketeer, and Bucky McCullough, a UDA gunman who had once taken part in a hand grenade attack on a Catholic pub, the Gem Bar on the New Lodge Road. Along with the two ex-Official IRA racketeers had come a third member of that organisation, Emmanuel Conway, who had abandoned it. But, unlike them, he joined the INLA.

Conway lived in the Unity Flats complex at the foot of the loyalist Shankill Road. His flat looked down into Denmark Street, where "Bucky" McCullough lived. With binoculars McCullough could be closely observed entering and leaving his house. He had two daughters, and each morning he brought one, then the other, to school. The INLA hatched a plot to murder the UDA man.

The two men involved were named in court as Rabbie McAllister and "Bronco", both Markets men. Watching from Conway's flat, they observed McCullough's morning routine.

Mishaps and delays frustrated the first efforts. However, on the morning of 16 October, as McCullough returned from having left his first daughter to school, the INLA unit struck. Using a motorbike, McAllister drove the short distance into Denmark Street with "Bronco" as pillion passenger. They arrived just as McCullough was leaving the house with his other daughter. In a signed statement, McAllister told the police: "As I was half-way down Denmark Street I noticed the target getting into his car. I slowed down the motor bike and Bronco jumped off. The target's motor was facing the Shankill Road. At this time I saw a child walking down the pathway from the house towards the car. I was just past the target's car and stopping on the ramp when I turned and saw Bronco firing several shots through the passenger's side window of the motor. I heard a girl screaming and saw her run towards the house again. Bronco jumped onto the back of the bike again and said, 'Let's go, Bob.'"

There was a hitch when the motorbike broke down; but by then they were not too far from the Divis Flats, and escaped into the organisation's traditional place of refuge.

According to McAllister's statement, he was surprised to learn later on the radio that the victim's name was William McCullough. "I said to Bronco, we hit the wrong man," he told police. McAllister had imagined that the target was Tommy Lyttle, a founder of the UDA and one of its leading members in west Belfast. But when McAllister expressed his concern to Steenson he was told, "It didn't matter. He was in the UDA anyway."[1]

Bucky McCullough's death took place a year and a day after the assassination of Ronnie Bunting. The UDA later came to believe that the McCullough killing was a result of collusion between Jim Craig and republicans. They also cited a whole series of other attacks on loyalists that claimed the lives of the Shankill Butcher Lenny Murphy, the UFF leader John McMichael, Belfast city councillor George Seawright and UDA man Fred Otley as proof that Craig was feeding information to both the IRA and the INLA. When the UDA assassinated Craig in 1988 it produced a detailed "collusion memo" to justify the killing of one of loyalism's most colourful characters.

By late 1981 there were suspicions within the INLA that collusion of a different kind was rife in its own ranks. Towards the end of September, Kirkpatrick helped set up an attack on a part-time UDR man who worked in Mackie's engineering factory on the Springfield Road in the fringe of west Belfast. Two gunmen shot Mark Alexander Stockman dead as he left work during the lunch hour. One of them was eighteen-year-old Martin "Rook" O'Prey, the other an ex-member of the Provisional IRA.

At the time of the murder, members of the anti-terrorist squad E4A were staking out the area around Mackie's. There was a large number of policemen belonging to the Divisional and Headquarters Mobile Units (DMSU and HMSU). However, their attempt to intercept the INLA unit's car failed. Under fire, O'Prey and the others escaped. Kirkpatrick and Steenson were a few streets away from the scene of the murder, along with Barkley and Paddy McAreavey, another INLA member from the Falls area. Steenson escaped, but Kirkpatrick, McAreavey and Barkley were arrested and held for three days of questioning. They were released without charge.

Clearly the police had intended an ambush. E4A was the same unit that the following year would be involved in a series of shoot-to-kill incidents that claimed the lives of six people, five of them IRA and INLA members. The police had obviously been forewarned, which meant that an informer was at work within the INLA's ranks.[2]

However, the dark clouds of doubt had not yet settled on Steenson and his band when on 19 September, ten days before the murder of Stockman, Kirkpatrick married his long-time girl-friend, Liz Meenan, whom he had met when he was working in the laundry. They were split up when he was jailed in 1975, and their relationship seemed over. However, within two months of Kirkpatrick's release he resumed his affair with her. By September 1981 Steenson was OC of the Belfast Brigade and Kirkpatrick had graduated to being his adjutant. But on 19 September, for once Steenson played second fiddle to "Harry O". He was Kirkpatrick's best man. At the wedding were Sparky Barkley, Seán Mackin, and other members of the gang. A lavish reception was held in the Martin Forsythe Club in the Turf Lodge estate, where the drink flowed freely. It was reported to have cost two thousand pounds.

When not on "active service" Kirkpatrick spent a considerable amount of time on active service of a different kind. He was quite promiscuous, before and after marriage. He haunted pubs, picking up women. He had four regular girl-friends, with whom he would often spend the night. He was an inhabitant of a moral universe completely at variance with that of the traditional republican, which, like that of the Irish priest, is associated with abstemiousness and sexual purity. Kirkpatrick and his friends were products of a different, urban culture, in which the old puritanism of Irish Catholicism had been swept away. A kind of confused hedonism had replaced it, in which drink played a leading role, as did drugs. A petty criminal who spent some time with Kirkpatrick in jail claims that he took Diconal, a heroin substitute, which he obtained from a dealer called Tony Butler in a city centre bar. He was a frequent user of cannabis and other drugs.[3]

Steenson and Kirkpatrick used a flat on the top floor of the Divis Tower, where they would bring their girl-friends. It was a sort of bachelors' pad, with nothing in it but two beds and some toiletries. There, directly under the British army observation post on the roof, they enjoyed their *liaisons dangereuses*. Something of the nature of Kirkpatrick's relations with women might be glimpsed from the anecdote about one of his girl-friends, who was nicknamed "Piggy". He once said that "she was so ugly I only did it from the back."

Some of the liaisons proved more dangerous than others. In February 1981, a few months after he had resumed relations with Liz, Kirkpatrick contracted a sexually transmitted disease. Steenson accompanied him to the clinic in the Royal Victoria Hospital, where they both had to receive treatment. Kirkpatrick told Steenson that it was Liz's fault; when he confronted her with the accusation she burst into tears and admitted that he was right. She had been attending the same clinic. Kirkpatrick learnt later that Steenson had been having an affair with Liz, and he blamed him for giving her the disease. This might help explain why he would turn so vehemently against his former idol.

In the autumn of 1981 the Belfast INLA seemed more dynamic and dangerous than ever. Yet it was on the brink of disaster. At least one informer was at work within its ranks. Meanwhile, the difficulties between Dublin and Belfast that had existed since the formation of the organisation were replicating themselves like a virus.

Steenson was worried that the Dublin leadership of Roche and Harry Flynn were plotting revenge for the coup he had organised against Harry's brother, Seán. Supported by Kirkpatrick, Jimmy Brown, now the Belfast Brigade's intelligence officer, Seán Mackin, the Markets man John O'Reilly, and Sparky Barkley, Steenson had more or less set up a parallel movement to the Dublin-run INLA. Seán Flynn and Jackie Goodman, concentrating on running the IRSP in Dublin, had control of and access to weapons and, though at odds with Steenson, continued to supply him and his units with small amounts of hardware. Obviously this made Belfast vulnerable to pressure.

In late 1981, in an attempt to establish an independent arms supply, Steenson, Kirkpatrick and Sparky Barkley set off to the United States, where they had one contact who arranged for a small arms haul of a dozen rifles or so to be shipped back via Dublin.[4] Clearly, it would not be enough. If Steenson's units were to operate effectively then they would have to have control over GHQ dumps and supplies.

Harry Flynn and Roche requested a meeting with Steenson in an attempt to heal the widening breach. They met in Dundalk. Along with Steenson came Kirkpatrick and Brown. The position of the Dublin leadership was that while they were not demanding that Seán Flynn be reinstated, they were saying that if changes were to be made then they should be made "through the movement". Steenson's reply was to demand total control of the movement. "Brown played his usual supportive role," commented one of the participants. The meeting lasted five minutes and resolved nothing except the determination of Steenson to push ahead with his ambitions.

Within the Army Council, Kirkpatrick and Brown were especially disliked. Kirkpatrick was regarded as a thief, and Brown was nicknamed "the Clown", partly because of a series of inept operations, beginning with his failure to supply Mick Plunkett with a car at Long Kesh prison (see chapter

8). When Brown applied to rejoin the IRSP in August 1981, Harry Flynn had vigorously opposed it. Brown's application was proposed by Gerry McKeaver, a Portadown man on the Ard-Chomhairle who was close to Steenson. When the matter of Brown's membership came up again for discussion, Flynn and Roche strenuously opposed it. The basis of their opposition was an incident that had occurred in 1977 during an INLA robbery in the Royal Victoria Hospital. Brown was acting as look-out. He failed to notice the presence of the Special Branch; as a result, Jackie Goodman and Hen Doherty (who had escaped from Long Kesh with Harry Flynn in 1976) were arrested. There were suspicions about Brown because of this incident.

After some argument, Flynn proposed "that we spend no more time presently on Jimmy Brown and we now reject his application." It was seconded by Naomi Brennan and passed. (Ard-Chomhairle minutes, 29 August 1981.) Brown's re-entry into the IRSP was blocked.

Steenson tried other avenues through which to extend his influence. He encouraged a Derry supporter and INLA member to set up a parallel group there, outside the influence of the Terry Robson-Tommy McCourt leadership, who were linked to the Dublin leadership. However, the Derry INLA found out about Steenson's plans and brought Steenson's man in for questioning, during which, he alleges, he was threatened with a blowtorch. In the end the Derry INLA took the less harsh but still painful measure of shooting him in the leg with a .303. This gun had been sent up to Derry on request because the organisation there said it was required for a sniping operation. (It was the same weapon that had been used in the attack on Paisley in July.)

Steenson was now more concerned than ever that the Dublin leadership around Flynn and Roche was going to launch a strike against him in Belfast, though they had shown no signs of wanting to do so. He took what for the INLA would prove a fateful decision. He ordered the murder of Harry Flynn.

Steenson was going to make it look like a loyalist job. On his instructions, Ta Power gave Rabbie McAllister, the quartermaster for the Markets unit, the money to buy a motorbike for the operation. McAllister went to the Ravenhill Road, a loyalist area of the city, where he bought a suitable bike. He drove it down to Dublin, where he spent the first night in the house of Tom McCartan. The next evening he met a Belfast man, "Bap" Hughes, as well as a former member of the Provisional IRA and a third man. At around ten o'clock the ex-Provo and the third man put on green combat jackets and woollen gloves. They each had a balaclava helmet. Two guns were produced: a Rhodesian-made submachine-gun modelled on the Israeli Uzi, and a P38 pistol. The two men left Bap Hughes and McAllister, who spent the rest of the evening in a pub in Baggot Street.

On the afternoon of 5 December, Harry Flynn was attending an Ard-Chomhairle meeting chaired by Naomi Brennan. Among the items on the agenda was a coming H-Block Committee meeting and the news that some prisoners in H-block 4 had started protesting again. It was noted that the Belfast IRSP was planning to hold a broad front conference. The members spent a considerable time discussing the instigation of "a national forum of public meetings to debate the demands and organisational forms of a new broad front." (Ard-Chomhairle minutes, 5 December 1981.)

When the meeting concluded, Flynn, along with his wife, Eilish, Naomi Brennan, and Terry Robson, went for a drink in the Flowing Tide pub at the corner of Sackville Place and Marlborough Street, not far from O'Connell Street.

Shortly before eleven the gunmen burst into the bar. One gunman stood at the door while the other rushed up to Flynn and fired into his back from almost point-blank range with the submachine-gun, leaving scorch marks on his skin. Flynn was hit by a hail of bullets in the neck and chest. But the machine-gun jammed—the Rhodesian model was not as reliable as the Israeli original. It saved his life. As it was, he was seriously wounded, and a bystander was hit in the leg. As the gunmen made their getaway, the motorbike too broke down, forcing them to flee on foot.

The gardaí swooped on McCartan's house, where Hughes and McAllister were staying; they were held and questioned, but released after a few days without charge. In the meantime the IRSP had issued a statement blaming loyalists or the SAS for the attempted assassination. The INLA issued a statement saying that talk of feuds was rubbish and that it stood behind the party.

The attack on Flynn was a turning-point in the history of the INLA. Before, though prone to constant factionalising, it had not resorted to killing as a means of settling its internal disputes. But Steenson had now crossed that Rubicon. He had set a precedent that would finally destroy the organisation.

True to his character, he pressed forward on his course of action. Following the shooting of Harry Flynn, he arranged a meeting with Seán Flynn and Jackie Goodman. When they arrived, he produced a gun and had them taken to a house in Andersonstown. There, with Jimmy Brown, he threatened to have them shot if they tried to revenge themselves for the attack in Dublin. Brown told Flynn that he had to resign his seat on the city council and co-opt him as a replacement. Flynn, along with Gerry Kelly and the two People's Democracy councillors, had just decided to end the boycott of the council and take their seats. Flynn refused. A few weeks later, word came to the Markets INLA from Steenson that they were to "shoot on sight Seán Flynn, Jackie Goodman, and Bernard Dorrian." Dorrian, Kirkpatrick's brother-in-law, had been involved in the IRSP and INLA from the 1970s, and before that in the Officials.

On the afternoon of 25 January, Flynn, Dorrian, Goodman and Michele were spotted in a bar in the Short Strand area of east Belfast. After O'Reilly was told, he collected a gun known as "the Silver Lady"—a Smith and Wesson Special that had been used in a hijacking operation before the McCullough murder. McAllister then drove John O'Reilly, an eighteen-year old youth from the Short Strand known as "Geeky" and a fourth man to search out their targets. O'Reilly asked Geeky to go into the bar and shoot the three men. O'Reilly told the hit-man that he could not do it himself as he was too well known to them, and they would flee if they saw him.

However, as Geeky made his way to the bar, Flynn and Dorrian, along with Michele, came out and started walking towards the Newtownards Road. "Where the fuck were you?" O'Reilly is said to have shouted at Geeky when he saw him. "They've just walked out the top of Seaforde Street; go and get them." Geeky obeyed. Along with a fourth man, he ran up to the targets. About six shots were fired, wounding Flynn and Bernard Dorrian in the arm. However, they escaped along the Newtownards Road.

The attacks seemed certain to provoke a feud. According to former leaders of the movement from Derry, a unit of the Derry INLA came down to Belfast to search out Steenson and his supporters and eliminate them. However, they couldn't find them, and they returned.

The *Starry Plough* condemned the attempt to murder the Flynns, Goodman, and Dorrian: "Their attackers, wittingly or unwittingly serve the interests of British imperialism by attacking the leadership." At the next meeting of the IRSP's Ard-Chomhairle a resolution was passed unanimously expelling Gerry McKeaver, Jim Marron, Liz Lagrua, and Denis O'Hearn. It accused them of causing "disarray" to the party in Belfast.

Steenson's attempt to eliminate the leadership had been a failure. It left the party demoralised and the INLA divided. Flynn eventually resigned his council seat and left the organisation in 1983. Kelly, the party's other city councillor, also resigned his seat at the same time. Dorrian resigned from the movement when he learnt that there was to be no action taken against Steenson for the shootings.

In spite of these efforts at restraint, Steenson's attacks seemed to be pushing the whole movement down a bloodstained slope towards a disastrous feud. Then events took a different course. Four days after the attempt to murder Flynn, Goodman, and Dorrian, the INLA targeted John McKeague.

McKeague was one of Belfast's most notorious loyalist leaders. Blond-haired, clamp-jawed, tense, he always exuded menace and an angry intolerance, looking and behaving like someone who would have been a suitable recruit to Hitler's SA. In August 1969 he had led loyalist mobs on their assaults on Catholic homes between the Falls Road and the Shankill. He had been an associate of the Rev. Ian Paisley's but later parted company with him. He was a founding member of the Ulster Defence Association, but broke with it after an acrimonious dispute about money. In 1971 the UDA petrol-bombed his shop in the Albertbridge Road, burning to death his elderly mother, who lived above it. In the early 1970s he founded the Red Hand Commandos, a small but vicious paramilitary group that carried out several of the nastier sectarian murders that marred those years. McKeague was among the first loyalists to be interned in February 1973. He was also a notorious homosexual, and usually surrounded himself with teenage boys.

It has since emerged that McKeague was linked to British army intelligence. An intelligence agent who says he was McKeague's handler confirmed to the authors that the former loyalist leader was supplying information to the British from the early 1970s. This man had been McKeague's handler up until 1976; after that his contact was less frequent, as the value of McKeague's information declined, mainly because of the fact that other loyalists intensely distrusted him. Still, his handler would visit him in his shop regularly to pick up whatever McKeague had to offer.

Towards the end of January, McKeague was questioned by detectives about the Kincora Boys' Home scandal. Police were investigating allegations that William McGrath, one of the housemasters, was sexually abusing boys in his care. It was also being alleged that boys were being prostituted, and among their clients were civil servants, loyalist politicians, and members of the intelligence community. McGrath was the chief of staff of "Tara", a shadowy loyalist organisation that dated back to the 1960s and was known mainly for issuing pamphlets full of esoteric nonsense, including claims that the Protestants of Ulster belonged to the Lost Tribe of Israel. Like McKeague, McGrath had formerly been close to the Rev. Ian Paisley; but he also had contacts in the intelligence services. In 1977 he was passing around an intelligence document that alleged that another formerly close associate of Paisley's was a homosexual.

The former British intelligence officer has said that some time in January 1982 he learnt that McKeague was about to "go public" on what he knew concerning the Kincora Boys' Home scandal. On Friday 29 January 1982, a few days after police had questioned McKeague about Kincora, he was shot dead in his shop.

The INLA claimed responsibility for McKeague's murder. Two men were involved, escaping on foot into the Short Strand. One of the men is known to have been working for the Special Branch, and the other is also alleged to have had security force connections.

On 5 February, Rabbie McAllister was arrested. After being told that he had been named in a statement made by Seán McConkey, an INLA member who had been arrested on 30 January, McAllister made a long statement detailing the activities of his fellow-members of the INLA. He included accounts of the murder of McCullough and the attempted murders of the Flynns. This led to the arrests of thirteen people, including Steenson, Ta Power, and Kirkpatrick. But on 18 March, McAllister retracted this statement and made another. It read: "In making this affidavit I swear all the following facts are true. Towards the end of 1981 as a result of constant arrests and psychological pressure I was trapped into working as an informant for the RUC Special Branch."

McAllister goes on to allege that not only was he coerced into giving information but that "on one occasion before my arrest on these charges the RUC asked me to 'set up' Tommy Power, Gerard Steenson, and John O'Reilly to be shot by the police. I refused to do this and was at that time seeking a way of freeing myself from their grip." Later, in court, it was revealed that McAllister had warned police about the plan to murder Stockman outside Mackie's.[5]

McAllister was involved in five murders and attempted murders that took place between September 1981 and January 1982. In court, the police revealed that he had made his statements when he realised that "his Special Branch handlers could not help him" (*Belfast Telegraph*, 4 November 1985). In November 1985, McAllister was sentenced to a total of 766 years for his part in a series of crimes, including the murder of the UDA man Bucky McCullough. This raises many questions, not least of which is how it was that McAllister, while working for the Special Branch, was allowed to commit serious crimes, including murder and attempted murder. The McKeague killing was not mentioned by McAllister in his statement, though he is alleged to have been part of the unit that carried it out. This raises another complex problem. A former leading member of the INLA reported that no-one in the organisation knew who gave the order for McKeague to be shot. This is more intriguing still in the light of the allegation that McKeague himself was working for British army intelligence. "It's too coincidental," said McKeague's handler, "that he's eliminated prior to exposing Kincora." He quickly added that he didn't think the RUC set him up. But he said: "There were few tears shed in Lisburn." (Interview, 12 December 1993.)

When McAllister was in jail, after withdrawing his statement, he approached a senior member of the Belfast INLA (imprisoned on the word of another informer) and told him that British intelligence had helped set up McKeague. They had guaranteed that there would be no foot patrols in the area when the assassination took place. It is also alleged that the eighteen-year-old gunman who actually shot McKeague made a long statement outlining his involvement in working for the security forces, and left it in the keeping of a Belfast priest. This raises the bizarre vista of one agent eliminating another—knowingly or unknowingly. McKeague's handler had intimated that at the time of the shooting he was no longer as useful to the security forces as he had been. Most embarrassingly, his name had been linked to the Kincora Boys' Home scandal. Whether or not his role in that case was an important factor in his death has never been satisfactorily determined. McKeague's death, like his life, remains surrounded by the murkiest kind of intrigue, through which it is difficult to perceive any clear and reliable outline of the truth.

Until 1981 the INLA had never been infiltrated by the security forces' intelligence services. Suddenly, within the period of a few months between September 1981 and January 1982, the whole organisation began to totter, worm-eaten with informers and touts. McConkey and McAllister were followed by Jackie Grimley, a petty criminal and police informer from Craigavon who had joined the INLA in 1979. Grimley had been arrested in February 1982, after the INLA had become suspicious of him. They discovered that he possessed information that could only have emanated from police sources about the arrest of three INLA volunteers who were caught with a bomb in Craigavon. Councillor Seán Flynn and Jackie Goodman were accused of holding and questioning Grimley, and threatening to shoot him. Instead he was freed, and told that he should go to Father Faul, who would help spirit him out of the country.

The INLA say that this was a ploy. The intention was to ambush Grimley as he met his two Special Branch handlers the following day at four o'clock in the car park of the Stables pub. However, the night Grimley was released by his INLA interrogators, unknown gunmen kicked in his door in an attempt to find him. (He was actually having a drink in a local pub frequented by the INLA.) When Grimley learnt of this he panicked and put himself in the hands of the police.

His subsequent statements led to a series of arrests. Among those he named were Seán Flynn, Jackie Goodman, Bernard Dorrian, Thomas "Ta" Power, Gerard Steenson, John O'Reilly, Harry Kirkpatrick, and Terry Robson. Altogether some twenty-two people were held on his word.

Grimley became the first of the INLA "supergrasses" to go to trial, in September 1983. After two months Lord Justice Gibson dismissed the case, on the grounds that Grimley was an unreliable witness. As the trial proceeded it had become embarrassingly evident that Grimley had been acting since 1979 with the knowledge of his Special Branch handlers, who had encouraged him to set up an INLA unit in Craigavon and recruit people into it, and then allowed crimes to be committed. Among the revelations during his trial was the fact that Grimley had given the Special Branch officers the dates of a proposed armed robbery that he and three other INLA men were planning, and the police had done nothing to prevent it.

The Grimley case is most interesting for the bearing it has on Rabbie McAllister. Like Grimley, McAllister was a self-confessed Special Branch informant who, during the time he was supplying the police with information, was allowed to commit serious crimes, including murder and attempted murder. The fact that Grimley was also given a free hand— including being involved in an attempted assassination (that of Calvert)— suggests that McAllister's situation was not unique.

As the extent of the collusion that existed between the police and Grimley became evident, the case against the defendants weakened. This might also give a clue as to why in McAllister's statement he did not mention the murder of McKeague. Clearly if there was some form of co-operation between elements within the security forces who allowed the killing to occur and the gunmen who carried it out, then it was best kept quiet. This would explain why in the otherwise lengthy and detailed statement McAllister made over a period of three days, beginning at 6:25 p.m. on 8 February 1982, McKeague's death is not mentioned.

A chain reaction had been set off. McConkey had led to McAllister; McAllister had led to Kirkpatrick; Grimley had led to Goodman. McAllister retracted, and on 23 March Kirkpatrick and others he had named left the Maze Prison, where a special remand centre had been set up to accommodate the sudden influx of suspects being held on the testimony of "supergrasses". But as they reached the gates they were rearrested and told that once more they had been implicated in serious crimes by another former colleague.

Kirkpatrick was charged initially with the murder of Constable McDougall. By the time he was seated in room BF4 at Castlereagh interrogation centre, facing Detective-Constables McCarten and Morgan at half past seven that same evening, he had already established who it was who was now testifying against him: Jackie Goodman. He sat silently for a while and, when asked if he was going to talk, replied: "Look, what's the score here?" Detective-Constable McCarten told him that if convicted he would possibly have to go to prison. About an hour after the interrogation started, Kirkpatrick said Goodman was a nobody in the organisation compared with him. "Do you want to know my rank?" he asked. McCarten said he did. "I'm brigade operations officer for the North; but I'm saying nothing more. I want to see someone higher." A Detective-Sergeant Henderson was brought in and said to Kirkpatrick: "I believe you want to talk to us." "I do," Kirkpatrick replied, "but I need an assurance." The RUC say that no assurance was given. But Kirkpatrick began to talk anyway, repeating his rank to the sergeant. When asked what he was involved in, he continued: "Murder and a lot of conspiracies." The sergeant asked for specifics. He was told: "I was involved in the shooting of a policeman in Great Victoria Street in January 1981, and Gerard Steenson and Fitzpatrick, the older one, was with me." According to the police statement of the proceedings, "we then discussed matters not the subject of these charges ... The interview terminated at 9.15 pm."

It was clear from this and what happened later that Kirkpatrick was letting out information bit by bit, feeling his way, in an attempt to see what kind of a bargain he might be able to negotiate with the police. He was prepared to lie—he was never "brigade operations officer for the North"—to increase his own importance. But it seems he was also partly motivated by a continuing resentment towards Goodman—his old nemesis, who had tried to prevent him rejoining the INLA. The idea that Goodman might be in a position to outdo him in the "supergrass" stakes irked Kirkpatrick, both for personal and opportunist reasons. This combination of cunning, personal vanity and opportunism was to become a feature of his performance as one of the North's most celebrated and reviled supergrasses as it unfolded over the next three years.

Goodman had been arrested after Jackie Grimley fled to the police. He had broken under interrogation and named thirty-six people allegedly involved in INLA activities. The police had granted Goodman immunity from prosecution, though he had been involved in very serious offences. Kirkpatrick, from his rearrest on 23 March 1982, seems to have been looking for a similar immunity. But he had probably already admitted too much to the police for that to be granted. When Goodman retracted his statements, Kirkpatrick and the others, including Steenson, Ta Power, Terry Robson, John O'Reilly, and Jimmy Brown, were held on Grimley's testimony.

From this point on Kirkpatrick was engaged in complex manoeuvres with the police and the authorities as he tried to put himself in the strongest position possible. As one sign that something was going on, he was held not with the other prisoners but in the Annex of Crumlin Road jail—a special unit where prisoners who were turning Queen's evidence were kept, along with sentenced members of the security forces and other special cases whose lives would be at risk if they mixed with other inmates. Among the informers being held there during Kirkpatrick's time were Tony O'Doherty, an ex-Provisional and the brother of the former INLA chief of staff John O'Doherty (see chapter 6), and supergrasses Kevin McGrady and William "Budgie" Allen. McGrady had been in the Provisionals and had experienced some kind of religious conversion. Allen was an ex-UVF man.

Life in the Annex was, from all accounts, very relaxed. Drink was freely available, prisoners were allowed to leave their cells and wander about, and special arrangements were made for visits, including, it was alleged, provisions for sexual relations.

It is not clear exactly when Kirkpatrick decided to go "supergrass". A prisoner who shared the Annex with him from March 1982 to January the following year said that at the start Kirkpatrick was very hesitant about giving evidence but "in the unnatural atmosphere of the Annex his mind was changed for him." Kirkpatrick told this prisoner that the police had only offered him a deal if the case against Grimley failed. The prisoner said that Kirkpatrick claimed that the deal "at that stage was for him to do seven years in an English prison and then be released. He seemed happy with this."

Kirkpatrick continued to see his solicitor, P. J. McGrory, who was also defending most of the others being held on Grimley's evidence. There was still uncertainty about what Kirkpatrick was doing, and Steenson tried to get word to him to rejoin his former colleagues, assuring him that he would be safe. But he told McGrory that he just wanted to be "left alone" and to assure the others that "there was no question whatever of his giving evidence."

On 28 April 1983, McGrory was told by Tony O'Doherty's solicitor, Ted Jones, that Kirkpatrick was "going to go supergrass." Jones also passed on the information that Kirkpatrick had been out of the prison, in Castlereagh interrogation centre, two days in a row. McGrory tried to see Kirkpatrick at Crumlin on 29 April and was told that he was not "in the building". After Easter, McGrory tried again. On 3 May he went to the jail and after waiting for twenty minutes was told by a prison officer that Kirkpatrick "was not available." McGrory asked what that meant; the officer replied that he knew nothing and was just passing on the message.

The solicitor wrote a letter of complaint to the Northern Ireland Office, demanding access to his client and threatening to apply to the High Court. Assistant Governor Campbell rang McGrory and apologised that he had been given the wrong information. He explained that on Friday 29 April, Kirkpatrick had been undergoing prolonged interviews with the police, on NIO authority. The following Tuesday, when McGrory had again visited the jail, Kirkpatrick had told the Assistant Governor that he did not wish to see him.

On 7 May, McGrory received the following letter, with the heading: *Number 386, Annex Base, Crumlin Rd.*

"Dear sir,

"I would like to inform you that I no longer wish you to represent me at my forthcoming trial. I would appreciate it if you would forward any documents or papers concerning myself to me at HMP Belfast.

"Yours sincerely, Henry Kirkpatrick."

The signature, but not the note, was in Kirkpatrick's handwriting. It was dated 4 May 1983.

On 3 June 1983, Kirkpatrick went before Mr Justice McDermott and pleaded guilty to 197 charges, including five murders. The judge said that he had been a dangerous criminal but "was probably disenchanted with the senselessness and lawless activities of the INLA." He said that Kirkpatrick realised now "that what you did over the years was indeed very wrong." Kirkpatrick was sentenced to five life sentences, without any recommendation, and concurrent terms of imprisonment on the lesser charges. Mr Justice McDermott added that a life sentence must mean imprisonment for life, unless and until the Secretary of State saw fit to recommend an earlier release.

Following the trial, two things happened that played a crucial role in Kirkpatrick's thinking. On the night of 26 October the naked corpse of "Sparky" Barkley, wrapped in a plastic bag, was found lying on a roadside near the Fermanagh-Monaghan border. He had been shot in the back of the head. The INLA claimed they had shot him because he was an informer (see chapter 10). A month later, the Grimley trial collapsed as the judge threw the case out of court.

Kirkpatrick's relationship with Sparky Barkley was unusually close. They had been friends since childhood; they had gone to school together, joined the youth wing of the Official IRA together, robbed and hijacked their way through adolescence side by side, ended up in jail together, and become members of the INLA at the same time. When Sparky got a job in the Royal Victoria Hospital as a porter, "Harry O" had tried to get one as well. A few days before Barkley was murdered he visited Kirkpatrick, along with Kirkpatrick's wife, Liz. "Harry O" reportedly told Barkley that he wouldn't name him if he looked after Liz while he was inside. He is said to have warned Barkley that the INLA were out to get him. (These assertions are based on a statement made by a prisoner who shared the Annex with Kirkpatrick.)

After Barkley's death, Kirkpatrick's father reported that during a visit to his son when he tried to bring up the subject of his giving evidence against his friends, he was cut off. Kirkpatrick said he didn't want to talk about it. Then he said, "They shouldn't have killed Sparky."

Barkley does seem to have enjoyed special protection from the police. After McAllister had withdrawn his statement, in March 1982, Barkley was not rearrested with Power, Steenson, O'Reilly, Kirkpatrick and the others as they left the remand centre in the Maze. Barkley then continued to visit Kirkpatrick while he was being held in Crumlin Road jail, though the police were undoubtedly aware of his involvement in INLA activities. It has been suggested that the failure of the police to rearrest Barkley indicates that even as early as March 1982, Kirkpatrick had reached some kind of understanding with them, and that as part of that deal his special friend, Sparky, was not to be touched.

On 23 November 1983, Lord Justice Gibson dismissed charges against seven of the eighteen INLA men being tried on the word of Jackie Grimley. Said Justice Gibson about the witness: "His whole life and evidence was characterised by instability—if not of mind, then certainly of motive, purpose, and behaviour." (*Fortnight*, December 1983.) The court did not find that he was a credible witness. Three others were jailed, three given suspended sentences, and five held on other charges. (One of the accused, Seán Flynn, was not in court, having jumped bail.) But among those cleared were some whom the police most wanted to put away: Steenson, Power, O'Reilly, and Bernard Dorrian.

The police now began to work seriously on Kirkpatrick. His fellow-inmate said: "After Grimley's evidence was rejected, police used to visit him more regularly. He told me he was to get £50,000 plus a new life abroad as well as the seven-year sentence."

Kirkpatrick used to talk a lot about McGrady, the Provisional supergrass who was also held in the Annex. It is likely that McGrady—having undergone a religious conversion of sorts—was influencing him in making up his mind to give evidence, as well as perhaps tutoring him on how best to get a deal with the authorities. From April 1984 to January 1985 Kirkpatrick shared a cell with "Budgie" Allen, the UVF supergrass, who doubtless gave him some tips.

His erstwhile colleagues in the INLA were far from inactive while this was taking place. Outside, they kidnapped first Kirkpatrick's wife and then his stepfather, Richard Hill, and daughter. The INLA threatened to "execute" them unless he withdrew his evidence. Kirkpatrick seemed unperturbed by all this. He was reassured by the RUC that nothing would happen either to his wife or to the others. And Kirkpatrick himself suspected that Liz had gone voluntarily with her captors. Indeed, he was jealous that she might be having an affair with them. They were all eventually released (see chapter 10). Liz issued a statement threatening to divorce him if he did not retract his evidence.

Inside the jail the INLA was also busy. There was a rather Jacobean plot to poison Kirkpatrick using a Eucharist. Kirkpatrick, it was learnt, frequently went to communion. Some ODCs ("ordinary decent criminals") were enlisted. One who assisted the priest was supposed to hand Kirkpatrick the poisoned wafer. But, not surprisingly, the plan fell through. There was also a scheme to smuggle a gun in to have him shot. It too broke down.

On 16 May 1984, Kirkpatrick faced the thirty-one people who were being held on his word in a preliminary hearing, during which he gave them the V sign. "He continued to look confident as he recalled various terrorist incidents and pointed out those he claimed were involved. The defendants, including his sister, Michele Dorrian, remained impassive as the informer, often smiling, calmly gave his evidence. On some occasions he stood up to pick out those he had named." (*Irish Times*, 17 May 1984.)

On 25 May, as Kirkpatrick signed his deposition, disorder broke out in the public gallery, and police moved in with batons drawn. The gallery and dock were cleared out. It was expected that a new preliminary inquiry or preliminary investigation would begin, but instead the Attorney-General intervened. Rather than subject his star witness to another showdown with his former friends and colleagues, he issued a voluntary bill of indictment, returning all the accused for trial. This meant that solicitors for the defendants had little opportunity to question Kirkpatrick to test his likely response to a full-scale cross-examination and assess his strengths and weaknesses before going to trial.

The Kirkpatrick trial began on 22 April 1985, and ran until 18 December. The defence's team of barristers decided not to challenge Kirkpatrick's evidence but to use their cross-examination to undermine his credibility. This ultimately failed. (McGrory was of the opinion that Kirkpatrick should have been challenged directly.)

There were discrepancies in his detailed reconstruction of the crimes. Take, for instance, the murders of the off-duty UDR man Colin Quinn and the Territorial Army man Hugh McGinn. In both cases an examination of the scientific evidence shows that it clashes with Kirkpatrick's statements about the incidents in telling ways. According to Kirkpatrick, Sparky Barkley and Gerard Steenson both shot Quinn. Barkley shot first and then, according to Kirkpatrick, Steenson fired. The tests showed that only one gun was fired, a Browning pistol. In the McGinn case, Kirkpatrick says he fired first at the victim, letting off between five and seven rounds, and then Steenson pushed past him and shot McGinn the same number of times. But tests revealed that only five shots were fired, four of them from the same gun.

It seems clear that Kirkpatrick was trying to give Steenson a greater role in both murders than he may have actually enjoyed. It was because of such testimony, as well as that of other supergrasses, that Steenson was nicknamed "Dr Death" in newspaper accounts of the trials. (Jackie Grimley was forced to admit that he had exaggerated Steenson's role in giving his evidence, which was one of the factors that helped to discredit it.)

There were also serious omissions in Kirkpatrick's evidence. The most glaring concerned the booby-trap bombing that killed two police officers in May 1981. He says nothing about this double murder. It is possible that Kirkpatrick simply bluffed the police that he knew nothing about it. But, alternatively, it is possible that the police agreed that these killings should be concealed or suppressed in order to protect Kirkpatrick's credibility. For him to appear in court as a participant in a double murder of RUC men might have undermined any hope the police had of using him as a witness and of obtaining a deal in exchange for his testimony. There is also evidence that Kirkpatrick tended to trim his evidence to follow subsequent police testimony, changing his original account of events to place it more in line with that of the RUC, as for instance in his various statements about the Great Victoria Street murder of 9 January 1981.[6]

Kirkpatrick's testimony finished on 29 April, and cross-examination began. He was cocky and cunning, ingratiating and at times self-righteous. When Desmond Boal, one of the defence team, pointed out that he had lied to the police when he claimed to have been brigade operations officer for the North, Kirkpatrick said it was an "error", adding: "We are all capable of making errors, my lord, and I am no exception." One telling exchange occurred when Boal, questioning Kirkpatrick about why he was giving evidence against his own sister, asked: "Any other social or human relationship that exists at the moment that you value?" Kirkpatrick answered:

"I don't understand the question, my lord." Quipped Boal: "I'm sorry if it appears to be a difficult one."

The trial was long, and marred by several delays. One of the most significant occurred on 22 May because a defendant, Micky Kearney, had had the tip of his nose bitten off in a fight in the prison courtyard with three other of his fellow-accused. This almost comic episode was in fact the prelude to what would turn out to be the worst internal blood-letting that republicans suffered since the Civil War (see chapters 12 and 13).

The trial finally ended on 18 December 1985 when Justice Carswell found twenty-five of the twenty-seven accused guilty. Some, like Steenson and Power, were sentenced to life for their crimes. Steenson, the judge said, was an "enemy of society". He had been impressed by Kirkpatrick, calling him "cool, composed and courteous." (*Irish News*, 17 December 1985). Though he accepted that Kirkpatrick had tried to bargain for immunity, and had subsequently lied about it, this did not undermine his evidence. According to Carswell, "the end result is that I am satisfied that Kirkpatrick did not fabricate his part in any incident nor did he invent the participation of any of the defendants." (Ibid.)

The Kirkpatrick trial represents the culmination of the supergrass system. By then there had been some thirty supergrasses, whose statements had led to six hundred arrests with nearly three hundred people being charged. Violence had declined dramatically between 1983 and 1986. However, the system was already beginning to unravel. Within a year most of the convictions resulting from the supergrass cases would be overturned on appeal.

The impact on the INLA had been devastating. Though many of its most active volunteers were incarcerated for several years, this proved not to be the most serious impact the supergrass trials and their aftermath had on the organisation. Far more important was the suspicion and bitterness within the organisation that was planted during those years. It would soon grow to deadly proportions.

This, in the end, is the ironic legacy of the man who was more than any other associated with INLA militancy: Gerard Anthony Steenson. Steenson had brought Kirkpatrick into the INLA. He had ignored the petty crimes committed by Kirkpatrick and others. Money from robberies meant for the movement regularly went missing. Kirkpatrick used to boast about how easy it was to rob the Twinbrook post office in west Belfast and how he would keep the money from INLA robberies for himself. He furnished his flat from such robberies, with, among other expensive items, a £500 music centre. According to a former Provo who joined the INLA under Steenson,

"Steenson didn't care what you did in your spare time as long as you were there in the morning to shoot cops."

Under Steenson, petty crime flourished in the Belfast INLA, and informing became rampant. And most importantly, he had introduced the gun as a means of settling internal disputes. He had accentuated divisions within a movement that had always been prone to factionalising.

Yet again, when the INLA seemed on the verge of collapse, it defied all predictions. Instead of breaking apart, it actually raised its violent campaign to levels of bloodshed and horror never equalled before or since in the organisation's history. One of the reasons it was able to do so was the rise to power of a man who became known throughout Ireland as "Mad Dog" McGlinchey.

NOTES

1. Kirkpatrick's equally detailed account in court of the killing of Bucky McCullough gives no hint at all that there was any doubt about the identity of the target. According to Kirkpatrick, the intended target was McCullough.

2. After the trial of Kirkpatrick in December 1985, documents became available that showed that the police knew of the planned attack and were there in unusually large numbers. When one E4A sergeant was asked during the trial how it was that the gunmen had escaped, he said he had been "taking a rest" when Stockman was killed. Though his colleague fired an Ingram submachine-gun at the INLA getaway car, he missed. Rabbie McAllister would later admit that he had forewarned the police about the attack on Stockman.

3. Butler was shot dead by the UDA in January 1993 in a house in south Belfast.

4. Before they reached Dublin, Steenson had been arrested. Two Dublin youths were paid to retrieve them from the dockside, which they did by crashing a car through gates, driving onto the quayside, scooping up the consignment, and speeding off again.

5. The revelations concerning the police presence when Stockman was shot suggest that it might have been planned as such a "set-up" to eliminate Steenson and his colleagues but one that went horribly wrong, costing the UDR man his life.

6. In all, Kirkpatrick made sixty-six statements between 24 March 1982 and 15 May 1984.

10

DOMINIC'S REIGN

As the prison gates closed once more on Gerard Steenson and his comrades in Crumlin Road jail, Belfast, the doors at Port Laoise opened for Dominic McGlinchey. His freedom marked a new departure in the INLA's fortunes when the movement seemed on the brink of breaking up. In taking over the reins of power, Dominic McGlinchey held the organisation together and oversaw a two-year period of mayhem.

McGlinchey had switched his allegiance from the Provisional IRA to the INLA inside Port Laoise following a dispute with the Provos' leadership. He had been serving a four-and-a-half-year sentence for hijacking a Garda car in Monaghan in 1977. While in jail he clashed with the IRA leadership, including the late Sinn Féin vice-president Dáithí Ó Conaill. He was punished by being exiled to a separate landing under the orders of the IRA's OC in the prison, Jimmy Monaghan. One former inmate of Port Laoise gave a hint of the character of the man who was to take over the INLA. "McGlinchey liked giving orders, but he could never take them."

Despite his insubordination inside the Provos, McGlinchey's paramilitary credentials seemed first-class. It was more than a coincidence that he came from south Derry, the region where Séamus Costello made a name for himself as a young IRA guerrilla in the 1950s and that became one of the INLA's strongholds in the North from the mid-1970s on.

McGlinchey, however, came from a different background from the volunteers who followed Séamus Costello out of the Official IRA. He was born in 1954, just two years before the doomed IRA border campaign began. He took part in some of the earliest civil rights marches in the next decade, but he only became involved in the Troubles following his internment in 1971.

On his release at the age of seventeen, McGlinchey opted for the Provisional rather than the Official IRA, both of which were vying for republican supremacy in south Derry at the time. He fought alongside another young militant Provo volunteer, Francis Hughes, who died on hunger strike ten years after internment.

Those who came to know him in the INLA regarded McGlinchey as first and foremost a nationalist. They also felt that he was someone who preferred to control others in positions of authority rather than take responsibility at leadership level. As one founder of the INLA put it, "McGlinchey was a cunning countryman. He liked to manipulate others but did not like to be in overall responsibility." (Interview, 10 April 1993.)

Shortly before his release, McGlinchey contacted a fellow south Derry man who had been INLA chief of staff from 1978 to 1980. He reached him by sending out "coms"—secret communications written on cigarette paper and toilet roll—from Port Laoise. These were smuggled out inside a hollowed-out section of a Celtic cross made by McGlinchey in prison. The former INLA leader confessed that McGlinchey came close to persuading him to rejoin the movement; but he recalled McGlinchey's more off-the-wall comments inside Port Laoise, where the two men were held together for several years. McGlinchey's unpredictable behaviour convinced the former INLA chief of staff that he was better off staying out of the organisation; he already feared there would be a bloodbath caused by internal feuding. With McGlinchey now on board the INLA, the ex-leader concluded that the organisation was inevitably heading in that direction.

McGlinchey had a reputation for being volatile and impulsive. INLA veterans remember McGlinchey advising volunteers, "If you're on the run you should be armed. If not, fuck off home." (Interview, April 1993.) This, the veterans claim, illustrates McGlinchey's one-dimensional militarism. But regardless of this he appeared to be the man who could solve the INLA's festering divisions following the mass arrests after the "supergrass" disaster.

Shortly after he was freed, McGlinchey rose through the ranks to become the INLA's director of operations, and managed with some success to maintain the INLA's reputation as a dangerous and feared paramilitary force. His release in early 1982 coincided with the robbery of explosives from the same place where Séamus Costello acquired the INLA's first explosives in 1975. The theft of a thousand pounds of Eversoft Frangex explosives from Tara silver mines in Nenagh, County Tipperary, was a significant boost to the INLA's arsenal. As a result the organisation embarked on an intensive bombing campaign that culminated in one of the biggest atrocities in the history of the current Troubles.

Throughout 1982 the INLA kept up its onslaught against Unionist political leaders. The RUC had issued a public warning to political representatives of increased risk, following an INLA threat that if loyalists continued to murder Catholics they would "take action against the individuals who were inspiring such actions." This, of course, meant

Unionist politicians.

On 20 May the Democratic Unionist preacher Rev. William Beattie narrowly escaped death after an INLA unit from the Upper Falls planted a fire-bomb outside his Derriaghy home. The Free Presbyterian minister was alerted to the bomb by a neighbour, who found the device outside his house. INLA active service units in Belfast and south Derry also stepped up attacks on Unionist politicians. They left a booby-trap bomb at the home of the Ulster Unionist assemblyman Robert Overend in south Derry on 18 October. His son was slightly injured in the blast at the family's farm. The next day the INLA in Belfast planted a car bomb outside the Official Unionists' headquarters in Glengall Street. The explosion failed to kill anyone, although it caused exterior damage to the administrative centre of Unionist power. Twenty-four hours later the INLA's Upper Falls unit planted another bomb outside a coffee shop in Crumlin where the Official Unionist leader James Molyneaux breakfasted every morning.

The INLA's use of explosives failed to kill any leading Unionists. Instead INLA bombs were to accidentally kill three young Catholics in Belfast in the space of five months. On 2 June sixteen-year-old Pat Smith had been walking along Rugby Avenue with two friends. He came from the Lower Ormeau Road and lived just yards away from the INLA's Belfast Brigade intelligence officer, Jimmy Brown, who had a house in Farnham Street. Brown had set up a bomb trap for RUC officers in Rugby Avenue. Two INLA volunteers from the Lower Ormeau placed a booby-trap device in a helmet attached to a motorbike. As Pat Smith passed by the bike he went over to look at the helmet; on lifting the helmet he detonated the device. In the explosion he was decapitated and his head was later found yards away in another garden. His two friends were injured but survived. The tragedy was a propaganda disaster for the INLA, particularly in the Lower Ormeau. Before the explosion the INLA had been picking up massive support among nationalist youths in the area. Hundreds of young people from the Lower Ormeau, Markets and Short Strand areas had been recruited into the INLA's youth wing. Pat Smith's death was a chilling reminder to them of the price innocent people had to pay for mistakes in their "war".

In July, with McGlinchey firmly established as director of operations, the INLA appointed a new chief of staff. He was a Belfast man who was related through marriage to the legendary Official IRA commander Joe McCann. But the new chief of staff's tenure was to be one of the most short-lived in the history of the organisation.

Despite the new leadership, fatal mishaps continued. On Thursday 16 September the INLA's unit in Divis Flats prepared a booby-trap bomb hidden in a pipe. Their target was a British army foot patrol walking along a balcony. As the patrol passed by, two local boys, fourteen-year-old Stephen Bennet and twelve-year-old Kevin Valliday, came into view. The pipe bomb exploded, killing both boys and a British soldier, twenty-year-old Kevin Waller. Another soldier was seriously injured, and three other children on the balcony were hurt.

Divis Flats had been renowned as an INLA stronghold. Despite this an estimated two hundred residents, most of them women, held a protest march to the IRSP's offices in the Falls Road following Stephen Bennet's funeral two days later. They left a protest note at the door of the offices accusing the INLA and IRSP of having "the blood of our children on your hands." It also contained a demand that the INLA halt its actions in the flats and "immediately remove explosives and other trappings of murder from our district."

In the face of this second propaganda disaster the INLA ordered the suspension of the men responsible for setting off the pipe bomb. In a statement the INLA said it had underestimated the force of the bomb exploding in an enclosed area.

With anger boiling over in the flats, several families with INLA connections moved out of Divis after the explosion, and waited until the community's anger waned. What was once one of the few INLA support bases in Belfast had now become a hostile environment for the organisation.

The Divis and Rugby Avenue explosions gave the INLA a reputation for recklessness. But they also signalled a new twist in the movement's armed campaign in the early 1980s. Within days of the Divis tragedy, INLA bombers struck again, this time at a target in the Republic.

The INLA had always been keen to stress its anti-imperialist and revolutionary credentials. It saw itself as part of an international left-wing terror network that struck out at imperialist powers throughout the world. On Monday 20 September the INLA bombed a radar tracking station at Mount Gabriel, near Schull, County Cork. Admitting responsibility, they claimed that the station carried out high-tech tracking work for NATO, despite the fact that Ireland was officially a neutral state during the Cold War. The Department of Defence denied the allegation, and five suspects were arrested, one of whom was a former captain in a British army tank regiment, Jack Liston, who was convicted and sentenced to nine years in jail.

Schull was targeted, according to a member of the INLA's Army Council, after a meeting between them and their contacts in the PLO. The Palestinians suggested that the INLA attack the radar base in Cork to demonstrate their commitment to the anti-imperialist struggle. To capitalise on the propaganda effect of the Schull bombing, the unit charged to blow the station up were ordered to take a camera with them. The photographs of the damage would be shown around the world in left-wing and pro-Palestinian magazines. But human mishap played its part. After the bombing mission the INLA volunteer detailed to take pictures forgot to take the lens cap off his camera. The propaganda coup was missed.

While IRSP spokesmen boasted about striking at an alleged NATO target and thus taking part in the global struggle against US and British imperialism, some of their comrades in Belfast were involved in more sordid communal squabbles.

The INLA had always been quick to respond to loyalist attacks on its members and the wider nationalist community. On Friday 24 September three people were shot at and one person wounded during UDA attacks in the Short Strand, a Catholic enclave in east Belfast. A day later INLA volunteers in the area retaliated. Two gunmen opened fire at random on Protestants along the Lower Newtownards Road. A pensioner, 68-year-old William Nixon, was shot dead at the scene; a 21-year-old Sunday School teacher, Karen McKeown, was badly wounded and three weeks later died in hospital from her injuries.

On 27 September the INLA set off another booby trap in west Belfast, this time killing a 22-year-old British soldier, Leon Anthony Bushe. Admitting responsibility for this latest explosion, the INLA warned it would increase its bombing attacks on the security forces. Within two months the INLA fulfilled its promise, but this time the bombing campaign shifted to Derry.

The INLA's Derry city brigade had been relatively inactive compared with units in the county and in Belfast. But over the summer months intelligence officers working with the brigade pieced together information on a target several miles outside the city across Lough Foyle. Ballykelly army base is a huge fenced-in military compound containing not only soldiers and their depots but housing estates where army families live. INLA investigations found that many soldiers from the base socialised in the town of Ballykelly. One of the soldiers' favourite haunts was the Dropping Well pub, where a weekly disco took place. According to a senior INLA member in the city, the pub's owner received constant warnings about serving British soldiers.

A small bomb containing about ten pounds of Frangex explosive was placed by an INLA unit in a holdall under one of the pillars holding up the roof of the Dropping Well. The bomb was to bring down the roof on the patrons, thus maximising the number of casualties. On Sunday 5 December an INLA volunteer and his girl-friend went to a safe house across the border in Buncrana, County Donegal. They were detailed to pick up the charger for the Ballykelly bomb; but when they arrived at the safe house there was no charger for them. The couple made the short journey across the border back to Derry. The bombing operation was almost called off at the eleventh hour because of the logistical mishap; but late on Sunday night the INLA volunteer decided to go back to Buncrana. This time the charger was in the safe house. He took the device back to Derry, where the bomb was being assembled.

Twenty-four hours later, on Monday 6 December, the INLA unit carried out their plan. Seventeen people, eleven of them British soldiers and six civilians, were killed instantly. Another civilian later died in hospital. Four of the civilian dead were young women; they were described contemptuously by the INLA as "consorts".

Dropping Well became one of the most notorious atrocities of the Troubles. The death toll meant that by the end of 1982 the INLA had outkilled the Provisional IRA for the first time. Although the INLA issued a statement of regret in relation to civilian deaths, the killing of eleven British soldiers had been a major morale-boosting operation for the organisation, and put the terror group back on the political map. As one Derry INLA volunteer described it, "Ballykelly to us meant sending scores of Brits in coffins back to England. It gave the movement a great boost in terms of morale and prowess. The mood in the movement was very, very buoyant." He also gave another explanation about why the INLA targeted Ballykelly. He claimed that the base's radar and communications centre was tuned in to the NATO defence and tracking network. "Ballykelly was not just a blow against the Brits but also an attack on a NATO installation. We knew the RAF at the base had huge transport helicopters which could be used in an emergency to carry nuclear missiles. That was why the North was on the Russians' nuclear hit list. Ballykelly was part of NATO's nuclear strike force." (Interview, 20 November 1993.)

The Ballykelly bombing caused widespread revulsion in Ireland and Britain. Within a day of the atrocity the Supreme Court in Dublin ordered the extradition of Dominic McGlinchey to the North, even though the INLA was still technically a legal organisation in the South and he was still at large. He was wanted by the RUC in connection with the murder of Hester Mullan, a postmistress shot dead in an attack on her Toomebridge farmhouse in March 1977.

McGlinchey now became public enemy number 1 to the security forces on both sides of the border. On the night of 12 December the RUC thought they had their chance. The E4 anti-terrorist branch had a tip-off that McGlinchey was in Armagh. They were given the exact route that was meant to have been taken by McGlinchey and other INLA members from County Armagh. On Sunday 12 December the E4A unit shot dead Séamus Grew and Roddy Carroll at a checkpoint in Armagh. Both Grew and Carroll had long pedigrees as INLA activists. Grew was the brother of Dessie Grew, OC of the Armagh organisation. He was regarded as an operator and, like his brother, was a close friend of Gerard Steenson, who frequently visited Armagh to see his girl-friend. Carroll had been named by Harry Kirkpatrick as having been involved in a whole series of actions, including robberies and killings.

The killing of Grew and Carroll sparked allegations that the RUC and British army were operating a "shoot-to-kill" policy against republicans, which led to the Stalker inquiry. The RUC squad drafted into Armagh that evening included officers from Belfast who had never served in the county. They also included Constable John Robinson, an Englishman and former soldier. During testimony later given in court, Robinson described how he fired off the fourteen-shot magazine of his Smith and Wesson double-action handgun at Grew and Carroll, who were travelling in a car on a road in the Mullacreevie housing estate. Scientific evidence showed that four of the shots that hit Grew were fired from a distance of between thirty and thirty-five inches. The force of the bullets hitting the two INLA suspects was so ferocious that there were powder burns on Grew's body. (*Irish Times*, 4 April 1984.)

At Robinson's trial in April 1984 an RUC superintendent told Belfast Crown Court that on the night Grew and Carroll were killed the police officers believed the two men were on their way to "ferry" Dominic McGlinchey out of the Republic, where he was on the run. (*Irish News*, 27 March 1984.) The case opened up a can of worms for the RUC. During his trial Robinson said he had been ordered under the Official Secrets Act not to reveal the facts of the incident. He claimed he was protecting Special Branch officers who operated in the Republic. (*Irish News*, 4 April 1984.) Robinson did admit that he was drafted into Armagh on a special operation. He also admitted he was part of a Special Support Unit that was trained at RUC headquarters in Knock in the use of firearms. The gun used to kill Grew and Carroll was not standard issue. He had no detailed knowledge of policing in County Armagh; he was simply told to expect an upsurge in terrorist activity.

Following the shootings the Catholic priests of Armagh issued a joint statement expressing "alarm" over the deaths. They said they were aware of threats by the RUC and UDR against Grew and Carroll just before the shootings. In their strongly worded statement the priests added that "in view of recent similar killings by the RUC in the Lurgan area, it seems that there is now a policy of summary execution without trial." (*Irish News*, 14 December 1982.)

Grew and Carroll were given a paramilitary funeral on 15 December. Four masked INLA volunteers fired a volley of shots over the two coffins just yards away from police and troops on the Cathedral Road. Mourners had formed a protective cordon around the coffins when the INLA members came forward to fire the final salute to their comrades. Several of Carroll's and Grew's families had strong republican connections. Tommy Carroll was given seven hours' parole from the Maze prison to attend the funeral. However, Grew's brother Dessie was refused parole by the prison authorities at Port Laoise. Ironically, Dessie Grew was eventually killed by security forces in disputed circumstances when his IRA unit was ambushed by the SAS near Loughgall, County Armagh, on 9 October 1990.

In the second week of 1983 a new phantom organisation emerged that had dark antecedents in the INLA. The "Catholic Reaction Force" announced that it intended to carry out attacks that would send "shock waves" across Europe if Britain did not act against police and troops allegedly involved in the murder of Catholics. The CRF, which was confined almost exclusively to south Armagh and Belfast, was in reality a cover name for members of the INLA as well as some leading Provos. Under this flag of convenience INLA members became involved in one of the most infamous sectarian atrocities of the decade. Indeed some of those who were to carry out attacks under the CRF flag were INLA volunteers with a shared vendetta not only against the RUC and British army but against the wider Ulster Protestant community.

In response to the threat the INLA posed under McGlinchey's growing influence, the Coalition Government led by Garret FitzGerald outlawed the organisation. Ten days later, on 18 January, an INLA spokesman predicted on an American radio programme that the Provisional IRA would at some time in the near future enter into a broad front with them. It was an arrogant and absurd claim.

Throughout the year differences and antagonisms between the INLA and the Provisionals sharpened. The INLA started to muscle in on rackets run by local smugglers along the Louth-Armagh border. Several of these smugglers approached the IRA for help: the INLA had been demanding amounts up to four and five thousand pounds. The two organisations grew further apart after the INLA blew up the only Protestant pub in Strabane, prompting Sinn Féin's newly elected assemblyman Martin McGuinness to condemn the no-warning attack. With this background of growing tension, a broad front between the INLA and the IRA seemed like wishful thinking.

Six months after the Grew and Carroll killings the INLA believed they had unmasked the informer who provided the information to the RUC on the two men's movements. On 7 May the body of a 43-year-old Portadown man, Eric Dale, was found dumped on a border road at Clontygore near Killeen in south Armagh. He had been shot three times in the upper lip, left temple, and right side of the neck. Four days earlier, Dale had been abducted from his home at Inishkeen, County Monaghan, by up to eight armed and masked men. When they forced their way into the house the only occupants were Dale's wife, Claire, and three of her children. The gang waited for Eric Dale to return home. According to his wife (who is a sister of Éamon McMahon, later murdered also by the INLA), Dale was dragged away by two of the men when he arrived back at the house. As he was taken out of their home, he shouted to his wife: "Claire, I never harmed anybody." (*Irish News*, 6 December 1985.)

Claire Dale recalled that one of the men, who was armed with a rifle, had a northern accent and kept reassuring her that everything was going to be all right. The gunman was lying. Eric Dale was taken to one of the INLA's safe houses in County Clare and questioned about Grew and Carroll. They accused him of setting up their comrades. Tom McCartan was one of Dale's interrogators and subjected him to severe torture. It is understood that Eric Dale admitted he had worked for the Gardaí and passed information about shotguns and handed over detonators belonging to the INLA south of the border. During the interrogation a hot poker was shoved under Dale's armpit to make him confess. He told his tormentors that he had set up Grew and Carroll, then withdrew the confession. Obviously doubt must be cast on any confession that is extracted by such brutal means.

According to several former INLA veterans, Dale's denial was genuine: he had no role in the deaths of Grew and Carroll. Following his murder, Dale's eldest daughter, Fiona Hughes, issued a strenuous denial that her father was an informer. She denounced his killers. "From what we have learned, following the post-mortem, my father was beaten and tortured by the INLA. They say he admitted certain things but nobody could withstand the terrible torture they inflicted on him. My father was no informer: he was a dedicated republican and gave the last eleven years of his life to the republican cause." (*Irish News*, 9 May 1983.) In a letter to the *Irish News* on 4 August 1984 she challenged the INLA leadership to lift the allegation. She mentioned the disappearance of a spy from Castleblayney. "It seems he was connected with the deaths of Grew and Carroll in Armagh—the reason the INLA gave for murdering my father. It is now common knowledge that my father's name has been cleared in the areas of Dundalk, Monaghan and

Castleblayney where he lived and worked for eleven years. I would like his name cleared North of the border." (*Irish News*, 4 August 1984.)

Fiona Hughes's information about another "spy" was accurate. In fact the real traitor was a veteran republican, George Poyntz, who lived in County Monaghan. Several leading INLA members and other republicans have alleged that this man passed on the vital information that led the RUC to kill Grew and Carroll. The suspected traitor owned a bar in Castleblayney and occasionally socialised with Eric Dale in the town. It has now emerged that on the night Grew and Carroll were killed, Dale had been drinking with this man. Dale had been detailed to provide a car when Grew and Carroll crossed the border on their way to meet Dominic McGlinchey. The rendezvous was a picnic car park area at the edge of a forest near the border. Instead Dale got drunk and failed to turn up. These revelations were a shock for many republicans, who regarded Grew and Carroll's betrayer as a solid and loyal supporter of the cause.

Tommy McCartan, the interrogator, had become a willing tool of McGlinchey's. He was used as a hatchet man to carry out some of the organisation's most unpleasant tasks.

McCartan's work for McGlinchey had brought him to New York in the previous summer. He had told the INLA Army Council that he had contacts with arms dealers in the United States and could get American weapons for them. The INLA's coffers were boosted by a robbery of £100,000 from a Securicor van in Cork. The Army Council earmarked £30,000 to buy arms in America. An elaborate plan was set up where Tommy McCartan would go to New York and pose as a clothes buyer, and he was given £10,000 to buy a consignment of clothes from New York's garment district. The idea was that the guns would be hidden in the clothing shipment—an unlikely scheme, given that the inclusion of such heavy material as weapons in a cargo supposedly carrying clothes would have aroused suspicions. The Andersonstown man did travel to New York and spent, some Army Council members estimate, about £7,000 on clothes. The promised arms deal, however, never came off, and McCartan was summoned back to Ireland.

Shortly before eventually becoming chief of staff, McGlinchey met Harry Flynn and Gerry Roche to discuss the direction of the movement. McGlinchey promised that money acquired from recent robberies in the Republic would be used to rebuild the IRSP as a political force. In reality the IRSP's coffers remained empty. McGlinchey's interest in the IRSP, according to Flynn, was minimal. His first concern was to make the INLA the most daring and ruthless paramilitary group in Ireland. In fact the party went into serious decline. At the beginning of 1983 the IRSP's two full-time office workers, Naomi Brennan and Eilish Flynn, resigned from their jobs. The office in Gardiner Street stopped functioning. Ard-Chomhairle meetings became a rarity. Politics was almost exclusively replaced by the gun.

McGlinchey's succession as INLA leader also came about at a time of renewed rupture in the military side of the movement. Before his appointment the then chief of staff was a west Belfast man who had followed Séamus Costello out of the Officials into the new movement in 1975. By June serious disagreements had emerged between the INLA's leader and a number of men loyal to Councillor Seán Flynn and his brother Harry. The INLA's OC in Belfast had threatened Seán Flynn during a bar-room row in the city. After this incident Harry Flynn went to the chief of staff to warn him not to move against his brother. It was a sign of the disintegration of discipline and comradeship within the movement that the men involved in this squalid row had once been founding members of the INLA in Belfast, and old friends besides.

When Harry Flynn warned the INLA leader not to move against Seán, the chief of staff panicked. He approached McGlinchey and accused Harry Flynn of attempting to set off another feud. The row precipitated an Army Council meeting, held at the farmhouse in Ardee that same month.

A motion was put down that Harry Flynn be expelled from the movement after his clash with the chief of staff. The vote went against Flynn. Though McGlinchey had intimated that he would support Flynn, he did not. In disgust, Flynn's old comrade and former IRSP Ard-Chomhairle member Gerry Roche walked out of the meeting. They decided to fight a charge hanging over them since their involvement in a riot outside the British embassy in Dublin two years before. Although they pleaded not guilty, Flynn and Roche were each given eighteen months' imprisonment and sent to Port Laoise prison. It was probably the safest place for an INLA or IRSP member to be at the time.

The upshot of this meeting was that McGlinchey was elected chief of staff of the INLA, more or less reluctantly, it has to be said. For the first time in the history of the organisation the INLA had a leader who was not from the old Official IRA stable. The loss of Flynn and Roche also led to a gradual withdrawal of the core of supporters they had in the Dublin and Munster areas.

McGlinchey's period in charge has been described as a regime of "direct military rule" or "DMR". This, however, is historically inaccurate. DMR dates back long before Dominic McGlinchey was ever a member of the INLA. As far back as the middle of the 1970s INLA prisoners in Long Kesh devised a document calling for direct military rule to be imposed on the party and army in order to forge a revolutionary republican socialist movement. Indeed in 1976 Tommy McCartan was arrested at a house in south-central Dublin with forty INLA documents outlining the necessity of DMR.

McGlinchey's iron grip on the INLA tightened during the summer of 1983. He was particularly concerned to control finance-raising operations and not repeat the debacle of New York. One of the INLA's main sources of finance was the series of frauds and robberies along the south Armagh border. One such scam involved the theft of £140,000 worth of stolen bankers' orders taken in a robbery by a gang operating along the border. One of the main figures in the gang was 35-year-old Éamon McMahon, whose job was to process the bankers' orders. By July no money from the bankers' orders had been channelled into the INLA's coffers. McGlinchey set up a meeting with McMahon and another member of the gang, Patrick Mackin. The two gang members met McGlinchey's wife, Mary, in the Imperial Hotel in Dundalk on 13 July. She managed to persuade the two men to come with her to a car park outside the town.

Trusting Mary McGlinchey was a fatal mistake. Armed INLA men loyal to McGlinchey were waiting for them. McMahon and Mackin were shot in the back of the head; their bodies were put into the back of a car and driven across the border to south Armagh, where they were dumped on a roadside. The message was simple: no-one was to cross McGlinchey while he was in charge. But McMahon and Mackin's friends and comrades did not forgive or forget. They waited for the chance to avenge the two men's death.

The INLA's desperation to persuade Harry Kirkpatrick to drop his allegations against twenty-seven suspects culminated in a kidnapping three months after Dale's death. Kirkpatrick's stepfather, Richard Hill, and his sister-in-law, Diana, were abducted by the INLA and taken to a holiday home near Gortahork, County Donegal. The leadership had ordered the Hills to be killed. However, their guard, Patrick Ward, objected to killing the two prisoners and decided to tip off the Gardaí as to their whereabouts. The Hills were eventually rescued when members of the Special Task Force surrounded the house and freed the captives.

Ward was later abducted by the INLA and taken to the house in County Clare to face McGlinchey's wrath. While there he was also tortured. His interrogation included being forced to sit down on a boiling-hot stove by Tommy McCartan. The Derry man knew he could be facing death for saving the Hills. Luckily for him his two guards fell asleep and he managed to escape and handed himself over to Gardaí. Eventually the Hills' reluctant executioner made a new life for himself in Canada.

Despite the failure to stop Kirkpatrick, military activity continued unabated throughout the summer. On Saturday 13 August Dominic McGlinchey took direct charge from Dundalk of one of two operations planned that day across the border. One was an attack on an RUC reservist at a security barrier in Markethill, County Armagh. The other was to be carried out in Dungannon, also against local police.

According to statements made by an INLA informant to the RUC in Gough Barracks, Armagh, after the incidents, both operations were to be carried out at ten o'clock in the morning. He claimed, however, that the INLA active service unit on the Dungannon operation drove into a trap. Armed police were waiting for them, and in a subsequent gun battle INLA volunteers Brendan Convery, aged twenty-five, and John Gerald Mallon, aged twenty-seven, were shot dead. One year after the two shootings, while being interviewed in Gough Barracks, an INLA suspect told RUC officers: "The Markethill job and the Dungannon job were to be done at the same time—ten o'clock. The Markethill one was done too early and the boys on the Dungannon job drove into a trap." (Interview notes from Gough Barracks obtained by the authors in February 1993.)

It was clear from the Dungannon debacle that inside information from at least one source had been passed to the security forces about the operation. The RUC were lying in wait for the INLA unit. The three-man INLA team that had gone to Markethill also failed to kill any of their intended targets, and they returned to Dundalk to face McGlinchey. The informant who admitted supplying guns for the Markethill and Dungannon operations described how McGlinchey reacted when his unit returned south that day. He was summoned to see McGlinchey and forced to explain the loss of weapons and men in Dungannon. "McGlinchey went mad and called us all stupid cunts." (Ibid.)

Throughout the interview about the Markethill and Dungannon operations, the INLA suspect from Armagh was pressed to outline McGlinchey's involvement.

"We want to know everything that you were involved in."

"It's hard for me to talk about these things."

"Why?"

"Because of McGlinchey."

"Are you scared of McGlinchey?"

"Isn't everybody?" (Ibid.)

Within a month, INLA members under McGlinchey's direct control on the Armagh-Louth border picked off another RUC target. This time they were more successful. On Tuesday 6 September an INLA unit shot dead 61-year-old RUC Constable Johnny Wasson outside his home in Duke's Grove. According to the statement made by the same suspect on the Markethill and Dungannon operations, the INLA shot Johnny Wasson because he was an easy target. "I was in Dundalk about a month before it happened. DMcG was talking to me and he said it would be easy to shoot an old cop Wasson in Armagh. I said it would be easy as he lives at Duke's Grove and travels in and out of the Barracks every day." (Ibid.)

While the border unit was extremely active in hitting security targets, the climate of fear and suspicion within the INLA intensified. Éamon McMahon and Patrick Mackin were not the only members suspected of double-crossing McGlinchey. He had his doubts about certain members in Belfast. Several Belfast volunteers were summoned to McGlinchey's headquarters at the Ardee farmhouse just off the main Dundalk–Belfast road on Tuesday 25 October. One of those McGlinchey suspected was Harry Kirkpatrick's closest friend, Gerard "Sparky" Barkley. Travelling with Barkley to Ardee were a Lower Falls INLA volunteer, Paul "Bonanza" McCann, Seán Mackin, and the current INLA chief of staff.

Once they arrived McGlinchey started to accuse Barkley of "doing homers" (carrying out robberies with INLA guns for himself). Barkley admitted he was involved in robberies for his own gain but stressed that he was no longer an INLA volunteer. Despite his criminal record, Barkley was extremely popular with many INLA volunteers in Belfast. He was known to be a "likable rogue" who built a strong friendship with Steenson and, of course, his old pal Kirkpatrick. Indeed Barkley was one of many petty criminals whom Steenson had recruited into the INLA during the early 1980s.

After admitting he was now an "ODC" (ordinary decent criminal), Barkley was formally dismissed from the INLA by McGlinchey. Barkley and his friend Mackin were told they could go; McCann remained at the farmhouse while the other three Belfast men drove away towards the main road. As they passed by another of the two farmhouses under the INLA's control near Ardee they were flagged down by other INLA members. They sent Mackin off on a spurious errand to separate him from Barkley. Barkley meanwhile was asked to return to the original farmhouse, as McGlinchey had one more thing to discuss with him. He found himself pinned between two heavies who sat on either side of him in the car. When he arrived at the front door of a nearby location known as the "Big House", Paul McCann stepped behind him and shot him in the back of the head.

McGlinchey had ordered McCann to "execute" Barkley—he did not take kindly to volunteers using the INLA to do "homers".

Mackin panicked when he heard that Barkley had been shot. He bolted for Dublin, fearing that he would be next on the list.

Barkley's body was dumped in the back of a car and driven around for several days. It was eventually found naked just south of the Cavan-Fermanagh border on Wednesday 26 October. His killers had driven his body across the border as far away as possible from Ardee. In a statement the INLA said their victim had been involved in criminal activities and was suspected of being a police informer. One issued from the Republic accused him of being an informer; another statement, purporting to come from the INLA in Belfast, denied the allegation and claimed that Barkley had been killed by British agents!

The death of Gerard "Sparky" Barkley proved to be a cause of bitter dissent within the INLA's ranks. The 27-year-old west Belfast man had many close friends within the movement in his native city. They did not believe he was an informer. Harry Kirkpatrick, on the other hand, was bolstered in his determination to testify against his former comrades (see chapter 9). The deadly divisions within the organisation were clearly illustrated by the two contradictory INLA statements released after Barkley's body was discovered.[1]

The killing underlined the growing belief among some volunteers that McGlinchey was intent on wiping out all dissenters in the organisation. Seán Mackin, who had gone to Dublin on learning of Barkley's death, contacted prominent members of the movement. It was suggested that they get McGlinchey before he got them. Unfortunately for Mackin, one of those present at the Dublin meeting was an ally of the chief of staff. He conveyed the potential threat to McGlinchey. Mackin was fortunate enough to discover this and, fearing retribution, fled to the United States. McGlinchey did send a message that assured Mackin and others that he had no intention of starting a feud. Mackin wisely ignored this peace offer.

Mackin remained in America fighting a deportation order; his defence was that if he returned to Ireland his life would be in danger. Luckily for Mackin, the US immigration authorities eventually offered him asylum in 1993.

As a result of the deepening paranoia within the ranks under McGlinchey's reign, several members of the Army Council would only attend meetings carrying guns. An even clearer sign of the deepening rift within the INLA came three days after Barkley's body was found, when his INLA friends and comrades staged a paramilitary funeral for him at his west Belfast home. The funeral display was a calculated gesture of defiance to McGlinchey's leadership.

Even along the border the INLA seemed fragmented and out of control. Personal grudges and an insatiable thirst for revenge took over from political thinking. On the evening of 21 November, Pastor Bob Bains was leading his congregation in hymns at the Mountain Lodge Pentecostal assembly hall in Darkley in south Armagh. As the service began, three gunmen, all known to have connections with the INLA in the border region, opened fire on the congregation. More than thirty-five shots were fired in the attack, eleven at the side of the pre-fab hut, twelve in the entrance hall, and many inside when the gunmen sprayed the worshippers.

Three people died in the attack. They were Victor Cunningham, aged thirty-nine, of Orlit Cottages, Beechill, David Wilson, aged forty-three, of the Temple, Keady; and Harold Brown, aged fifty-nine, of Annvale Road, Keady. Seven other people, four men and three women, were injured. They included Pastor Bain's daughter Sally, who was shot in the elbow and leg.

In a statement admitting the attack on the Pentecostal hall later that evening, the "Catholic Reaction Force" threatened to make the Darkley murders "look like a picnic" unless Protestants ceased attacks on the nationalist community. They said the killings were in direct retaliation for "the murderous sectarian campaign in County Armagh and County Down over the past two years by the Protestant Action Force." (*Irish News*, 22 November 1983.)

The aftermath of Darkley produced not only the expected revulsion but also hysteria. RUC spokesmen blamed Dominic McGlinchey for being involved in the triple murder: they linked the weapons used in the atrocity to INLA killings such as that on 26 May of Reserve Constable Colin Carson in the centre of Cookstown. The Ruger rifle used in the Darkley killings had also been linked to the murder of RUC Constables Snowden Corkey and Ronnie Irwin in Markethill on 16 November 1982.

An IRSP spokesman, Kevin McQuillan, was quick to condemn the Darkley shootings. But his condemnation was coloured by a rather ludicrous claim that the guns used in the murders were seized by the security forces in an arms haul and that the attack was the work of British intelligence. (Ibid.) McQuillan should have been looking closer at home for the source of this latest sectarian atrocity.

Now McGlinchey not only had his own dissidents to contend with. Following the Darkley killings, his name became associated with the sectarian atrocity. In fact McGlinchey had nothing to do with the murders. A member of the INLA nominally under his control had carried out the shooting, along with two others, using INLA weapons. One of those who pulled the triggers was a member of a well-known republican family from Armagh; he travelled from Dublin to carry out the attack in revenge for the death of two relatives, one at the hands of the RUC and the other slain by the UVF. The other two were also part of an INLA team that operated under McGlinchey's auspices along the border and are known to the RUC.

The INLA chief of staff was quick to distance himself from the Darkley massacres. Six days after the shootings he gave an interview to the *Sunday Tribune* in which he condemned the killings. He admitted, however, that the INLA was indirectly linked to the incident. Later that same month McGlinchey, still on the run, gave a detailed interview for the November 1983 issue of the *Starry Plough*. Asked about the Darkley killings, he replied: "I condemn them. Those people were only hillbilly folk who had done no harm to anyone. They are in no way a legitimate target. These killings are contrary to republican socialism. They cannot be defended."

Despite McGlinchey's condemnation of the Darkley atrocity, it was a painful symptom of a deeper malaise afflicting the INLA. The organisation sworn to build a secular workers' republic found it hard on occasion to resist the temptation to get involved in Catholic revenge attacks. In rural areas in particular, INLA members were all too often drawn into bitter personal disputes with loyalists. The murder by the UVF or UDA of nationalists closely associated with the INLA or IRSP sucked them into a vortex of sectarian reprisals and revenge attacks. Darkley was simply the latest bloody milestone on the degenerative path taken by a deeply sectarian element within the INLA.

During the latter half of 1983, Ireland and Britain were gripped by "Mad Dog" fever. McGlinchey was sighted all over the country as the nationwide manhunt for him continued. The INLA leader gained the same reputation as Gerard Steenson: he could be everywhere at the same time. He was also blamed for almost every paramilitary operation, including (initially at least) the kidnapping of the Quinnsworth supermarket executive Don Tidey. Indeed it was during a Garda search for Tidey that one of the more farcical incidents of the McGlinchey manhunt occurred.

During house-to-house searches on 2 December, gardaí stumbled on McGlinchey and some fellow INLA members at a house in the Carrigtohill area of Cork. At around 2:20 p.m. Garda John Dennehy and Sergeant Tim Bowe knocked on the front door of the bungalow. At first there was no reply. The gardaí attempted to force their way into the house; as they did so McGlinchey and his men appeared. The gardaí were forced at gunpoint into the house and then stripped of their uniforms; they were then tied up. After about three hours the two gardaí managed to struggle free. By that time McGlinchey and his entourage had escaped in a neighbour's car they had hijacked. It had been a deeply embarrassing incident for the Garda Síochána.

McGlinchey had eluded them again.

His luck ran out, however, by the following spring. On St Patrick's Day 1984 a joint Garda-army operation finally cornered McGlinchey at a house in County Clare. Such was the determination to catch the INLA leader that eleven members of the Gardaí, all armed with Uzi submachine-guns, arrived at the house in Rathlaheen South, Newmarket-on-Fergus. An officer attached to the Special Detective Unit, Superintendent Seán O'Mahony from Dundalk, said he saw his men open fire after gunfire came from the besieged house. He said his men fired a total of ninety shots, eighty-nine from Uzis and one from a Walther pistol.

Detective-Sergeant Joseph Egan, also from the Special Detective Unit, led a party into the house. He called on the people upstairs to lay down any weapons and surrender. As he did so there was a burst of machine-gun fire. On his radio Egan was told there was man armed with a machine-gun on the roof. "I looked up through a skylight on the flat roof and saw a man overhead with a gun pointed in my direction. I fired a short burst of shots from my Uzi at this man and he disappeared from sight." (*Irish Times*, 22 February 1986.) He then heard a man's voice shout down that he was a spokesman for the INLA and he wanted to negotiate the end of the gun battle. The man asked for a priest to be brought to the house. At about a quarter past seven Rev. Timothy Tuohy arrived at the siege. When he got to the door of the house, he went inside and negotiated with Dominic McGlinchey. Eventually McGlinchey and his comrades gave themselves up. It was the end of Dominic's reign.

After his arrest McGlinchey became embroiled in a legal quagmire that saw him extradited once from the Republic to the North and then back to the South again. Three days after his arrest he was handed over through a funnel of gardaí to the RUC at the Killeen border crossing point. The huge cross-border security operation marked a legal landmark, as the INLA leader was the first republican paramilitary to be extradited from the Republic to Northern Ireland.

McGlinchey was eventually brought to trial in December 1984 and on Christmas Eve was convicted of the murder of the Toomebridge postmistress, Hester McMullan. He was sentenced to life imprisonment.

However, the saga of Dominic McGlinchey took another twist the following year. On appeal, his murder conviction was quashed at Belfast Crown Court because of a legal technicality. The decision by Lord Justice Gibson to quash the life sentence rested almost entirely on the contents of sworn affidavits McGlinchey gave to gardaí. These admitted his membership of the Provisional IRA in south Derry at the time of Mrs McMullan's murder.

The intention was to show political motive and thus avoid extradition. In a 45-minute judgement Lord Justice Gibson said membership of one active service unit did not necessarily mean that every member was engaged in every terrorist operation in that area. He even dismissed the use of McGlinchey's fingerprints on the car used in the attack on Mrs McMullan's home as evidence. The fingerprints could have been put there thirty hours after the attack, and did not support a conviction.

Once again Dominic McGlinchey was in the headlines. On 11 October 1985 he became the first person to be re-extradited from Northern Ireland to the Republic. The RUC handed McGlinchey back to the Gardaí at the spot where he was first extradited to the North over a year before. He was then arrested on charges relating to the siege in County Clare where he was captured on St Patrick's Day 1984. Around twenty spectators looked on as he was passed through a cordon of gardaí shortly after 4:00 p.m. at Killeen. One man held up a placard that read, *Céad míle fáilte*; another placard said, *Welcome home, Daddy*.

Dominic McGlinchey was eventually convicted in March 1986 for his part in the Newmarket-on-Fergus siege two years before. In Port Laoise prison he became a model inmate and spent a great deal of time studying. His own troubles, however, were far from over. Bitterness left by his legacy as INLA leader would bring tragedy to his own door just a year after his final conviction.

Dominic McGlinchey was probably the most famous and most charismatic INLA chief of staff since Séamus Costello. But the INLA under Costello was run on the lines of collective leadership. McGlinchey's reign was a period of one-man rule. The organisation became associated with the fortunes of one man. A founding INLA member was scathing about McGlinchey's effect on the organisation. "Under McGlinchey, collective leadership collapsed. There were no more Army Council meetings. It was just him running the whole show. Once he was gone the group faced collapse." (Interview, 15 December 1993.)

McGlinchey's leadership left another bitter legacy, which was to affect him personally over the next decade. Because he was the personification of all that happened to the INLA from 1982 to early 1984, those who suffered under his reign blamed McGlinchey personally. Those associated with Éamon McMahon and Eric Dale were among many nursing dark grudges against him.

McGlinchey had only been a free man for three months when some old enemies tried to kill him. On the night of Saturday 14 June 1993 he drove to his son Dominic's birthday party at a house in Newtowndarver, County

Louth. As he arrived at the house at around eight o'clock two men armed with a handgun and an automatic weapon fired at him. McGlinchey ran into the house for cover. Before diving inside he put both his hands on the top of his head to protect himself; the gunmen shot him in the hands and one bullet struck his skull. He was operated on in Louth County Hospital in Dundalk and recovered quickly.

In the aftermath of the shooting McGlinchey blamed British intelligence for the murder attempt. Other erroneous reports alleged that former INLA veterans close to Gerard Steenson tried to kill him. The choice of venue to gun down one of Ireland's most notorious paramilitary figures, however, pointed to the real identity of the gang. It was not an accident that they had chosen the spot near Ardee, County Louth, because it was there that he assumed the leadership of the INLA almost exactly ten years before.

McGlinchey must have realised that it was unlikely he would die peacefully in his bed. The men who tried to murder him at Ardee were still determined to settle scores. McGlinchey himself was keen to avenge the murder of his wife (see chapter 13). When he was released from Port Laoise he was known to have a list of fifteen enemies he wanted to eliminate.

At about eleven o'clock on the evening of 10 February 1994, McGlinchey was gunned down in front of his sixteen-year-old son, Dominic, outside a telephone booth in Drogheda. As he lay dying in front of his son, eyewitnesses reported that he cried out, "Jesus, Mary, help me." Even with his bloody reputation, his last moments were strangely moving. A ruthless paramilitary activist who had once led an organisation that claimed to be Marxist was calling out in his dying moments for Christ's help. The horrifying impact of witnessing such cold brutality on McGlinchey's son can only be guessed at.

At McGlinchey's funeral three days later in Bellaghy, the former mid-Ulster MP Bernadette McAliskey called him the finest republican of his generation. But McGlinchey's effect on the organisation Mrs McAliskey once supported was negative. His anarchic activities and murderous paranoia brought the INLA/IRSP movement into disrepute within the republican community. The killings he personally carried out or ordered others to do fuelled a vicious blood feud that may still not have run its murderous course.

The former MP also launched into a bitter attack on journalists, whom she branded as "dogs, curs, scum of the earth." (*Guardian*, 14 February 1994.) Such an irrational outburst against the media was proof that Mrs McAliskey, once the darling of the world's press, had retreated into a cul-de-sac of bitterness.

But the "mad dog" image conjured up by sections of the Irish and British media did not give the full picture of Dominic McGlinchey. Undoubtedly he was motivated by ideological rather than personal reasons. Shortly before his death he gave an interview in which he denounced the Downing Street declaration and urged the Provisionals to reject it. McGlinchey was not simply a dog of war; it was clear that he was not mad either. As a result of his imprisonment and extradition he spent hours in prison cells studying constitutional law. By the time he was released he was well versed in constitutional matters.

While on the run in 1983 the INLA chief of staff played down the effect on the movement of his possible capture. In the interview with the *Starry Plough* he was asked about capture or even death at the hands of the Gardaí. "I'll deal with these situations as they arise. I think it is important to realise that the movement will not end with me. I'm only one individual, not God." (Ibid.)

Shortly after the Darkley massacre, McGlinchey re-emphasised that the INLA would be unaffected if he was to be arrested or killed. "I will be remembered for nothing. I have no illusions about myself. There is no glory or anything to this. The only people who will remember me will be my family and particularly my children." (*Sunday Tribune*, 27 November 1983.)

It was a chilling prediction of his own sordid end. After all, there was hardly anything glorious about being mowed down in front of his son outside a telephone booth on a cold winter's evening. There was nothing admirable or momentous in a death caused by what was in essence a Sicilian-type family feud.

His comments in 1983 were a modest assessment of his contribution to the INLA's history. Such modesty, however, masked an underlying problem for the INLA once McGlinchey was removed. As a formidable and ruthless operator, McGlinchey had acted like a makeshift bolt that held the INLA machine together when it seemed on the verge of breaking into pieces. Once that bolt was removed on 17 March 1984, that terror machine finally broke into disparate parts. The descent into chaos had begun.

NOTES

1. Though a minor figure in the INLA, "Sparky" Barkley is in a way one of the most memorable. He made a deep impression on many who knew him as a charming rogue. Shortly before McGlinchey had him murdered, he had helped organise a robbery for the organisation near Sligo. Though it didn't work out, Barkley paid for the rented cars that were to be used in the job

out of his own pocket. A former member of the Official IRA at whom Barkley had taken a pot-shot during the 1975 feud reported that afterwards Barkley had apologised, saying it was "nothing personal". He later accompanied the Official IRA man on a visit to the man's ailing mother. The Official said he cried when he learnt of Sparky's death. A former INLA leader said of Barkley: "He enjoyed life. He loved money, and he hated the Brits."

11

BROTHERS ABROAD

Overhead the leaden-grey sky of a Paris winter promised nothing but rain. To the long straggle of visitors, mostly women, who waited to enter La Santé prison, which reared up in front of them, its massive grey stone walls promised, if possible, even less. There were no concessions to comfort in this oppressive institution: no seats to sit on, no shelters to huddle under from the weather. Only a railing along the pavement and the high granite walls of the prison itself are there as support for those who grow weary after hours of waiting in the biting cold to be filtered in, ten at a time, to see their menfolk.

The prison population is made up mostly of Arabs, Africans, and Indonesians: comparatively few Frenchmen find their way into its dungeon-like cells. However, in the winter of 1983 the prison held an Irishman: Michael Plunkett.

Plunkett, a founding member of the IRSP, for four years its general secretary and for a few months in 1979 its chairman, had been arrested along with Stephen King and Mary Reid in Paris in August 1982 and charged with possession of explosives and weapons. The pinkish-coloured explosives were of the type that had been used in the assassination of Airey Neave and were allegedly found above the toilet in Plunkett's flat at 82 Rue Diderot in the Vincennes area of Paris. It was but the beginning of one of the longest political intrigues ever to consume French politics.

Stephen King, from County Tyrone, was wanted on an arms possession charge in the Republic, having jumped bail. Mary Reid joined the IRSP in 1977 and had been the party's education officer and editor of its monthly newspaper, the *Starry Plough*. She had married Cathal Goulding's son, but the couple parted soon afterwards. Reid had a son by the marriage, who was named after his grandfather.

Mick Plunkett was one of the movement's most important figures. He had been a close friend of Séamus Costello. A Dún Laoghaire man, he had come to the Official republican movement through Costello's influence. Like many others who Costello influenced and who went with him when the

Officials split, Plunkett did not come from a republican background. His roots lay in the left. As a member of Official Sinn Féin, Plunkett first rose to prominence as chairman of the Dún Laoghaire cumann, one of the most militant in the movement. In 1971 the Dún Laoghaire unit of the Official IRA wanted to take action against auctioneers who were demolishing houses. When the Official leadership demanded proof that such action would have popular support, the Dún Laoghaire activists produced a petition with five thousand signatures demanding that something be done. The operation was still rejected; instead, the militants had to make do with destroying demolition machinery and bombing the headquarters of MBK auctioneers in Dublin.

In May 1972, after the Official IRA called its cease-fire, Plunkett's cumann withdrew from Official Sinn Féin in protest. Plunkett wanted Seán Garland and Cathal Goulding to reassure its members that the armed struggle would not be abandoned. At that time, according to Plunkett, there were twenty-three units of the Official IRA in Dublin alone, comprising a minimum of two hundred activists; but the cease-fire and the developing revisionism of the leadership saw many of them fall away. Some joined Costello two years later when he formed the IRSP and INLA. According to Plunkett, "the leadership was overtaken by the North: they didn't see the revolutionary potential of the northern situation." (Interview, December 1993.)

Plunkett became one of the driving forces behind the new movement. He was in the unusual position of being trusted by Costello and respected by the Belfast activists. He had been the IRSP's representative during the prison negotiations over political status in 1976 (see chapter 8). He had acted as Costello's election agent in the 1977 general election. Two years later, Bernadette McAliskey wanted him to organise her election campaign when she was running for a seat in the European Parliament. However, by June 1979, when the election was held, Plunkett had vanished from the Irish scene, having jumped bail on a charge of possession of bomb-making materials that had been found in his flat (see chapter 7).

Plunkett fled to Paris. He was no stranger to the Continent. While still a member of the Officials he had visited West Germany and France several times. In West Germany he was close to Rudolf Raab[1] and Heinz Joachim Stemler, members of the Revolutionary Cells organisation, and in France he knew Roger Faligot, a left-wing journalist who supported Irish republicans and frequented their expatriate circles in Paris and elsewhere. (Top-ranking Provisionals such as Ruairí Ó Brádaigh would stay with him when visiting the city.)

When the Officials split, Plunkett made further trips abroad for the breakaway group in 1978 and in January 1979, when he was in Frankfurt speaking about the H-block issue. On the run in the spring of 1979, he was given a refuge by Faligot on the sixteenth floor of an apartment building in the Rue Saint-Fargeau in the twentieth arrondissement of Paris. Then Faligot introduced him to Bernard Jegat.

Jegat was one of those French petty-bourgeois leftists who looked like the perennial student, sympathising with various Third World liberation movements and drawn towards the political underground with its ambience of menace, political intrigue, and illegality, a cloak-and-dagger world where just occasionally, as Jegat discovered, there is a real dagger under the cloak. He went to the University of Vincennes, an alternative, working-class university, and studied "Cinema and the anti-imperialist struggle", for which he obtained two credits. He set off for Lebanon in 1976 to make a film on "the legitimate Palestinian resistance struggle". However, his main aim seems to have been to join a guerrilla training camp. History intervened in the form of the Syrians, who, when they invaded Lebanon in 1976, forced him to leave Beirut and return to Paris. After a brief spell as a freelance journalist for Belgian radio and television in Paris he found his next great cause: the Northern Ireland struggle. One of Faligot's books on the Irish problem inspired Jegat to contact the author to ask him if he would help him join an Irish guerrilla training camp. Jegat was interested in the INLA, with which he could identify because, like him, it was left-wing.

Instead of finding him a training camp, Faligot brought with him a bearded, rather burly Irishman called James McCabe—one of the pseudonyms that Plunkett had adopted for his Continental existence. They first met in a café near the Forum des Halles, and Jegat was given to understand that McCabe was in danger. The British secret services were seeking him; he needed a safe house for a time. Jegat agreed to put him up for three weeks, by which time "McCabe" would have found other accommodation among sympathisers.

This was the beginning of Jegat's involvement in the Irish scene. Gradually, he was drawn into the INLA's gun-running network on the Continent by agreeing to store small amounts of weapons and explosives.

That network had originated in 1977 with West German members of a solidarity group who had Palestinian contacts (see chapter 6). The main contact between 1977 and 1981 was a PLO representative studying in Germany who, according to INLA men who met him, looked like Ronnie Bunting. The contact belonged to F18, the intelligence section of Arafat's Fatah, which remained the INLA's only Middle Eastern arms link. Though other, more extremist Palestinian factions did approach the organisation with proposals to establish connections, they were rejected.

The network developed between 1977 and 1981, channelling arms from Palestinian sources in Lebanon via West Germany (and later Switzerland) to France and thence to Ireland. The first shipment that Jegat held for the INLA arrived in July 1979 and consisted of six Herstal GPA pistols, 35 automatic pistols, and 4 Uzi submachine-guns. Among the weapons that came down this route and passed through Jegat's apartment were several hundred VZORs—the Czechoslovak pistols frequently used by Steenson's units when at their peak in 1981. Jegat reported that between 1979 and 1981 there were ten deliveries of these pistols in lots of twenty-five. (Jacques Derogy and Jean-Marie Pontaut, *Enquête sur Trois Secrets d'État*, Robert Laffont, Paris.)

The most the INLA ever spent on acquiring this hardware was £25,000, but it put them in possession of SKS rifles, Rhodesian submachine-guns, Browning pistols, and AK47 automatic rifles. The organisation also acquired some Skorpion pistols from al-Fatah, but these were donated free of charge. As well, there was the pink Soviet-made explosive that claimed the life of Airey Neave, among others.

Late in 1979 another important link in the chain was established when James Kerr, an ex-employee of Tara silver mines, Nenagh, and an old friend of Séamus Costello's, went on the run in Europe. Kerr, then in his sixties, had a varied and colourful past. As an IRA man he had served time in the Curragh in the 1940s; but he signed himself out, renouncing the IRA in order to fight the Nazis, which he did by joining the RAF and becoming a rear gunner on a bomber. He returned to republican circles and took part in the 1950s IRA campaign and later was a strong supporter of Costello. He was wanted by the Gardaí in connection with explosives that went missing from the silver mines. In late 1979 he ended up in Basel, Switzerland, where he used the aliases Anthony Herbert and James MacCharra. In Basel he lived with a young German woman who was a member of the Revolutionary Cells organisation. The French police acquired photographs of Kerr showing him in Plunkett's company. They also believed he was part of the Palestinian-linked INLA arms network. In November 1984, Kerr was extradited from Switzerland to Ireland, where he served a ten-year prison sentence.

Jegat would later tell French police that "James McCabe" and another Irishman, Harry Flynn, were involved in helping establish his apartment as a staging-post in the arms run from Lebanon across Europe to Ireland, and later for arms that came from PLO sources in Prague. He says that they proposed he adopt the code-name "Hennessy", and they established a procedure for telephoning him: a mute call, cut off as soon as his voice was recognised. This would mean that one of them would be arriving within forty to forty-five minutes. (Ibid.)

However, Jegat began to have a change of heart about his underground connections after François Mitterand, a socialist, was elected President of France on 10 May 1981. It seems he tried to interest Regis Debray in his credentials. Debray was a left-wing expert on Third World guerrilla movements who had been appointed a special adviser to Mitterand at the Élysée Palace. Jegat imagined that Debray would give him some sort of role in the new regime; instead he was ejected from the building as a suspected agent provocateur.

On 24 November 1981 the INLA launched a short-lived "European offensive"—which was among the first of such endeavours in the current Troubles. It planted a bomb outside the British consulate in Hamburg, which failed to explode. A day later it bombed the headquarters of the 7th Signals Regiment of the British army at Herford in north-eastern Germany. The attack on an accommodation block went awry as the device rolled off the roof of the barracks, where it had been left, and landed against the wall. It exploded, smashing windows and damaging the wall of one building, but caused no casualties. A day after the Herford bombing, West German police stopped a car speeding on the autobahn between Saarbrücken and Mannheim, not far from the scene of the attack. It was driven by the Revolutionary Cells activist Heinz Joachim Stemler. His passenger was carrying a passport in the name of Patrick G. Monaghan, but it bore the photograph of Mick Plunkett. Stemler was fined and released. Later, however, the French police would use this as evidence that the INLA was operating from its base in Paris to strike at installations elsewhere on the Continent, with the aid of other left-wing groups.

According to his own account, Jegat was by now becoming uneasy about the developing terrorist strategy of the INLA. He claims that the INLA asked him to take control of a "command centre" that would link up with German, Swiss and other extremist organisations. This alarmed him, as such activities seemed increasingly unrelated to the Irish cause. (Derogy and Pontaut, *Enquête sur Trois Secrets d'État.*) But he still permitted the INLA to use his apartment to store their weapons and explosives. In June 1982 he took delivery of a box of detonators, two Italian pistols equipped with silencers, and a set of blank identity cards. On 6 August, Jegat claims Plunkett and Flynn visited him and discussed the possibility of co-operating with Palestinian extremists based in Paris. Jegat alleged that Plunkett planned to meet Palestinians the next day. The two Irishmen, according to Jegat, said that they might telephone him over that weekend to arrange a meeting for the following Monday, 9 August.

No call came. Instead came the news of a massacre. Goldenberg's, a Jewish delicatessen and restaurant in the Rue des Rosiers, the main street that runs through the Mairie—Paris's Jewish quarter—had been attacked by Arab terrorists. Six people had been killed and twenty-two injured and mutilated. It was the latest in a series of terrorist outrages in France that year, including an attack by the left-wing extremist group Action Directe on a synagogue in the Rue de Pavée. It was also the most brutal. The atrocity electrified France and the socialist who had recently become its President. Eight days later, France heard Mitterand declare war on terrorism. Following this declaration, the Élysée Palace issued a statement claiming that the French police were on the verge of an important breakthrough against the international terrorist network operating on French territory.

Jegat, according to his own account, waited two weeks after the Goldenberg killings for Plunkett and Flynn to show up. When they did not, and disgusted by the massacre in the Rue des Rosiers, he approached some contacts in the world of journalism with his story about Irishmen with links to Arab terrorists. He told them he wanted to get in contact with the authorities, and asked that he be put in touch with Commander Christian Prouteau, special security adviser to the President and the founder and former head of the élite Groupe d'Intervention de la Gendarmerie Nationale (GIGN), or one of his subordinates. The Socialist government, distrusting the normal police because of its right-wing political sympathies, had come to rely on the GIGN. Eventually, on 24 August, Jegat was introduced to Captain Paul Barril.

Captain Barril, short, with a powerful, taut physique and wild, staring eyes, was a different kind of political animal from Jegat. Barril seemed like a creature of the world of the extreme right, a marginal world like that of Jegat's, which attracts its own mixture of unstable individuals, some of whom are Walter Mittys and others deadly fanatics. He had been involved in operations against a banned Corsican nationalist organisation. He was linked to an attempt to import arms from Belgium into France, arms which Barril said were to be used to entrap would-be terrorists. But Barril was in fact more apolitical than anything. His overriding impulse was ambition. He wanted medals. His policy was to get to know his enemy well by whatever means, then crack them by whatever means; then collect the medal, with which came honour and glory.

These two men from the outer fringes of the political world now became inextricably linked in a series of events that would scandalise French politics.

Barril, in plain clothes, drove Jegat to his office in the headquarters of the GIGN. Jegat had with him Identikit photographs of the killers of the Rue des Rosiers that had appeared in *France-Soir*, as well as photographs of Plunkett and Flynn that he claims he took from a bag left at his house by Plunkett in November 1981. Barril told Jegat that he was "95 per cent sure" they were the same people.

They talked for a while; then Jegat brought Barril to his apartment and produced the photograph that appeared in a June 1979 issue of *Paris Match* to accompany an interview Roger Faligot carried out with the INLA representatives. It was taken in Jegat's apartment and apparently shows two men in hoods, one bearded, both waving AK47 rifles, while in the background hangs a Starry Plough flag. At any rate, the men interviewed had told Faligot that they were on the GHQ staff of the INLA, and justified their assassination of Neave, giving some hints about how it was carried out.

Jegat claimed that the two INLA members in the photograph were Mick Plunkett and Harry Flynn. In fact one was a woman in disguise, and the other was a well-known French journalist, who was talked into posing for the picture.

Jegat also showed Barril a rent receipt bearing Plunkett's address, 82 Rue Diderot.

The accounts given by Barril and Jegat of what happened next now diverge sharply. Jegat alleges that he unveiled the INLA arsenal in his apartment: a lump of the Soviet explosives, five detonators, a role of Bickford tape, a dozen CZ70 7.65 mm pistols, an Italian automatic pistol with a silencer, and boxes of ammunition for Spanish and Swedish-made pistols, Lugers, and Remingtons. As well, he claims he showed Barril a pile of blank identification papers, photographs, and other documents. The GIGN captain strongly denies this and says he merely looked over some documents. While in the apartment, according to Jegat, Barril telephoned and spoke to Christian Prouteau, declaring, "I may have something interesting to tell you." Jegat says that Barril told him: "You must understand that because of his responsibilities at the Presidential Palace he cannot meet someone like you for the moment." (Ibid.)

On 25 August, Barril told Prouteau that a contact in the Irish police had informed him that the INLA's leading bomb-maker was due to arrive in Paris to carry out an attack. Barril again visited Jegat, who says he surrendered another pistol, one he alleges was given to him for his personal protection by "McCabe". When Jegat took a cloth to rub off his fingerprints, he was told not to bother—that the police would do it later. Barril denies this. A day later, Barril informed Jegat that he had been tailing "McCabe" and discovered him in the company of "two Arabs" (ibid.)—proof, to Barril, that he was on to something big. In fact photographs show that the so-called "Arabs" that

"McCabe" met were an Irish couple, who were on holiday in Paris at the time. (One of them is now on the Ard-Chomhairle of Sinn Féin.) However, Barril's radar screen did not register such blips as he homed in on his prey.

A day or so later, Jegat said that he received the "mute" call, signalling the imminent arrival of "McCabe". It came at around noon. He called Barril with the news. According to Jegat's account, Barril came round at once with another member of the GIGN, who was wearing gloves, even though it was August, and carrying a long sports bag. They took two short-barrelled shotguns out of the bag, and moved furniture around to give themselves a clear view of the passageway leading to the door. Fearing that a gun battle might ensue, Jegat pushed his girl-friend and their two cats out of the apartment.

Barril and the other policeman waited tensely for Plunkett and Flynn to arrive. All this time the captain stayed in contact by radio with the police outside. He was nervous. At an unspecified hour the telephone rang with a call for Barril, which resulted in a change of plan. "We'll wrap things up here," Barril said to his subordinate; "we'll corner him at his place." The two policemen packed up their bags, one of which, according to Jegat, contained explosives, and left. (Ibid.)

The ambush was abandoned. Plunkett had met Flynn, but, instead of visiting Jegat as planned, they had gone off on a drinking session around the cafés in the Bastille area. The INLA men believe that this saved their lives, and probably that of Jegat as well. Earlier, Jegat had been asked by a policeman to handle the explosives stored in his apartment; the policeman had also allowed Jegat's fingerprints to remain all over a handgun.

The scene now switched to Vincennes. On 28 August at around 8 a.m. Barril received a call from a tenant who also lived at 82 Rue Diderot informing him that a group of men had gone into Plunkett's apartment earlier that morning carrying a heavy case. By ten o'clock two plain-clothes policemen were watching the building. Barril by now was in touch with Prouteau again, warning him that the Irish-Palestinian terrorist cell was about to act.

There now arose the question of French legal bureaucracy. In French law, if the police suspect a crime and wish to intervene they have to be accompanied by the Équipe Judiciaire scene-of-crime officers, one of whose functions is to accompany magistrates as they gather evidence. Jean-Michel Beau, a commander of the judiciary police for Vincennes, had already been forewarned by Prouteau to expect a request from Barril. Barril may have balked at this: the GIGN was not accustomed to having its hands bound by such bureaucratic ties. However, Prouteau reassured the captain that the

Minister of Defence, Charles Hernu, had given him the green light. Beau reportedly was dubious about the entire operation and protested that he did not have the authority to help Barril, but was reassured that it was "covered". The issue of who had the authorisation from whom to do what would remain at the centre of the long legal wrangle that was destined to engulf the whole case.

What is fairly well established is that at about 1 p.m. a bearded man— "McCabe"—was seen leaving 82 Rue Diderot accompanied by a young boy of about ten years old. The latter was Cathal Goulding, grandson of the former Official IRA chief of staff and son of Mary Reid. About five hours later one of Barril's surveillance team saw a tall man appear at the window of "McCabe's" apartment. Barril ordered an immediate intervention.

Ten plain-clothes officers with guns drawn burst into the building, much to the shock of the concierge, who asked one of the other tenants to call the police. Barril bounded up the stairs, to meet the man he had seen at the window leaving the apartment. They grappled and tumbled down the steps, until Barril thrust the barrel of his gun into his opponent's mouth. Another officer placed a gun on his neck. He was then gagged, blindfolded, bound, and brought back into the apartment. Barril then dashed from the building to block the police cars that were coming in response to the emergency call.

Shortly afterwards "McCabe"—alias Mick Plunkett—came on the scene. He too was gagged and blindfolded, his hands tied with wire. Hustled into his apartment, he assumed it was an SAS job and that he and his companion—identified later as Stephen King—were to be executed on the spot. At around 8 p.m. the boy who was seen leaving with Plunkett returned with his mother. They too were arrested at gunpoint. Back at the police station, when Cathal Goulding was returning from the toilet, Barril took him aside. When they were alone, the captain asked him, "Is there anything you can tell me that will help the little children of Ireland?" The boy replied right away: "I don't know anything." Goulding, reared in republican and left-wing circles, was well used to seeing his mother being questioned by Special Branch police and knew that the cardinal rule was to keep your mouth shut. He was then separated from his mother and brought to a holding centre for children.[2]

The police had searched the apartment, which was full of mattresses lying on the floor; they claimed to have found two handguns, one of them under a mattress, and a small quantity of pink-coloured explosives, the same as was held in Jegat's cache, near the toilet. Present during the search were Barril, Jean-Michel Beau, and José Windels, who was in charge of the procedure.

The Élysée Palace had issued a statement the weekend of the arrests that claimed there had been a breakthrough in the fight against international terrorism. It did not prove that simple.

Over the complex story of *les Trois Irlandais de Vincennes*, as they had become known in the French media, hangs the shade of Airey Neave and the shadow of the British police. On 27 May 1982, three months before the three were arrested, the British secret service had sent a four-page note to the French police about a Belgian arms dealer with links to Irish and Basque guerrilla groups and al-Fatah. The note singled out "two other dangerous terrorists" who were said to be in Paris at that time. "One of them Michael Plunkett (INLA terrorist, specialist in arms supplies for the organisation) author of a series of attacks in the Federal Republic of Germany, is a friend of James Kerr (member of INLA probably linked to attacks carried out by this organisation in Federal Republic of Germany) ..." (Ibid.)

The French had been advised of Plunkett's presence probably a lot earlier than this: they undoubtedly had a French informer close to the Irish fugitive who pre-dated Jegat. But they had chosen to ignore the activities of the INLA in France as long as it did not involve itself in any terrorist acts on French soil or embarrass the government in any overt way. The British, however, had already singled out Plunkett, and warned the French police of a nebulous conspiracy involving the INLA, Palestinians, ETA, the Provisionals, and others. After the massacre in the Rue des Rosiers, when pressure was placed on the GIGN to produce results in the war against international terrorism, Plunkett may have seemed like a convenient target.

Within two days of his arrest, a superintendent and an inspector from Scotland Yard Special Branch arrived in Paris and tried to get in touch with those in charge of the Vincennes investigation to see what they had discovered. They spoke to Barril, who supplied them with some photographs that had been found in the Rue Diderot. On hearing the news of the arrests, a leading British diplomat, who was close to Margaret Thatcher, telephoned the Élysée Palace to congratulate the French for their work.

After the arrests, Commander J. Wilson of Scotland Yard's Special Branch sent a seven-page memo to the French authorities. Part of it was reproduced in *Enquête sur Trois Secrets d'État*. It read: "Michael Oliver Plunkett, alias Mike, alias James McCabe, was born on 11th October 1951 in the Republic of Ireland ... [He] was introduced to Irish extremism in 1969 when he entered the CP. Was a member of Official Sinn Féin from 1971 to 1974. Later he was a founding member of the [IR]SP and became a world-wide organiser. This position hides his activities within the INLA. He is the author of articles in the *Irish Times* and the *Starry Plough*, official organ of the IRSP protesting against accusations that the IRSP was responsible for killings and murder in Ulster. His name has been associated with those of various confirmed terrorists, among whom — and Vincent Ford, two of the suspects in the Airey Neave murder in London on 30 March 1979, claimed by the INLA. He was also in Holland during the assassination of the British Ambassador in 1979, for which he is still a suspect.

"His girlfriend Corinne Marie Carole Cheronnet, was arrested and then detained in conformity with the Prevention of Terrorism Act upon arrival at the port of Holyhead. Born 14 August 1952 in Grandville (France), she was in 1978 an unemployed French teacher ... When she's released she says she's hitch-hiking to Amsterdam ... Plunkett was arrested in 1976 for having taken part in the hold-up of an Irish post train where £210,000 was taken, but was released through lack of evidence ... Plunkett is a central figure in the extreme left movement. He has solid relations ... with left-wing extremists in Germany and Holland."

Of course the memo does not say that the train robbery for which Plunkett and other members of the IRSP were charged was carried out by the Provisionals. Brendan O'Sullivan, who joined the IRSP in the autumn of 1979, seems to have found his way onto the Special Branch memo in relation to Airey Neave because of a photograph of him leaving the House of Commons with Bernadette McAliskey that was taken around 1970. Vincent Ford, a priest, was held on various charges by the Gardaí, including bank robbery, in 1980, when he jumped bail. He was later rearrested and spent time in Port Laoise. In spite of the seriousness of these allegations against Plunkett—which were soon leaked to the tabloid press in Britain—no attempt was ever made by the British to extradite him from France.

When Mick Plunkett was interviewed by one of the authors on that cold February morning in 1983 he had been sitting in La Santé prison for about six months, locked in a tiny cell with three other men for twenty-three hours a day. Their only exercise was a walk around the prison yard, where convicts still broke rocks, wearing a ball and chain.[3] The only source of water was the flush of the toilet in one corner: that was where the dinner plates got washed. For visits, the prisoners were locked in cubicles behind thick glass screens. The cubicles looked like large microwave ovens, equipped with small grilles through which the prisoner spoke. After half an hour a bell would ring loudly, signifying that the visit had ended. "That means you're cooked," Plunkett joked.

However, by February 1983, far from being cooked, the case of *les Trois Irlandais de Vincennes* was proving to be a recipe for disaster, becoming an ever-growing embarrassment to the French authorities. Indeed, within days of the arrests of Plunkett, King, and Reid, information was being leaked about the origin of the explosives and the weapons found at 82 Rue Diderot. It was being suggested that they had been taken from the INLA arms dump in Jegat's flat and planted there deliberately by the police.

Jegat was thrown into a panic by the rumours following the arrests. He felt sure that once the material found in the Rue Diderot was identified, the INLA would know from where it originated and identify him as the informer. On 8 September, *Le Monde* had run an article saying that *les Trois Irlandais de Vincennes* had been arrested thanks to the work of an informer. He plagued Barril with his anxieties, but the GIGN captain told him that he had nothing to worry about, that he had not used the material he had found in his apartment. According to Jegat's deposition, Barril told him that "the leaks to the press were meant to sabotage the work of the Gendarmerie. He led me to believe that the security forces were all the same closing in on the Rue des Rosiers killers, who were to be found in Plunkett's entourage, that he was continuing to work on it himself." (Ibid.)

In truth, the police were not linking Plunkett, Reid and King to the anti-Jewish atrocity that had shaken France; nor did they seriously pursue that avenue of enquiry. The events that unfolded regarding their arrests have more to do with the complex rivalries within the French security force bureaucracy than with the history of the INLA.

The three were released in May 1983, and all charges against them were dropped the following September, when a gendarme with the technical unit present during the raid said in a sworn statement that he had been "ordered by his superiors to lie about the affair." There were many irregularities in their arrest. The three had not been physically present when the evidence against them was uncovered, contrary to French law. The gendarme was also hinting that the evidence had been planted by Barril.

In 1989 the three won a case against the French state, which acknowledged that they had been wrongfully arrested; they were awarded damages of 1 franc. "The bastards haven't paid us yet!" laughs Plunkett, who now works as a plumber in Paris.

The case dragged on into the 1990s. In June 1991, Prouteau, Beau and Windels appeared in court charged with subverting evidence in order to frame Plunkett, Reid, and King. Under the stately panelled ceilings of chambre 17E of the Palais de Justice—the very room where some two hundred years earlier Marie-Antoinette faced her accusers—the extraordinarily complex case wound its way, with more twists and turns in it than a French Restoration drama. To one side sat a bearded Jegat. Prouteau—whom François Mitterand had once described as his "prototype of a soldier"—listened as Beau pointed the finger at him, saying that he was responsible for the mess. Prouteau replied that he was no longer in charge of the GIGN at the time of the raid in the Rue Diderot. Windels said that he had been under orders from Beau.

However, throughout the hearing, which lasted for three days, the name that was most often mentioned was that of the man who was conspicuous by his absence: Barril. And to the judges' repeated question, *"Qui commandait le Capitaine Barril?"* which resonated throughout the trial, there was no answer. Barril was under sub-poena to appear, but no-one believed he would respond. Rumours that he was in France were dismissed as wishful thinking.

Since his involvement in the Vincennes affair Barril had gone on to even more scandalous intrigues, including that of the sinking of the Greenpeace ship *Rainbow Warrior* in 1985, in which the French secret service was involved. On the second day of the trial, after Plunkett had spoken and Mary Reid had given an emotional account of how the whole affair had damaged her life, Jegat stood up and in an angry mood tore his deposition into shreds. Flinging them on the floor he proclaimed his "shame at being French" and his disgust at the whole procedure. It was a dramatic scene and might well have been the most memorable of the trial. Unfortunately it was upstaged minutes later when word buzzed around the ornate but stiflingly hot courtroom that Barril was arriving.

People flocked around him as he strode up the steps of the Palais de Justice. He had flown in from Qatar, where he worked advising oil sheikhs on personal security matters. He was tanned, greying elegantly around the temples but still with a taut physique and in good trim. He caused a sensation when he announced to the court that in 1982 he had been acting under a carte blanche given to him by the former Minister of Defence, Charles Hernu. Hernu had been forced to resign after the sinking of the *Rainbow Warrior* and had died in 1990. Eight years earlier, according to Jegat, Barril had told him: "I'm clean in this Irish affair. All these defamations of my character are just a politically motivated set-up. If anything happens to me, four ministers will go down: Beregovoy, Hernu, Deferre, and Franceschi. I have a cassette and file on Hernu, who threatened me with death." (Ibid.) At the trial, Barril also said that they had raided Plunkett's apartment after being warned by British intelligence that there was to be a terrorist attack that weekend. He continued to assert that he had not done anything wrong.

Barril's name was not on the charge sheet, and he departed after giving his evidence, followed by a flock of reporters. The three policemen left behind were convicted and given light sentences, which were later quashed on appeal. Prouteau went on to become head of security at the Winter Olympics in Albertville. As for Barril, he now designs and markets bullet-proof underwear, as well as acting as security adviser to oil-rich Arabs.

Two of the three *Irlandais de Vincennes*, Mick Plunkett and Mary Reid, fought for political asylum. Eventually, however, Reid followed King, who had left earlier, and returned to Ireland. Plunkett continued his struggle to stay in France, which he eventually won. Even though charges against him in Ireland were also dropped, he remains in Paris. At present Plunkett and Reid are carrying out a civil court action against whoever was responsible for the planting of the explosives and weapons at 82 Rue Diderot.[4]

That the INLA was not linked to the Rue des Rosiers massacres must have been obvious from a very early stage. Yet the fact was that the INLA did have links to the Arab world—but always to al-Fatah, the "moderate" wing of the PLO. Rue des Rosiers was carried out by the People's Front for the Liberation of Palestine (PFLP), a breakaway from the mainstream PLO. Any approaches from this wing of Palestinian extremism had always been rejected by the INLA.

In spite of this, there were further attempts to associate the organisation with terrorist attacks in Paris. In 1985 a bomb went off outside the Paris Marks and Spencers, which stands behind L'Opéra. It was blamed on Arab terrorists; but it was alleged that the INLA had carried it out on their behalf. The evidence: a map of Paris found in Plunkett's apartment in 1982, three years before the attack, with an X marked near L'Opéra.

Plunkett had explained at the time of his arrest that Mary Reid's nine-year-old son had done it. "He also drew an X on a map we had of the solar system—on Mars," Plunkett said. "Does that mean the INLA wanted to bomb Mars?" (Interview, 2 December 1993.)

In spite of the attention focused on the INLA's activities in France by the affair of *les Trois Irlandais de Vincennes*, the organisation continued to use the country as an important staging-post in its arms-running operations.

A second conduit developed, linked to Action Directe, the left-wing terrorist group that carried out a series of attacks against property and individuals in France in the 1980s. Action Directe was a loosely knit organisation with a highly politicised leadership and a cadre who more or less bombed and robbed as they wanted. They acted on the principle, almost anarchistic, that every individual had the right to attack the state. The original, "mainstream" INLA Continental network that had grown up in the late 1970s had not been linked to such groups. But from 1982, through an INLA member, Seán "Bap" Hughes, contacts between it and Action Directe were established. Hughes, from the Divis Flats in Belfast, had fled to France at the beginning of that year after the murder of Garda Patrick Reynolds. Reynolds was shot dead when he called at a house in Avonbeg Gardens, Tallaght, Dublin, while investigating a post office robbery. Hughes was wanted for questioning in connection with the shooting.[5]

Hughes had also been linked to Gerard Steenson in Belfast, and had taken part in Steenson's failed attempt to remove the Flynn-Goodman leadership. Between 1982 and 1983, during the rule of Dominic McGlinchey, the movement received a few weapons from France; but these were purchased in the country itself or in Belgium, in small lots, often employing Action Directe contacts. There were no major arms shipments to the INLA from the Continent for some two years. The original INLA arms route that ran from the Middle East remained in the hands of the older leadership, who were increasingly marginalised during the McGlinchey years (see chapter 10).

After the demise of McGlinchey and the movement's splintering (see chapter 12), "Bap" Hughes aligned himself with the John O'Reilly faction, which was desperate for arms and needed to bypass the Dublin leadership. In late 1984, Hughes linked up with an Irish-American couple, Bill and Eleanor Norton, who agreed to help them procure weapons. Theirs is one of the most unlikely stories in the history of the INLA. On the face of it, the Nortons hardly seemed like the stuff out of which INLA supporters are made.

Bill Norton was a sixty-year-old successful Hollywood screenwriter, who scripted many films both for the big screen and television. Among the fourteen feature films for which he wrote the scripts were *Brannigan*, starring John Wayne, *Gator*, starring Burt Reynolds, and *Dirty Tricks*, starring Elliot Gould and Kate Jackson. In 1984, Norton signed a $100,000 contract with Walt Disney Productions to develop ideas for a television mini-series. (*Irish America*, January 1987.) Norton, however, was a dedicated socialist, who often opened his two-storey house in the Los Angeles suburb of Hancock Park to refugees from Central America. He also devoted much of his spare time to helping "street people". According to one of his colleagues, "Bill would go down to the Rescue Mission and dole out the soup. A lot of us would give money, but he would go much further. He had deep religious convictions and would give of himself." (Ibid.)

The INLA made contact with Norton through "Peter McCormick". This was the alias used by a high-ranking member of the Provisionals who had joined the INLA and was part of the John O'Reilly faction; later, he became chief of staff. "McCormick" had been in the United States in the late 1970s doing arms deals for the IRA.

Norton agreed to help the INLA. He purchased arms and ammunition, including rifles and handguns, in the United States, then concealed them in his camper, which was loaded onto a freighter in Los Angeles harbour bound for Europe. After arriving in Rotterdam, the vehicle was driven to Le Havre, where it was put on a ship bound for Rosslare. However, the first arms shipment sent across this way was intercepted when it arrived by the Dublin INLA leadership, who were opposed to O'Reilly (see chapter 12).

In March 1986, Bill Norton retired from Hollywood and bought a house near Omeath, County Louth, to which he intended to move in June that year. Among the items he was to move with him was a camper. Once more Norton agreed to try to get weapons to O'Reilly's faction. The shipment he acquired consisted of two machine-guns, twelve AR15 rifles, twenty-four revolvers, a rifle scope, silencers, and around 2,200 rounds of ammunition, which were concealed in the woodwork of the mobile home. (*FBI Law Enforcement Bulletin*, October 1987.) It followed the route of the first shipment, arriving in Rotterdam on 5 June 1986. From there it was offloaded and transported in a truck with an Irish registration to Le Havre. But the second effort proved no luckier than the first. The FBI, which had been investigating Norton since February 1985, had forewarned the French police. On 11 June 1986 they searched the vehicle and uncovered the weapons haul. Bill and Eleanor Norton were arrested, along with "Bap" Hughes (under the alias Anthony James MacKenzie), Jim McLaughlin, and Suzanne May. In August 1987 the gang were convicted of illegally importing arms. Norton, Hughes and McLaughlin were each sentenced to four years; Eleanor Norton received three years, of which two were suspended.

Upon his release, Bill Norton, who because of his arms running was also wanted by the FBI, moved with his wife to Managua in Nicaragua, which has no extradition treaty with the United States. He spent the last few years of his life there, where he died in 1992.

In the mid-1980s, before Hughes's arrest, the INLA—or at least one faction of it—took part in several major robberies on the Continent, along with left-wing terrorists from Action Directe and Belgian, Italian and Spanish groups. The biggest was a multi-million-pound haul in Brest, of which the INLA was supposed to receive a cut of between £300,000 and £400,000. In fact some £30,000 of their portion of the proceeds was supposed to be in the

Norton arms shipment that was intercepted by the Dublin INLA en route to O'Reilly in late 1985 (see chapter 12).

There was one more affair in France involving O'Reilly and his supporters: the murder of the former gunrunner and IRSP Ard-Chomhairle member Séamus Ruddy. That tragedy formed part of the prelude to the 1987 feud (see chapter 12).

The O'Reilly faction was not the only one that was busy in Europe in the mid-1980s. The old links that had provided the INLA's major arms shipments were reactivated in the post-McGlinchey era by the remnants of the original organisation. In 1984 a few of the INLA's founding members, based in Dublin and Munster, set about trying to build an infrastructure in order to either create a new socialist republican movement or reform the existing INLA. (At that time it was not certain how things would evolve within the group, which was then in turmoil.) They wanted to avoid the mistake that Séamus Costello had made ten years earlier: he had created a movement before he was able to properly equip it. They were going to make sure that they had the weaponry with which to equip their movement before they set about fixing plans for its structure.

Between late 1984 and 1986 the INLA held a series of meetings with representatives of al-Fatah and other Arab sympathisers in Prague, East Berlin, Warsaw, and Tunisia. One former member of the GHQ staff was mainly involved; he acted as a sort of ambassador from the INLA to the PLO.

Prague, where the PLO had a headquarters, was becoming the major link in the international terrorist arms chain. The PLO could operate freely there, without supervision from the Czechoslovak security services. The INLA's representatives were met at the airport by a PLO man, who spirited them through customs and immigration checks. On one occasion the INLA "ambassador", who was already in Prague, went to meet a second who was coming in to join him, but when he got to the airport he found that his newly arrived colleague had not got a visa. A telephone call was put through to the PLO office in Prague; it required little more than a quick chat between the Czechoslovak immigration officials at the airport and the Palestinian official at headquarters to clear the matter up, and the visitor, regardless of the fact that he had not got the proper papers, was permitted to enter the country.

East Berlin and Warsaw were very different. The East German secret police, the Stasi, shadowed the PLO representatives everywhere they went, and it was impossible to conduct any business in the open. Negotiations with the INLA had to be carried on in secret.

In 1984 the arms began flowing again, at first in modest amounts.

Skorpion pistols, VZORs and grenades were acquired, as well as some "remotes" for detonators. These offered the potential for building remote-control bombs.

For small quantities of weapons, an arms route was established. The INLA "ambassador" would fly to Prague to meet his PLO F18 contact. From 1985 onwards it was a Palestinian activist who had been involved in an attack on a yacht in Cyprus in which three British people were killed. (The PLO had accused them of spying for Israel.) They met in one of the flats the PLO owned throughout the city. When the deal was arranged, the INLA "ambassador" was taken by car to East Germany and into West Berlin. There he was given a twelve-hour visa to visit East Berlin. During the time in East Berlin he had a diplomatic car to escort him. He was told where he could pick up the weapons, which were left in a car parked in West Berlin. From West Berlin the "ambassador" drove to Strasbourg and then Paris.

After the United States bombed Libya in April 1986, things began to change dramatically. According to a former high-ranking INLA member, "the Arabs were ready to give you anything. You could have got anything you wanted then." (Interview, 8 January 1994.)

Several offers came to the "ambassador". In Prague he was introduced by his PLO contact to the Deputy Minister of Security from South Yemen. The Irishman was told that the South Yemen government was prepared to arrange for the training of five volunteers from the organisation in Yemen itself. Then, because British intelligence was known to be extremely active in that area, the venue was later shifted to Tanzania, where the deputy minister promised to arrange for the INLA men's training. He even suggested that he help the INLA to buy a ranch there and convert it into a permanent INLA training camp. However, these schemes collapsed when there was a feud in the South Yemen government that sparked off a shoot-out during a government meeting. This led to the Deputy Security Minister's arrest. Though later released—through PLO pressure, it is thought—he was never able to renew his offer.

In return for the PLO's help in setting up these and other meetings, the INLA agreed to provide the Palestinians with false Irish passports. At one time the INLA spent £2,500 on a single batch.

It was during this period that the INLA had approaches from Libya. There had been an earlier contact between the organisation and Colonel Gaddafi, a man regarded as a sort of international terrorist "godfather", but it had led to nothing. As a result the INLA had regarded the Libyans as unreliable. But in 1986 a Libyan came with another offer. It sounded interesting enough for a representative from the Dublin-Munster faction to make the trip to Malta to discuss it. When he got there his Libyan contact asked him, "What kind of ship have you?" His mind was boggled by the quantities of weapons Gaddafi's man had to offer: he was talking in tons. The INLA's representative had to turn down the offer: his organisation simply could not absorb the amounts in which Libya was dealing. But another organisation could—and did. Between 1985 and 1987 the Provisional IRA received four shiploads of weapons, amounting to some 120 tons. The shipments were all organised out of Malta. (*Economist*, March 1990.)

However, weapons did reach the INLA from Libya, albeit in a small amount and in a rather surprising manner. After the bombing of Tripoli, the "ambassador" got to know a high-ranking Libyan official in Dublin who liked to go fishing in one of the small seaside towns on the coast near the city. He fell into conversation with them and soon made it known that he was sympathetic. He agreed to help, and an arrangement was made for him to deliver a few weapons. He arrived at the rendezvous in a limousine that he said belonged to a member of the family of a very high-ranking politician in the Irish Government. The Libyan was on friendly terms with the family, one of whom had put the car at his disposal. He explained that he thought it would make the ideal cover for transporting weapons. In it were concealed four pistols. He handed them over to the bemused INLA activists and drove off in the car.

It was thanks to the anti-western mood among the Arabs that in 1986 the INLA had a breakthrough in its arm procurement efforts. A £70,000 arms haul was clinched through the PLO Prague contact, which included a hundred light anti-tank weapons. These were easily handled rockets that enabled an infantryman to destroy a tank. It also contained forty AK47 rifles, three 12.5 mm machine guns, and two 80 mm mortars. An operation was set in motion to move the weapons from Prague to East Germany and thence to the Polish port of Szczecin, from where the shipment was supposed to leave in April, destined for Cyprus. From there it was to be moved to France. However, things began to go wrong. The Stasi blocked the shipment; it was eventually cleared only after weeks of waiting. Preparations were then made to receive it. In July, William "Boot" Browning (who had stood with Flynn's brother Seán as a candidate in the Northern Ireland local elections in May 1981) was identified by police as he arrived in France. He was followed to Paris. There he met George Kevin McCann, John Gormley, and Harry Flynn. The men were arrested by the French police as they were getting ready to move detonators for remote-controlled bombs, and were charged with illegally transporting weapons.

Flynn, who had already escaped from custody twice in the North and had been involved in some other escapes—some due to his own ingenuity and some to good luck—made one more effort. The police who were escorting him between police stations had unhandcuffed him. He was Irish, they were French and none too fond of the English. Flynn thought he saw his chance as he was being escorted down the street. He leaped over the bonnet of a parked car. Hitting the road, he dashed through the Parisian traffic. However, one of the escort proved to be a powerful runner. Within minutes he'd brought Flynn to the ground. *"Je suis un marathon man,"* the French policeman declared as he clutched his prey. "I decided at that point I should learn French," Flynn recalls.

He had plenty of time to do so. In October 1987 he was sentenced to five years' imprisonment, two of which were suspended. Browning got three, with eighteen months suspended; McCann, whose Volvo car was being used to transport the equipment, was given a three-year suspended sentence and Gormley a suspended sentence of one year. Before sentencing Flynn, the judge explained that he was very impressed by the demeanour of all the accused and that he recognised that they were acting for deep political motives. He had therefore decided to suspend two years of Flynn's sentence, and follow suit with the others.

During the trial the prosecutor did not mention the word "terrorism" once. The most controversial moment came when the accused, having been allowed to explain themselves, compared Margaret Thatcher to Klaus Barbie. The prosecutor jumped to his feet to protest, and the president of the court did intervene, but without demanding that the comparison be withdrawn.

Following the sentencing, the British applied for Flynn's extradition on the charge for which he was originally arrested on 12 April 1975: the armed robbery of a bank in central Belfast. Flynn was being held on that charge when he escaped for the first time, a month after his arrest. It was a puzzling request, since the British had already attempted to extradite him from the Republic on the same charge in 1978 and failed. The High Court in Dublin had ruled that the charge was "political" and rejected the request. It was unlikely that the French, who have always demonstrated that they prefer placatory measures when dealing with international terrorism on their own soil, would depart from the precedent set by the Irish court. And they did not, turning down Britain's request in May 1988. Flynn was released (speaking fluent French), and returned to Dublin.

The arrests had made it impossible for what was left of the original INLA leadership to carry out its plans for a major arms shipment from the

Continent. By 1988 it had so splintered and been reduced that, though the weapons—including the light anti-tank weapons—were still available, neither it nor its offshoot, the IPLO, was ever able to enact any scheme to bring them into Ireland.

The INLA's main arms supply links had always been with the Near East and eastern Europe. However, the organisation did succeed in getting arms from two other sources, one of which was in the United States (see chapter 12). The other, much more important source was in Australia and had been activated by Séamus Costello. Between 1977 and 1983 the INLA received four shipments from a sympathiser in Sydney. The first comprised only seven weapons and was used to test the route. (Because of a strike, this shipment was kept in a warehouse in Dublin for over a year before the INLA could gain access to it in June 1978.) The second came in 1980 and a third two years later, each comprising between twenty and thirty weapons. The rifles included Ruger Mini-14s, a Springfield M1A, Garrand M1s, Egyptian Mauses, and Simonovs (SKS). They were usually sent in boxes marked "personal belongings" through shipping agencies.

In late 1983, however, Séamus Ruddy was arrested by the Gardaí. On his person was found a document that led to the discovery of the fourth (and last) Australian shipment. Ruddy was not actually involved in gun-running at the time but had been given the document to hold simply because he was a trusted person.

The discovery also led to the arrest in Sydney of Patrick Joseph Feehan, an Irish immigrant who had lived in Australia since 1968 and had become an Australian citizen in 1973. In February 1984 he told a Sydney court that the guns were for "the defence of my own people against an invading army." (*Sydney Morning Herald*, 21 February 1984.) He was convicted of arms running and fined $17,000.

NOTES

1. Raab was forced to go on the run in late 1979, when he fled to Ireland. There he took part in several INLA operations, including a bank robbery. He later returned to Germany, where he died in 1991 after refusing medication for a liver disease.
2. After a few days without seeing her, young Goulding threatened to go on hunger strike unless he was granted a visit. However, after a brief fast, French food got the better of him. He was allowed to see his mother only after some three weeks had passed.

3. In the French penal system, prisoners are expected to pay for their own upkeep while in jail. Those who can't are forced to do hard labour.

4. As late as March 1993 the case of *les Trois Irlandais de Vincennes* was still making news in France. The newspaper *Libération* revealed that the GIGN had organised illegal wire-taps of a journalist's telephone line in 1986. The journalist, Edwy Plenel, who worked for *Le Monde*, had been investigating the background to the story.

5. The Ard-Chomhairle meeting of 27 February 1982 notes that in the wake of the killing of Reynolds there were several resignations from what was left of the IRSP. From London came notice that it had been a "bad collection week and comment was passed about 'the lot that shot the guard'."

12

PRELUDE TO DISASTER

The frenzy of activity generated under the rule of Dominic McGlinchey masked the seriousness of the crisis facing the IRSP and the INLA. By 1984 the movement had degenerated into a loosely knit group of often mutually suspicious fiefdoms. The IRSP was politically irrelevant, having paddled into the backwater of "Marxist-Leninist" politics, where the distance from reality was in direct proportion to the volume of left-wing rhetoric coming from party leaders.

To say that the movement founded by Séamus Costello in 1974 was facing a crisis may seem almost tautological. Had not the INLA and the IRSP confronted a crisis in every year of their existence? But the problems facing it as it celebrated its tenth birthday were of a different order of magnitude.

In the military wing the usual organisational procedures had been abolished. McGlinchey had made the post of chief of staff a matter for his disposal. On going into jail he had handed it on to a Newry man nicknamed "Jap"; the Army Council was not asked for its opinion. Another of McGlinchey's men, Tom McCartan, had fled north, afraid that "Mad Dog" would make him pay for failing to carry out an operation as ordered.

With the leading Belfast INLA figures such as Hugh Torney in jail because of Kirkpatrick, McCartan declared himself OC of the city. He quickly became involved in widespread extortion rackets in west Belfast. By the summer of 1984 reports were pouring in alleging that the INLA was moving in on racketeering in the city, causing friction with the Provisionals. The *Sunday Times* quoted an unnamed Catholic businessman who complained about the INLA: "They don't care whether you have a security camera or not. They tell you to pay up or else. They are bad people. They don't care a damn about the Provos. In the past, the Provos could sort out people like this. But not now. INLA is just a bunch of psychopaths. The Provos were always more flexible. But these guys don't mess. You pay up or go on the list. People are frightened. You're not dealing with reasonable people. They can just shoot you." (*Sunday Times*, 17 June 1984.) Another described the INLA as "less civilised" than the Provisionals. (Ibid.)

The leadership decided it was time to get rid of McCartan—partly because his racketeering was so blatant that it was becoming an embarrassment, and partly because it thought the money should be directed into its coffers.

One of the activists close to Torney was twenty-year-old Paul "Bonanza" McCann, brother of Francis McCann, who is now a Sinn Féin Belfast city councillor. Paul McCann, who the year before had shot dead "Sparky" Barkley on the orders of McGlinchey, was regarded as one of the INLA's up-and-coming operators. He had joined the INLA when still in his teens and was soon a "staff officer", and became OC of the Divis Flats. In 1984 he was involved in a dispute with the Official IRA in Belfast, allegedly stealing an AK47 rifle from an Officials' arms dump in the Lower Falls.

McCann was ordered to remove Tom McCartan. On the night of 14 June, along with three other INLA men and a woman, McCann was in a flat in Lenadoon, west Belfast. A radiator was rammed up against the door to prevent it being opened easily from the outside. The four drank into the early hours. McCann was armed with an AK47 with the words *Black Widow* burned into its wooden butt. According to a former INLA man, he was carrying the weapon to protect himself against McCartan.

At three o'clock on the morning of 15 June someone tried to force the door. McCann may have thought that McCartan was making a pre-emptive strike, or that the Officials were coming to claim back their gun. Then someone in the flat shouted: "It's only the peelers. Use the AK47 and shoot them." (*Irish News*, 7 May 1987.) As the first three constables squeezed in past the radiator they were hit by a burst of fire. Constable Michael Todd was killed and two others were seriously wounded. There was a second burst. When the police switched on the light they found McCann lying dead, still clutching his rifle, with "a gaping hole" in his head. An inquest later found that the fatal wound had been caused by McCann's rifle. None of the police had fired their weapons, and the coroner returned a verdict of suicide.

McCann's family protested. Francis McCann told the court: "My brother never talked of suicide." (Ibid.) Another theory was that McCann had been felled by a ricocheting bullet. The President of Sinn Féin, Gerry Adams, carried the coffin at McCann's funeral, during which McCann was praised as "one of the finest soldiers ever to fight for national liberation and socialism." (*Irish News*, 19 June 1984.)

In any case, "Jap" and his supporters blamed Tom McCartan for McCann's death. Had it not been for his criminal activity, they reasoned bitterly if not logically, McCann would not have been armed and the chain of events that had led to the freakish incident in Lenadoon would not have started. The loss of McCann added to the growing hostility towards McCartan within the INLA.

The racketeering and corruption became so bad in Belfast that the Green Cross stopped making payments to INLA prisoners arrested after a certain date. The Provisionals had clashed with McCartan in May, when some of his men appeared at a hunger strike commemoration organised by Sinn Féin. They were armed, and forced their way onto the platform, though Sinn Féin had barred the IRSP and INLA from taking part in the demonstration.

The Provisional Army Council, provoked principally by McCartan's racketeering, sentenced him to death, but then did not carry out the execution for fear of sparking off a feud in Belfast. It was left to his former colleagues in the INLA to settle accounts.

If this was the sordid reality of what the INLA had become, the political mask it had adopted presented a contrasting image. The face of Jim Lane, who became the IRSP's chairman in 1983, encapsulates it perfectly. Round, bland, and bespectacled, it is the face of a bureaucrat or petty civil servant.

Lane, a Corkman active in the IRSP since the H-block crisis, was a Marxist-Leninist of the fundamentalist variety. In December 1982 he had stood as the IRSP candidate for Cork South-Central in the general election and received a mere four hundred votes. It was not surprising that he tended towards political theory rather than practice. He said that his goal for the party was "to see a greater emphasis on political education ... We must research, study and discuss, so as to further develop the necessary revolutionary theory which is required to bring to fruition national liberation and socialism in Ireland." (*Starry Plough*, September 1983.) The interview appeared a few months before the sectarian massacre at the Pentecostal Hall in Darkley; Lane could not ask for a greater testimony to a lack of "political education" than the shooting of three Protestants in a church hall. The bitter irony is that it was carried out by people linked to an organisation whose political wing was now proudly proclaiming its "Marxist" credentials.

Those political parties that the gods want to destroy they first make theoretical. At the 1984 ardfheis, held in September of that year, the IRSP would "declare" itself formally a Marxist organisation and adopt the works of Marx and Engels as their bible. A motion from the Belfast Comhairle Ceantair proposed "that the Republican Socialist Movement takes appropriate steps to ensure that all members become familiar with the writings of Marx, Engels and Lenin." In Belfast the party was in the hands of Kevin "Bap" McQuillan, who had been a member of the Officials up until 1977.

While Lane's politics and those of his party were in the realms of left-wing fantasy, the INLA's were increasingly grounded in petty criminality, bitter fratricidal disputes, and naked sectarianism.

It was the working class, moreover, that seemed to be bearing the brunt of the INLA's campaign. Its activities in 1984 had been characterised by punishment shootings and disputes over whether this or that petty robbery was carried out by the INLA or "hoods" using the organisation's name. On 13 April the INLA had gunned down a 26-year-old man, John George, at his home in Twinbrook, west Belfast, in front of his young daughter. They accused the man of engaging in "criminal activities and using the name of the INLA to carry out these deeds." (*Belfast Telegraph*, 27 September 1984.) In her statement the girl said: "A man came up the stairs with a green mask and a big black gun. He said if I didn't get into bed he would shoot me." (Ibid.)

At the beginning of June in Kilkeel, County Down, two armed and masked youths tried to rob a teenagers' disco run by the well-known priest Father Pat Buckley. They claimed they were from the INLA. When Buckley refused to hand over the takings they threatened him. "I answered, if they were the kind of people hoping to lead us to a new Ireland, then God help us," the priest said. (*Irish News*, 4 June 1984.) The INLA denied involvement; but it was becoming increasingly academic, given the racketeering activities of McCartan and his group, whether any particular set of hoods was in the INLA or were mere freelances.

In September the armed wing of the newly refurbished party took its military campaign to new heights when it declared war on bouncers. It accused them of being "sadistic rent-a-thugs". In Derry the INLA shot a 33-year-old doorman, Paddy Bonner, in the leg after it said it had received complaints that he was using "excessive force". Three weeks after he was shot his leg had to be amputated.

Shortly after this the crisis of confidence facing the organisation surfaced when several of its leading activists imprisoned in Port Laoise left it. Among them was Dessie Grew, former OC of Armagh, who late in 1984 cut his links with the INLA and moved onto the landing occupied by the Provisional IRA. (He did not actually join the Provisionals until his release.)[1] However, the INLA still postured as a revolutionary guerrilla army in spite of the ridicule and contempt its activities had inspired. It attempted to cover itself by occasional efforts at making political statements. They appeared in the party paper, the *Starry Plough*, which by 1984 was often reduced to a two-page broadsheet. But these only reinforced the sense of the political bankruptcy of the military wing.

An interview with a member of the GHQ staff that appeared in the

Starry Plough of December 1984 to mark the tenth anniversary of the birth of the movement made the lack of political coherence glaringly obvious. Asked how the INLA viewed the recent decision of the IRSP to become a Marxist organisation, the INLA spokesman replied: "Remember, that we trace our origins to the Irish Citizens Army founded by James Connolly. Now Connolly was a Marxist. He made no secret of the fact himself. So it comes as no great surprise to see the IRSP developing in a more consciously Marxist direction." The replies that follow are equally vague and perfunctory, giving a distinct impression of someone going through the motions, lacking any serious interest in or commitment to the matter under discussion. The GHQ representative clearly felt it sufficient to utter the vaguest generalities about defending the interests of the working class to pass himself off as a Marxist. Asked about the low level of INLA activity in 1984, he answered: "Yes, the level of INLA activity has dropped off recently and some media commentators have said we are a spent force ... Let our actions speak for themselves in the coming months. We in many ways are a relatively young organisation. Ten years is not a long time in politics. We were borne out of turmoil and subject to constant pressures. In many ways we were organisationally and politically immature. But we have learned a lot of lessons. We know where mistakes were made in the past. We are quietly confident of the future."

The interview ends: "The British ruling class has tried every method to smash us as the fighting voice of the Irish working class. They have failed and as time goes by we become more capable of carrying on the struggle until victory. We, like Séamus Costello, owe our allegiance to the working class."

As the year ended, the INLA's armed campaign went on to a more ambitious plane—or at least tried to—with a spasm of attacks. The most notable was an attempt to assassinate the Derry DUP councillor Gregory Campbell. On 17 December a booby-trap bomb was placed under his car; but it dropped off, and was defused. The same day an attempt to murder British soldiers as they returned from a night-club in Hollywood to the east of Belfast failed when the bomb exploded after they had gone past.

In the *Starry Plough* interview the INLA spokesman had rebutted accusations that his organisation was weakening by saying, "Let our actions speak for themselves in the coming months." They did: but the tale they told throughout 1985 was not one of revolutionary success. Throughout much of the year the campaign seemed desultory and spasmodic, characterised by miscalculation.

It had begun with a failed attempt to assassinate Rev. Ian Paisley. However, when John O'Reilly took over as chief of staff the campaign escalated with a series of bomb attacks, which he organised. Three incendiary bombs concealed in duffel bags were left on the Belfast–Dublin train, forcing the evacuation of a hundred passengers. The devices went off fifteen minutes later, gutting three coaches. Later that same month an elaborate trap for the security forces went wrong in south Armagh. The INLA told police they had left a bomb under a bridge. Instead they had placed a device behind the door of a house nearby, after abducting the occupant, Francie Maginnis. The bomb was attached to the doorbell. They clearly expected the RUC to go to the man's home to evacuate him; instead a neighbour, Peter Begley, went to warn Mr Maginnis. When he rang the bell it detonated the bomb, and he was seriously injured.

In another incendiary bombing at a Newry disco a month later, a DJ had his hand blown off.

A more ambitious plot was hatched in November 1985. The INLA had not struck in England since 1980. A bombing attack was planned in London, but the original target was changed at the last moment. Chelsea Barracks was chosen instead. Explosives had been obtained from "Bap" Hughes in France, who had got them from his Action Directe contacts, and they were brought in a camper van to London. On 11 November three separate explosive devices were left outside the barracks in a package. The overall weight of the explosives was about thirty-seven pounds. Packed with nuts and bolts, it was a package meant to kill. Instead, it was defused. The camper was also recovered in London six weeks later. In it were traces of explosives consistent with those from which the Chelsea Barracks bombs were constructed.

The van belonged to James McLaughlin, a friend of Bap Hughes. When the police raided McLaughlin's Belfast home in March 1986, among the items they uncovered were a map of London, electrical circuit boards, and a roll of film that, when developed, showed a picture of McLaughlin and Peter Stewart, a close colleague of O'Reilly's, in Paris. McLaughlin was later arrested with Hughes and the Nortons attempting to smuggle weapons from Le Havre to Ireland in a camper (see chapter 11).

When the bombs had failed to go off and were defused, the bombing team seem to have panicked, abandoning their van.

A follow-up investigation led to the arrest and conviction of a Derry man, Patrick McLaughlin (no relation to the van owner). McLaughlin is almost certainly an innocent man. He had been in London for a week supposedly looking for work but actually spending his money and time drinking. His links to the bomb team seem to have been no more than accidental. He claims he was on a drinking spree with an acquaintance from Derry called Peter O'Loughlin and accepted a lift in the camper, in which were three men whom O'Loughlin knew. The camper took them from one pub to another. McLaughlin was carrying a bag of washing he had earlier done in a launderette, and a puzzle magazine with his home address on it. The magazine was found in the camper, and helped lead the police to his home in Derry, where he had returned before Christmas after making up with his wife. In spite of the flimsy evidence against him, McLaughlin was sentenced to life imprisonment.

The bungled London bombing was just one of many failures that characterised INLA operations in 1985. The truth was that during the year the energies of the INLA were absorbed not in the armed struggle but in an internecine battle for control of the organisation, from which John O'Reilly, the former OC of the Markets area, emerged the winner. It was the prelude to a tragedy that was to engulf the INLA and from which it would never recover.

O'Reilly was a man with a decidedly mixed reputation. There were those within the INLA who regarded him with deep distrust, going so far as to accuse him of being an informer. Others who estimated him highly describe such allegations as "despicable". He impressed some with his bravery. According to Terry Harkin, "as an operator, he was quite courageous and highly committed." (Interview, 21 January 1994).

However, suspicions about him dated back to the late 1970s, when he was arrested by the RUC after a shooting attack on the High Courts, which it is alleged he carried out after a night's drinking. A gun was recovered by the police with O'Reilly's fingerprints on it—he had not been wearing gloves. However, he managed to avoid going to jail. O'Reilly is said to have told fellow INLA members that he had agreed to work as an informer for the police in order to get them to release him. Ronnie Bunting, then OC of Belfast, held an inquiry into the incident; afterwards he ordered O'Reilly to be dismissed with ignominy from the organisation.

Within a year he was back in the INLA. When Gerard Steenson rose to power, O'Reilly once more became active in the Markets and Short Strand areas. He was again arrested and held between July and November 1981. Later that year O'Reilly was involved in Steenson's plot to assassinate Harry Flynn in Dublin, and took part in the attempts on the lives of Flynn's brother Seán, Jackie Goodman, and Bernard Dorrian. O'Reilly was OC of the Markets INLA when the decision was made to murder the former loyalist leader and British agent John McKeague, a killing that has been linked to various undercover intrigues (see chapter 9). He may, indeed, have given the order for McKeague to be shot. A series of informers, including Goodman, McAllister, and Kirkpatrick, named him in early 1982, and he was arrested along with Steenson in the swoops that followed.

In jail the INLA began to break up into warring factions. By late 1984 they had crystallised into three bodies. There was that around Gerard Steenson, a group who opposed him, and one that associated itself with Tom McAllister. (McAllister had been jailed in 1978 after being shot by the RUC when allegedly on a bombing mission.) Steenson's men, who included Jimmy Brown, were angry and disillusioned at the course the INLA had taken since their arrest in 1982. Incidents such as Darkley, as well as the prevalence of informers and the growing tales of corruption in Belfast, had forced them to the conclusion that the INLA was no longer the organisation to which they had given their allegiance.

Those who opposed Steenson were a more loosely knit body and included the INLA chief of staff "Jap", O'Reilly, and a few INLA veterans such as "Ta" Power and Hugh Torney. Though Power was also in favour of reforms, their overriding aim was to preserve the organisation. O'Reilly seems not to have been much interested in the debate about reforming and restructuring that was going on inside and outside the prisons. He was ambitious to take charge of the INLA and make himself chief of staff.

McAllister shifted position as time went by, at first drawing close to the O'Reilly group and then changing course and aligning with O'Reilly's opponents.

In 1984, John O'Reilly, though facing serious charges in the Kirkpatrick trial, was released on bail. On 18 October, along with Kevin McQuillan, he staged a token one-day fast in Dunville Park on the Falls Road in protest at the use of supergrass evidence. Soon afterwards he jumped bail and fled south. He was determined to solidify his position within the INLA and remove anyone who got in the way. He ordered the shooting of two INLA men, John Boyd and Jimmy McCrystal; he also planned to shoot Róisín McDonough, the girl-friend of Jimmy Brown, but the men sent to carry out the task could not find her.

Meanwhile O'Reilly established himself in Dundalk. "Guys had to rob fish-and-chip shops so he could go to the republic" was the bitter comment of one of the founding members of the IPLO, who later opposed O'Reilly. In Dundalk he joined forces with "Peter McCormick", the former high-ranking Provisional IRA man from north Belfast who had been involved in arms procurement for the IRA in the United States (see chapter 11). O'Reilly carried out a "bloodless coup" against Jap, to whom the post of chief of staff had been handed on by McGlinchey. He despatched McCormick to tell Jap that he was "stood down". The ease with which O'Reilly became chief of staff of the INLA did not characterise the methods he used to hold on to his position.

O'Reilly saw the veterans of the INLA's original leadership, based mainly in Dublin and the Munster area, as a threat to his rule. Harry Flynn and Gerry Roche had been released from Port Laoise in 1984. They had not given up the hope that the organisation founded by Costello might yet be reconstructed. The foundation for their work was a narrow one, but it was a beginning. They had support in Dublin, some in Belfast and in parts of Munster, and the remnants of an IRSP cumann in Waterford, as well as connections in England and other countries. On this small base they hoped a new organisation might arise.

Their efforts posed a threat to O'Reilly's own legitimacy as chief of staff. A dispute broke out between the two factions in the usual way. Two of O'Reilly's supporters lifted weapons and a sum of money from a dump that belonged to the Dublin-Munster group. O'Reilly contacted Roche to arrange for a meeting to patch up a peace between them. The meeting was to take place near Shannon; but as Roche was waiting at the designated place, a gunman drove up and opened fire. Roche dived for cover in a nearby bungalow, which happened to be the home of a Special Branch officer. Dangerous invitations were to become a hallmark of O'Reilly's rule.

The attempt on Flynn was to take place in Lower Gardiner Street in Dublin as he arrived to collect the dole. But he spotted the hit-men's scout, whom he recognised. When he confronted the scout, the gunmen panicked and fled. One of them was O'Reilly.

The new chief of staff was in charge of an organisation that was desperate for weapons. He suspected that Stephen King and Séamus Ruddy, who were living in Paris, were still supplying the Dublin faction, or at least knew where its arms dumps were hidden. Towards the end of May 1985, O'Reilly and "McCormick" arrived in Paris, where they met "Bap" Hughes and a fourth man from Derry. Hughes, who had been in Paris since 1982, was sympathetic to the O'Reilly faction and had agreed to help them. They first approached Stephen King, who had been one of *les Trois Irlandais des Vincennes* but had not been involved in the movement for a long time. When he told them he knew nothing about arms shipments, O'Reilly and Hughes badly beat him. They decided to try their luck with Séamus Ruddy, who they knew had been involved in arms procurement. Acting through an intermediary, they got in touch with him.

Ruddy had been an active member of both the IRSP and the INLA from the late 1970s. From April 1980 he was on the party's Ard-Chomhairle; by 1981 he was national organiser, and during the hunger strike he played an active role as a go-between for the families of the INLA hunger strikers. He was popular and well liked by many in the movement. His last known involvement with arms running was in the autumn of 1983, when the Gardaí found documents on him relating to an arms shipment from Australia (see chapter 11). After this incident, Ruddy broke all links with the INLA and settled into a teaching job in Paris.

Ruddy was wary of the invitation from O'Reilly, Hughes and McCormick when they asked him to meet them. But his safety was guaranteed by another, whom he did trust. He agreed to meet O'Reilly and the others at a bar in Montparnasse. From there they left to go to the apartment of the Derry man, who was a friend of Hughes. In the apartment Ruddy was questioned by the former Provisional, who specialised in "debriefings" and interrogating suspected informers. He was asked to reveal his arms-running operations to Ireland. When Ruddy told them he was no longer involved they allegedly beat him badly (though "McCormick" denies this). After further "interrogations" and beatings, he was then shot in the head and buried.

Séamus Ruddy's body has never been recovered. His anguished family and friends have made repeated appeals for information about the fate that befell him. Two months after he vanished, his English girl-friend, Cecilia Moore, was still uncertain what had happened. She told the *Sunday Tribune*, "I hope he's not dead but I think at this stage he must be." (*Sunday Tribune*, 7 July 1985.) The INLA lied to her, and continued to lie. In August, Moore said that she had met an INLA man in Paris who told her that her boy-friend had been sent back to Ireland to face an inquiry. After the meeting the organisation issued a statement that said: "After an exhaustive enquiry in the Newry area, we find no evidence to suggest that members of the INLA were involved. We are issuing this statement to clarify our position on this matter." (*Irish News*, 17 August 1985.) Cecilia Moore commented: "If they were making serious enquiries into his disappearance, surely the first place they would make exhaustive enquiries would be Paris, not Newry." Nine years after Ruddy's brutal murder, the two men who know where his body is refuse to divulge the information, for the simple reason that without a body the French police have no crime to investigate.

"It was a macho thing," said a former member of the INLA Army Council; "Séamus was murdered for no reason at all. They killed him for their own ego." (Interview, 7 January 1994.) He compared the situation faced by the Ruddy family to that of the families of the thousands of Argentines who had been "disappeared" by the regime. This man was one of those for whom the murder of Ruddy was a turning-point in their opposition to O'Reilly and his regime. Among the factions that were formed or forming, the notion of revenge began to take shape.

In jail in Belfast, Gerard Steenson was on trial as one of some twenty-seven facing charges on the word of Harry Kirkpatrick. He had time to think about his situation and that of the organisation whose fate he had been so influential in determining. In April he initiated a series of contacts with people on the outside, former INLA members and those who constituted what was left of the original movement, in an effort to forge a course for the future. One of those he wanted to contact was Harry Flynn, the man whose murder he had planned less than four years earlier.

The contact began indirectly. Jimmy Brown communicated with Terry Robson, the former IRSP leader from Derry, that Steenson was interested in opening up lines of communication with Flynn, Roche, and Robson himself. Robson went in to see Brown to convey to him that Flynn and Roche were "interested in dialogue—and nothing more!" (Letter from Robson to Flynn, 14 April 1985).

Robson wrote: "As one can expect with Jimmy he had plenty to say— some of value but most consisting of rhetoric. In short, he said that they were about to distribute 'coms.' to yourself, Gerry Roche, and I consisting of their ideas and suggestions for a future 'democratically' structured movement. He said that he and GS [Steenson] were concerned to ensure that any subsequent developments would guarantee against attempts by relatively strong areas such as Belfast having a veto on any future agreements. He was concerned to make us aware that if the 'coms.' give an appearance of arrogance that we were to ignore it as merely their difficulty in conveying ideas satisfactorily through the medium of coms.

"On a more positive level he said that there is a need to return to the reason for the existence of the movement and trace its development throughout the last eleven years—a view which somewhat echoed what you had to say. Clearly, they are not at all happy with the newly discovered 'Marxism/Leninism' and wish to see a return to basic Republican values (presumably) vis-a-vis the national question. More specifically they are of the opinion that they have a great deal of influence within Belfast and feel that their emergence on to the streets will transform present allegiances (I think I've heard that one before). They believe McQuillan [Belfast IRSP leader] is an idiot—and worse—an opportunist.[2] Their former friend O'Reilly is just exactly that—a *former* friend. Dornan is a disaster. The litany, as you can imagine, becomes endless and boring ... Of course, the whole question of J.B. [Jimmy Brown] and company maybe entirely academic as Harry Kirkpatrick may prove to be an acceptable witness in which case a great many people can breathe sighs of relief. I'm not too sure how you would view that as a development but I wouldn't be too optimistic. Perhaps all that we are doing is creating a new monster for ourselves.

"Finally, you will probably be aware that the conflict inside Crumlin Road has degenerated into a slanging match about who made statements to the RUC and who didn't. They (JB and coy) allege that 'Ta' [Power] made a few damaging statements the last time he spent time inside. And so it goes on—and on—ad nauseum!"

There followed a series of coms from Steenson, some thirteen of which have survived, most of them undated. However, his first is dated 9 April, and was therefore written within two weeks of the beginning of the Kirkpatrick trial. Like the others that followed, it was meticulously written on cigarette papers and sheets of toilet paper that had been smuggled out of the prison. Each is a densely packed essay and shows an extremely articulate young man, possessed of analytical skills and a burning political ambition.[3]

Steenson declared to Flynn: "We see a potential realignment of progressives as absolutely crucial in the ongoing crisis affecting the remnants of the movement in its present form ... No movement presently exists resembling the movement, organisation, we were once part of. On what basis should the 'disjointed elements' reform? How is our republican socialism distinct from SF's and the PD [People's Democracy]? They are far from bland questions and are issues of great importance to us here, who, after years of disillusionment with the pathetic L/ship [leadership] of recent times seek a return to roots ...

"The word L/ship is a misnomer as none effectively exists or functions. There is no national movement under their control. They have pockets of larger or smaller groups in B/fast, Derry, perhaps Newry, a few in D/dalk but examination of these loose affiliates reveals no cohesion, no direction, little structure, few quality personnel though ample IRA security rejects and other assorted undesirables ... Those claiming L/ship status: their self-appointed legitimacy is invalid based on no mandate other than gangs earlier described."

He asks if the current INLA leaders have the potential to further the movement's aims, and answers: "No. Even worse, they permit Darkley, and murder old men, Sunday school teachers." The "old man" was William Nixon, a Protestant shot dead at random by the INLA in Belfast in 1982, as was the teacher Karen McKeown in the same incident. It is interesting to note that Steenson, in contradiction to his "Dr Death" image, was outraged by these random murders. In fact under his leadership there were no random sectarian killings carried out by the Belfast INLA.

He continues: "I'll not develop the roll of dishonour further ... suffice to say they have collectively distorted, misrepresented and corrupted the m/ments objectives in an intolerable way. Our intention is to quite simply suppress the gang leaders and effectively disperse the remainder on a national basis. Eradicate the vile influence of their few mouthpiece trendy lefties and support a nucleus of men comprised of men here in the blocks (soon free) and others outside already. We feel that this tried and tested corps can establish a proper organisation within a short period ...

"Ideological consistency, clarity, organisational cohesion and unity, strategical direction and tactical purpose. These are not cliches, these are our aspirations and objectives. We want to build, to construct, lasting structures ... Consensus and unity. That is our goal. Whatever happens, we are going forward."

Flynn replied on 26 April. He wrote that Tone, Lalor and Connolly provided the basis for the movement and the "understanding of the roots and class nature of the national question and its underlying problems." He criticised the "triumphalist fashion in which our party was declared a Marxist-Leninist Party. These sudden declarations show a lack of consciousness of what the terms actually mean." He calls it "empty rhetoric", which bore no relevance to the situation in the Six Counties. Answering Steenson's enquiry about criteria for membership of a restructured organisation, he says that "it is necessary that a uniform standard exists nationally. A dept. to oversee this is best. In our view it would be:

1. Anyone who agrees and accepts the objectives of the organisation and who is able to satisfy certain conditions.

2. They must be above suspicion of being touts or possible touts.

3. That they are not hoods.

4. That if they have recently resigned or been dismissed from any other organisation they state the reasons so they can be checked out.

5. Non-Irish nationals should need special ratification from a nationally accepted body.

Prospective members should undergo classes in 1. counter-interrogation, 2., History and objectives of movement. These should be used to weed out various weaknesses ... ratification should be considered carefully."

Flynn continues, concurring with his former enemy: "Our overall assessment would approximate with yours, i.e. scattered individuals and groups who lack cohesion and [are] in most cases low calibre or worse.

They draw their confidence from their *apparent* strength in Belfast and from their *apparent* legitimacy. This is through their tenuous control of structures and resources. Within their own camp there is reasonable evidence to suggest conflict between Jap and MQ [McQuillan]. How important these are we cannot assess at this time ...

"The present A/C [Army Council] has been constituted outside of any procedure ever used in past history of army by any of us. It was constituted on the basis of Yes men. C/S [chief of staff] was selected by Dominic McG some days before his arrest. Again a procedure never before given credibility. The C/S used this body to ratify him as true heir apparent." Flynn then outlines the support that "Jap" (not yet replaced by O'Reilly as chief of staff) could command.

"The following is what we know of their present condition: Newry, 4 or 5 members, no party. Dundalk: 4 incl. J. O'R who has there no party. Dublin southside: three members. Northside: three recently recruited in Ballymun, 2 undesirables and 1 ex-IRA tout. Party collapsed. Cork. No real army. Chairperson of party and wife and 1 other. Derry is not a loyal force.

"Their most important contact is Bap [Hughes] in Paris. How would he stand with you? If they lost him they would be in serious trouble. He is their only source [for weapons]. In view of all the above if we can achieve unity of purpose, disposing of present clique does not present great problems."

Steenson's reply is undated. He begins: "No major contradictions exist between us to threaten the all-important foundation stone of unified action ... I have written to P [go-between and later one of the founders of the IPLO] requesting material assistance of a specific nature which I need not repeat though I would ask your help in this matter if its in your power to do so owing to threatening behaviour and avowed intentions of Jap and co. to defend their ill-gotten gains by violent means." He writes of the IRSP/INLA "wandering in the wilderness," of the organisation being subject to the "reigns of assorted lunatics" during the past few years, and admits: "I am totally aware of my own faults and responsibilities but admittedly this is not long the case.

"At some point the unruly house must be put in order," wrote Steenson, "or the disastrous tradition of factionalising will continue." The irony of this was surely not lost on the recipient of the com, shot on Steenson's orders in 1981. "If I am freed I will come to meet you in a first declaration of trust. There will be attempts to kill myself and others though any success would owe more to luck than competency. Nevertheless, I don't propose to foolishly attempt any constructive work whilst awaiting some juvenile's bullet. Consequently, first on the agenda is the total suppression of all negative forces. This we must discuss and decide upon. If this trial collapses, we have no problems of a serious nature in B/fast. Derry fence-sitting as you observed will hardly enter the fray in defence of interests at the expense of their own." He predicts that outside of Belfast, the rest of the North "will soon understand wisdom of subordinating themselves to the newly constituted L/ship.

"This must be the last dispute of this nature," he wrote, contemplating the prospect of another feud. "Let's determine to do the thing correctly. Accept a period of press hostility. What could eclipse Darkley anyhow? ... The whole publicity aspect of these actions are of vital importance. We must project the proper image. We would like to conclude this diversion quickly by channelling all resources towards this end, the achievement of which makes possible the beginning of our real work."

However, there are problems. "Our own situation regarding materials is frankly dire in that we have only 2 shorts [handguns] and base our hopes on trawling among friends." No doubt remembering the attempted RUC ambush in September 1981, when Steenson and his unit shot dead the off-duty UDR man Alexander Stockman, he cautions: "The streets aren't what they were. Covert surveillance is a daily feature and encountering undercover RUC men now means 4 car patrols, 1 or 2 men armed with subs. This is reality today."

He adds: "I can get gear from the USA. But until actually here it may as well be on the moon."

Steenson was later informed from Dublin that the old leadership gave money, explosives, arms and its arms-running contacts to McGlinchey's predecessor as chief of staff, and then the bulk of what was left to McGlinchey himself when he took over in July 1983. There was little or nothing, clearly, that Dublin felt it could do at that time in furnishing Steenson's group with the guns it required.

Flynn replied on 12 June. "We did stay together as a nucleus of people with a common political/military purpose," in the hope that people would see the necessity of "reconstituting the whole thing ... Unfortunately that is a dead breed ... When Gerry [Roche] and I went into jail [Port Laoise, 1983–84] we were still a reasonably strong core on the outside. The months in jail took their toll on that ... I have known of talk to kill me since before Xmas [1984]. But with their failure in Munster [to kill Roche] it became more prevalent. In February they discussed it at an A/C meeting. It was in fact around that issue that an opposition was formed. In attempting to purge all opposition they created the very thing they wanted to destroy."

The old leadership had decided to "give it one last chance" and try to rebuild the organisation. They set about acquiring money and weapons, as well as starting a newspaper, *Freedom Struggle*, which appeared in the Munster area for a time. Moves were set in motion to contact "European sources" for weapons. It was at this point that the Prague PLO link was reopened (see chapter 11).

"We are very solid in Shannon, Limerick, Tipperary and have a strong unit in Dublin. We all had contacts here and there. We were happy to build slowly but correctly ... We were very aware that Jap and co. wanted to finish us, especially before the conclusion of the trial."

The com outlines problems with Dominic McGlinchey's wife, who, from being close to the Dublin-Munster axis, seems to have switched to the O'Reilly faction. "Mary McGlinchey concluded that we were not as respectful to her as she expected. She seen herself playing a leading military role. For months she wanted us to kill Jap, O'Reilly. She was well looked after in Shannon." Mary McGlinchey played a role in the building tension between the Jap-O'Reilly-McQuillan group and the others. When attempting to reconstruct the movement, Flynn and Roche had opened an old wound between two men involved in the INLA. One was in charge of a farm where the movement had concealed weapons and six thousand pounds. Mary McGlinchey, realising he was disaffected, brought people from the O'Reilly faction to see him, whereupon he surrendered the weapons and the money to them. They used him to entice a member of the Dublin leadership out to the farm, where he was "dismissed". They then made off with the six thousand pounds.[4]

In an undated com that was probably written in the early summer of 1985, Steenson describes the growing tension within the jail between his group and "the others", as he refers to them. He mentions that Jimmy Brown had been assaulted in a "clearly planned" attack. Brown had been punched in the face, and his attackers had attempted to shove his glasses into his face. Twelve of Steenson's men fought twelve of "the others", three of whom "received a fair going over." According to Steenson, "it gained us credibility in the eyes of the IRA who later reported to their B/B [Belfast Brigade] that the others had always been the aggressors and we acted only after much provocation ... The situation here is very unstable and dangerous for me because the others have a .32 revolver which our men saw under different circumstances some time ago when McGlinchey was here."

In the worst incident, in late May 1985, Paul Donnelly, a friend of Steenson's, was attacked allegedly by "Ta" Power and a Ballymurphy man, Micky Kearney. In the vicious mêlée, Donnelly bit off the tip of Kearney's nose, causing a six-day adjournment in the men's trial. Steenson reported hearing from a visitor, who had been told by the IRA, that the O'Reilly faction intended killing him before the end of his trial. "But clearly in the light of the att. on Gerry [Roche], your material going missing and the good prospects of my being acquitted these people are verging on hysteria and are capable of rashness without consideration of consequences." In the event, Steenson was found guilty and given multiple life sentences. It would take another year and a half for his appeal to run its ultimately successful course.

During that period Steenson and his supporters considered several options for their future involvement in the republican socialist movement. One of them, that of forming a new organisation altogether, is first broached in the letter tentatively dated to around May 1985. He wrote: "Some of our men have been discussing the merits and demerits of reconstituting the PLA or otherwise completely dissociating ourselves from the disreputable INLA legacy of recent years by launching a new organisation. The crux of the matter being: not only are the present L/ship irredeemable but the entire structures and grass roots members are also in the same category as is the INLA image ... the name is now associated with trendy leftism, thuggery, sectarianism etc. ..."

The idea of a clean break will reoccur, finally becoming the preferred course. In the meantime, Steenson warns Flynn: "They may attempt a 'lift' [kidnap] to discover from their captive where arms are dumped. They have been trying to catch a couple of our men in Belfast but haven't succeeded to date. Odds on they will kill some fringe person and use the resulting publicity to issue more ridiculous statements to the media threatening mayhem to bolster their own faint hearted." This warning proved prophetic: it came shortly before Séamus Ruddy was "lifted" and murdered in Paris in just such an attempt to find arms.

"I feel we need a deterrent in here now," Steenson continued, "because it's only a matter of time before an attempt is made to shoot, stab or otherwise debilitate me, their theory being if I'm removed the rest will break up ... If you have a miniature weapon of any description: pistol, Dillinger, zip-gun, pen-gun, anything of that nature I would appreciate the use of it ... But the nearer I get to the street the move panicky I expect them to get. They speak of the dangers of being caught in a pincer movement by you in Dublin and me in Belfast ... keep you head down, G."

One of Steenson's group, nicknamed "Geek", later confirmed that the O'Reilly faction plotted to murder Steenson in jail. "He was the target of a poisoning attempt by O'Reilly's crowd. O'Reilly feared Gerard. Then we got wind of an attempt to strangle him with cheese wire in a toilet inside the Crum. But we managed to stop that in time. No wonder Gerard wanted to get back at this gang." (Interview, 19 August 1993.)

After the May 1985 local elections, which Sinn Féin fought, winning fifty-nine seats, Steenson diverges from the main theme of his coms to reflect on the role of the IRA's political wing and its future strategy. Ironically for the man who had opposed the IRSP entering the 1981 local elections, he praises Sinn Féin's efforts.[5]

In a com undated but probably written in the spring or early summer of 1985, Steenson writes that he is satisfied with the quality of the men who will support him, who, he says, are of "particular quality and calibre. Others", he writes, "are committed in principle on the basis of mutual aspirations and political harmony. These must ultimately, being natural allies, come our way irrespective of short-term misgivings as to the inevitability of violence of an internecine nature.

"Understanding these people as I do and realising that the almost monastery atmosphere of the small self-contained communities that are the H/Block wings affects men strangely by narrowing perspectives, creating false illusions about outside conditions etc., I know it is virtually impossible to force objectivity upon them and consequently they tend to see things through rose-coloured glasses and imagine everywhere else is the same as their little wings. It is quite startling at times to read some of the writings that emerge from there, completely at odds with reality. What matters is their attitude a month after hitting the streets. We have been successful in that those we need we have, those we want we have good prospects of getting, and none of crucial significance actively oppose us ... Should we get out coinciding with the suppression of Jap and co., the remnants of their supporters in the blocks will be neutralised and control of all m/ment's prisoners placed in our own men's hands."

The problem of corruption in Belfast and the attitude of the Provisionals is referred to. "Due to widespread extortion in W/Belfast instigated by Tom McC [McCartan] the Green Cross no longer makes payments to INLA prisoners arrested after a certain date. The IRA A/C decided to kill Tom McC some time ago over the extortion issue but then declined in case of feud.[6] But this is 100% so keep it in your mind only. Indications (no more) are it's possible some attempt short of feuding will be made to bring the B/fast crew to heel if we get convicted. The IRA wish to close that side show down. Overt hostility is apparent at times towards IRSP-INLA. This in keeping with [Martin] McGuinness proposal to the closed session of the Ard Fheis regarding refusing support or assistance to anyone outside the Rep/m/ment.[7] No other bodies figure in their plans."

In this com Steenson also reveals that he had little time for "Mad Dog"

McGlinchey: "McGlinchey continues to have a divisive role in the blocks as he did here. He's now thought of as a Walter Mitty and only taken seriously by youths impressed with fairy-tales. Jap was an IRA-reject himself ..."

The main concern, however, is the future of the movement. "I would like to hear your views on how exactly we should proceed regarding Jap and Co. What are the immediate objectives as you see them, what sequence of events do you envisage? What of the party offices in Dublin, other southern cities, Derry? Any thoughts on army structure? Relation of North-South, various departments, relationship of Party-Army, control of either or both?"

However, by August the plan to constitute "a separate body" was firmly entrenched. Of the INLA leadership he writes: "They are a hotch-potch varying from Lane [IRSP chairman] to O'Reilly ... There is nothing to salvage ... We think it's pointless for HF [Harry Flynn] to fight these wasters by himself because he cannot gain anything from victory, there being nothing of value anyway ... There is a twisted logic in that fighting for something implies it's worthwhile ... We have all drank from the bitter cup of factionalism and it's sour."

In a com dated the seventh of that month, which was addressed to P, the go-between, Steenson says that he has heard that Flynn has reached an accommodation with the other main player in the complex power game, Tom McAllister, and it is obvious from his attitude that he is annoyed. McAllister was due to be released after serving a fourteen-year sentence (see chapter 6). In July 1985 he was out on parole. Steenson clearly did not trust him: he believed that McAllister was only interested in becoming chief of staff of the organisation. He tells Flynn that any approaches from McAllister will be rejected. "We are out and will not return" to the INLA, he writes. But, he adds, if Flynn stays in "and comes to prominence we would consider good relations worthwhile but that apart future disputes within the [INLA] will not concern us and HF must rely on himself. Not that he hasn't always done so—I give him credit for it but let's understand where we stand. This McA will come to nothing. He will inherit a slag heap but the weight of the 'clever' prince crown on his head may distort his *perception* of reality for awhile."

Replying in a com dated 19 August, Flynn lists a series of positions, the last three of which are concerned with relations between McAllister, Steenson, and the "old gaurd". "3 ... We firmly believe that McA is a progressive force; 4: We have not worked out any accommodation with him; 5: We did not exclude you or your people from any accommodation, as ... none exists; 6: We firmly believe that you and your comrades are a progressive force which cannot be excluded."

Flynn says that they had accepted two proposals from McAllister: that a "convention" be held to resolve the serious difficulties and that "we would engage in no provocative actions while this was being arranged. We met him in July and were informed that the l/ship had refused the proposal of a convention" and that "they intended to pursue attacks on G/R [Gerry Roche], H/F [Harry Flynn] and another. We agreed to facilitate further attempts by avoiding conflict with the 'others'." The com ends by arguing that it is too soon to make a final decision on the INLA's future, as too many factors remained unresolved. Flynn writes that it would be "tactically disastrous" to take such a decision now; the outcome of the Kirkpatrick trial was still unknown, and meanwhile the bulk of Steenson's supporters remain in jail making, Flynn says, the whole exercise "abstract".

Steenson wrote back to Flynn on 13 September that an alignment between him and McAllister was "a logical extension of the points you made. As yet I know nothing of McA's position regarding us here though much ascribed to him is of a contradictory nature. Your note omitted to mention his attitude to us but it must have been stated during discussion. As it is McA failed to deliver a convention and the B [Belfast] leadership threatens you still. How will McA overcome this difficulty? Hypothetically, say McA approaches us with a view to reconciliation. First question. Who does he represent? Himself alone, sections of B/fast or the L/ship?" Steenson points out that if McAllister is in a minority "his influence is negligible as are the prospects of reconciliation under such conditions. If he could effect change peacefully then his willingness to engage in dialogue would be worthy of response and we will meet with him if invited to do so ... He meets with Ta Power tomorrow (14). I expect him to be criticised because of his association with you." In the meantime, Steenson reported, his group would remain "open minded" about a possible alliance with McAllister. "Until McA the option was to feud or dissociate. Is negotiation an alternative?"

To this Flynn replied two weeks later: "Once again let us state our position i.e. McA. 1) We do view him as a progressive force. 2) We do not believe he on his own can effect radical change. 3) We believe that given the right circumstances he could play an important role towards constructive 'reconciliation'."

However, Steenson continued to drift away from the notion of reforming the INLA with or without an alliance with McAllister. When he learnt that O'Reilly was chief of staff, this seemed to strengthen his opinion that the organisation was past redemption. In an undated com he wrote: "I feel

[INLA] is creditless, at its lowest ebb ever ... It's useful to find O'R in the position of C/S. I'm sure it will work wonders for their credibility in the eyes of the IRA who think him an informer. Let me know what's going to be done."

Following his meeting with "Ta" Power, McAllister at first drew closer to the O'Reilly faction. Upon his release from the Maze in the late summer of 1985, with the agreement of the O'Reilly leadership he became OC of Belfast and began to consolidate his position there. He was committed to cleaning up the movement. However, things did not go well in the relationship with O'Reilly. McAllister was increasingly critical of O'Reilly's behaviour. At one point O'Reilly delivered explosives and weapons to him in a known car. This caused a dispute. McAllister called O'Reilly a "cowboy". There was a rupture. It was then that McAllister became aware that O'Reilly and his men had discussed a plan to have him shot.

In early 1986 a meeting was arranged between McAllister and the O'Reilly faction, which by then included Peter Stewart, a republican from north Belfast who had joined the INLA and was close to its chief of staff. At McAllister's insistence it was held in Dublin Airport, where the stringent security would ensure that no-one could show up armed. (McAllister had known of O'Reilly's reputation.) The meeting seemingly patched things up, and confirmed McAllister as OC of Belfast.

However, after his return to Belfast, McAllister was alerted to the fact that O'Reilly was about to import an arms shipment from France. The arms had been purchased after a robbery in France in which INLA personnel were involved with Action Directe. McAllister was told that O'Reilly intended to use the arms to carry out a St Valentine's Day-style massacre of him and his supporters in Belfast and elsewhere. He fled to Dublin and pleaded with the old guard to intervene and prevent the weapons from falling into O'Reilly's hands. He offered them half of the haul, which was supposed to include £30,000 from the proceeds of the robbery. The Dublin-Munster leadership agreed to help him but declined to accept the weapons. All they wanted from McAllister was a commitment that he would "reform" the INLA and IRSP.

The plan went ahead. O'Reilly had sent two men to meet the vehicle carrying the weapons when they arrived in Ireland in the spring of 1986. McAllister and his men were there, including members of the Dublin faction. McAllister said they had come to "escort" the haul. They took it over without opposition. O'Reilly's men were left unaware that the gear was in fact being appropriated. However, when the haul was examined there was no trace of the £30,000. This joint operation meant that by 1986, McAllister had drawn close to the Dublin-Munster axis, as had Steenson. This alliance was to stay intact through the bloody feud of the following year.

However, attempts were still being made to avoid that conflict. In Steenson's coms he writes: "The others now have a proposition before us which amounts essentially to this: They want a guarantee to be given by me in person to Fr. Des Wilson that we do not intend attacking them upon release. They agree to the same terms to be made in person by one we nominate from their side. No negotiations of any sort were proposed save this mutual non-aggression pact before a witness. In return they pledge to desist from further threat or attack on our people. Central to this reduction in tension is we cede them the name and current structure of the [INLA] which we had decided to do regardless. They say our business is then our own affair; whatever we constitute ourselves as is no concern of theirs. This is attractive to men here and in the [blocks] who primarily want to engage the enemy and not waste time feuding." But he adds: "We are not naive and don't accept the word of such as these." He reserves the right to strike back if attacked. He goes on: "Disputing with that band of rabble will accomplish nothing. Unless totally suppressed their negative influence will remain. That's why we say, abandon them, ignore this corps of thugs and join together with us in preliminary work to build anew." Steenson says he will not agree to the pact with O'Reilly unless Flynn and Roche are included in its terms.

Clearly, his reasons for accepting the pact were heavily qualified by the circumstances, which he admits. "When they propositioned us we were in the position where if we agreed the possibility of a solution was raised and if we refused they would likely come together in their collective fear and maybe attack someone outside we are unable to protect. Besides all of these factors, there are those of culpability and diplomacy to consider. Who wants to be seen as negative to peaceful resolution and therefore responsible for any trouble arising? ... I would appear a feud-monger if I refused to try for peace. Once they avow to Fr. Wilson what light will they appear in should they break the terms?"

His intentions to avoid a feud were obviously conditional, and Steenson was still pursuing possibilities of getting arms, including one in which the IRA would be unknowing helpers. In a com of which part is missing he writes: "I have been in touch with an old contact dating back to 1981. This man imports material for the Provies. His association with me is discreet and he declares a willingness to assist me in a material way when recently asked. As you can imagine this must be treated very confidentially. This person met the bearer of this note and accepts any approach from this quarter as legitimate. It's not a question of stealing their stuff. The proposition is we buy from their sources, paying their prices, unknown to them and they unwittingly transport it into the country for us. The cost is no more because of this but you pay the 'shop' price. I haven't went into details with him yet so don't know what numbers he can supply. Because of what I told him he might think I only want a 'personal' [weapon]! But he may be able to supply several ...

"This is totally above board, not a case of us having material and trying to raise cash. I want that absolutely clear because anything we later come upon won't have to be bought or sold but given freely among comrades. This is an option in response to an emergency. Use it or not as you decide. Anything you get is your own. Just be very quiet about it because this person's neck is on the chopping block if the Provies learned of his sympathy for us, especially now when the material might be used in a feud ... I understand our contact can facilitate us only periodically, in other words only when the Provies are receiving themselves can something be added. This is a serious matter, P. A man not to be endangered ... I can't get any of the material in the USA released to anyone other than myself were I to beg for it on my knees, it's impossible ... That's another reason for us to end this little trial soon. I have to negotiate for the material personally. Regards, G."

The Dublin-Munster group shied away from this proposal to act as a cuckoo in the Provo nest.

The last com from Steenson to Flynn is dated 12 June 1986, six months before the Appeal Court quashed his sentence and he was released. By that stage O'Reilly had gone to jail, on foot of a British extradition warrant. A close colleague of O'Reilly's (whose name is left blank below for legal reasons) had temporarily taken over from him. But McAllister continued to consolidate his position within the INLA, effectively gaining control of Belfast, which as always was the key to controlling the organisation.

Steenson describes these events and reports that he and his comrades were now "civilians", i.e. unaligned to any movement. He writes: "What information I have re. recent takeover is scant because detailed intelligence has not been sought. As communications improve more will be known ... What is known: Bap [Hughes] has agreed to supply McA with material. Bap, McQ mediated between McA and — after a raid on —'s place. McA declined to take over fund-raising activities of —. McA gave an undertaking to Sinn Féin re. the same. They think him open to influence ... That is all I know. None of it can be verified just yet. Re. Torney and Co.[8] Torney received visits from McA since sentencing. Nothing to suggest any change from that already known. Power—offered Adj, Camp. First report unsure if offer accepted or rejected. Has been openly calling for disbandment of IRSP m/ment in favour of rev. vanguard party!

"Politics of it unknown as yet. My own position and that of my comrades—civilian status under SF. Involvement offered by Camp OC, Inky. Declined. Asked if group existed. Replied, No. Situation here different to Crum [Crumlin Road jail]. Group structure unnecessary. No threat posed. All factions dispersed throughout H/Bs [H-blocks]. S/F defacto control. IRSP extinct. Exceptions—Torney and Co. Gerry Dowdall, John Knocker—ex-stalwarts—civilians also.[9] No question of us propping up IRSP structure at behest of outside. My standard response re. to future intentions—plan retirement. See no merit in discussing anything with IRSP in here, S/F in here, re. future before actual presence on streets. That no hostility is planned is true. But possible participation politically is private matter for those concerned. Existence of group fanned fires of Torney and Co. who cried wolf, civilian status comfortable, non-threatening in penal setting. Calming effect."

He continues: "Basic view of McA coup—for a year or so McA sought change via manipulation of others, ineffective. Front-running from rear lead to inevitable dispute with [O'Reilly's successor]. Coup expected. Onus on McA to produce results, operational, organisational. Any group capable of sporadic success, McA the same. Improvements—discipline—personnel—likely in relative terms. Genuine attempt to develop acknowledged. Long term survival doubtful ... McA lacking quality middle-management in sufficient numbers. Edicts from above ineffective below. If forced to get exposed via activity arrest follows, development halts, reverses. Expect McA exhausted in 6 months. What ideological basis of McA's alliance? If founded on op. [operational] success will split first crisis. Are people politically committed to McA or just seeking excitement? Your possible realignment—you see McA less harmful than previous C/S and think him preferable on that basis. I accept—on that basis."

There then follows a consideration of the IRSP's fate, and Flynn's group's relationship to it. Soon Steenson, obsessively, returns to the burning question: "Are we to realign with McA and secure control then clean house? It's necessary for clarity now. Don't want to waste energy without gain. Once central question is clarified realignment—in or out—can begin to work. To ensure McA's position you need to give more material aid. He needs direction and L/ship. If he survives, he may do some good. His intentions probably are but he is or was aligned with —.

"Torney—If freed, McA's influence wanes, Torney's waxes. That troublesome—Torney or us—no possibility of unity—any circumstances. If

McA ousted what gain your co-operation? Practical view. Central question is what basis realignment? I appreciate your view that to allow IRSP to deteriorate to c.rev. [counter-revolutionary] state by withdrawing your people was dangerous and you said this last year. You have to get in or get out and develop something otherwise it's time-marking fruitlessly. Could in theory back McA for short periods and be no further in five years time. Must decide if McA represents good bet or best likely and do what's necessary to consolidate, or develop alternative. I stated this before and it still needs resolution. For a re-al. [realignment] there has to be a rallying point. What is it? I don't know about McA. I expect little. None of them, IRSP, L/s [leadership] have been effective. You can assess more accurately than I. I would like to hear your views on what I have said. As you requested I *will not* discuss the contents of our exchanges with *anyone*—regards, G."

Flynn did not reply to this com. Within three weeks of it being written he was in jail in France, where he remained until 1988 (see chapter 11). The realignments would take place without his participation, as would the blood-letting that followed. Steenson would find himself aligned to McAllister, the Dublin-Munster axis, and a new force that had appeared on the scene.

By the autumn of 1986, for the INLA the writing was, literally, on the wall. In Catherine Street North in the Markets area a new four-letter acronym appeared on a gable end: *IPLA*. This was a throwback to 1975 and the People's Liberation Army. It would soon be amended to IPLO—"Irish People's Liberation Organisation". A cabal of disaffected INLA veterans had met in June and decided that a total break with the organisation was the only way forward. Steenson had heard rumours about them in jail, but nothing was certain.

On 12 November, the IPLO struck. Constable Derek Patterson was shot dead in University Avenue. At the end of November it issued its second claim of responsibility after one of its volunteers threw a grenade through the security grille at Queen Street RUC station in Belfast. Six policemen lay injured as the bomber melted into the pre-Christmas shopping crowd.

The new group turned its attention to fellow-republicans whom it regarded as renegades. The first to be targeted was John O'Reilly: the IPLO sentenced him to death. On his release from Port Laoise he was invited to a meeting with them. They were intending to shoot him. However, he did not show up.

The IPLO then decided to move against Tom McCartan, an INLA figure who was isolated from all factions and hated by most. "He made thousands on the back of the struggle," commented an IPLO leader. McCartan's death sentence was confirmed when he was accused of threatening a republican and spreading black propaganda against another former INLA leader. Three days before Christmas, as he was returning to his Andersonstown home, two gunmen stepped out of the shadows and cut him down. The IPLO claimed responsibility for ending the life of the man who had been denounced for his extortion rackets. "He was killed because he abused the Republican struggle for his own selfish ends. Any other cause other than this is totally irrelevant and purely opportunistic," said the IPLO's statement. "We have no connection with any other republican organisation."

The very day that the IPLO slew McCartan, the Appeal Court freed the twenty-four men still in custody on the evidence of Harry Kirkpatrick. In spite of Steenson's affirmations about the necessity of avoiding a feud, it was clear that the splinters into which the INLA had fragmented had one thing in common: their sharpest ends were pointing at the heart of John O'Reilly and his men.

NOTES

1. Grew had been one of the INLA's most active members. He was one of the few to have been questioned about the Neave assassination. On his release he became part of an IRA unit operating on the Continent, where he is believed to have carried out attacks on off-duty British military personnel in 1989 and 1990. On 9 October 1990 he and another member of the IRA were killed by an SAS unit in County Tyrone. Grew's brother Séamus, also in the INLA, had died in a shoot-to-kill attack along with Roddy Carroll in late 1982.

2. McQuillan was later shot in the face by Steenson in an attempted murder during the 1987 feud (see chapter 13).

3. There is a striking contrast between the image of Steenson that emerges from these "coms" and the "Dr Death" psychopathic gunman image that was beginning to appear in the media at this time. Steenson certainly was ruthless but far from thoughtless.

4. Mary McGlinchey was murdered in appalling circumstances in 1987. Though the killing took place during the feud, it had no direct link with it (see chapter 13).

5. Steenson shows himself a shrewd analyst, correctly predicting that the Provisionals would have to abandon their abstentionist policy in relation to the Dáil. "If they wish to elevate the national question onto the top of the agenda they will have to take this step ... The unifying force within the Provos is the continuing A/struggle." He also reflects on IRA tactics and targets and how they affect the movement's political standing. "I feel the

Provos have harmed themselves these last few years by an over-dependence on off-duty targets. There's no question of morality here but a purely tactical objection in that I think it is very important in light of the Ulsterisation and criminalisation policies of the Brits to portray the A/S [armed struggle] in its proper light as an anti-colonial war especially for international consumption. Okay most nationalists can identify off-duty targets for what they are and have little sympathy but how does this look internationally? Can other peoples acknowledge these actions as guerrilla operations or could the F/O [Foreign Office] gain ground at our expense and distort issues?"

6. McCartan was shot dead in December 1986 by the IPLO (see below).

7. Martin McGuinness, a high-ranking member of the republican movement from Derry and vice-president of Sinn Féin, had been strongly opposed to the IRSP and the INLA from the start and had tried to curtail their growth in Derry.

8. Hugh Torney was a veteran INLA leader who sided with O'Reilly. He was one of those named by Kirkpatrick. In 1993 he was named in court as INLA chief of staff.

9. Dowdall and Knocker were serving long sentences for murder and related offences. Dowdall had been wounded in a shoot-out with the British army in south Derry in 1977 (see chapter 4).

13

THE PROPHETS ARMED

Within weeks of Steenson's release, the anti-O'Reilly forces coalesced. Two years of tentative approaches ended in an embrace that would have murderous consequences.

John O'Reilly's INLA was caught in a pincer movement. In Belfast the IPLO had emerged and was spoiling for a fight. Tom McAllister's core, consisting of twenty experienced activists, was well armed and in control of a large arsenal of weapons, some of which had been hijacked the year before from O'Reilly's men. Then the men who followed Gerard Steenson were back on the streets, nursing deep grudges against their former comrades, while in Dublin and Munster there was the remains of the old guard led by a former IRSP general secretary, who completed the coalition ranged against the INLA leader.

Steenson's talk of pacts with O'Reilly was put aside when he saw the weaponry available to the anti-O'Reilly forces. This convinced him that the time had come to "clean house", which he believed could be done in one swift, brutal blow. The blow had to be aimed at O'Reilly, Peter Stewart, his close associate, and Hugh Torney, who had become identified with the Markets man's leadership. The fourth important person who was close to John O'Reilly was "Ta" Power—well respected and well liked in republican circles.

Like Gerard Steenson, Power was also putting down his thoughts on the future of the INLA/IRSP movement. Unlike Steenson, however, he still saw a future for the INLA/IRSP, albeit radically different from what it had been in the past. A native of the Markets area in Belfast, he remained solidly loyal to John O'Reilly. Both men had joined the Official IRA Fianna in the Markets when they were in their early teens, and they had operated together in the Markets when the INLA was at its height in Belfast during the hunger strike. Unlike O'Reilly, however, Power also saw himself as a political strategist. He was widely schooled in the classic works of Marxism, and espoused communist ideas while held in the Maze.

While imprisoned on the word of Harry Kirkpatrick, Ta Power started to muse on the failings of the movement he joined while still an Official IRA prisoner in Long Kesh in 1975. He expressed concern about where the INLA/IRSP was heading. Just like Steenson, Ta Power saw that the organisation was reaching a crisis point.

In an essay that eventually became known as "An historical analysis of the IRSP", Power wrote: "Another trend arises of prestige building, of wanting to be seen and known as being the 'lad'. This in turn attracts the ambitious power-seeking individual who begins to consolidate his position to build a power base. This was manifested in periods 1979–81 and from 1982 onwards. A lowering of standards eventually comes into being where criminal type elements are allowed entrance and rise to prominence. The result is constant crises, factions, instability and discredit." (*Starry Plough.*)

Oddly, these were the very same problems that Gerard Steenson highlighted in his "coms". Although in opposing camps, both men had indirectly prophesied the bloody feud that was just around the corner.

On the outside, John O'Reilly's faction decided to show the world they still meant business. Ten days after the murder of Constable Patterson (see chapter 12), two journalists and a photographer were invited by O'Reilly to witness a show of strength near Dundalk in response to the IPLO's emergence. On a border farm, nineteen armed and masked men put on a display of Heckler and Koch rifles, AK47s, Uzi submachine-guns, and an M16 rifle with a laser scope that O'Reilly's faction claimed was capable of shooting down a helicopter.

O'Reilly himself joined the display. He was pictured in a Dublin magazine, masked, wearing a green combat jacket, and brandishing an M16 rifle.

Yet throughout 1986 the INLA under John O'Reilly's leadership had not killed a single member of the security forces in Northern Ireland. By the end of that year the fledgling IPLO had killed one RUC man and seriously injured two others.

On the political front the IRSP was falling apart. Five members of the Ard-Chomhairle resigned in November 1986, having been urged to do so by the southern-based leadership of the faction opposed to O'Reilly. No ardfheis was held that year. And on the military level there had been no INLA convention since 1985 to elect a new Army Council.

The Markets man already knew that his enemies were closing in on him. Several days before he was shot, O'Reilly told his close friend and comrade Peter Stewart that someone was following him around Dundalk. One week later, on 19 January, Tom McAllister and another man called to the house of Ta Power in Friendly Street in the Markets area of Belfast to confirm arrangements for a meeting outside Drogheda. McAllister was still sincere in his pursuit of a convention at which the different factions would settle their differences peacefully; but unwittingly he was party to an elaborate trap in which the IPLO and their allies planned to turn the table on O'Reilly and his men. McAllister proposed that each of the rival groups hold a meeting to hammer out their differences. The venue for the discussion was the Rosnaree Hotel on the main Belfast–Dublin road. According to the faction loyal to John O'Reilly, the atmosphere that evening was extremely cordial.

The Rosnaree talks were supposedly intended to decide what weapons would go to each group, the welfare of both groups' prisoners, and the division of rackets raised in areas of the North. But Gerard Steenson and some of his comrades had other ideas. The negotiations were set up by inter-republican mediators, including the west Belfast priest Father Des Wilson. The mediators, it must be said, were unaware of Steenson's plans.

John O'Reilly, Ta Power, Hugh Torney from west Belfast and Peter Stewart from Newtownabbey travelled to the Rosnaree in a Ford Capri car. They arrived there at around twenty to five and ordered tea and sandwiches. Shortly before five o'clock John O'Reilly telephoned Des Wilson to find out why he had failed to turn up. He only managed to reach Wilson's secretary, who told him the priest was not available. Reliable sources say there was a plan to shoot all four in the car park before they went into the hotel. This was abandoned, however, because the gunmen and their driver arrived late.

One of the two survivors of the shooting, Peter Stewart, recalled that on leaving Belfast for Rosnaree his wife remarked that it was a lovely day. Stewart, fearing the worst, replied as if he had just experienced a premonition: "Yes, it's a lovely day to die." (Interview, 19 November 1993.)

"I was sitting between Power and O'Reilly. Torney was at the far end of the table. Suddenly somebody came in from a side door. O'Reilly jumped up. He was nervous. But it was only a customer." (Ibid.)

Then Stewart noticed that two men had arrived at the front door of the hotel. His suspicions were aroused. "Both men had beards. But I realised they were false beards when I saw the sticky stuff which was used to put them on glistening under the lights." Alert to the newcomers' real intentions, Stewart jumped up and rushed towards them. As he got close both men drew their guns from combat jackets they were wearing. In what Stewart described as a "very military-like operation", the gunmen opened fire. Stewart was hit three times in the stomach. He fell on a stool and lost consciousness. "All I can remember is a woman whispering a prayer into my ear. I asked her were my friends okay. She said everybody was fine." (Ibid.)

Afterwards Stewart found out that O'Reilly had got up and was hit in the spine as he tried to flee. He reached the front door and collapsed. One of the gunmen finished him off by firing three times into his head.

The next thing Stewart recalled was waking up in an ambulance lying beside Ta Power. Paramedics were using shock-pads to revive Power. "They were too late," Stewart said. "I knew he had gone." Hugh Torney meanwhile had escaped by running across a line of chairs behind which the INLA leaders had sat. He was wounded in the hand by Power and O'Reilly's killers.

One of the killers is a former member of the Irish army who is now a drug runner and hit-man in Dublin, nicknamed the Chef. The identity of the other killer is still a matter of dispute. Though Gerard Steenson has been named as the second gunman involved, Peter Stewart insists that Steenson was not there. He believes the mystery gunman came from the Walkinstown area of Dublin. Moreover, according to one of Stewart's comrades, Steenson was in Belfast at the time of the murders. However, the man who drove the getaway car revealed that Steenson was one of the killers. A close comrade of Steenson who sided with him inside Crumlin Road jail also claimed he was at Rosnaree.

During the next few murderous months it would not have been a surprise if Gerard Steenson had been blamed for sinking the *Titanic*, such was the myth that had grown up around him. History is supposed to be written by the victors; but in such a fratricidal struggle where there are no victors it becomes difficult to arrive at any fully consistent version of events.

After the double murder the Gardaí sealed off roads around the hotel while a widespread hunt for the killers was launched throughout Louth and Meath. Torney and Stewart were taken to the intensive care unit of Our Lady of Lourdes Hospital, Drogheda, and put under armed guard.

Within hours of the double murder the two rival factions released statements accusing each other of the same thing. A communiqué issued in Belfast from a faction calling itself the INLA Army Council alleged that Power, O'Reilly, Torney and Stewart had "served the interests of British imperialism in Ireland." A second statement, released through the IRSP in Belfast, said: "The cowardly murders are just another example of the depths to which those who would aid British imperialism will stoop to." According to the two factions, each were guilty of being British agents.

A further statement from the comrades of Power and O'Reilly in the Markets threatened revenge for the double murder. It referred to Ta Power's popularity in the organisation. "Thomas Power was very, very well respected. There will be people looking for blood. There could well be reprisals for this double murder."

There was further confusion in the war of words between the rival groups. Those loyal to O'Reilly and Power insisted that they were the only organisation worthy of the name INLA. The killers belonged to the IPLO; the term Army Council was only a fiction. There is some degree of truth in this claim. Séamus Costello did not want the INLA's name sullied in the initial feud with the Official IRA in 1975. Instead the defenders of the IRSP used the temporary title People's Liberation Army. Twelve years later the IPLO was adopting the same tactic by using the Army Council title in its war with the INLA. It was obvious that the IPLO also wanted to avoid having its name blackened by a sordid feud.

On the night of the Rosnaree murders the IPLO/Army Council faction in Belfast moved swiftly to stamp out any retaliation. According to a Lower Falls activist who eventually became the IPLO's leader, the Army Council personnel captured seven INLA GHQ members in the city loyal to John O'Reilly. Their captives were held at a variety of safe houses around Belfast.

They also moved swiftly to annihilate the IRSP in Belfast. Their target was the party's spokesman, Terry Harkin. Once the official voice of the IRSP was dead, the rival faction would claim that they were the legitimate IRSP/INLA movement and could then move quickly to dissolve it.

Terry Harkin had a lucky escape. His version of events throws a question mark over claims that Gerard Steenson was at Rosnaree. Minutes before Power and O'Reilly were slain at the Rosnaree, Harkin had been drinking in a nearby bar. As he went out the door he claims he spotted Gerard Steenson and Martin "Rook" O'Prey getting into a car. At that stage Harkin was unaware that his two comrades were dead. He made his way to the top of Castle Street, where he got into a taxi to go up the Falls Road.

As the taxi passed by Divis Flats, Harkin saw Steenson and O'Prey rapping at his door in Gilford Walk inside Divis Flats. It was not until he arrived at a house in Ballymurphy where an IRSP meeting was taking place that he learnt about the Rosnaree shootings. Harkin then got a phone call from his wife, who told him Steenson and O'Prey had tried to force their way into their flat and that they were armed. It was the first of several brushes with death Terry Harkin was to have throughout the feud.

Meanwhile Steenson's long-time friend "Geek" asked older veterans siding with the IPLO what they should do with the captives. Their answer raised some suspicions in his mind as to the real motive behind the feud. "On the night Power and O'Reilly were killed we had seven of their mates held hostage in different parts of Belfast. It would have been over in one night. But R— and McD— argued against us wounding or killing any of them. Why did they hold us back? I think they wanted the feud to go on for quite some time. Their aim wasn't just to dissolve the INLA, it was to end anything coming out of the movement at all. They weren't interested in starting up a new organisation. Maybe they wanted us all to join the Provos." (Interview, 19 August 1993.)

Ta Power's popularity was reflected in the number of people who attended his funeral on Saturday 24 January. Hundreds turned up outside his parents' home in Friendly Street. They included leading Provos, local Workers' Party activists, IRSP members, and many non-committed mourners. Many turned up out of respect for the murdered man's mother. Margaret Power was and is a well-liked character in the Markets area. She was known as the woman who recorded the ballad of Joe McCann, and she remained friendly with both INLA and Official IRA volunteers after the 1975 split. Mrs Power had already lost one son, Jim, in 1981. Once again she and the rest of her family followed a coffin through the narrow streets where he grew up to St Malachy's Church.

Ta Power's funeral was joined by John O'Reilly's from his parents' home in Eliza Street Close. While he undoubtedly had enemies, many also turned up to pay their respects, particularly in support of his father, Tommy, a quiet, likable man in the Markets who, like Margaret Power, remained friendly with many of his son's political opponents in the small enclave. There were, however, just yards away from O'Reilly's home known supporters of the IPLO/Army Council alliance, including one man who helped lead that faction into war with the murdered INLA leader. In such a small area tempers were bound to erupt and recriminations explode.

Trouble initially came in the form of swarms of RUC officers who ringed the funeral cortege and the entrance to St Malachy's Church in Alfred Street. They tried to prevent a paramilitary display, and got involved in ugly scuffles with mourners in the grounds of the church as the coffins were being carried out after Mass.

The bitterness was reflected in obituaries for both men. One particularly harrowing memorial notice inserted by Ta Power's mother reflected the depth of hatred towards the IPLO/Army Council alliance. "Like Judas of old, they lied and deceived. They killed my son for he believed in the people in Ireland, in honesty too, but his big mistake was he trusted you; youse took my son, youse left me hurt, but the people that's left recognise youse as dirt." (*Starry Plough*, February 1988)

There was a tragic twist to the double murder at Rosnaree. One of Ta Power's sisters revealed that her brother should have been on holiday in Cyprus instead of travelling down to the hotel that fateful afternoon. She said the only reason he didn't go on holiday was because his flight was overbooked. It would have been his first foreign holiday in thirteen years.

Despite the crowds who turned up to honour O'Reilly and Power, the IPLO/Army Council continued to call for their rivals to disband. The rival INLA group retorted by urging their enemies within to wind down and join the Provos.

The men's killers attempted to gloss over the deed and excuse one of the deaths as a mistake. Following the murder the IPLO/Army Council axis claimed that Ta Power had been killed by accident. In a statement, the rebel group claimed the gunman panicked when Power lifted up the table to hurl it at him. Doubts must be cast, however, on this excuse. Ta Power had been involved in several brawls with supporters of Steenson in Crumlin Road. INLA old guard members in Dublin who supported Steenson admit that killing Power was a major setback for the Army Council/IPLO alliance and alienated many potential supporters.

As the two sides squared up to annihilate each other, older scores were settled that had little or nothing to do with the IPLO/Army Council drive to dissolve the INLA.

On the evening of 1 February, Mary McGlinchey was bathing her two children at the family's home at Sliabh Foy Park in the Muirhevnamore estate in Dundalk. At around twenty past nine two men wearing balaclavas burst into the home. They ran upstairs to the bathroom and fired a burst of shots at Mrs McGlinchey. Both her sons, nine-year-old Dominic and ten-year-old Declan, stood screaming as the gunmen murdered their mother. Declan ran out of the house and down the road towards the McEneany family's home. According to Adrienne McEneany, young Declan screamed and shouted that his mother had been shot. "Call an ambulance, call an ambulance for Mammy," he cried. Another neighbour, Lil Traynor, ran into the McGlincheys' house and found Mary lying with her head in the bath, covered in a pool of blood. She had been shot in the head and died almost instantly.

Mary McGlinchey had made many enemies within the movement. She had been blamed for snaring victims into murder traps. It is alleged that among those she set up was Éamon McMahon. With the feud raging, McGlinchey's sworn foes saw their chance for revenge.

The former INLA leader was powerless to retaliate: he was still locked in Port Laoise prison, serving a ten-year sentence for firearms offences. His grief was compounded by the Government's decision not to allow him to attend his wife's funeral. A spokesman for the Department of Justice said the decision was taken because of potential threats to the prisoner, his guards, and members of the security forces. There was the added complication that Mary McGlinchey would be buried in County Derry, and that meant taking her husband into Northern Ireland, where the RUC had no authority to detain him. The then Taoiseach, Charles Haughey, expressed regret that McGlinchey could not attend his wife's funeral, but he defended the decision on security grounds.

A lot of reports have erroneously laid the blame for Mary McGlinchey's death at the IPLO's door. Gerard Steenson's name was also mentioned as one of the culprits. Indeed the IRSP's spokesman, Kevin McQuillan, described Mary McGlinchey as a "tireless worker" for the party. Party sources claimed that the same gang that killed Ta Power and John O'Reilly was behind the McGlinchey murder. The truth is that Mrs McGlinchey was gunned down by a gang based in south Armagh who had close associations with Éamon McMahon. They knew she had been actively involved in the murder of McMahon and of his brother-in-law, Eric Dale. Following the McGlinchey murder, the suspected killer fled to the United States. His gang had connections with IPLO personnel, but their primary motive for killing Mary McGlinchey was pure revenge.

The latest feud was taking on a whole new dimension. Previous battles between the Officials and the INLA and the Provisionals were clear-cut conflicts with two recognisable sides motivated by opposing ideologies and policies. The current feuding brought to the surface several complex, over-lapping animosities and personal hatreds.

Hopes that John O'Reilly's loyal followers would fold and surrender after the Rosnaree killings were ill-founded. Many INLA volunteers were still loyal to the memory of John O'Reilly and Ta Power. One of those who fought against the IPLO/Army Council alliance believed O'Reilly's political thinking was developing at the time of his murder. "John was a highly committed young man, whose ideas on politics were just forming. He was not in Power's league when it came to political thinking. But John was a good operator and loyal to the ideals of the movement. His death motivated us to fight on." (Interview, February 1994.) Those volunteers formed the INLA GHQ faction, and they drew up a death list of rivals. Their targets included the men who they believed were behind the Rosnaree killings.

Within a fortnight the GHQ hit back. The target they chose was not in Belfast but across the border in County Monaghan.

In the early hours of 6 February an armed and masked gang burst into a house at Rossmore Park, Mullaghmat. They were looking for Tony McCloskey, who came from County Armagh and had been associated with the rebel faction that eventually formed into the IPLO. The gunmen believed McCloskey had provided vital information to the killers of Power and O'Reilly. The INLA GHQ later claimed that McCloskey had been in the Rosnaree hotel and telephoned the Army Council assassins to inform them that Power and O'Reilly were there. But according to Peter Stewart, McCloskey was only spotted following John O'Reilly around before they arrived at Rosnaree.

What was to happen to Tony McCloskey illustrates the depths to which fratricidal violence had sunk within the IRSP/INLA movement.

Accompanying the gunmen in the attack at the McCloskey home was a masked woman who wielded a knife. After breaking down the door, the two men and their female accomplice burst into a bedroom where Tony McCloskey and his wife, Patricia, were sleeping. According to Patricia McCloskey, one of the men pointed a gun at her and said to her husband: "If you have any ideas I'll put six of them into her." The gang then dragged her husband into another room while she was held at knifepoint by the female member of the gang. A neighbour who was in the house at the time, Fergal Lavery, and his brother Michael, were also held by the gang.

During a brief interrogation in the kitchen, Patricia McCloskey remembers one of the gang asking something of her husband. She recalled that the masked inquisitor had an Armagh accent. Her husband simply replied: "I've got nothing." Tony McCloskey was then brought into the living-room, where the gunmen were shouting and cursing at his captive. After about fifteen minutes Patricia McCloskey remembers that her husband was taken upstairs. The next time she saw him he was dressed, and the first gunman asked if he had anything to put round his face. Another gunman handed his comrade a black scarf.

At around 12:30 a.m. Tony McCloskey was asked for his car keys and then taken from his house by one of the gang. The remainder of the gang were told: "If we're not back in half an hour, grab the keys and get the fuck out."

Patricia McCloskey, Fergal Lavery and Michael Lavery were kept in the kitchen. At one point the female gang member allowed Mrs McCloskey to go upstairs to the bathroom, although her captor followed her, still carrying the knife. The woman holding the knife, several republican sources have confirmed, was the wife of the gang leader.

Patricia McCloskey's husband returned with the first gunman. Everyone was brought into the sitting-room. Michael and Fergal Lavery were tied up. Patricia McCloskey saw her husband sitting on a chair. She was also tied up and gagged. It was the last time she saw her husband alive. The 32-year-old father of two left the room with the gang. As he walked out he smiled at his wife and said, "Be back by three o'clock." He was never to return.

It took Patricia McCloskey and her neighbours about thirty minutes to wriggle free. She went to bed feeling ill. At around eight o'clock she got up and woke her son, Kieran, and daughter, Paula, to get them ready for school. Their father had not returned. He was already dead by the time her children left the house.

A few hours after his abduction Tony McCloskey's body was found by a passing motorist lying by the side of the road at Knockbane, near Middletown, on the south Armagh border. His hands and feet had been bound. He had been struck by five bullets from a high-velocity weapon in the head and body. His burnt-out Fiat estate car, in which the gang had taken him to his place of death, was left close to the entrance of a nearby field.

RUC officers who later examined the body made another grim discovery. There were clear signs that Tony McCloskey had been tortured. The pathologist's report later showed that his abductors had severed the lobe of his ear and the tip from the right index finger. He had also been severely punched and kicked. It later emerged that the gang had used a bolt-cutter during the horrific interrogation. This kind of gruesome brutality between former republican comrades had not been seen since the Civil War.

Who was behind the McCloskey killing? One IPLO leader has no doubts who carried it out. He lays the blame squarely at the feet of an INLA maverick who later broke away to form his own gang, the so-called "Border Fox", Dessie O'Hare. The man the IPLO leader claimed used a bolt-cutter to cut pieces of flesh from Tony McCloskey employed the same horrific torture tactic during an infamous kidnap in the Republic a year before.

Tony McCloskey was buried on 8 February in a cemetery just a few hundred yards from St Patrick's Cathedral in his home town of Armagh. The late Cardinal Tomás Ó Fiaich appealed directly to both sides in the feud to call off the blood-letting. "Is there no-one amongst the relations and friends of those responsible who can convince them of the madness and selfishness of what is going on?" he asked mourners. "In God's name let them cry out with me today: Stop it, stop it now, stop it for good." But, like many other churchmen's appeals to paramilitary leaders in the past, the cardinal's demand for an end to the internecine killing fell on deaf ears.

Meanwhile in Belfast a collective paranoia gripped nationalist areas. Activists on both sides of the fighting were asked to leave republican drinking clubs for fear that neutrals would be caught in the cross-fire. Both factions stalked the streets looking for their enemies. Those who felt under threat followed standard procedures during feuds and moved out of their homes, sleeping in a series of safe houses around the city and beyond. Once again the most striking thing about this latest republican feud was the fact that these rivals lived cheek by jowl with each other.

Target number 1 for the GHQ faction, Gerard Steenson, had several safe locations to hide in. These included a house in Glengormley and a relative's home in Antrim town.

There had been a series of unsuccessful murder attempts by both sides after the deaths of Power, O'Reilly, and McCloskey. On 28 January the IPLO/Army Council side tried to kill a Lower Ormeau man, Emmanuel Gargan. The 25-year-old, who had been a friend of Power and O'Reilly, escaped by running along the Ormeau Road.

Two days later they tried again. Gargan was standing outside a taxi booth in the Belsteele Road in Poleglass along with John O'Reilly's brother Michael. They had been spotted by an IPLO/Army Council gang roaming the area. Two gunmen fired a burst of shots at Gargan outside the taxi cabin. Gargan was hit in the hand, stomach, hip, and shin; but he managed to escape death by rolling down a grass bank nearby.

The gun used in the second murder attempt on Gargan had already been used before by the IPLO. The 9 mm CZ pistol had been the weapon used to murder Thomas McCartan; it had also been fired during the IPLO attack on Queen Street RUC station and in another murder attack on rival INLA members in early February. (Inquest into death of Thomas McCartan, 5 August 1987.) The link between this weapon and IPLO operations in late 1986 cast a cloud of doubt over claims that the IPLO and the Army Council of the INLA were separate organisations.

Patrick McCrory and Bobby Tohill were ambushed by an Army Council/ IPLO gang led by Martin "Rook" O'Prey in the Suffolk Road on 16 February. According to one of O'Prey's accomplices, he fired at both men. He alleges that O'Prey was within point-blank range of Tohill but refused to fire the fatal shot. "Rook was a good operator but for some reason he couldn't kill Tohill. He wasn't afraid to kill you. Maybe it was old loyalty in Tohill's case. Whatever it was he was very lucky." (Interview.)

O'Prey also tried to kidnap and kill the IRSP's main spokesman during the feud, Terry Harkin. On 13 February, Harkin became the last man to be acquitted on charges related to the Harry Kirkpatrick trial. As he walked from Crumlin Road courthouse a free man, O'Prey and another accomplice were waiting in a car. Harkin spotted the two Army Council members and ran along the Crumlin Road to escape. He recalls spotting a Downtown Radio news car that had been parked outside the courthouse with a reporter inside waiting to interview survivors of the last Kirkpatrick supergrass trial. "I shoulder-charged Rook out of the way when he got out of the car and approached me outside the Crum. Then I bolted up the road after the Downtown car. I managed to catch up with the reporter, who drove me away from the courthouse to Bap McQuillan's house.

"When I got to Bap's house I noticed something hanging from the tree in the front garden. Ten of us had been billeted in Bap's house during the feud. It was a measure of how we were getting on top of each other that the lads had hung my white baseball boots outside on the tree. I had almost been abducted and killed by O'Prey, yet all Bap could talk about was the stench of my baseball boots. It was absurd." (Interview, 11 November 1993.)

The CZ pistol used in the murder attempt on Tohill and McCrory was used again to murderous effect on 17 February. Another INLA GHQ member who had been a target of the rival faction was Mickey Kearney from Ballymurphy. Hostility to Kearney had been simmering since the brawl inside Crumlin Road jail. As the feud intensified in February, Kearney had been planning to ambush his killers. Instead they ambushed him.

The 33-year-old father of five had learnt of the presence of the rival group in Ballymurphy that evening. The Army Council gang, which included Gerard Steenson, had taken over two houses in the district. They spotted three men, including Kearney, walking along Springhill Gardens. According to an Army Council statement, their volunteers confronted their three rivals, and there was an exchange of fire.

During the gun-battle Kearney was shot dead. The statement gloated about the killing: "Kearney and his colleagues learnt of our volunteers' presence in the area and they decided to take advantage of the situation. They were ambushed. They fell into their own trap. They were coming to get us but they were met with a heavily armed gang with superior firepower."

As with all feuds, murder was followed by character assassination. The INLA GHQ, through the IRSP, claimed that Mickey Kearney was on his way to visit his wife, Jeanie, and his children at the time of his murder. The Army Council alleged that Kearney may have been hit accidentally by bullets fired by his own comrades during the fatal exchange of fire. They claimed he had been shot for hiring out INLA guns for Belfast "hoods" in return for a cut in the takings. It is known that Kearney had a working relationship with several west Belfast criminals, including Jimmy Campbell, who was shot dead by the Provisional IRA in 1985 in the Pound Loney Social Club, and Thomas "Wee Buck" Valliday, who died from choking on his own vomit after taking an overdose of drugs stolen from a local chemist's just weeks before Kearney's murder.

Kearney's widow denied these allegations. Regardless of the alleged criminal accusation, her husband was killed primarily because of his opposition to the demand that the INLA dissolve. Among the people who visited her home the day after the murder were Margaret Power and John O'Reilly's wife, Agnes.

Jeanie Kearney was critical of the security forces after her husband was murdered. She claimed they did not go near the murder scene until hours after the shooting, even though the heavily fortified New Barnsley RUC station, which bristles with high-tech surveillance equipment, overlooks Springhill Gardens.

The Upper Springfield area became a bitter battleground between the two factions. An attempt was made on the life of the IRSP chairman, Kevin "Bap" McQuillan, at his Springfield Park home on 10 March. A group of gunmen including Martin O'Prey and Gerard Steenson burst into his home at around 1:30 a.m. Terry Harkin remembers that he was lying on a quilt in Kevin McQuillan's living-room when their enemies arrived. "I was ballock-naked except for the quilt wrapped around me. I was reading Tom Sharpe's *Riotous Assembly* when there was a knock on the door. Kevin went out to answer it and I remember hearing a voice at the door. I heard Steenson's voice. It's a voice you'll never forget. Steenson's voice was very calm, very clear, and very calculating." (Interview, 15 October 1993.)

Harkin acted quickly. He boarded himself into the living-room, placing a sofa against the door. He believed Steenson was particularly determined to kill him because he was the IRSP's main spokesman during the feud. Killing him and Kevin McQuillan would have effectively decapitated the movement's political wing.

The gang led by Steenson shot Kevin McQuillan twice. One of the bullets went through his eye. Gerard Steenson also shot his nineteen-year-old brother Éamon in the nape of the neck. Harkin remembered the scene after Steenson and O'Prey fled. He was standing in the hallway watching Éamon McQuillan cough up blood; then he saw Kevin McQuillan coming towards him with a towel wrapped around his head, dripping in blood. Harkin also remembered a curious odour in the air caused by a mixture of gunpowder and Bacardi. From the smell he deduced that Steenson and O'Prey had been drinking before embarking on their murder attempt.

During the shooting one of the gunmen, Rook O'Prey, even spoke to Kevin McQuillan. "All right, Bap," he shouted out as he opened fire. Kevin McQuillan later signed himself out of hospital and managed to give an interview for Ulster Television the following evening, during which he labelled his attackers "apolitical gangsters". He attacked the rival group for singling out his brother, Éamon, for attack. He had no political connections and was simply an innocent bystander.

Once again the shooting took place under the very noses of police and troops in New Barnsley RUC station. McQuillan said he telephoned the RUC station four times to tell them there was a critically injured man who needed emergency first aid. He claimed it took over two hours for the RUC to come a hundred yards across the street to investigate the incident. (*Irish News*, 10 March 1987.)

Following the attack on the McQuillan home the IRSP called on all other republican organisations to link up and fight the IPLO/Army Council. (Ibid.) Terry Harkin told the Provisionals and others that "the time has passed when you can sit back and issue press statements in the hope that the IPLO will go away." His demand for wider republican support was futile. The Provisionals were never going to get involved in the squabble. They simply sat it out and waited for the blood-letting to come to an end.

The feuding also continued along the border area. On Saturday 7 March the INLA GHQ faction killed a nineteen-year-old Newry man, Thomas Maguire. His body was discovered with three gunshot wounds to the head at a crossroads near Ballinliss, County Armagh. It was the sixth body to have been shot and dumped in the area in the past two-and-a-half years.

The dead man was the son of Seán and Mary Maguire, who came with their family from the Falls Road in Belfast to live in Newry in the early 1970s. Like many other casualties in the internecine fighting, Thomas Maguire, who lived at North Street flats in the town, had been released from prison several months before. When he was kidnapped by his killers he was wearing a green army jacket. He had been dressed as if he was going to war, but he never got the chance to fight. Although an initial statement was issued to the press claiming the IPLO carried out the murder, a second communiqué from the organisation denied this. Jimmy Brown later told the authors that the "O'Reilly gang and its remnants" were responsible for the Maguire murder. Brown's statement was the accurate one, at least on this occasion. Thomas Maguire had been a personal friend of Brown's and was known to have supported the policy to dissolve the INLA.

On 14 March the gang that killed Thomas Maguire and Tony McCloskey struck again, but this time against one of their own members. After the Maguire murder, a 31-year-old Newry man, Fergus Conlon, had told the *Irish News* that he feared for his own life. He said that events were closing in on him and that he would be "safer out of the country and away from it all." Several days after that interview Fergus Conlon's body was found on the side of the road in the border townland of Clontigora. He had two gunshot wounds to the head. Following his killing, the INLA GHQ issued a statement accusing Conlon of working for the security forces for several years. The INLA communiqué alleged that their victim had been responsible for the discovery of thirty arms dumps and the arrest of fifty people.

The "informer" label attached to Fergus Conlon was, according to Army Council/IPLO sources, a fiction. They claimed Conlon was killed because he disagreed with the leader of the INLA gang that murdered Thomas Maguire. These sources pointed out that Conlon opposed Maguire's murder. Indeed the gun used to kill Thomas Maguire was also used to shoot Fergus Conlon. The Conlon killing further illustrated the depths of paranoia and delusion afflicting the leader of the GHQ gang operating in the south Armagh area.

The INLA GHQ was fighting back in Belfast as well. On the same date it finally struck at the heart of the Army Council faction's leadership. Once again the Upper Springfield area was the chosen killing ground.

Mediators had tried to force both sides to call a cease-fire. Leaders from both factions met at Clonard Monastery to hammer out a peace agreement. On the night of 14 March both sides had officially agreed to a cease-fire. It was meant to have come into operation from midnight.

Gerard Steenson took advantage of the prospect of peace to go for a drink that Saturday evening. He decided to go to a city centre pub with an old friend from Twinbrook, Anthony "Boot" McCarthy. The two men remained on friendly terms, even though McCarthy had resigned from the INLA in 1977. Indeed, according to the future IPLO chief of staff, the 31-year-old father of three had been suspected of working for the security forces and was not trusted either by him or Gerard Steenson.

After a heavy night's drinking in the Washington Bar, McCarthy and Steenson decided to go back to west Belfast. The pair learnt that the GHQ had burned a taxi place in Poleglass that, they alleged, the IPLO/Army Council side had used to ferry men and weapons around the city. The GHQ had indeed taken the initiative. Several of their volunteers the same evening kicked in doors and displayed weapons on balconies in Divis Flats. The operation in the flats was an act of provocative bravado by the GHQ, as the complex was regarded as a stronghold for the rival faction.

Steenson and McCarthy were furious about the GHQ attacks. They headed up to Springhill Avenue, where McCarthy's mother-in-law lived. The men were armed when they drove into the area with a Browning pistol and a Scorpion machine-pistol. They arrived in Springhill Avenue at around ten past twelve—ten minutes into the cease-fire. As their car stopped, a group of armed and masked men appeared in the street. One of the gang at the top of Springhill Avenue, closed a security gate that leads onto Springfield Road. As the pair in the car saw this and the armed gang approach from a nearby entry, McCarthy was heard to shout, "We're fucked."

The GHQ members fired a volley of up to twenty shots into the car. Residents in Springfield Avenue dived for cover in their homes as bullets ricocheted everywhere. One bullet went through the living-room of a house and lodged in a picture of Pope John Paul II. One local man said the car in which Steenson and McCarthy were travelling crashed into wooden railings. He recalled going over and seeing the two men slumped in the front. (*Irish News*, 16 March 1987.) One of the gang that ambushed the pair claimed that some of the weapons used in the killing came from the cache displayed by John O'Reilly outside Dundalk at the start of the year. The Colt Commando rifle (a slimmed-down version of the Armalite) used to kill Steenson and McCarthy had been part of the arms haul smuggled into Ireland from France in 1985.

The guns in the car were taken away and eventually, according to an INLA volunteer who was there, ended up in the Provos' hands.

After the shooting, one of the GHQ members phoned the organisation's chief of staff, who was staying at a safe house nearby. The lad shouted down the phone, "We nailed him. I'm 99 per cent sure. I emptied a full magazine from the Colt Commando into him." (Interview, 20 November 1993.)

To be absolutely certain about Steenson's death, the GHQ boss telephoned the Royal Victoria Hospital's emergency unit. Pretending to be a friend, he asked to speak to someone about Gerard Steenson. The person who picked up the phone was Jimmy Brown's girl-friend, Róisín McDonagh. She confirmed that Steenson was dead. The GHQ leader was jubilant.

According to one of the INLA GHQ members who ambushed Steenson and McCarthy, the man who closed off their only escape route was Alexander "Sandy" Lynch, an INLA volunteer from Turf Lodge. What the INLA gang that gathered to ambush Steenson and McCarthy did not know was that Lynch was an RUC agent. He had been working for the police inside the INLA for several years. Despite this he was allowed a certain amount of freedom of action in his paramilitary career. After the INLA-IPLO feud ended, Lynch was advised by his handlers to leave the INLA and link up with the Provos.

Lynch was finally unmasked as an RUC agent on 5 January 1990. He was held at a house in Carrigart Avenue in Lenadoon and interrogated for two days. He was saved, however, by a British army patrol that surrounded the house on 7 January. Among those arrested at the scene was Sinn Féin's publicity director, Danny Morrison, who is now serving a prison sentence related to Lynch's abduction.

During Morrison's trial, on 29 October 1991, Lynch admitted under cross-examination that he had been working for the RUC Special Branch for seven years. He confessed to tipping the RUC off initially about INLA arms dumps and later IRA weapons hides in west Belfast. On the night of Gerard Steenson's death Lynch played a key role, and no doubt his RUC handlers would not have lost much sleep over his involvement in the death of one of their most feared and hated enemies.

Sandy Lynch was actually detailed to dump the weapons used to kill Steenson and McCarthy. One of the GHQ volunteers involved in the ambush claimed that the guns were lifted by a joint RUC and British army patrol within twenty-four hours of the shooting. Up to then the GHQ faction had not lost a single weapon in the feud.

One of Steenson's closest confidants has confirmed that his comrade was drunk at the time of his murder and would not have gone into what was regarded as a GHQ stronghold had he been sober.

Ironically, Steenson's name was linked to the killing of John O'Reilly and Ta Power. They had been lured to the Rosnaree hotel under the false pretences of a peace conference. The INLA GHQ had taken the chance to turn the tables on Steenson by agreeing to a cease-fire and then at the first opportunity ambushing their prime target. The manner of Steenson's and McCarthy's deaths was all the more ironic because they were killed only yards away from where Michael Kearney was shot dead just weeks before.

Steenson's death was a body blow to the IPLO/Army Council axis. He had been one of the organisation's most seasoned and ruthless operators. At his funeral on St Patrick's Day, Jimmy Brown referred to Steenson as a "valued comrade". Brown described Steenson's paramilitary career, which began at the age of thirteen when he joined the Official IRA Fianna, two years later progressing into the Official IRA proper and eventually the INLA.

Jimmy Brown's bombastic portrayal of Steenson as a "committed and highly efficient military activist and a dedicated revolutionary" was predictable. There was, however, a more objective and unintentional compliment dished out to Steenson at the time of the Kirkpatrick supergrass trial. Sentencing Steenson to six life sentences, Lord Justice Cardwell described the Lower Falls man as an enemy of society, "a most dangerous and sinister terrorist. A ruthless and highly dedicated, resourceful and indefatigable planner of criminal exploits who did not hesitate to take a leading role in assassinations and other crimes."

The future IPLO chief of staff remembered Steenson as an articulate and completely dedicated volunteer who would not hesitate to kill an opponent. "Steensy was only a wee lad. There was nothing macho or hard about him. To look at him you would never have imagined he would hurt anyone. But he was completely ruthless. He would not think twice about killing you if he thought it was necessary. That's why they all feared him." (Interview, 19 August 1993.)

Both his friends and enemies still speak in a tone of awestruck admiration about Steenson's paramilitary prowess. One of the founders of the IPLO described Steenson as "in the same class as Michael Collins. Like Collins, he was a military genius." (Interview, 10 October 1993.) Coincidentally, one of the men Steenson tried to murder during the feud paid him exactly the same compliment. Terry Harkin suggests that Steenson was one of the most formidable paramilitaries to have emerged from the current Troubles. "Steenson was a student of the psychologist B. F. Skinner. While in jail he tried to learn about how to manipulate groups of people. Gerard was into psychological manipulation on a big scale. He was able to influence you to do anything for him. There was a time when I was really taken in by him. During the hunger strike, Steenson played an invaluable role in the war. He believed in what he was doing, for republicanism, the movement, and for Ireland. The only person I can compare him to in Irish history is Michael Collins." (Ibid.)

Gerard Steenson blooded himself as a sixteen-year-old volunteer by murdering the Official IRA leader Billy McMillen twelve years before his own death. McMillen's young wife, Mary, had watched Steenson murder her husband in front of her own eyes. It was an experience she never forgot or forgave. On the day of Steenson's funeral a woman who had been close to McMillen was drinking in the Lower Falls Social and Recreational Club with some old friends of the Official IRA commander. As the funeral cortege of around seventy mourners flanked by twenty RUC and British army Land Rovers made its way up the Falls Road, the women left the social club. She headed up the Grosvenor Road, halting at the junction of the Falls as Gerard Steenson's coffin was carried past. Former comrades of the widow told the authors that after it passed by she returned to the club and ordered a bottle of champagne.

14

OPEN DOOR

Despite the loss of Steenson, the Army Council/IPLO alliance was far from finished. Within eight days they had avenged the death of Steenson and other comrades slain by the INLA GHQ. One of their targets was the Lower Ormeau man Emmanuel Gargan, and it was Steenson's close friend Martin O'Prey who settled the score.

Even his enemies admit that 25-year-old Gargan showed remarkable physical courage during the feud. Despite being wounded during the gun attack on 28 January, he signed himself out of hospital to carry on the fight.

On the evening of 22 March, Gargan was drinking in the Hatfield Bar in the Ormeau Road. He was still walking on crutches and, according to local sources, was wearing a flak jacket and carrying a pistol. He had been in the bar for about an hour when he got up to get another round. As he stood with his back to the door, a man with a hood rushed in and shot him in the head with a shotgun. He died instantly. The gunman was Martin O'Prey.

Local people and his family later claimed that Gargan had been set up. They said that one of the men he was drinking with that evening left the pub and was seen making a telephone call. One youth who was in the Hatfield at the time claimed that Gargan's betrayer was seen with his arm wrapped around the INLA activist minutes before he made the telephone call to the IPLO/Army Council alliance. Gargan's suspected betrayer is now living in north Belfast.

The murder of Emmanuel Gargan caused outrage among the Lower Ormeau community. He had been a well-known and popular character in the area. Local people were disgusted at the way he had been set up for assassination by someone with whom he was seen drinking. The collective disgust was reflected on the wall of an entry between Dromara Street and Artana Street, where local youths daubed the slogan, *IPLO scum*.

The same evening the IPLO struck at another target, this time in Armagh. Kevin Barry Duffy had lived with his parents, Paddy and Philomena Duffy, close to the parents of Tony McCloskey. Throughout the feud the 20-year-old single man was warned that he should dissociate himself from the INLA.

A local Sinn Féin councillor, Tommy Carroll, revealed that he had told Duffy he was "in out of his depth with the wrong people." Carroll said he was aware that Duffy was involved with an INLA grouping that was responsible for the mutilation and murder of Tony McCloskey.

Duffy was ambushed by an IPLO hit team around midnight as he walked to his home in D'Alton Road. He was abducted by the gang and then dragged towards a wall in the grounds of St Brigid's School in Nursery Road. They fired several shots into his body with a shotgun. According to one senior IPLO source, they used a shotgun in order to cause maximum mutilation to Duffy's body in revenge for the horrific torture marks on Tony McCloskey's body.

Kevin Barry Duffy was the last victim of this latest republican feud. Several key participants in the fighting were beginning to question the logic of continuing the struggle. The Lower Falls activist who was soon to be elected chief of staff of the IPLO explained the feelings of his group following the Gargan and Duffy murders. "We came to the conclusion we had done enough, that it was over now after we killed Duffy and Gargan. To be honest, I was reluctant from the very start to move against the O'Reilly faction and dissolve the INLA. It was easy enough for anyone to call themselves the INLA. Four people could do it. But we knew we were in danger of being attacked by O'Reilly's crowd, so we moved against them. As for others who were on our side, they did little or no fighting. They encouraged us but sat by on the sidelines." (Interview.)

During the feud, Jimmy Brown explained in his usual purple style that the IPLO would not desist from destroying any memory of the INLA. After the murder of Michael Kearney he said: "They can call themselves the Islamic Jihad for Ballymurphy so far as we are concerned, or the INLA mark 4—but not the INLA." (*Irish Times*, 20 February 1987.) By that semantic standard the Army Council/IPLO had failed. Indeed the organisation's future chief of staff in hindsight accepts that the feud resulted in "needless deaths".

As a result of inter-republican mediation, the INLA was allowed to continue in existence alongside the IRSP. It was, however, a mortally wounded organisation, reduced to a rump membership in the Ballymurphy-Springhill area along with some personnel scattered around Belfast, Dublin, and Armagh. Regardless of which group claimed victory, the truce that had been negotiated by two priests from Clonard Monastery, Father Alex Reid and Father Gerry Reynolds, at least ended the bloodshed.

Paradoxically, the real winner in the conflict was the Provisional IRA. It had new recruits who were seasoned political and military operators, some of whom had access to weapons, intelligence, and arms routes abroad. The

Provos also faced two rival republican organisations that were fatally weakened as a result of the feud. This weakness was eventually to be exploited by the Provisionals.

The IPLO alliance held a post-feud conference at a hotel in Portumna, County Galway, in April. There were two strategies on the agenda. One was to disband the organisation and apply en masse for membership of the Provos; the other was to continue as the IPLO and concentrate on their real enemy: the security forces and loyalist paramilitaries.

A younger, more militarily active element based mainly in Belfast decided to carry on fighting under the IPLO banner. Politically they organised themselves around Jimmy Brown. The Portumna conference elected one of Gerard Steenson's closest friends, a Lower Falls man with a reputation for ruthless activism, as the IPLO's chief of staff. Predictably, the old pattern of North-South division was emerging again. The bulk of the IPLO who remained with the organisation was concentrated in Belfast, Newry, and south Armagh; the majority of those who chose to link up with the Provisionals or to opt up of out active republican politics altogether were almost all based in Dublin. The fragile alliance that had precipitated the bloody feud with the INLA was already breaking up only weeks after the fighting was over.

One IPLO member from the Markets area of Belfast who was extremely active during the feud described Portumna as a disaster. Like the future IPLO chief of staff, he felt let down by older comrades who had helped set the organisation up and then decided to abandon it after the feud. "Portumna was a real bombshell. Suddenly, after all that fighting, the old guard members turned around and said they were leaving. After it was over I asked one of them from my area what the hell the feud had been for. He replied that it was to do with personalities; that it was in revenge for Séamus Ruddy. I couldn't believe it. To this day there are people who won't speak to me because of my involvement in that feud. Now I wonder what it was all for. Were we used by these people?"

While some felt let down by older comrades, others in the IPLO/Army Council alliance smelt a rat. They believed the IPLO had been encouraged and perhaps even fostered by the Provos in order to smash the INLA. The GHQ's chief of staff at the end of the feud laid the blame for this conspiracy at the door of a senior IRA man and former hunger striker from north Belfast. "The IRA created a monster in the IPLO, which ran out of complete control," he contends. (Interview, 2 November 1993.) He pointed to the evidence that most of the older veterans who set up the IPLO immediately joined the Provisionals after the fighting. His belief is that the IRA wanted to sweep aside any potential armed opposition from its left in the republican community in the event of a possible cease-fire or truce.

This conspiracy theory is implausible. It does not explain the already existing divisions and contradictions within the INLA/IRSP movement. A leading figure in the anti-O'Reilly faction did hold negotiations with the IRA in the autumn of 1986 with a view to bringing over his faction into the Provos; however, once it became clear that Steenson and his supporters might be freed, the ex-INLA man decided to fight his corner against O'Reilly and his allies, with the aim of restructuring the INLA/IRSP movement.

The Provisionals may have helped those who saw no future for the smaller republican organisation. But the feud would have erupted anyway without the interference of the IRA. Undoubtedly the Provos must have realised that an element of the Army Council/IPLO alliance would want to carry on as an independent force.

Under the new leadership of the Lower Falls activist, the IPLO set out in a more openly sectarian direction. In the next five years of its short existence the terror group would concentrate its attacks on loyalist figures as well as drinking clubs and other commercial outlets in Protestant areas. Only occasionally would the IPLO shoot at British army or RUC targets.

The IPLO's onslaught on suspected loyalist paramilitaries fitted in with the new chief of staff's personal views on the entire unionist community. He still refers to unionists as "Afrikaners who are irreformable". His "analysis" of the wider unionist family is analogous to the policy of the extreme Pan-African Congress in South Africa, whose attitude towards the white population is summed up in the chilling slogan "One Boer, one bullet."

Many in the nationalist community, including current and former IRSP members, expressed outrage at the more blatantly sectarian nature of IPLO attacks after the feud. But what they tend to forget is that from the INLA/IRSP movement's very conception a sectarian element, forged by the loyalist pogroms on nationalist areas at the start of the Troubles, had latched on to the organisation. For young men such as the IPLO's new chief of staff who witnessed Catholic streets burning at the hands of loyalist mobs, the politics of socialist revolution were occasionally submerged in the politics of revenge.

The remnants of the INLA GHQ/IRSP movement took longer to recover from the carnage. Politically the organisation spun out of the traditional socialist republican orbit into a black hole of extreme Marxist-Leninist fundamentalism. In 1984 the IRSP had already adopted the works of Marx and Engels at a single vote at its ardfheis. Now under the leadership of Jim Lane the IRSP retreated further into an ideological cul-del-sac.

In December the first edition of the *Starry Plough* to be published since the feud outlined the new political path the movement was taking. In an editorial steeped in rhetoric and Marxist verbiage, the IRSP referred to the necessity to "break away from Left Republicanism and embrace the scientific socialism of Marx and Engels in order to analyse and thus formulate a political programme for the Irish revolution."

The editorial stated that the "petit bourgeois politics of the Sinn Féin leadership, who deny the leading role of the working class and thereby class struggle, offers no way forward for the Irish revolution." Naturally the IRSP believed it had the strategy to bring about such a revolution. The editorial spelt out what was to be done: "While it is a simple matter by the stroke of a pen to call oneself a Marxist-Leninist party, it is quite another matter to build such a vehicle ... But by breaking with left republicanism/militarism, we feel that we have made the first steps along that road."

This campus left rhetoric was light years from the reality in Belfast. Even months after a split and bloody feud, another rupture in the ranks was visible. While the *Starry Plough* criticised the militarist tendency within republicanism, a hard-line military-minded faction was plotting to seize control of the organisation.

On the one hand there were political activists such as Terry Harkin and Kevin McQuillan, who wanted the INLA/IRSP to pursue a joint military and political struggle totally independent of the IRA. On the other hand there was a faction led by a man based in the Springhill area who called for a strategy of outright military action against the security forces and loyalists. The latest internal battle was a more long-drawn-out, bloodless struggle. Eventually Terry Harkin was edged out of the movement and Kevin McQuillan left isolated. The INLA's current leader in Belfast expelled everybody who did not agree with him and eventually founded a cadre of young militants willing to carry out any order given to them.

Throughout the next five years Harkin and McQuillan tried to push the IRSP along an independent socialist republican path. They frequently clashed with Sinn Féin, particularly when in 1991 the IRSP was denied a place on the speakers' platform in Dunville Park off the Falls Road during a demonstration to mark the tenth anniversary of the hunger strike. Kevin McQuillan distributed leaflets at the march accusing Sinn Féin of élitism and reminding nationalists that three of the dead hunger strikers had been INLA/IRSP members.

The INLA suffered a further demoralising setback with the erratic behaviour of Dessie O'Hare. After the feud O'Hare broke off from the INLA's leadership in Belfast and formed a new group based around the border region called the "Irish Revolutionary Brigade". Others in the INLA in Belfast had a more colourful name for this latest break-away: O'Hare and his men were nicknamed the "Castleblayney Zulus".

O'Hare's handful of disciples had a short but illustrious terror career. On 13 October they kidnapped a Dublin dentist, John O'Grady, from his home in Cabinteely. Their intended victim had been O'Grady's father-in-law, the millionaire Austin Darragh. For the next few weeks the Republic was gripped in a near-farcical story of botched rescue attempts and narrow escapes as O'Hare's gang travelled across Ireland with their victim in tow.

Labelled the "Border Fox" by the media, 29-year-old O'Hare became the most famous republican paramilitary since Dominic McGlinchey. There were, however, sinister twists to the nationwide chase to catch O'Hare and rescue John O'Grady.

As a demonstration of their seriousness, the kidnappers hacked off the tips of the dentist's little fingers and then sent them to Carlow Cathedral with a ransom note demanding one-and-a-half million pounds. The O'Hare gang gagged O'Grady and put a pillowcase over his head, and used a hammer and chisel to cut off his fingertips. After severing the tips they then cauterised their victim's wounds with a hot instrument. This gruesome behaviour was a repeat of the torture inflicted on the INLA Army Council supporter Tony McCloskey during the feud.

In a statement during the kidnap, O'Hare's gang accused Austin Darragh of being a lackey of "international capitalism" who peddled mind-bending drugs for multinationals. John O'Grady was eventually rescued after a shoot-out at a house in Carnlough Road, Cabra, Dublin, on 5 November.

Later, when O'Hare was brought to trial, he raged against his enemies. The former Provo from Keady, County Armagh, said: "May all my deeds reverberate until bloody war is waged against the British and their southern allies."

Dessie O'Hare had been useful to the INLA GHQ during the feud, but by the end of that year he was ostracised by his former comrades. In the December issue of the *Starry Plough* the INLA released a short statement pointing out that "he is not a member of the INLA." The curious mix of fiasco and brutality created by Dessie O'Hare and his gang had brought the INLA movement into deeper disrepute. Those who still clung to the original ideals of the INLA/IRSP were attempting to rebuild the organisation as a left-republican alternative to the Provisionals. The O'Grady kidnap was another blow to the INLA's shattered credibility. For others opposed to the INLA for one reason or another, the antics of O'Hare and his "Irish Revolutionary

Brigade" were just further proof of the anarchic legacy created by the incessant feuding.

In the immediate post-feud period the IPLO became far more militarily active than the INLA. From the summer of 1987 the IPLO had started to pick its own targets; they were to be almost exclusively loyalist ones. They decided that their first victim would be a "popular hit".

The IPLO's offensive began against the man who was probably the most reviled loyalist politician in the North: George Seawright. The Glasgow-born Belfast city councillor gained notoriety in May 1984 when, during a meeting of Belfast Education and Library Board, he called for Catholics to be incinerated. Seawright was subsequently expelled from Ian Paisley's DUP for this remark.

Gaining the title of "Burn-Again Christian", Seawright set himself up as a super-Protestant bigot, launching a series of political stunts to win support within the loyalist community. During the summer of 1984 he staged a night raid on Whiterock Leisure Centre in west Belfast and removed a Tricolour from the roof. Two years later, at the height of loyalist protests against the Anglo-Irish Agreement, he was captured on television physically haranguing the then Secretary of State, Tom King, during a visit to Belfast City Hall. Seawright leaped onto his car, screaming abuse at King and his entourage.

These antics gave Seawright a double reputation, not only as a hardline bigot but also as a political clown. Despite his overt sectarian politics, Seawright was the only loyalist on the council who spoke to Sinn Féin councillors during tea and biscuits in the members' room before city council meetings. Perhaps this was because Seawright was regarded with contempt by fellow-Unionist councillors, whom he constantly ridiculed and verbally attacked as traitors, hypocrites, and sell-outs. The outspoken loyalist firebrand had no-one else to talk to.

Seawright's willingness to talk to republicans extended beyond Sinn Féin. A week before his death Seawright met Jimmy Brown in the Europa Hotel. This odd union was arranged by a close friend of Brown's who worked for the City Hall's community services division at the time and knew Seawright personally. Seawright wanted assurances from Brown that he would not be a target for assassination. The loyalist councillor felt under threat after the Provisional IRA shot dead his close friend and top UVF killer, John Bingham, at his home in Ballysillan on 14 September.

After Bingham's death, Seawright called openly for revenge. Two nights later the UVF shot dead 33-year-old Raymond Mooney in the grounds of Holy Cross Catholic church off the Crumlin Road.

Seawright's liaisons with Jimmy Brown did him little good. In fact

Brown, according to two senior IPLO members from Belfast at the time, knew nothing of the plan to kill Seawright.

About lunchtime on 19 November, Seawright was sitting in a car on waste ground between Dundee Street and Northumberland Street off the Shankill Road. The car was parked close to the offices of a local taxi firm, Standard Taxis, for which Seawright had just started working. At around one o'clock a van pulled up beside Seawright's car. A gunman got out and walked towards the passenger seat where George Seawright was sitting, and opened fire with a handgun several times.

The gunman got back into the van and made off towards the Falls Road, abandoning the vehicle in Ross Road, near Divis Flats. Seawright was hit in the chest and head. He survived for more than three weeks on a life support machine in the Royal Victoria Hospital, but finally died on 3 December from his injuries.

The Seawright legacy lived on, however, with his wife, Liz Seawright, standing as a Protestant Unionist candidate in the by-election caused by her husband's murder. Ironically, the only candidate to stand against her for the Court ward was Peter Cullen of the Workers' Party. While former Official Republicans undoubtedly risked their lives canvassing for Cullen in hard-line loyalist areas of the Upper Shankill and West Circular Road, the several hundred votes cast for the WP was an illustration of the failure of the Officials to build their imagined cross-sectarian working-class unity. Sectarianism rather than socialism won the day as Liz Seawright romped home.

In singling out George Seawright for assassination the IPLO had hoped to win new support within the nationalist community. He was clearly loathed by many Catholics for his bigoted outbursts. But within nationalist Belfast there is always a tension between the desire to strike out at loyalist targets and the fear that in doing so republican organisations may provoke a fierce Protestant paramilitary backlash against the wider Catholic population.

The organisation also continued on another familiar path, shooting people it believed were part-time members of the security forces. An IPLO hit team in Armagh shot a 41-year-old woodwork instructor in November, claiming he was a part-time member of the UDR. It turned out that their victim, who survived the murder attempt, had never been a member.

In 1989 the IPLO's actions raised sectarian tensions to heights not experienced since the 1970s. During the first half of the year the IPLO employed another tactic to try to win new support among working-class nationalists. On 5 March workers at the Department of Health and Social Services in Derry received threats over the phone from a caller purporting to be from the IPLO. At the time a twelve-member team of department investigators was in the city investigating social security fraud. As a result of the threat the entire department staff walked out in protest. The IPLO claimed it was fighting a war of liberation on behalf of the Irish working class. It saw an opportunity to gain respect among the unemployed in Derry by issuing threats to dole snoops. Instead the populist tactic backfired, as low-paid trade unionists went on strike against threats from the working class's self-declared defenders.

In contrast to the IPLO, it took the INLA more than a year to recover from the feud. In the first *Starry Plough* after the internal war the IRSP criticised the militarism of the rival faction and accused them of being devoid of politics. However, the INLA followed the IPLO down the same violent path. It pledged in an interview with the London listings magazine *City Limits* in February 1988 that the INLA was here to stay. Arguing that the movement was now recovering, the spokesman also branded Dessie O'Hare as a maverick. The INLA was determined to continue its armed struggle despite the aftershock of the internal war the previous year. "We are small, with room to grow. People who left, high-profile people known to Special Branch both in England and Ireland, are coming back into the movement. There is still a need for us."

Their first major operation was directed against a British army border checkpoint at Clady, outside Strabane, on 10 August 1988. It was a disastrous rebirth. An INLA unit attacked the heavily armed checkpoint armed only with handguns. During the attack an INLA volunteer, James McPhelimy, was shot dead by a British soldier. He was one of three masked INLA volunteers who opened fire on the permanent checkpoint at around half past nine in the evening after shouting to local children nearby to get down. Two of the INLA team escaped across the border after a short gun-battle between them and British troops at the base. James McPhilemy lay badly wounded near a stream that marks the border. After the shooting, he was taken to Altnagelvin Hospital in Derry, where he died a short time later.

To use small arms during the sortie at Clady had been undeniably suicidal. Four days after the Clady attack the president of Sinn Féin, Gerry Adams, called on the INLA to disband. (*Sunday Tribune*, 14 August 1988.) It was to be the first of many such calls by Sinn Féin leaders on both the INLA and the IPLO.

The IRSP later held a commemoration in Strabane in honour of the INLA's first martyr since the feud, at which Patsy O'Hara's mother, Peggy O'Hara, unveiled a memorial stone for James McPhelimy.

In Belfast the INLA was more successful one week after its botched operation at the border checkpoint. At around ten o'clock on the morning of 14 August a lone gunman wearing dark glasses and a scarf walked into Fred Otley's grocery shop in the Shankill Road, only yards away from where the IPLO shot George Seawright dead a year before. The gunman asked a shop assistant, "Where's the boss?" When Otley appeared at the counter, the man pulled out a handgun and shot him several times at point-blank range.

By the time the INLA killer and his back-up team abandoned a hijacked red Renault in Divis Flats, the organisation had released a statement explaining why they had singled out Fred Otley. The statement alleged that Otley was a UVF terrorist and had a direct role in the murder of Francis Notorantonio in Ballymurphy the same year. The INLA referred to the fact that Otley was implicated by the UVF supergrass Jackie Gibson. Otley had been freed when the trial collapsed in April 1985.

Several informers were still operating within the INLA's ranks. Up to the end of 1988, Alexander "Sandy" Lynch, an RUC agent, was active inside the organisation. Indeed in that year he took on a new position as one of the group's interrogators, questioning INLA volunteers and others suspected of being informers. In January, Lynch, along with several other INLA members, lured a County Down man to an interrogation house in Downpatrick. Peter Duggan, a former member of the French Foreign Legion, fell under suspicion after several conversations with women in the town connected with the INLA. One of the women he became friendly with was Mary Clinton, whose husband was serving time in prison on paramilitary offences. After Duggan had asked questions about other INLA members in the town, Clinton became suspicious. She reported to the local OC, who relayed what she said back to the INLA in Belfast. It is possible that the INLA was also angry with Duggan because they suspected he might be trying to sleep with Mary Clinton. Whatever the reason, Duggan was invited to Clinton's house for coffee. When he got there, Sandy Lynch was waiting for him, along with the then INLA chief of staff.

"I was locked in a room and asked questions: who I was, where I was from, etc. I wasn't hooded. They introduced themselves to me and shook hands. Lynch said, 'We represent a couple of organisations.' S— said, 'I am from the INLA.'

"Lynch was there all the time. He tied me up, stripped me, assaulted me in certain ways, and then eventually sent me away to another house, interrogated me a bit more with him and a couple of others, then took me to a derelict house, put me up against a wall. They told me, 'I'll be back in a minute,' and then *click, click, bang, bang*. He left me for dead, and they boarded up the house. I eventually made my way to the maternity hospital in Flying Horse Road." (Interview, 12 May 1991.)

In fact Peter Duggan had been lucky that it was Lynch and not any other INLA man who had been assigned to shoot him. Lynch may have been under orders from his handlers not to directly involve himself in murder. Duggan, who denied ever being a spy, left Downpatrick shortly after the incident and fled to London, where he now lives.

The then INLA chief of staff came suspicious of Sandy Lynch when he failed to give an adequate explanation why Duggan did not die. Eventually the INLA leader came to believe that Lynch was the real police agent. By that time, however, Lynch had parted company with the INLA and joined the Provisionals.

The tables were turned on Lynch when the Provos eventually unmasked him as an informer (see chapter 13). One wonders whether he ever thought back to when he was on the other side of the interrogation room. The hunter had now become the hunted. Lynch must have realised that his captors would not show the same reluctance to kill their quarry as he had demonstrated in Downpatrick two years before.

While the INLA struggled to weed out remaining informers in Belfast, the IPLO concentrated its offensive on targets in the Unionist political establishment and the loyalist paramilitary leadership. On 9 August, the seventeenth anniversary of internment, the IPLO sent a letter bomb to the home of the Mid-Ulster MP, Rev. William McCrea. The DUP man had become suspicious after noticing that the package had a Dublin postmark.

On 12 August 1988 a bomb was planted outside a house in Bendigo Street, off the Ravenhill Road in east Belfast. The device failed to go off and was later defused by a British army bomb disposal team. In a statement admitting responsibility, the IPLO claimed that the house was used as a loyalist meeting place.

A week later a parcel bomb was posted to the Dungannon offices of the Fermanagh-South Tyrone MP Ken Maginnis, the Ulster Unionist Party's security spokesman. The suspicions of one of the workers in his advice centre were aroused when she noticed that the parcel came from Dublin. The security forces were called out and the bomb defused. It was clear from the parcel bombs sent to McCrea and Maginnis that the IPLO was desperate to strike at another prominent loyalist target to raise its national and international profile.

The IPLO failed, however, to pull off anything close to a spectacular operation throughout 1988. The organisation killed two people in that year: a loyalist and one of their own members. On 7 September 1988 an IPLO unit from the Lower Falls shot dead a 32-year-old UDA member, Billy Quee, outside a corner shop in the Oldpark Road in north Belfast. Just over a month later, at around two o'clock on the morning of 3 October, a former IPLO volunteer, Henry McNamee, was shot dead in front of his girl-friend at their home in Lenadoon Avenue. A statement from the organisation accused McNamee of working for the RUC. The IPLO alleged that the murdered man had been recruited as an informer after being questioned at Castlereagh holding centre over a bank robbery in June 1987. They claimed McNamee had travelled to London to meet his handlers under false identity, using the name John O'Neil. In their statement admitting responsibility for his murder the IPLO also claimed that their victim was planning to travel to Amsterdam to meet his contacts in the security forces. For their part, the McNamee family denied these allegations and branded the IPLO "renegade gangsters". (*Irish News*, 4 October 1988.)

The McNamee murder caused intense bitterness within the ranks. The authors have learnt that Henry McNamee was actually asked by Jimmy Brown to offer himself up to the RUC Special Branch as an informer. Brown's scheme was to lure McNamee's handlers into a trap. McNamee handed over a weapon to the RUC in 1988 and indicated that he wanted to work for them. The Special Branch obliged. According to reliable republican sources who were once close to McNamee, he played his part in the Brown plan. For some unknown reason, however, the IPLO failed to trap McNamee's handlers. On the orders of Jimmy Brown, Henry McNamee was then sentenced to death for allegedly working as an informer. The sources deny that he had ever betrayed the IPLO: they believe to this day that McNamee was simply caught in a web of intrigue spun by Brown, which the IPLO boss tried to wriggle his way out of. The most convenient means to escape the mess Brown created, they say, was to label Henry McNamee an informer. Whatever the truth behind the episode, the death of McNamee caused further dissension in the organisation and brought it into even more disrepute with the wider republican community in Belfast.

The following year was to prove a watershed for the IPLO. It continued its round of murder attempts on loyalist targets in Belfast. The organisation also became involved in an activity that all republican groups had until then carefully avoided: drug dealing.

Republican paramilitary organisations have run building site scams, extortion rackets, bank robberies, drinking clubs, cattle smuggling, gambling dens, and even brothels. Drugs, however, were a complete taboo. While individual volunteers may have smoked marijuana or occasionally taken other drugs, the official policy of groups like the Provisional IRA was to prevent the spread of drugs in nationalist areas. Indeed the Provisionals were extremely active in the Concerned Parents Against Drugs movement in Dublin during the heroin crisis of the early 1980s. In contrast to Dublin, Belfast's working-class areas—both nationalist and loyalist—were relatively drug-free, because of the hard line taken by paramilitaries on both sides.

The IPLO's decision to get embroiled in the drugs business opened a Pandora's box. High profits from drug dealing produced infectious greed, which would lead to new rivalries and splits within the movement.

A former IPLO leader in Belfast who resigned after the feud claimed that the organisation became involved in drug trafficking at the beginning of 1989. The drug trail started in the Netherlands and led to France along old INLA arms routes to the port of Rosslare. Most of the drugs purchased in Amsterdam were "ecstasy" tablets. These were then shipped to Belfast via a hiding-place in Swords, County Dublin. In Belfast, IPLO personnel and criminal elements associated with the organisation would sell the tablets at huge "acid house" and "rave" discos around the city.

The mastermind behind the IPLO drugs operations was Jimmy Brown. According to former comrades, Brown used not only old INLA arms routes but also tried-and-tested smuggling methods. The drugs were packed beneath the floorboards of camper vans, which were driven across Europe towards French ports. Ecstasy tablets were then put inside paracetamol bottles, which were placed inside fridges on arrival in Belfast.

Brown never liked to admit his involvement in the drugs trade. He would always skirt around the issue, only muttering about the need for funds to fight their war. He pointed to the Palestinian guerrilla groups in Lebanon that ran the country's lucrative hashish trade until the Israeli invasion of 1982. He argued that, like the Palestinians, the IPLO needed to use any means necessary to raise funds for its revolution.

It has to be said that Jimmy Brown probably believed his own propaganda. Forever the romantic, Brown was constantly promising his volunteers that the drugs trade could net them enough money to buy sophisticated weaponry that would change the "war" against the security forces in Northern Ireland.

The IPLO was offered the chance to pick up an arms shipment in 1988 on the Continent, which included shoulder-held light anti-tank missiles. The weapons had the capability of knocking out British army and RUC Land Rovers and the larger Saracen armoured personnel carriers. The man offering the arms haul had a long-standing connection with the old INLA/IRSP movement and had considerable experience shipping weapons to Ireland. His offer was rejected, however, by Brown, who informed him that the IPLO had not got the capability to transport such a large cache to Ireland at the time. With enough money from the profits of the drugs trade, however, the IPLO, Brown reasoned, could become large enough to bring such weapons to Ireland. Brown's logic was crude and reductionist. He discounted one crucial factor: greed. If he believed drug dealing could indirectly help the IPLO build up a more sophisticated arsenal, many of his comrades around him saw the chance to get rich quickly.

So determined was the IPLO to protect its new source of income that it was willing to wipe out small-time rivals. The IPLO was also prepared to collude with the very people they were trying to kill. Over the next few years IPLO members met loyalist paramilitaries, mainly from the UVF, to divide the spoils from drug peddling in the North.

Perhaps one of the more bewildering aspects of the Northern crisis is the cross-over between deadly enemies involved in paramilitary rackets. As IPLO and UVF members connected with the new drug trade started to cut across each other, a series of meetings was organised to iron out differences and divide the spoils. They met each other in a Belfast city centre bar and agreed to stay out of each other's territory and to eliminate minor drug dealers who stood in their way.

The stakes were high, after all. Almost overnight young men from west Belfast had large amounts of money stuffed in their pockets. The drugs known on the "rave" scene as "Es" were sold for £25 a tablet. The trade created a new class of paramilitary in west Belfast. Young, brash, and arrogant, they strutted around Castle Street as proud as peacocks, unashamed of their new business. One former IRSP member described them as "wide boys who did little or nothing to hide their newly found wealth." One drug dealer from Divis Flats could be seen strutting around Castle Street in £300 suits carrying a portable telephone while he peddled the tablets from a nearby entry.

As the trade mushroomed, the IPLO bought over a city centre taxi firm and used it to ferry drugs around Belfast to "rave" venues and to various pubs and clubs. The American gang-style culture sprouting up in the Divis Flats and the Lower Falls was a far cry from the days of Séamus Costello and the search for the socialist republic. The decision to deal in drugs also sparked off a new round of defections in the movement, particularly of older veterans who were fed up with the tag of criminality.

The IPLO was suffering from a unique form of paramilitary split personality. Despite the creeping collusion over drugs, the IPLO onslaught against loyalists continued. On 18 February it came close to killing most of the UVF's Belfast Brigade. The IPLO attacked the Orange Cross social club off the Shankill Road. A lone gunman ran into the bar and opened fire with an Uzi sub-machine gun; 36-year-old Stephen McCrea of Ebor Street died in the hail of bullets. Two other men and two women were wounded in the attack. In a statement admitting responsibility for the "spray job", the IPLO, through Jimmy Brown, claimed that McCrea had been an intelligence officer for the UVF. Whatever the accuracy of that claim, it is true that McCrea had at one time been involved with loyalist paramilitaries. A former member of the outlawed Red Hand Commando, McCrea had just been released after serving a long prison sentence for his part in the murder of a Twinbrook man, James Kerr, at the Lisburn Road garage on 31 October 1972.

There were, however, more prestigious targets the IPLO missed in the Orange Cross attack. The IPLO's last chief of staff revealed afterwards that the UVF brigade staff had been holding a meeting upstairs above the bar when he burst in with the Uzi submachine-gun. "It's a pity we couldn't have wiped out their entire brigade staff in that attack. That would have really given us a great boost among nationalists in Belfast, who wanted action taken against loyalists then." (Interview, 14 August 1993.)

The Uzi submachine-gun used to kill Stephen McCrea had almost set off another feud with the INLA the previous year. The weapon had in fact been stolen from an INLA arms dump by IPLO volunteers in west Belfast. The theft of the highly prized machine-gun infuriated the INLA.

One former INLA volunteer who played a key role in the 1987 feud explained how the Uzi incident brought both organisations to the brink of war again. "The weapon was stolen around the second week of January 1988. We were determined to do something about it, so the INLA kidnapped an IPLO member. We informed the IPLO we'd only let him go if they gave us the Uzi back. A republican mediator came back to us with a message from Jimmy Brown that we could shoot his man if we wanted. The IPLO wasn't giving the gun back.

"In the middle of this tension Ian Catney was shot dead by the UVF in Smithfield. At first we thought the IPLO had shot him, so we all went to ground. Catney had been wounded by the IPLO in the feud the previous year. We were holed up in safe houses rearing to go. Once it emerged that the UVF shot Ian we went to the mediators.

"Unfortunately the mediators used in the '87 feud were not called upon this time to negotiate. Old republicans were called in, and to be honest it was a waste of time. The IPLO were allowed to keep the Uzi. It's funny that it nearly resulted in another feud, and the weapon ended up killing a loyalist." (Interview, 1 November 1993.)

The incident over the machine-gun demonstrated how volatile relations were between the two factions. Many in the INLA GHQ were still smarting from the wounds inflicted on the organisation by former comrades. Terry Harkin, then the IRSP's main spokesman, described the bitterness about the IPLO. "Brown and his cronies had shattered a once-great organisation. The INLA/IRSP movement had managed to merge the national and class question together. Despite our difficulties, we were building a movement with real revolutionary potential. It was really criminal that the IPLO killed a volunteer of the calibre of Ta Power. Ta was the greatest revolutionary leader Ireland never had." (Ibid.)

Relations between the IPLO and the Provisionals were also facing new strains throughout 1989 and 1990. The Provos and others in west Belfast noticed a disturbing new pattern within the IPLO. Petty criminals and paramilitary rejects started to swell the IPLO's ranks. Concentrated in the Divis Flats, Lower Grosvenor, Lenadoon and Markets area, the IPLO embarked on an "open door" policy. Many hardened Belfast criminals sought sanctuary from the Provos' own brand of street "justice" by joining the IPLO.

Within a year the IPLO lost several key volunteers who still had some military and republican credibility. One month after the Secretary of State, Peter Brooke, finally got around to proscribing the organisation, the IPLO launched an attack at the home of an off-duty RUC man at Lislalley Road, Kinnego, County Armagh. As an IPLO unit led by Martin Corrigan approached the garden of the house, a group of British soldiers opened fire. Corrigan, carrying an M1 carbine, was killed in the gun-battle. Martin Corrigan was to be the IPLO's only member shot dead engaging the British army.

Corrigan came from a strong republican family. He had drifted away from the Provisionals in Armagh towards the IPLO at the end of the 1980s. Eight years before the gun battle at Kinnego he had witnessed the murder of his father, a Sinn Féin activist, at the hands of the Protestant Action Force in 1982 as he stood outside Armagh social services office in Alexander Road. An ex-UDR man, Geoffrey Edwards, was later arrested and convicted of Peter Corrigan's murder.

The IPLO was dealt another serious blow, this time on the Continent. The organisation had already suffered a serious setback in Europe the year before when a 42-year-old west Belfast man, Peter McNally, was arrested in Amsterdam on 8 September. The Dutch police found a 9 mm pistol, ammunition, a bin liner full of documents and cocaine in his flat. After his arrest McNally insisted that a British agent provocateur had lured him into drug dealing. In a detailed declaration handed to a Dutch court two years later McNally said he and Anthony Kerr were offered drugs and guns by the alleged agent in a café in Amsterdam's red light district. Both men faced extradition to Belgium, Kerr on a charge of smuggling guns from Antwerp and McNally for an armed robbery in 1987. During a later hearing, on 26 November 1991, McNally alleged that the cocaine was planted on him by the "agent".

The IPLO had become a haven for former IRA members who had either been expelled from the Provisionals or left after disagreements with the leadership. One such dissident Provo was 23-year-old Eoin Morley from Newry. He had enraged local Provos by defecting to join the IPLO. On Easter Sunday 1990, Morley was sitting in his girl-friend's home at Iveagh Crescent in the Derrybeg estate when a team of IRA men burst into the house. His girl-friend and her three children were forced into an upstairs bedroom. Morley tried to escape but was caught and dragged outside. In a back garden nearby he struggled with his captors; in the confusion he was shot twice in the back.

The IRA gang fled and left Morley bleeding to death. He was found by a number of local people and rushed to Daisy Hill Hospital, where he died two hours later.

In admitting responsibility for the Easter Sunday murder, the Provisionals accused Morley of being an informer whose treachery led to the loss of IRA weapons. The Provos alleged that Morley had been guilty of passing "sensitive information". But there was something curious about the killing of Eoin Morley. When the IRA execute an informer they normally shoot their victim through the back of the head, earning the IRA's internal security unit the nickname "the Headhunters". Eoin Morley's wounds, however, were different. He was wounded in the back, and bled to death from his injuries.

Shortly after the Morley murder, Jimmy Brown met IRA representatives in Newry. He later told the authors that he believed the Provisionals had not intended to kill Eoin Morley; he felt they had intended to wound him as an example to other republicans in Newry not to join the rival IPLO. Brown claimed that the Provos were also angry that Morley may have handed over IRA guns to the IPLO when he defected.

The Morley killing caused a great deal of anger in Newry. The murdered man's family were respected republicans. Eoin Morley's father, Dónal Morley, had served time in the early 1970s, and was OC of the Provos in the jail for a period. On his release from prison, however, he had distanced himself from the organisation.

A feud in the border town between the IPLO and the Provos was averted by the inter-republican mediation process. Easter Sunday, the most sacred date in the republican calendar, had been marred by the sight of republicans killing other republicans in Newry.

A veiled admission that Eoin Morley was innocent of the informer charge was made by the Provos two years later. In the 16 November 1992 edition of *An Phoblacht* the Provisionals issued a terse statement that read: "Eoin Morley was never suspected by the IRA of being an informer."

The deteriorating relationship between the Provos and the IPLO got worse after the Morley killing. On a June evening in 1990 a group of young IPLO members, along with two brothers on the fringes of the organisation, were waiting for a "carry-out" in a Chinese takeaway in the Falls Road. Also inside the takeaway was a young woman from Bangor. She became friendly with the young men, and they invited her to a party in Divis Flats. After arriving at the flat, the woman was brutally raped by the two brothers, with at least one IPLO member also involved. When news of the rape started to filter out to the community there was outrage. On Wednesday 20 June a group of women held a demonstration to show public abhorrence over the rape. Sinn Féin joined the protest. Some of the party's female members and supporters held up anti-IPLO placards.

Brown hit out at Sinn Féin's party politicking during the anti-rape march. He claimed that the protest had started out to raise the issue of a serious assault on a young woman but ended up as an attack on the IPLO's very existence.

In a statement that Brown drew up after the incident he gave details of an IPLO punishment shooting against six of the youths involved, including the IPLO volunteer he admitted took part in the rape. Whether the IPLO bore any collective blame for the gang rape at Divis is debatable. But at the very least the Divis rape showed a serious lack of discipline among IPLO personnel.

Beyond debate, however, was the IPLO's continued involvement in other forms of anti-social behaviour, namely drug dealing. On 15 July 1990 the IPLO killed a rival drug dealer, William Sloss, at his home off the Lisburn Road and three weeks later sanctioned the death of another, Emmanuel Shields at, the hands of a loyalist. Both men's murders were the result of collusion between the IPLO and loyalists in the drugs business.

The IPLO's rivals in the INLA continued to follow on a parallel path. They too lost another volunteer in a shoot-out with the security forces in 1990. On 13 November part of the INLA unit in the north-west that had carried out the botched operation at Clady checkpoint picked a softer target. They had singled out the home of a UDR man at Victoria Bridge. What the INLA unit were unaware of was that British army intelligence also knew of their plans. According to the BBC reporter John Ware, the man driving the

INLA gang to kill the UDR man was working for the security forces.

When the gang arrived, heavily armed undercover soldiers from the British army's 14th Intelligence Unit (a regiment trained and organised on SAS lines) sprang out of nearby bushes. The soldiers raked the INLA car. When the shooting was over the car's driver, 31-year-old Alexander Patterson of Church Mews, Strabane, was dead. Unknown to the soldiers or to his INLA comrades, 24-year-old Gerard McGarrigle and 30-year-old Samuel Joseph McNulty, Patterson was alleged to be a double agent; it was his information that led to the undercover army squad staking out the UDR man's home. The Patterson incident was a major embarrassment to the security forces; but it also exposed the success of the RUC and British army in penetrating the ranks of the INLA.

The INLA failed to launch any significant operations for two years after the Victoria Bridge debacle. The fall-out from the feud, however, forced some volunteers to revise their support for armed struggle. On 6 August 1991 a Newry INLA volunteer, Damien McShane, publicly called on his comrades to renounce violence. McShane had just been released after six years in the H-block for INLA membership.

McShane joined a fledgling peace organisation set up by a former Provisional IRA volunteer, Mark Lenaghan, from the Twinbrook area of Belfast. Lenaghan had been one of Bobby Sands's pall bearers. On his release from prison ten years later, Lenaghan came to the conclusion that the armed struggle was an obstacle to peace. He set up an All-Ireland peace petition that called on the republican movement, loyalist paramilitaries and the British government to pursue political aims only through democratic and peaceful means.

For Damien McShane the turning-point came after the 1987 feud ended. In an interview he explained: "I knew a lot of lads who were killed during that feud. After it I said to myself, 'What's the point?' I realised finally how futile violence was. Every sacrifice we made was not a victory at all." (*Irish News*, 6 August 1991.)

Damien McShane's plea to his former comrades in both the INLA and the IPLO was ignored. In Belfast the IPLO kept up its wildcat attacks on loyalist-owned pubs, clubs and businesses throughout the city. On 5 June 1991 an IPLO hit team tried to assassinate Eddie McIlwaine, a member of the notorious Shankill Butchers gang who had just been released from prison after seven years for kidnapping the only survivor of the Butchers, Gerard McLaverty. McIlwaine was wounded while driving a black taxi at the junction of Lower North Street and Bridge Street. Again the IPLO had tried to go for a "popular hit"; but, unlike the Seawright killing, this time they were unsuccessful, as McIlwaine survived.

Loyalists had taken note of the threat posed by the IPLO. Two months after the McIlwaine shooting the UVF hit back. On 16 August 1991 two gunmen burst into the home of Martin "Rook" O'Prey in Ardmoulin Terrace, just two hundred yards below the heavily fortified British army look-out post on top of Divis Tower in the Falls Road.

The UVF gang had entered O'Prey's house by the back door. As they barged their way through the house they were confronted by O'Prey's girl-friend, Yvonne. One of the UVF killers punched her in the face before bursting into the living-room. Martin O'Prey was found watching television. One of the UVF opened fire with a handgun, killing him instantly. Both loyalists fled out of the back of the house to a waiting car, which sped off towards the Shankill Road.

The O'Prey killing left the IPLO without one of their most experienced and ruthless operators. O'Prey had been number 2 in the IPLO, with a fearless reputation within republican circles. His assassination posed several questions. The UVF team's daring in entering a strong nationalist area and attacking O'Prey at a specific location threw into doubt accepted republican wisdom about the lack of efficiency among loyalist killer gangs. IPLO comrades admitted that the murder had been carefully planned and professionally executed.

After O'Prey was buried with paramilitary honours, including a masked colour party outside his father's home in Leeson Street under the noses of the British army and RUC, it emerged that the UVF had received inside information on O'Prey. The IPLO "arrested" a member from the Grosvenor area and interrogated him for several hours at a house in the Lower Falls. They accused him of colluding with the UVF, and claimed that he passed on details of O'Prey's house. Worse still, they alleged that the suspected traitor was in O'Prey's home less than an hour before the UVF struck. According to the IPLO's chief of staff, this man tipped off the UVF gang and before leaving had left O'Prey's back door open.

O'Prey's alleged betrayer managed to escape. While held in an upstairs room of the interrogation house, he managed to cut himself free and jump from a bedroom window. He had undoubtedly avoided execution. His alleged involvement in setting up O'Prey exposed the dangers posed by drug dealing and collusion with loyalists in the trade. The IPLO's suspect had been involved in drug peddling around Belfast and had met several senior UVF figures. It was during these liaisons that plans were hatched to kill O'Prey. According to Brown, money is understood to have changed hands, with one businessman associated with IPLO drug dealers being offered £30,000 by the UVF to set up O'Prey.

The IPLO's lethal cocktail of drug peddling and attacks on loyalist targets continued after O'Prey's death. Jimmy Brown, along with the IPLO's chief of staff, threatened to kill "selective loyalist targets" in revenge for O'Prey's murder. Instead their volunteers opted for safer and softer operations. The "spray jobs" on loyalist bars and businesses continued. On 11 October the Diamond Jubilee Bar in the Shankill Road was machine-gunned by the IPLO. One man, Harry Ward, a worker for loyalist prisoners' aid, was killed in the attack. Two months later, on 21 December, the IPLO struck again at another loyalist pub, the Donegall Arms, in Roden Street, Belfast. In that attack, carried out by an IPLO unit from across the "peace line" on the other side of the M1 motorway, two men, 55-year-old Thomas Gorman and 25-year-old Barry Watson, died. None of them had any known loyalist paramilitary connections. Patrons in the pub reported hearing the gunmen scream as they fired indiscriminately across the bar, "Orange bastards! Orange bastards!"

On the same evening a group of IPLO members were drinking in the Frames Too night-club, facing the *Belfast Telegraph* offices. Following a drunken row with the club's floor manager, Colm Mahon, several IPLO members left the bar. About half an hour later the IPLO volunteers returned with a handgun. Once inside, they sought out Colm Mahon and shot him dead in front of hundreds of patrons. Following Mahon's murder the IPLO put out a statement saying that the shooting had been a tragic mistake: they claimed their intended target was a prominent loyalist drinking at the bar. But no-one believed the IPLO. Sinn Féin described the explanation as a "blatant lie". The murder of Colm Mahon was the result of a drunken brawl with the floor manager. Once again the IPLO had demonstrated a complete lack of internal discipline.

It was the second time in six years that the Mahon family had suffered at the hands of republican paramilitaries. Colm Mahon's brother Gerard and sister-in-law Catherine were shot dead at the bottom of an alleyway in the Turf Lodge estate in west Belfast on 8 October 1985. The Provisionals had alleged that the couple were working for the RUC as informers.

The INLA also incurred the Provos' wrath after the murder of a 19-year-old student in Moy, County Tyrone, on 21 December 1991. Robin Farmer had just returned from university in Scotland for the Christmas holidays. The INLA had targeted his father, who was a former UDR soldier. They entered his gun-shop in Main Street and opened fire. But instead of hitting Farmer the bullets struck his son, who dived into their path to protect his father.

In the aftermath of the murder Sinn Féin's Mid-Ulster representative, Francie Molloy, called for the INLA to disband. What Councillor Molloy forgot to mention was that the Provisional IRA had tried to kill Robin Farmer's father earlier in he year when they put a booby-trap bomb under his car. Hitting back at the Provos' latest disbandment call, the INLA said: "Councillor Molloy has a small memory when it comes to mistakes and accidents that occur. He should have a good look at the IRA's track record on accidental deaths." (*Irish News*, 23 December 1991.)

After a year of sectarian blood-letting and drug dealing, the IPLO, through Jimmy Brown, promised great things for 1992. In a statement he wrote (on letter-headings belonging to a consultancy firm in Lower Camden Street, Dublin), Brown outlined the IPLO's strategy for the coming year. "1992 will see an increase in the political and military activity of the IPLO. Recent increases in supplies and improved training means that the organisation is now in its best position since its formation five years ago."

He went on to boast that "for the first time we are now prepared to conduct selective interviews." It was as if Brown was recruiting for the consultants' firm on whose letter-headings he was writing rather than seeking volunteers for the IPLO! "The organisation runs a very rigid vetting process and has little difficulty in attracting recruits. Our membership is strong and growing," he claimed. Within eight months of drafting the IPLO's strategy for 1992, half of those he had recruited would rebel against his leadership and plot his eventual death.

As for the IPLO's promised political strategy, the closest Brown came to political activity in the North was a threat to stand against Gerry Adams in West Belfast during the Westminster general election campaign. Brown boasted he would split the republican vote because, he alleged, IPLO prisoners in Crumlin Road jail were being harassed by IRA inmates and had to be put on 24-hour lock-up for their own safety. In the end the imagined challenge to Adams's voting base in the Lower Falls never materialised. By the time the election took place Brown was too busy trying to hold his own organisation together.

On the military front the IPLO started the new year where it had left off in 1991. On 17 February an IPLO unit struck at an alleged "selective loyalist target" in north Belfast. Its intended victim was a loyalist from the Ballysillan area who owned a video shop in the area. When the IPLO burst into the shop in the Upper Crumlin Road at eight o'clock that evening they singled out a seventeen-year-old working behind the counter. Their "selective loyalist target" turned out to be Andrew Johnston, a "born-again" Christian voluntary worker for the Ballysillan Elim Pentecostal church. Ironically, he belonged to the same Pentecostalist sect as the men who died in the Darkley massacre in 1983. The same sectarian patterns were replicated in the IPLO's armed offensive.

The IPLO's random attacks and drug dealing put further pressure on the IRA to move against its smaller republican rivals. The Provos were outraged that during mediation meetings Jimmy Brown made it known that senior Sinn Féin figures such as Gerry Adams would be regarded as legitimate targets if the IRA attacked the IPLO. Over the year the Provos had to watch and wait as the IPLO began to break apart.

Yet while relations between the two groups were plummeting to new depths, Jimmy Brown still promoted a strategy of co-operation with the Provisionals. While the Provos champed at the bit, holding back from wiping out the IPLO, Brown fantasised about building a new broad front of republican and nationalist organisations to force Britain out of Ireland. Expounding on the concept, Brown addressed other republicans and appealed for unity. "We are determined to see that the Broad Front is put on the agenda for the Irish left in the coming period. Our members and supporters are active in single issue campaigns, increasingly they will be advancing the arguments for the creation of a Broad Front to oversee a minimum programme capable of completing the national struggle in terms favourable to the working class of this island as a whole. Without such a unified approach we are destined to further marginalisation and the prospect of protracted defeat."

Defeat, however, was already staring Jimmy Brown in the face. He was naïvely clinging to the old idea articulated by Séamus Costello of a broadly based republican alliance. But the knives were already out for Brown.

In his document the IPLO's spokesman enthused about his members' capabilities. "In 22 years of activity I have never seen a more security conscious organisation. The membership are highly motivated and increasingly politically conscious." The "open door" policy, however, let petty criminals, paramilitary dissidents and drug dealers drift into the IPLO's ranks. The organisation Brown helped set up was walking blindly towards its own destruction. And the man who advocated the broad front was now trapped within a narrow, isolated splinter group that was ready to tear itself apart, not through political differences but rather through personal hatred and individual greed.

15

ENDGAMES

The story of modern Irish republicanism is punctuated with a constant series of "what ifs". Each generation has uttered these words when faced with vital questions about the direction of republican struggle. "What if Michael Collins had refused to sign the Treaty? What if the Republican Congress's left-wing programme had been adopted by the IRA in the 1930s? What if the IRA had been able to stay together in 1969? What if the Officials called their cease-fire later than 1972? What if the Provisionals had not been lured into a cease-fire by the British in 1975? What if Séamus Costello had not been assassinated? What if Thomas Power had survived the feud and headed the IRSP?

Republicans of all hues have been tortured by the "ifs" of their history. Reflecting on his lifelong involvement with the republican movement, Cathal Goulding cites his own great "if". He believes the pivotal moment in the IRA's post-partition history was the rejection of the Republican Congress in 1934. "Republican Congress members were wrong to leave the IRA," Goulding maintains. "They were only beaten by one vote at the 1934 Army Convention. If they had stood their ground they could have won in another, later IRA convention. If the IRA had adopted their programme we would have had a serious republican left-wing party long before the 1960s. We would have got rid of the element that later formed the Provos much earlier. Instead we lost thirty years. That was crucial." (Interview, 11 November 1993.)

Goulding also reflects on more modern turning-points, particularly the 1972 Official IRA cease-fire. In hindsight he admits that the Officials probably called off the armed struggle too soon. He accepts that the decision (while morally and politically correct) caused unnecessary trauma and divisions within the movement. Perhaps if the Officials' armed struggle had been run down at a slower pace and eventually brought to a halt by the mid-1970s, Goulding feels the second split may not have been as damaging. His theory now is that the leadership could have slowly but surely edged out some of the young militants who later formed the nucleus of the INLA and maybe even have won a few of them away from militarism through political education.

In an interview in January 1990, twenty years after the Sinn Féin ardfheis walk-out that formalised the creation of the Provisionals, Goulding gave a telling reflection on the changes set off in Irish republicanism in the 1960s. "We were definitely right, but right too soon. Adams may be right in pushing the Provos towards politics, but he's too late. And Ruairí Ó Brádaigh will never be right." (*Irish News*, January 1990.)

This hearkening back to what might have been also permeates the thinking of those who supported Séamus Costello. Tony Hayde and Rose Doyle from the Séamus Costello Memorial Committee felt that Irish republicanism lost its most charismatic leader since James Connolly.

A daughter of the 1916 Rising's left-wing hero compared Costello to her father. "Séamus was the greatest follower of my father's teachings in this generation," wrote Nora Connolly O'Brien, "and I hope that his example will be followed and that his vision for Ireland will be realised in this generation."

For the supporters and fellow-travellers of the IRSP/INLA movement, Costello was the lost Messiah. After his death the organisation was left without a proper leader and thinker. If only he had survived, they ask themselves; what if he had been allowed to develop the party? Things then might have been different.

Just before he was assassinated, Thomas Power wrote a detailed analysis on the history of the IRSP. He too described Costello in near-mystical terms. Awestruck by his legacy, Power wrote: "The sheer stature of the revolutionary Séamus Costello is far too great for what can possibly be expressed in feeble words." ("Historical analysis of the IRSP", *Starry Plough*, December 1987.) The language of Power's adulation reads like John the Baptist's humbled description of the man who is to come after him.

This idea of the lost leader is not a new concept in Irish politics. It leads back to the fall of Parnell and perhaps even beyond to the death of Tone and Emmet. In the story of Irish nationalism and republicanism there is a constant biblical sense of loss for the prophet-hero who is cast out and betrayed by the ungrateful masses in each generation. Séamus Costello is another of those figures who fit that sentimental pattern of betrayal and loss in Irish history. Added to the lost leader concept is the reductionist argument that only spectacular individual acts by these heroes and their men would stir the slumbering masses to revolt.

It was this psyche that prevailed throughout the INLA's bloody history. The plot, for instance, to kill the British ambassador in St Patrick's Cathedral, the INLA thought, would result in widespread state repression, perhaps even internment. The working class would then be forced to choose in a state of political crisis whether they backed the establishment or revolutionary republicanism. The worse the better, the strategists of such acts believed.

This logic was similar to ultra-left thinking in Britain in the early 1980s. Far-left activists believed mass unemployment would worsen the condition of the British working class. The theory was that as misery piled up, British workers would eventually rebel and throw out the Tories, by the ballot box, general strike, or even armed uprising. In reality mass unemployment weakened the trade union movement and helped the Conservatives pick off isolated groups of workers, such as the miners.

The INLA leaders concluded that creating a climate of state repression in the Republic by one spectacular act of terror in St Patrick's Cathedral would have hastened Ireland's revolution. But in fact the widespread revulsion caused by such an atrocity would probably have weakened the republican cause among the southern population. The masses would have remained at the very least indifferent towards the national revolution.

Those who keep his memory alive believe Costello would have made it into the Dáil and become an influential republican-left TD capable of swaying public opinion on the national question. One man, they argue, could have been the pivot for so much change. This thinking is analogous to that of the followers of Leon Trotsky, who cling to the view that socialism would have succeeded in the twentieth century if their hero had taken over the Russian Communist Party instead of Josef Stalin. However, it ignores wider factors and deeper reasons for fundamental political realities. While the followers of Séamus Costello rightly believe he could have held together the movement for some time, they fail to admit the existence of internal contradictions, which were visible from the day he founded the IRSP. Splits would have occurred even with Costello still at the helm. He may have staved off further feuding for a while, but the divisions existed and could not be healed or, eventually, halted.

It was ironic that in his analysis of the IRSP, "Ta" Power regurgitated Costello's concept of the broad front uniting all anti-imperialist groups and organisations around a minimum programme for Irish unity. While Power was developing this idea some of his own former comrades were plotting to kill him. This was more common than not with the movement. The supreme irony of its history is that the party most prone to internal feuding was also the party of the broad front.

Although hopelessly naïve in its demand for a new liberation front, Power's document is a well-written historical essay that touches on the some of the inherent failures of the INLA/IRSP movement. He suggested that the organisation adopt a Bolshevik-style structure, where the armed wing would be subordinate to the party political strategists. In other words, the INLA would be the cutting edge of the IRSP's politics. This position was similar to the left bloc that, under Bernadette McAliskey, split from the IRSP in late 1975.

Power believed the central contradiction in the organisation was the domination of militarism over party politics. Employing crude Marxian terminology, Power called the political wing A and the military wing B. His vision of the future was that A would dominate and dictate to B. (In fact B in internal IRSP documents was the INLA.)

"Out of the predominance of A over B definite psychological traits will emerge: of discipline, unity, work, theoretical strength, comradeship, solidarity, confidence." These traits had certainly been lacking in the INLA/IRSP for a long time before Ta Power wrote his last political testament.

Power quoted Lenin's critique of the ultra-leftist Social Revolutionaries, who employed terrorist tactics to bring about revolution in Russia. Lenin wrote: "Their terrorism is not connected in any way with work among the masses, for the masses, or together with the masses. It distracts our very scanty organisational forces from their difficult and by no means completed task of organising a revolutionary party."

Lenin, Power was inferring, could have been writing about the state of the INLA/IRSP at the end of 1986 as well as the Social Revolutionaries in Tsarist Russia at the start of the century. The Irish revolution was being impaired by the historical tendency to subordinate politics to the gun. The task ahead, Power argued, was to reverse that process.

The INLA's last theoretician had touched on the central dilemma of modern Irish republicanism: the fragile relationship between politics and armed action. Unlike the movement Séamus Costello founded, the Provisionals did succeed in mixing armed action with street politics. The INLA failed because of an inherent instability. The movement lacked middle-ranking leadership. It had taken the axe to the root of historical republicanism when it broke from the Official IRA. After Séamus Costello's murder, most remaining links with the republican past were lost. There was a lack of mature and experienced leadership, which has always been available to the Provisionals and the Officials. A founding member in Belfast admits that the INLA was run more like a family organisation than a traditional republican movement. In fact those who replaced Costello came more often from a communist and extreme-left tradition than from a republican background. This led them to attempt the kind of spectacular exploits more in keeping with the activities of a European anarchist group.

Throughout the INLA/IRSP's history the organisation has been noted for its pathfinding. It was the vanguard behind the early H-block struggles. The party broke the electoral ice by entering city councils in Northern Ireland four years before Sinn Féin did. The INLA found fresh arms networks and developed new bomb-making technology that were later adopted and refined by the Provisional IRA. The IRSP became embroiled in issues that traditional republicans would regard as distractions from the main struggle. As far back as 1975 at the IRSP's first ardfheis three hours were devoted to women's issues, and controversial topics were debated such as the right to contraception and abortion. And, as has been noted before, women played a much more prominent role in both the INLA and the IRSP than ever was accorded to them in the other republican groups.

Subordinating military struggle to carefully thought-out political strategy had been Ta Power's dream for a long time. In the 1980s Sinn Féin and the IRA made that a reality with their ballot box cum Armalite policy. The Provos learnt well from the lessons and mistakes of the IRSP/INLA.

Ta Power recognised that the IRSP needed to build a political base in the South as well as the North. The IRSP would become a "revolutionary party" capable of harnessing working-class discontent in the Republic to the wider struggle for a united Ireland. But, as with so many other proposals Ta Power mapped out for the future, he was far too late. By the time he got around to musing on the necessity of a Marxist-oriented republican party organising among the southern working class, the IRSP's old rivals the Officials had stolen their thunder.

The Workers' Party entered the Dáil during the 1981 "hunger strike election" in the South when the Cork East TD Joe Sherlock was elected; within eight years it had seven TDs and one European Parliament seat in Dublin. The party the Official IRA had set out to create in the late 1960s had became the voice of urban working-class dissent in cities such as Dublin, Cork, and Waterford. By 1989 there were fears in the southern establishment that the Workers' Party could eventually eclipse the Labour Party in Dublin.

The relative success of the Workers' Party reflected their grasp of new realities in the Republic. One of the most striking fault-lines within modern Irish republicanism is the divergence between the demands of Dublin and Belfast. By the end of the 1960s many republicans brought up in Belfast would not have recognised the new Ireland emerging south of the border. With the economic revolution created by Seán Lemass in the 1960s, a new working class had emerged. Ireland was no longer a predominantly rural nation. The Dublin metropolitan area bulged westwards as new satellite estates grew larger and people flocked to the capital.

It was no accident that within two decades the Workers' Party was able to build a support base in these new areas of Dublin. Interestingly, the party found it more difficult to break into the electoral areas in traditional working-class areas of the city. These older areas were sewn up particularly by Fianna Fáil through a complex network of clientelism and old historical loyalties. Tallaght, Kilbarrack, Finglas, Ballymun, and Clondalkin—these new population centres of Dublin were the areas that elected Workers' Party candidates to the Dáil.

The enemy for the Workers' Party was no longer simply British imperialism. By the late 1970s, under the intellectual guidance of thinkers like Eoghan Harris and IRA veteran Éamon Smullen, the Workers' Party created a new adversary, "Anglo-American imperialism". In a deluge of political pamphlets and theoretical journals, the Workers' Party argued that foreign domination of Ireland had changed. Britain was no longer the dominant power in the world: it was now led by the nose from Washington. Imperialism no longer meant gunboats steaming up the main rivers and foreign troops marching on the streets. Multinational capital was now the main power exerting influence over Ireland through a complex network of political patronage and economic intimidation. Workers' Party theorists concluded that the movement of foreign capital in the boardrooms and financial houses around the industrial world had created a new monopoly-capitalist order. It was time to adapt and change in order to cope with these new times.

The Workers' Party built up an efficient organisation in the new urban Ireland and slowly but surely offered a radical alternative to the Labour Party, which was dogged by constant condemnations of merely acting as a crutch for right-wing parties like Fine Gael.

But the Workers' Party's analysis of the changing Ireland south of the border had a negative effect on its small support base in Northern Ireland. Captivated by the desire to introduce class politics in the entire country, the Workers' Party ended up arguing against power-sharing within a Northern Ireland devolved government. The thinking behind opposition to power-sharing was that it merely institutionalised sectarian divisions—and anyway the only real majority in the north was the working class, not unionists or nationalists. Locked into class reductionism, the Workers' Party failed to win over enough unionists, who were still suspicious of its republican roots, while nationalists saw the position as at best extremely naïve and at worst a betrayal of republican principles.

Protestant workers were seen as ripe red apples. All the Workers' Party needed to do was shake the tree of economic and social discontent and they would fall into the party's lap. The existential question about the Northern Ireland state was either ignored or lost in a mist of rhetoric.

This type of left-wing wishful thinking left the Workers' Party open to accusations that it supported a return to majority rule at Stormont and the union with Britain. Undoubtedly traditional republicans within the party were unnerved by such accusations. There were others, however, who were not bothered by such claims. By the end of the 1970s a new element, particularly in the Republic, had latched on to the Workers' Party. Many came from an oddball pro-union leftist group known as the British and Irish Communist Organisation. The uneasy marriage between Workers' Party members, many of whom had joined the movement as Official IRA volunteers in the early 1970s, and leftist intellectuals who supported the union helped sow the seeds of bitter divisions within the party.

In January 1992 the Workers' Party went through another acrimonious split. Those who later formed the Democratic Left claimed they no longer wanted to be associated with people they alleged were still running the Official IRA. Party members loyal to the republican faction led by Seán Garland and Cathal Goulding accused Proinsias de Rossa and his supporters of abandoning socialism for a mushy form of liberal social democracy. The Official IRA excuse, it seems, was a red herring. If the Official IRA was still in existence then, how did senior party members like de Rossa and Pat Rabbitte not know anything about it for such a long time?

In reality the central reason for the split was the desire of the parliamentary-based faction to dump ideological baggage, including the remnants of the republican tradition within the Workers' Party. It was worth noting that the backbone of opposition to Proinsias de Rossa's plans to liquidate and reconstitute the Workers' Party was the Northern membership. There were deep north-south divisions under the surface of the Workers' Party's united image, just as were found in the IRSP.

In the aftermath of the split the Workers' Party seemed to flip back in the direction of republicanism. The party's Dublin regional secretary, Seán Ó Cionnaith, even accused the Democratic Left leadership of adopting a "two-nationist" policy. He criticised the Democratic Left leader, Proinsias de Rossa, for calling on the British Labour Party to organise in Northern Ireland. Ó Cionnaith said the statement was a "clear illustration that DL has adopted the 'two-nationist' policy of the old British and Irish Communist Organisation." He alleged that de Rossa's comments at the 1993 British Labour Party conference in Brighton "expose what their break-away was all about—an abandonment of the ideal of a unitary democratic socialist republic." (*Irish Post.*)

The contradictions within the Workers' Party fit the pattern that also dogged the IRSP/INLA movement. For the Officials the emphasis after 1972 was on building a political base in the Republic at the expense (if unintentionally) of the North. For the IRSP it was the reverse. The pressure of organising in two separate states created conflicting demands. How to concentrate the movement's resources in both Dublin and Belfast? The rival organisations failed to square that circle.

The rise of the Workers' Party south of the border left the political stage too packed for an alternative radical republican party such as the IRSP or Sinn Féin. The trail of lost deposits that followed Sinn Féin's failed electoral campaigns in the Republic also reflected a wider indifference among southern voters towards the Northern issue.

After the "hunger strike election", in which two prison protesters, Kieran Doherty and Paddy Agnew, were returned to the Dáil, the North nose-dived down the South's political agenda. As the recessions of the 1980s pulverised the Republic's economy, issues such as job creation, the lack of a proper national health service, crippling taxation on urban workers and rising domestic crime became the central questions in the minds of the electorate. The Workers' Party was able to tap in to the well of discontent among urban workers and the unemployed in the South.

Growing indifference to the Northern question in the Republic threw up serious questions about the old Connollyite idea of welding together the national and class issue into a revolutionary front. Most people in the Republic piously aspire towards a united Ireland. But the working class of Dublin and other cities in the South seem unlikely and perhaps unwilling to become the vanguard of a new national revolution.

If the leaders of the IRSP/INLA overestimated the revolutionary potential of southern workers, they severely underestimated loyalist opposition to a united Ireland. At the IRSP's first public meeting in Dublin in February 1975, Séamus Costello gave a rather simplistic explanation for the activities of the UDA and UVF. "The loyalists murder gangs were comprised mainly of members of the British army or the Ulster Defence Regiment going about at night out of uniform to murder innocent people because they opposed imperialism or just took a nationalist position." (*Starry Plough*, April 1975.) In other words, Ulster loyalism simply did not exist as an independent force.

Republicans have suffered from a unique form of political solipsism. Their world is one-dimensional. Their struggle is a noble conflict between them and their British colonial masters. In this equation there is no room for loyalism. It is a central failure of republicanism that it cannot either accept or understand indigenous loyalist opposition to a united Ireland. However, there does seem to be a recent shift in perspective within the Provisionals, as has been revealed in the Hume-Adams dialogue. In this, Adams seems to accept the reality of unionist opposition to republican goals, albeit begrudgingly.

Loyalists have been an unwelcome addition in republicanism's one-dimensional world. At the very least loyalists are seen by republicans as simply puppets of British imperialism. The language republicans and nationalists use to describe the UDA or UVF is an illustration of this solipsism. Loyalist paramilitary groups are described as "British-inspired death squads". The wider unionist population are portrayed as merely "dupes of British imperialism". Unionists are either ignored as a nonentity or caricatured as spoiled children who constantly cry "mother" to Britain. At its most extreme, this misunderstanding of the loyalist community produces the kind of approach the IPLO held towards Northern Protestants in labelling them "irreformable Afrikaners". Such an attitude ultimately leads to the indiscriminate machine-gunning of Protestant bars and businesses.

Remove the British, republicans argue, and unionists will come to their senses and sit down with nationalists to negotiate for a new Ireland. This view is still widely held within republican ranks, despite a century-long loyalist opposition to home rule and a united Ireland. But when fact does not fit theory, those who live by ideology alone must ignore uncomfortable realities

The inability to acknowledge loyalism as an independent internal enemy of republicanism was a crucial denial of reality.

As time went by, the INLA/IRSP movement degenerated into pure militarism. The absurd posturing of the "Marxist-Leninist" faction did nothing to conceal this fact. The militarism was seen at its purest in the last days of the IPLO, when Jimmy Brown excused the murder of a shop owner by linking it to the second Gulf War. This exposes a lack of reality as startling as that of Charles Manson, who thought the murders of Sharon Tate and her friends would spark a Black uprising in the United States and lead to revolution, controlled by him. By this time the IPLO in particular were suffering from an alarming strain of political psychosis.

As the INLA/IRSP's political base disappeared, it was not susceptible to popular pressure. However, their international heroes, such as the ANC and the PLO, retained a mass base, which gave them the authority and confidence to suspend the armed campaign when they thought it was appropriate. Irish republicans still involved in armed struggle today find it extremely hard to give up their holy grail of armed struggle. In many ways the military campaign became an end in itself. Republicans are still ultra-sensitive to charges of sell-out and betrayal. They are also open to internal criticism that calling off the armed campaign without getting anywhere near a united Ireland means that the last two decades of sacrifice and struggle have been in vain. The result of this is that republicans have been impaled on their military "cutting edge" for too long.

And so each new generation is condemned to ask the wrong question of their history—"what if?" But it seems there are no more "ifs" left to ask. The modern republican movement has exhausted every available option open to them, from the ballot box cum Armalite strategy to the search for new kinds of high-tech weaponry that could deliver a knock-out blow to Britain. The "ifs" and "buts" keep the armed struggle alive. Calling up the dead and quoting from sacred texts gives the campaign a historical legitimacy. However, in the real world the people of Ireland are no longer overwhelmingly in favour of either the IRA's or INLA's violent activities. The Provisionals' self-declared "national revolution" is confined to working-class nationalist ghettos in Belfast and Derry, and the border areas of Armagh, Fermanagh, and Tyrone.

As for the INLA, there is little or no base left. In twenty-five years of struggle the Provos and the INLA have never got beyond this narrow social stratum that provides their main support. Unlike other republican struggles, such as the War of Independence, Sinn Féin has not harnessed enough support beyond their traditional working-class base and penetrated into the urban middle class. The Catholic middle class in Northern Ireland have been bought off by British public money and turned off by the excesses of the armed struggle. Nor have any republicans convinced their fellow-Irishmen who prefer to be British that they have nothing to fear from their New Ireland.

On a wall in Beechmount Avenue off the Falls Road there was a mural that depicted the old and the new IRA. On the left was a classic portrait of the twenties volunteer, with the old trench coat, a Sam Browne belt and floppy hat. At his side he carries a First World War issue Lee Enfield rifle. On the opposite end of the mural is the modern volunteer. He is masked, wearing a green flak jacket and carrying an Armalite rifle. The mural's message is clear: there is an unbroken connection between the War of Independence and the IRA's current campaign.

The mural's message, however, illustrates the intellectual poverty of violent republicanism today. Ireland, north and south, has undergone profound change. There are deeper divisions now between the two states, the two northern communities and among the classes in the country. The world is a different place from what it was in 1916 or 1969. When republicans begin to grasp these new realities, perhaps then the only worthwhile question they should start asking themselves is not "what if?" but "what now?"

16

NIGHT OF THE LONG KNIVES

Jimmy Brown sipped his cup of black coffee and promised another scoop. "When I get back from Belfast I'll have a great story for you," he boasted to one of the authors in a cramped café in Tara Street, Dublin. From his look and demeanour, Brown did not seem to be a man who knew his time was nearly up. He cheerfully loved to impress his contacts, offering stories about internal republican gossip, splits, and petty rivalries, all lightly sprinkled with some half-cooked ideological spice.

Within three days of his latest promised scoop, Jimmy Brown was dead. He was killed by a lone assassin at point-blank range in his native west Belfast. The leader of the Irish People's Liberation Organisation had travelled to the city to try in vain to patch up a new split within a group that had been born in fratricide.

On the afternoon of 18 August 1992, Jimmy Brown met Provisional IRA leaders inside Clonard Monastery, near where the Falls and loyalist Shankill converge at the so-called peace line. Brown attempted to get back IPLO weapons the Provos had stolen from their arms dump in the Lower Falls. The guns included AK47 rifles and Skorpion machine-pistols. Among those present was a Sinn Féin city councillor who acts as the Provos' main go-between in negotiations with rival republican groups, as well as leading Provisional IRA members and two local priests.

Brown finished the meeting just after two o'clock and left the monastery in his car. As he drove down Clonard Street he noticed a fellow IPLO member walking along the pavement. Unknown to Brown, this man, a former Provo, was armed.

Besides his killer, the last man to speak to Jimmy Brown was another IPLO volunteer, who sat beside his leader in the front passenger seat of the car. The man, who comes from the Andersonstown area, described what happened. "We got to the bottom of Clonard Street, outside the GAA club, when Jimmy said he was going to pull over to the side. He saw someone he knew. Jimmy was driving. He stopped the car and shouted to the fella walking by. Then I heard Jimmy shout, 'No, no!' and then there were shots. I remember turning round and seeing Jimmy getting it in the head. I bolted from the car with my head down. My heart was beating real fast. I could still hear shots ringing out as I ran onto the Falls Road towards Divis Flats."

This man described the murder to one of the authors in the Blue Lion pub in Parnell Street, Dublin, twenty-four hours after the killing. He was wearing the same clothes he had on him when his leader was assassinated, including a blue denim jacket and jeans. They were still smeared with streaks of Jimmy Brown's blood.

The witness to the murder was also acquainted with Brown's killer. He knew that the assassin was from the Clonard area and had joined the IPLO after falling out with the Provisional IRA. The ex-Provo already had plenty of experience in close-quarter killings; he is known to have been part of the IRA team that killed the notorious Shankill Butcher Lenny Murphy in November 1982. He is now in prison for an arms offence, and cannot be named for legal reasons.

Inside the Blue Lion lounge, the only witness to the Brown killing still looked shaken after his ordeal. He was certain the murder had been a spontaneous act: the killer had seen his chance to eliminate his rival and used it to deadly effect. "I'm absolutely certain we weren't followed. This guy acted on his own. The killer must have believed he was in danger and then opened up. I saw him draw his gun from the front of his trousers. He wasn't wearing a mask or gloves, so it couldn't have been well planned—or planned at all," he said.

Around him were about twenty-five young IPLO volunteers who had travelled south like him to meet the new leader of the organisation, a Lower Falls man who fled to Dublin after allegations that he was involved in the murder of the snooker hall manager Colm Mahon.

They all looked nervous and bewildered that night. Many were barely out of their teens. By their look and dress they seemed they would be more at home at a "rave" party than waging war on the streets of Belfast. But this band of young men swaggered about with the cockiness of an American drugs gang.

When open war finally broke out within the IPLO after Brown's death, the two rival factions behaved like the youth gangs of Los Angeles. One side bunched around the Distillery estate at the end of the M1 motorway, the other in Divis Flats. The geographical dividing line between the two gangs became the Grosvenor Road. And, like their American counterparts, there was little ideological divide between the two groups. Their row flared up over the division of profits from drug dealing.

Jimmy Brown's murder was another break in the fragile chain back to the origins of the INLA, from which the IPLO was spawned. Whatever Brown's own level of involvement in drug dealing, it is fair to say he was motivated by political principles rather than profits.

The warning lights had been flashing all around Brown for several months. Fatally, he chose to ignore them. In a series of minor skirmishes with the IRA in June that year, the IPLO sorely tested the Provos' patience. In one incident in the Lower Ormeau area of Belfast, an IPLO member shoved a gun into the mouth of a former INLA member (now in Sinn Féin) after a row about the allocation of a house in the nearby Markets area. Both men had been drinking at the time in the Hatfield Bar. The role of heavy drinking as a catalyst for feuding and murder cannot be underestimated in Belfast.

It is clear that many leading Provos blamed Jimmy Brown personally for the deteriorating relationship between them and the IPLO. One Sinn Féin spokesman referred to Brown as "a very dangerous man". Within the rank and file there was a frustrated desire to finally put the IPLO in its place: to finish the group off for good. The fear among the IRA leadership in the city was that if the IPLO were attacked, it would target prominent Provisionals, such as the Sinn Féin president, Gerry Adams. This held them back from immediately striking at the IPLO. All they had to do was sit back and wait for their chance to come. The impending split within the IPLO provided that opportunity.

Motivated by greed over drug profits and personality differences, the organisation Jimmy Brown and his comrades helped set up after the feud with the INLA in 1987 was threatening to atomise into a myriad of rival factions.

Amid the drip-drip of accusations of drug dealing and other sordid criminal deals, Jimmy Brown still strutted around Dublin with a far-left entourage in tow. With his Soviet army hammer-and-sickle belt around his ample waist, John Lennon glasses and nascent beard he resembled a 1960s-style revolutionary student. The mobile phone he always carried about was the only gesture to the age of the yuppie. The phone was still ringing when the ambulance crew took his body out of his car minutes after he was shot.

Before his death Brown had been working for a north Dublin community radio and media group called "Patch". It was through his community work in the north inner city that Brown scored a personal coup that he often recalled to members of the media. A year before Gerry Adams's famous handshake with President Mary Robinson in west Belfast, Jimmy Brown managed to shake hands with the head of state. He was part of a delegation of community workers invited to Áras an Uachtaráin. The IPLO's spokesman was tickled by the fact that his visit to President Robinson's residence was recorded for all time in the visitors' book at Áras an Uachtaráin. He signed it *Jimmy Brown—Belfast.* One wonders if President Robinson remembered the signature when news of Brown's death hit the headlines. Did she realise she shook hands with the leader of one of the most violent republican factions in Irish history?

The stunt at Áras an Uachtaráin was part of Jimmy Brown's political play-acting. He successfully cultivated contacts with journalists, far-left activists and the radical chic in the capital. Unlike most of his golden circle, however, Jimmy Brown came from a working-class nationalist background. He remained close friends with several of the hard men who would no doubt have little time for Brown's trendier friends in Dublin.

Jimmy Brown straddled two worlds. He quoted Marx, Lenin, and Trotsky, and then enthused about his beloved Tottenham Hotspurs. On his penultimate journey to Belfast, Brown took up soccer programmes with him for the son of an IPLO comrade who was on the run in Dublin.

Brown grew up in a sub-culture of violent republicanism. He died just yards away from the shop where his old friend Gerard Steenson murdered the Official IRA leader Billy McMillen seventeen years earlier.

The IPLO leader was liked and loathed with equal force within republican circles. One former INLA Army Council member dismissed him as a "clown". Others nicknamed him the "Professor" for his role in planning shootings and bombings.

The contradictions Brown lived under eventually consumed him. Whatever his "terror credentials", Brown was affable and extremely charming, if unbending and dogmatic at times. In another time perhaps his skills and enthusiasm could have been harnessed for better things. Unlike others in the IPLO, he was a political animal who threw himself into a variety of causes. The last political battle he was involved in was the left's campaign against Ireland signing the Maastricht Treaty.

There was also a devious and manipulative side to Brown. He had been attempting to set up a bogus computer firm with a former INLA man in Derry. The fraud Brown thought up was to obtain a grant from the IDA and then quietly close down the company, redirecting the finance into the IPLO's war chest.

The drive for profit poisoned the IPLO. Over the summer of 1992 the rumblings within the organisation began to grow louder. The movement led by Jimmy Brown was tearing asunder. A month before Brown was gunned down, his faction shot at a house in the Malone Road area. The attack was not reported at the time. Inside was the nucleus of the gang of dissidents that later broke away.

The murder of the 36-year-old IPLO leader seemed absurd. An indication of what the killing was really about was the fact that Jimmy Brown had a substantial amount of money on his person when he was shot.

But there was more to the latest republican feud than just rows over drugs money. Ten days after Brown's murder, one of the authors was invited to meet a leader of the IPLO rebels, who referred to themselves as the "Belfast Brigade". Inside St Malachy's Church in Alfred Street, Belfast, a former INLA activist who sided with the IPLO and Brown in 1987 explained now why "Jimmy had to go." Ironically, he joined the IPLO at the start of 1992 at the behest of Brown. Indeed, just weeks before his murder, Brown had spoken enthusiastically about his erstwhile comrade, who was to lead the gang that eventually killed him.

"He was protecting a drugs baron living in Dublin. I asked for assurances that we would not be involved in drugs. Jimmy lied to me, even though he persuaded me to come back into the organisation. He threatened one of the people who thought like me. And when the lad felt under threat in Clonard Street, he opened up and killed Jimmy."

The Magnum revolver the IPLO Belfast Brigade used to murder Brown had a grisly history. It had been used by IPLO assassins in three other murders, one of which Jimmy Brown made an absurd excuse for. On 18 July 1991 two IPLO gunmen walked into McMaster Brothers' tool shop in Church Lane, Belfast. One of them singled out 47-year-old John McMaster and opened fire, killing the shopkeeper instantly.

After the murder, Jimmy Brown offered an unusual explanation. John McMaster had been a member of the Royal Naval Reserve, which has no active security role in Northern Ireland. Brown explained, however, that McMaster had been a reservist in a navy that took part in the US-led naval bombardment of Iraq during the Gulf War. "Our friends in the Middle East," as Brown called them, would take note of the IPLO killing a member of that same navy in Belfast. The prospect of Saddam Hussein, Abu Nidal or George Habash taking note of a merciless killing of a well-liked businessman in Belfast and as a result offering physical support for the IPLO seemed remote. But it was an eerie twist of fate that the man who limply excused the murder would himself be shot dead with the same weapon.

The McMaster murder also illustrated the IPLO's "open door" policy regarding criminals. One of the young men jailed in connection with the murder (he drove the getaway car) was Chris Montgomery from Friendly Street in the Markets area. In February 1991 he had been forced to flee

Northern Ireland after a death threat from the Provisional IRA. But within months he was back in the city, using the IPLO as a protective shield. His price was involvement in the murder of John McMaster.

The murder weapon's history indeed tracked the degeneration of the IPLO. It was also used to kill a retired security officer, William Sergeant. He had been enjoying a pint at the Mount Inn in the Tiger's Bay area of Belfast on the night of 5 May 1992 when IPLO gunmen burst into the bar and opened fire, killing 66-year-old Sergeant, who was hit twice in the back of the head and neck. During the inquest a year later the Belfast city coroner, John Lecky, described the attack as "purely random and sectarian." No other words could have been more appropriate.

Throughout the summer of 1992 journalists, commentators, politicians and ordinary citizens were on a morbid watch for a macabre milestone. According to the RUC's figures, Jimmy Brown was the 2,999th person to die in Northern Ireland's present Troubles. The vigil was now being held for the landmark 3,000th victim. Some expected the Provisionals to kill a high-powered politician, soldier or leading loyalist and reap the historical-propaganda benefits. Perhaps loyalist paramilitaries would take the opportunity to murder a top republican or nationalist political figure.

In the end the 3,000th victim died on the night of 27 August in the continuing IPLO feud. 21-year-old Hugh McKibbon had just finished playing a Gaelic football match for his team, Dwyers, against Lámh Dhearg at Hannahstown on the edge of west Belfast. The match ended at around half past eight. The Dwyers team showered and then boarded their bus. There were at least twelve women on board, as well as several children, along with the players and older supporters. Suddenly two men, neither of whom were masked, boarded the bus, told everyone to sit down, and then said they were from the IPLO Belfast Brigade. They singled out Hugh McKibbon in the third row, and shot him several times at close range.

As the first gunman finished firing, his accomplice screamed: "Get out of the road, let me at him!" The second gunman then fired another burst, and terrified passengers heard him shout jubilantly, "He's dead!"

Two other young men were injured in the shooting, including the son of murdered Official IRA man Éamon "Hatchet" Kerr. The next day the IPLO Belfast Brigade, which admitted the killing, sent a message to the Royal Victoria Hospital apologising to young Kerr and his friend. No such apology, however, was offered to Hugh McKibbon's family.

The callous nature of the McKibbon murder spoke volumes about the general turn of an organisation committed to the ideal of a workers' republic through armed revolution. That "revolution" now lay bleeding on a bus in front of terrified women and children who had gone out for an evening simply to watch a football match.

Just over a week before his murder Hugh McKibbon had been one of the IPLO colour party that flanked Jimmy Brown's coffin as it was carried to Milltown Cemetery. According to the IPLO Belfast Brigade, McKibbon had also been involved in driving gunmen to a bar in Springfield Road after that funeral in a botched attempt to kill the man suspected of gunning down Jimmy Brown.

Futile appeals were made by local politicians and clergy to end the feud. Their calls fell on deaf ears. On 11 September the IPLO faction still loyal to Brown's leadership hit back. They gunned down 31-year-old Seán Macklin outside his home in Whiterock Gardens. The faction styling itself the IPLO Army Council accused Macklin of driving the killer of Hugh McKibbon to Lámh Dhearg GAA club.

Macklin's sister, Patricia McKee, made a desperate plea for no retaliation and called on the killers to stop. Speaking from her home in Ballymurphy, she reflected the view of many ordinary people caught in the madness. "It's been in the papers that there's going to be retaliation. We don't want retaliation. We don't want any other family going through what we're going through ... My mother's heart is broken, and the family's been shattered for a second time." The murdered man's sister Geraldine was shot dead by the UVF in a gun attack on a garage off the Springfield Road in 1974.

Following Macklin's murder, the feud seemed to peter out. Negotiations were held between the two factions, and an uneasy truce was established at the end of September. The IPLO's short, violent life, however, was about to come to an end. The organisation was now fatally weakened and vulnerable to outside attack.

It was a senior loyalist who actually made the most devastatingly accurate prophecy about the IPLO's future after Jimmy Brown. The former leader of the UDA in west Belfast made the prediction during the inter-IPLO fighting. Inside the UDA's west Belfast headquarters, which was later destroyed in the IRA Shankill bomb, he confidently claimed that "the big tiger would pounce on the wee tigers once they had finished tearing each other apart." (Interview, September 1992.) The "big tiger" the UDA leader was referring to was the Provisional IRA. After the IPLO had been weakened enough through internal blood-letting, the Provos would take their chance and move in for the kill.

This prediction proved absolutely correct. The Provisionals had been watching and waiting for their chance. Now the time had come to pounce. By the end of October 1992 the Provos had already chosen their number 1 target after Jimmy Brown had been assassinated. The man they wanted to kill had already signed his own death warrant.

Sammy Ward, a thirty-year-old father of four from the Short Strand in east Belfast, had been part of the IPLO team that Jimmy Brown ordered to threaten leading Provos in June. Ward produced a weapon at the home of a top IRA man in north Belfast. He even placed the gun at the Provo's head and warned him that IPLO members were not to be messed about. Ward also led an armed IPLO unit that raided the Gregory Pub in the Antrim Road the same evening. When the gunmen burst in, staff and customers dived for cover, fearing a loyalist attack. Instead the IPLO unit held up their arms and read out a statement about "not taking Provo aggression lying down." Several Provisionals from north Belfast were drinking in the bar at the time.

Ward's provocation was the final straw. The Provos had been under constant pressure to deal with the IPLO. Drug dealing, a gang rape, wildcat sectarian attacks and now a minor humiliation at the hands of the splinter group had left the Provos smarting. Their volunteers were bursting for revenge.

The IRA leadership chose a significant date on which to make their well-planned move to wipe out their rivals: Halloween.

On Saturday 31 October, Sammy Ward and two comrades from the IPLO's Belfast Brigade went for a drink in Seán Martin's GAA club in Beechfield Street in the Short Strand. One of the men who accompanied Ward to the club was the Belfast Brigade's second-in-command, an experienced former INLA veteran whom Jimmy Brown had persuaded to join the IPLO at the beginning of 1992. In the club's snooker room the three men shared a drink together. Customers said they watched the door every time it opened, no doubt still worried that their rivals in the IPLO Army Council faction might be hunting them.

Two men entered the club. At first Ward and his friends were not unduly concerned by their presence. They were not members of the Army Council. The newcomers crossed the room. Ward was at the bar ordering a round of drinks. Suddenly the two men drew their guns. One shouted to the customers to lie down on the floor. Then they singled out Ward, who was returning from the bar. The other IPLO men were warned not to move from the table. The blast from the short-arms fire was deafening. Ward was struck in the chest by two bullets. As he slumped to the floor, one of the gunmen fired again into his head.

As the two gunmen left the snooker room, one of them fired, this time into the ceiling. Customers were warned that "they had seen nothing." Sammy Ward, the effective leader of the IPLO Belfast Brigade, was dead. It later emerged in interviews with witnesses that one of the men who provided logistical back-up for the gunmen was a former INLA member from the Lower Ormeau area who had been a personal friend of Emmánuel Gargan and had backed the INLA GHQ during the 1987 feud. This man, still in his early twenties, had been given his chance at last to get revenge on part of the organisation that had killed his friend five years before.

During the latest feuding the IPLO Army Council's Dublin-based leadership had singled out Sammy Ward as being top of their death list following Brown's murder. But within half an hour of Ward's death it emerged that his killers were taking part in a huge Provisional IRA operation to wipe out the IPLO in Belfast.

Throughout the city, the Provos launched a wave of attacks on IPLO personnel as well as petty drug peddlers on the fringes of the organisation. Up to a hundred IRA volunteers with back-up teams providing cars and weapons hunted down both IPLO factions.

At the time Sammy Ward was killed, the Provos carried out raids on pubs and clubs in west Belfast. In the Lower Falls several IRA foot patrols, each carrying a G3 assault rifle, were walking the streets looking for their rivals. In Divis Flats twenty IRA members marched across the balconies. Several IPLO members were dragged from their homes. Some were told simply to leave the country; others were shot in the legs and hands. Rifles were used instead of handguns in kneecapping, to cause greater injury to their victims' limbs.

The size and ferocity of the operation stunned both sides of the IPLO. A "hit list" was distributed throughout west Belfast. Many heeded the warning and headed for ships and planes to Britain. Confusion reigned in the first few hours of the purge as the two IPLO factions thought they were under attack from each other. During this period fifteen separate places were raided by the Provos.

This operation became known in Belfast as the "Night of the Long Knives". The Halloween operation was billed by the Provos as a purge against drug dealers; in reality it was more than that. The Provisionals had removed a potentially dangerous foe in their own back yard. Undoubtedly the drive to expel drug dealers went down well with working-class nationalists; but many of the dealers were small fry. They included drug users as well. One nineteen-year-old man from Twinbrook was knee-capped merely for smoking cannabis. His father later wrote a letter of protest to the *Sunday World* accusing the Provos of hypocrisy. He asked if the IRA would knee-cap the Sinn Féin councillor Hugh Brady from Derry, who had been caught in possession of cannabis on a fishing trip.

By the morning of 2 November 1992 the IPLO was more or less finished. The Provos' adjutant in the city arrived in the Short Strand to accept unconditional surrender by the IPLO Belfast Brigade second-in-command. At first the IPLO Army Council faction issued a statement in Dublin defying the Provos' demand to disband. But eventually the Army Council's leader also accepted surrender. He made a deal with the Provos, who allowed him to live in return for the dissolution of his gang. He is still living in Dublin and has begun a new career operating with criminal gangs in the capital.

The Provos had prepared themselves for losses in the purge. They were undoubtedly surprised that not a single member had been arrested or killed. It might have been different, some seasoned observers suggested, if the man who had killed Jimmy Brown had been around at the time. But by then he was in jail on arms charges.

Both IPLO factions had folded without resistance. Their leaders had come forward and asked for their death sentences to be commuted to exile. The IRA had one target left, who was at the top of their death list: the IPLO's chief of staff in Dublin. He communicated to the Provisionals through a third party that he would hand over all the IPLO's weapons in the capital if the death sentence was lifted. The Provisionals were stunned when the IPLO's small arsenal in Dublin, which included shotguns and a few Browning pistols, was given to them at a meeting in the Ballybough area a week after Sammy Ward's death. But the IRA leadership agreed to give the IPLO chief a reprieve. The IPLO had accepted the Provos' terms unconditionally. It was total surrender.

It was ironic that the Provisionals had chosen Halloween to stage their "Night of the Long Knives" operation. Seventeen years before almost to the day the Provisional IRA had launched a similar wide-scale operation against the Official IRA throughout the North. In October 1975 the Provos organised a concerted series of attacks on the Officials. They killed several Official IRA members, including one in the Markets, Lower Ormeau, and Short Strand. Their target in the east Belfast area was one of the few Protestant members of the Official IRA, Tom Berry. He was killed only yards away from where Sammy Ward was to be slain. Over thirty venues, including pubs, clubs, and homes, were attacked in the 1975 operation. Most of the shootings on Officials' houses took place around supper time, when local Provo leaders could be certain their enemies would be at home having tea.

The aim of the attacks was to smash the Officials' organisation in Belfast. At first the Officials were reeling on the ropes. There was, however, an important contrast between Halloween 1975 and Halloween 1992. Unlike the IPLO, the Officials fought back ferociously in a struggle for political survival. The Provos had accused the Officials of "gangsterism"; the real reason for the attacks, however, was that the Provisionals were at the time involved in a cease-fire with the British government. They were given a free hand in nationalist areas of Belfast. Incident centres were opened that monitored complaints against the security forces during the cease-fire. The Provos believed they had the right to run nationalist communities. The Officials were the main opposition in those communities at the time. It was also useful to turn the volunteers against a common enemy at a time of cease-fire. Hitting the Officials held the movement together. During the feuding the Provisionals shot dead six-year-old Eileen Kelly, the daughter of an Official supporter in the Beechmount area.

The Officials have never referred to the 1975 fighting as a feud. To them it was a "pogrom" aimed at wiping them out of political existence on the streets of Belfast. The experience still haunts them today.

By the end of the feud the Officials had reorganised and had killed several Provisionals, including the Provisional IRA's chief intelligence officer in the North, Séamus McCusker. His murder outside the Artillery Flats complex off the New Lodge Road in Belfast effectively ended the blood-letting.

Seventeen years later, both sides in the IPLO conflict faced the same threat from the Provisionals. They failed, however, to fight back as efficiently as the Officials had. In fact they refused to stage any kind of fight-back at all. The reason for this was primarily political. The Officials retaliated because they had a political raison d'être: they were fired by an ideological drive towards building a political party. The IPLO, on the other hand, had degenerated into an apolitical gang. The last of their politicos, Jimmy Brown, was dead. A vacuum had been created within the IPLO's leadership. The quality and the will was simply no longer there to fight back and survive.

Those holding onto the name of the INLA can claim at least to have survived. They are also particularly lucky not to have been contaminated with involvement in drug running.

In the years leading up to the IPLO's destruction, the INLA tried to stage several Lazarus-like come-backs. During the late 1980s it carried out a handful of operations. These included a bomb attack in June 1989 on Ward Park, Bangor, during an international bowling tournament. The INLA said that the bomb, which was a crude device consisting of fertiliser and petrol, was aimed at the Israeli bowling team. The operation was carried out, the INLA said, "in solidarity with Palestinians expelled from their lands." This absurd operation, which was more reminiscent of the Baader-Meinhof gang's solidarity killings in Germany, was symptomatic of a swing towards ultra-left extremism in the movement after the feud.

The organisation started to reactivate contacts both in Britain and Ireland with a far-left group known as Red Action. This had broken away from the Trotskyite Socialist Workers' Party because the latter were regarded as not revolutionary enough. Red Action believed in violent political activity, including support for terrorism in Ireland; the SWP, however, took a more critical stance on the issue of republican violence. Many in republican circles were mistrustful of tying themselves too closely to British ultra-left groups, which they suspected would be heavily infiltrated by MI5. Several former INLA activists claimed that Red Action had been penetrated by the British secret services and used to spy on republican groups in the North and the Republic.

From the late 1980s until 1992 the INLA had failed to kill or seriously injure a single member of the security forces. Their first big operation of the year, however, was a deadly reminder that the depleted republican splinter group should not be written off too prematurely. On Monday 12 April, Sergeant Michael Newman, an NCO serving in a British army recruitment office in Derby, left work. As he went into a local car park and walked towards his car, two men approached him. They opened fire, shooting him in the head and chest. He died instantly from his wounds.

In a statement issued through the Socialist Republican Publicity Bureau in Belfast, the INLA admitted responsibility for the murder. They explained why they had singled out Sergeant Newman. "Army recruiting officers have a vital role to play in the British war machine. Their highly sophisticated propaganda campaign is aimed at the thousands of unemployed youth, offering them a chance to travel and see the world with the British Army. Whereas in reality they are recruited to be used as cannon fodder on the streets of Belfast and Derry against the Irish working class. The ordinary British soldier is just a tool in the hands of the British government which has had to use force and naked repression to maintain its domination of the Six Counties. Whilst the British continue to occupy our country and pursue a policy of repression against our people then we reserve the right to attack all those who actively participate in the British war machine."

The shooting in Derby was clearly a morale boost for the INLA. It was the first INLA operation to claim a life in Britain since the assassination of Airey Neave. But the net propaganda effect of this squalid killing of an army sergeant not even involved in an active security role in Northern Ireland should not be overestimated.

There was a chasm of significance between the shooting of Sergeant Newman and the blowing up of one of Margaret Thatcher's favourite political allies in the heart of the British establishment. The message from the INLA in the Derby killing was simple: "We are still here." The political signal sent out thirteen years before in the House of Commons car park was much more significant. Members of Britain's ruling elite were prime targets for assassination by the INLA. What is also important to note is that the team behind the Neave killing were never caught. In contrast any ambitious operation the INLA has undertaken in more recent years has been followed by arrests. This suggests a widening gulf in both quality and training between the original INLA activists and those who have been recruited to its ranks since the late 1980s.

The INLA is now controlled by one man, who comes from the Upper Springfield area of Belfast. He is a seasoned paramilitary activist who survived three feuds. Known variously as "Cueball" and "the Ball" to his ex-comrades, he is admired at least for his staying power and tenacious commitment to a shrinking movement. One former comrade who fought alongside him against the IPLO in the 1987 feud described him as "incorruptible". "The Ball is really dedicated to the cause. He does tend to centre power around himself and doesn't trust anyone else. But while I disagree with him over his militarism you can say he is his own man. He is not in it for money or glory. He really believes in what he is doing." (Interview, 20 November 1993.)

Some observers cast doubt on whether the INLA's current Belfast-based leader really is his own man. Many in nationalist areas believe the INLA has simply become an auxiliary force for the Provos. They point to several operations, mainly against loyalists, which were carried out after a nod of approval from the Provisionals' leadership. The INLA, according to this view, carried out "dirty jobs" that the Provos won't do themselves for fear that they will be accused of sectarianism.

Support for this claim that there is tacit agreement between the two organisations can be detected from the silence of Sinn Féin after recent INLA killings of Protestants. On 9 January 1993 the INLA killed Samuel Rock, a Protestant man, at his home in Rosewood Street, north Belfast. Unlike previous killings of loyalists and Protestants, Sinn Féin failed to say anything about this murder.

At the very least there is clearly some degree of collusion between the Provos and the INLA. The latter group is no longer absolutely independent of the "big tiger", which would undoubtedly pounce on the smaller organisation if their interests diverged. Paramilitary logic would dictate that the Provos have no other option. The last thing the IRA leadership can afford at a time of possible cease-fires and vaunted peace initiatives is an independent fledgling paramilitary force in its own back yard willing to absorb Provo volunteers who want to carry on fighting if the armed struggle is called off. That is, in spite of suspicions to the contrary it seems the INLA is still an independent force.

Despite a tacit understanding with the Provisionals, there have been flashes of autonomous INLA action. Perhaps the most significant INLA operation in Belfast was at around twenty minutes past midnight on Christmas Eve 1992. The IRA's seasonal cease-fire was just twenty minutes old. In this annual ritual the Provos call off the campaign for seventy-two hours as hundreds of republican prisoners are released for three days on Christmas parole and reunited with their families. The INLA, however, ignored the cease-fire. A unit from the Lower Falls fired a volley of shots at Grosvenor Road RUC station. No-one was injured in the attack; it was, however, a small but symbolic reminder to the security forces that another republican paramilitary force exists and might continue if the IRA finally decides to lay down its arms.

The INLA, of course, deny that it is a proxy force operating under the Provisionals' umbrella. The organisation and its supporters lay claim to the legacy created by Séamus Costello. One of Costello's oldest friends and comrades, Tony Hayde, believes the current INLA are the true inheritors of the republican socialist tradition. But the original movement founded by Costello was not simply a physical force phenomenon: it contained some of the most able political activists of the time. The departure in 1992 from an almost non-existent IRSP of its political spokesmen, Terry Harkin, Éamon Mullan, and Kevin McQuillan, signified the near-total exclusion of politics. Tony Hayde may argue that the existence of an INLA disproves this. But this argument seems theological from the perspective of Belfast, where the organisation seems exclusively bound up with militarism.

Séamus Costello's dream was fading further into memory by the end of 1992. At Jimmy Brown's funeral, on 21 August 1992, some of Séamus Costello's old comrades turned up to pay their respects. They included Brigit Makowski, the Shannon councillor who had written so bitterly about the "treacherous comrades" who purged Costello from the Officials in 1974. Beside Brigit Makowski in Milltown cemetery on that windy Friday in autumn was her daughter, Stella, a formidable woman from Derry who was close to Brown.

It was fitting that Stella Makowski gave the oration as the pallbearers laid Brown's coffin into a grave close to where his great friend and comrade-in-arms, Gerard Steenson, was buried. Around the grave stood about fifty of Brown's IPLO disciples, along with old friends and his family. As the wreaths were placed beside the earth mound next to his grave, Stella Makowski read off cards stating where the flowers had come from. "Lower Ormeau IPLO," she said defiantly; "Lower Falls IPLO; North Belfast IPLO; Newry IPLO," and so on. One of the wreaths was tackily arranged to spell out the letters *IPLO*. It was an epitaph not only for Jimmy Brown but for the whole organisation.

Every wreath and message of sympathy was a signal to the mourners and the media present as to which areas of the North were still faithful to Brown's faction. The clusters of beefy young men in ill-fitting suits and streaky black ties nervously surveyed the scene. They were no doubt taking note of those who had failed to turn up for the funeral. In the confusion caused by internal feuding, a funeral was one sure way of divining who was on your side and who was not.

A helicopter purred overhead as Stella Makowski picked up the megaphone to give the traditional graveside speech. She started with a summary of Jimmy Brown's life in republican paramilitarism. She described how he worked secretly for Séamus Costello within the Officials' intelligence department even after the initial split. Brown, she told the mourners, then left "the Sticks" and became active in the INLA/IRSP. She reminded his comrades that Brown combined political and military activity; she noted his contribution during the hunger strike protests and his later involvement in the Stop the Show Trials group aimed at highlighting the injustices of the "supergrass" system. Parallel to this was Brown's work as an intelligence officer in Belfast, firstly for the INLA and later the IPLO. With all the grit of a true believer, Makowski outlined how Brown saw the necessity of dissolving the INLA in the mid-1980s as it had degenerated into an apolitical gang. Those who opposed dissolution were "agents of British imperialism". Other, new British agents, she insisted, had slain Jimmy Brown and were now working for that same imperialism by smashing the new movement he helped set up.

After her embittered invective against the rival IPLO faction, Stella Makowski turned around. She pointed her megaphone at the long legion of RUC officers ringing the graveside. She cried: "You are the enemy and we are going to kill you. We are going to defeat you." The verbal broadside did not seem to trouble the lines of RUC men. A few overlooking Brown's grave smiled and chuckled when Stella Makowski uttered these words. They knew the truth: they had no longer any need to worry about the IPLO. An organisation those heavily armed officers had once feared and loathed so much had been smashed to pieces by its own internal contradictions. It had been destroyed, not by British imperialism or loyalist gangs but by its own hands. The dream had been betrayed and eventually consumed by the enemy within.

EPILOGUE

The casualty wing of Belfast's Royal Victoria Hospital was as busy as ever. We stood at the head of the escalator near the entrance, waiting nervously for the arrival of the man nicknamed "Cueball", who now leads the Irish National Liberation Army. For months, meetings had been arranged but for one reason or another were either abandoned or aborted.

Casualty seemed as good a place as any to have one last try at a rendezvous. It was public, people came and went, and the very activity of the place was somehow reassuring.

The minutes went by. It was past the time we had arranged to meet. One of us went down the escalator to the floor below to check that we had not somehow missed him. A squad of soldiers and policemen who had come into the hospital from another entrance were swarming around. Our last attempted meeting some weeks before had ended when the place of the rendezvous was suddenly swamped by policemen.

He turned and went back up the moving stairway. As he reached the top, the INLA's last chief of staff came through the entrance doors of heavy flapping plastic. He wore a black leather jerkin, into which his hands were thrust. He walked past the porters and came straight towards us.

"We can't talk here," he said. He nodded towards the road outside. A car was stopped by the kerb, its engine running, a short-haired young man with one gold earring at the wheel. For a few moments we hesitated. One of our terms for meeting the INLA leadership had always been that it would take place in a public area. Cueball looked at us impatiently. He told us there was a safe house in the Lower Falls area; we could go straight there. He assured us there was nothing to worry about. We agreed. It had to be done.

Seconds later we were heading down the streets of the old nationalist ghetto, now unrecognisably transformed into a development of neat, modern houses with little gardens. There were only two landmarks that told us where we were: the twin spires of St Peter's Cathedral, and the rectangular block of Divis Tower—all that remains of the place once known as the Planet of the Erps. Under the shadow of that block we drove into a cul-de-sac and pulled up. "We're here," the INLA's leader announced.

He jumped out of the car and opened the side door of the safe house and waved us in. The door closed behind us. The sitting-room was decorated with Irish dancing medals. A young girl's dancing shoes were wedged into the opening of an electric fireplace. Beside the shoes were the child's clothes. There were other trophies on the mantelpiece marking the child's triumphs at Irish dancing.

Underneath a brown plaque where the medals were displayed sat the INLA's current leader, slumped in an armchair, while we took the couch. He wanted to go over the book. He was anxious about certain things: possible distortions, misinterpretations. Most of all he wanted to talk about 1986 and 1987. He explained that the feud was not a feud but an attack on the INLA by the IPLO. He and Ta Power wanted to build a consensus with McAllister and Roche, he explained, excluding Steenson, whom he refused to accept back into the movement. Why? we asked. "Do you think anyone could control the likes of Steenson?" he replied.

He believes to this day that the feud was deliberately planned to remove the INLA from the scene by people who were really only interested in joining the Provisionals, which many of them did when the feud ended.

When he speaks of Steenson he taps his temple with his finger, indicating that he believes the man was mad. Cueball speaks quietly, calmly about the man nicknamed "Dr Death" who wanted him dead. But he is confident that Steenson was not among the gunmen who almost succeeded in bringing that about in Rosnaree in 1987.

He agrees the INLA made many mistakes. "Dessie O'Hare should never have been brought into the organisation," he affirms, referring to the man known as the "Border Fox". What happened to Séamus Ruddy was also wrong, he continues, and the INLA had not sanctioned it. He also lamented the fate of Tony McCloskey, who, during the 1987 feud, was tortured and killed by elements of the INLA connected to O'Hare's gang and aligned with O'Reilly.

There was indeed much to lament in the blood-stained past. But what about the future, he was asked. He explained that there was a debate going on within the movement about the IRSP. Should it reform or continue— shrunken as it had to a handful of members who still proclaim their faith in Marxism? And what happens when the Provisionals agree to a cessation of violence and an end to the armed campaign? That would be a problem, he muses. The INLA would have to look at what was on offer.

"We'll oppose British imperialism whatever way we can," he says, as quietly as ever.

He produces a battered and creased photograph. It is eighteen years old, and shows a group of smiling INLA men, some of them founding members of the organisation, gathered on a sunny day outside their prison hut behind the barbed-wire fences of Long Kesh camp. It was taken by a smuggled camera a few days before the successful break-out of May 1976. These were men who would one day end up killing each other.

"You wonder how it happened," he says, shaking his head, perusing the picture.

APPENDIX 1: INTERVIEW WITH INLA CHIEF OF STAFF, MARCH 1994

Why should you keep going? Why is there a need for your organisation now?

In 1974 Séamus Costello outlined the political position of the Republican Socialist movement. He stated that the struggle for socialism and the struggle for national liberation were part of the same struggle. That the British presence in Ireland was the basic cause of the division between the protestant and catholic working class in the North. "It is the principal obstacle preventing the emergence of class politics in Ireland." But he also saw the struggle for national liberation taking place side by side with the class struggle in the entire country. Reaffirming Connolly's view that the struggle for national liberation and the struggle for socialism are one and the same struggle.

The Republican Movement on the other hand is a nationalist movement, fighting against the British with its objective as a united Ireland. It has restricted its activities to resolving the national question whilst neglecting the social question. Adams himself is on record as stating that "socialism is not on the agenda."

Our movement believes in revolutionary socialism and our objective is to establish a revolutionary state in Ireland. Whilst British imperialism remains in Ireland, whilst the Irish working class remains exploited, there is a need for a revolutionary alternative. Despite all the difficulties, we intend to fulfil this role.

What happens if the Provisionals accept the Downing Street declaration? Would you, and could you, fight on?

Whether we would continue or not with our campaign would depend on the prevalent conditions at that time. We would have to be convinced that gains are to be made and in turn see how the situation develops. We have always believed that armed struggle is but an extension of politics and is a tactic to be used when the prevailing conditions dictate that it is right to do so.

As revolutionaries, we do not believe in the constitutional road to socialism. As Costello said, "in the long term the lessons of history show that the robber baron must be disestablished by the same methods that he used to enrich himself and retain his ill-gotten gains, namely, force of arms. To this end we must organise, train and maintain a disciplined armed force which will always be available to strike at the opportune moment."

Where is your membership concentrated, both in the North and the Republic?

We are a 32-county organisation and our membership is spread throughout the 32 counties.

Most of the operations you have carried out have been directed at loyalist targets. Why have you been relatively unsuccessful in directing attacks against the security forces?

Although our movement enjoys much support within the nationalist community for our stance against loyalism, we are not a reactive force. Of course we will defend the community against vicious sectarian attacks, and we reserve the right to punish those responsible and disrupt their activities, but there is no deliberate intention to concentrate attacks solely against loyalists. All targets, whether loyalist or Crown forces are selected according to intelligence and feasibility.

In recent years, we have carried out attacks in Britain, killing a soldier and causing extensive firebomb damage; such attacks entail much finance and organising. In Belfast, a CID member was executed, RUC members were shot at whilst in their own car park, and we launched a daring attack on an RUC check point. We have also carried out numerous sniper attacks upon crown force bases and checkpoints in Derry and Belfast. In themselves they may not have caused heavy casualties upon our enemy but they certainly demonstrate our ability and determination to attack military targets whenever and wherever possible.

Given the history of your movement, which has been dogged with splits and feuds, can you be confident there won't be further schisms in the near future?

It is true that since the foundation of our movement, there were divisions, which has on occasions manifested itself in vicious armed attacks by ex-members. This culminated in 1987 with the attack on our organisation by the IPLO, an organisation already formed before the attack, with the prime objective of destroying our movement. At its inception, our movement was forced to defend itself from armed attacks from the Official IRA, and as such never got the breathing space to develop a strong political base. Now we have a programme of political education for our volunteers and strict vetting procedure. We encourage widespread debate and we believe that divisions are part of our history but not part of our future.

Many observers would perceive some of your attacks in loyalist areas as purely sectarian reactions to UFF and UVF murders directed against the Catholic community. How can you seriously refute the allegation of sectarianism?

As we have already stated before, our armed attacks are not reactive and we make no apologies for defending our own community against loyalist murder gangs. As for sectarianism within our movement, it simply does not exist. Anybody involved in an attack against Protestants would be punished and dismissed. What happened at Darkley, which was unsanctioned could never be repeated. Our struggle is based on socialist principles, which means that we are struggling as working class people whether we be catholic or protestant. Any attacks against the UFF or UVF are derived from a purely political basis and are not sectarian attacks.

In 1984 the IRSP adopted the entire works of Marx as part of its political ideology. Do you still follow that Marxist line? Isn't that a retreat into ideological extremism?

As revolutionaries, we base our ideology on Marxism. We believe that Marxism as a scientific guide to understanding the world and the social forces at work is as relevant today as it was when it was first written. Connolly was the first Irish Marxist, and it was through using Marxist analysis that he was able to produce *Labour in Irish History*, a history of the Irish working class. With the collapse of the Soviet Union and the Eastern communist bloc, it has been said that the communist system does not work, can never work. We believe that socialism was distorted for many different reasons and the systems which emerged were bureaucratic, creating a bureaucratic elite which abused its power. But the emergence of capitalism has created even bigger problems for the working class in these countries; where once they had subsidised housing, full employment, free education, health care, now there is little food, crime has risen, thousands are homeless.

Capitalism has not resolved the problems, by its very exploitative nature, the working class will get poorer and the rich richer. We believe in the inevitable collapse of capitalism and the need to create a system where the working class will be in control, a system where exploitation no longer exists and real justice and freedom will flourish.

And what about the party itself? Is the IRSP now effectively dead, or will a new party arise from the ashes?

We cannot speak for the IRSP, as we are a separate organisation. What we can say is that we are going through a period of reaction, and for any revolutionary party it is an uphill struggle. The IRSP has been in existence for twenty years, it has been consistently involved both in the national and class struggle throughout the 32 counties.

During the past few years it has taken the time it needed to debate internally the way forward. No doubt in the near future it will have reached a decision as to how it proposes to move forward. We believe that it is essential that a revolutionary party is built in Ireland, which can represent the interests of the working class. We hope that the IRSP will form the basis for such a party.

When does the armed campaign stop? At what stage would you be prepared to call it off?

The situation must be created where the British withdraw politically, economically and militarily from this country. Once there is an end to partition and both parts of our country are united then a different scenario develops into a straightforward struggle between Irish labour and capital. How the struggle is pushed forward at that historical moment will be determined by the relevant conditions of the day. But as revolutionaries we have no interest in some form of cosmetic change. We believe that eventually the state must be smashed and the working class established in power. As we have said before, all armed actions are an extension of politics, they are only a tactic to be used when the conditions are right to do so. As a tactic, armed struggle is constantly reviewed, and will constantly be reviewed in light of the prevailing conditions.

Have you tried to re-establish links with international groups which provided your movement with weapons in the 1970s and 1980s?

As revolutionaries, we are also internationalists, and we believe that our struggle is part of the international struggle against capitalism which is being waged in many parts of the world. We have always believed it is important to forge links with other anti-imperialist forces, and will continue to do so.

It has been alleged that your organisation is now merely an auxiliary force for the Provisionals. How do you respond to that?

Our organisation was formed twenty years ago, and it has always acted independently from the IRA. Whilst our short-term objectives may be the same, our long-term political objectives are very different. As we said earlier, we believe in the establishment of a revolutionary socialist state, which we do not believe can be achieved through the parliamentary road to socialism.

There are still some unanswered questions relating to the movement in the 1980s. In particular there is still the issue of Séamus Ruddy's disappearance in Paris. Can you throw any new light on this mystery?

We can state categorically that our present leadership was not involved nor had any knowledge in the disappearance of Séamus Ruddy.

A Derry man is currently serving a long sentence for offences connected with the bomb at Chelsea Barracks in 1985. Patrick McLaughlin has consistently protested that he is innocent. Can you confirm that Mr McLaughlin is innocent?

We can confirm that Patrick McLaughlin was not involved in the planning or involved in the active service unit which planted the bomb at Chelsea Barracks. He is totally innocent. Like many other Irish people, he is serving time in an English jail for something he didn't do, his only crime that of being Irish. We fully support the committee which has been set up to campaign on his behalf.

Will there still be a movement to talk about in the next five years?

During the past twenty years, we have endured British murder gangs, loyalist death squads, the paid perjurer system, and armed attacks. Our members have faced imprisonment, maiming and death. Yet we have survived this, and continue to struggle. We intend to continue our struggle for national liberation and socialism, until it is achieved.

APPENDIX 2: CHRONOLOGY OF INLA ACTIONS

The INLA did not begin claiming responsibility for its actions until January 1976, by which time it had killed at least twelve people. None of the killings in the feud were ever claimed by the INLA. Some attacks, including sectarian shootings, especially in the early days, also went unclaimed, as did a few "mistakes". These are marked "unclaimed". Also, in April 1975 a list of attacks was claimed under the PLA label. Where appropriate, these have been acknowledged, while it is fully understood that the PLA was simply the INLA under a different name.

Where a precise date cannot be given, the month or months alone are indicated.

1975

8 February. Princess Bar in Ormeau Road sprayed with bullets; barmaid wounded. Unclaimed.

24 February. Republican club in Turf Lodge burnt down. Unclaimed.

25 February. Official IRA man, Seán Fox, shot dead in Divis Flats. Unclaimed.

March. Series of shootings as feud with Official IRA escalates, none of which were claimed by the INLA. The most significant were:

1 March. Seán Garland shot and wounded in Ballymun, Dublin.

13 March. Seán Morrissey shot and wounded in Belfast.

3 April. Republican Club burnt in St Agnes Drive, Belfast (PLA).

4 April. Burning of car in Andersonstown (PLA).

6 April. Des O'Hagan, leading member of Officials, shot and wounded. Two other Officials kneecapped in Moyard, Turf Lodge (PLA).

7 April. Officials fired on in Beechmount, Belfast (PLA).

12 April. Paul Crawford shot dead, Springfield Road, Belfast. Unclaimed.

28 April. Billy McMillen, OC of Official IRA in Belfast, shot dead. Unclaimed.

24 May. Constable Noel Davis killed by booby-trap bombs, south Derry. First member of security forces to die at hands of INLA.

18 June. RUC man wounded in Derry.

26 July. Constable McPherson shot dead, Dungiven, south Derry.

9 August. Two soldiers wounded in Armagh. Two soldiers wounded in separate attacks in Ballymurphy and Lower Falls, Belfast.

6 September. Shooting attack on Rosemount RUC station, Derry. One policeman wounded.

12 September. Two soldiers wounded in booby-trap bomb in Whiterock area, Belfast.

13 September. Two soldiers wounded in attack in Derry.

26 September. Private David Wray shot dead in Derry.

30 October. Garage burnt down in Armagh.

2 November. Soldier wounded in Armagh.

2 December. Alexander Mitchell and Charles McNaul, Protestant businessmen, shot dead in Derry; mistaken identity. Unclaimed.

31 December. Richard Beattie, William Scott and Sylvia McCullough killed in pub bombing, Gilford, Co. Down (claimed by "Armagh People's Republican Army").

1976

7 February. Thomas Rafferty killed by booby-trap bomb meant for security forces near Portadown. Unclaimed.

3 August. Private Alan Watkins killed by shotgun blast, Dungiven.

25 September. James and Rosaleen Kyle, father and daughter, shot dead in south Belfast. Possible mistaken identity (there was a Special Branch inspector named Kyle). Unclaimed.

24 November. Private Andrew Crocker shot dead by sniper, Turf Lodge.

22 December. Constable Armour killed in booby-trap bomb attack in Kilrea, south Derry.

26 December. James Ligget, security man, dies of his wounds after being shot in Portadown.

1977

23 January. Private Muncaster shot dead by sniper in Markets area.

March. Attempt to kidnap West German consul fails.

26 May. Soldier seriously wounded by gunfire in grounds of Royal Victoria Hospital, Belfast.

September–December. INLA claims it carried out six attacks in Belfast, Derry and Armagh on prison officers and their property.

1978

26 February. Soldier wounded in west Belfast; grenade thrown at RUC

station in Springfield Road.

10 May. Henry Taggart Barracks attacked; UDR patrol fired on in Ormeau Road, Belfast. Grenade attack on Springfield Road RUC station.

9 August. INLA carries out series of sniper attacks with AK47 rifles on British patrols and bases throughout west Belfast.

13 August. British soldier wounded in Roden Street, Belfast.

14 August. Observation post hit by snipers in Markets area.

16 August. Three soldiers wounded in Cromac Square, Markets area.

November, Remembrance Sunday. Attempt to assassinate British Ambassador, Sir Robert Haydon, in St Patrick's Cathedral, Dublin.

17 December. Maze prison officer slightly injured when mercury-tilt bomb explodes under his car near Lisburn. (First time INLA used this type of bomb.)

1979

23 January. RUC man seriously wounded in Belfast.

15 March. UDR man Robert McNally dies after being injured nine days earlier by booby-trap (mercury-tilt switch) bomb in Portadown.

30 March. Airey Neave, Conservative Party's shadow Secretary of State for Northern Ireland, dies after mercury-tilt bomb explodes under his car in Palace of Westminster, London.

19 April. Agnes Wallace, prison officer, dies after a grenade and gun attack in Armagh.

27 July. Jim Wright, former RUC man, killed by under-car mercury-tilt bomb in Portadown; his 21-year-old daughter is seriously injured.

31 July. Constable George Walsh shot dead outside Armagh courthouse.

9–10 August. Two soldiers wounded in sniper attack in Belfast.

7 November. David Teeney, wages clerk in Crumlin Road jail, shot dead at a bus stop.

1980

7 March. Bomb attack on Netheravon British army camp in Salisbury, England.

8 March. Booby-trap bomb seriously injures UDR man in Belfast.

18 March. Bomb destroys Gate Inn in Derry, following a series of attacks in the city, including the wounding of a UDR man at Gransha Hospital.

3 April. Bomb planted under RUC man's car in east Belfast.

9 August. One soldier seriously injured by grenade in New Lodge Road.

19 August. James McCarron accidentally shot dead during sporadic rioting in west Belfast. Unclaimed.

29 August. Frank McGrory killed in booby-trap bomb meant for soldiers in Armagh.

19 November. Thomas Orr shot dead by mistake in west Belfast. Unclaimed.

10 December. Off-duty UDR man, Colin Quinn, shot dead in Belfast.

28 December. Member of Territorial Army, Hugh McGinn, shot dead in Armagh.

1981

14 January. Constable McDougal dies after being shot near Belfast city centre on 9 January.

21 January. Attempt to murder off-duty UDR man in west Belfast.

8 February. Alexander Scott, off-duty reserve constable, shot dead in east Belfast.

25 March. Belfast city councillor and UDA member Frank Millar shot.

27 March. Off-duty UDR man, John Smith, shot dead in Markets area.

3 April. Attempt on life of south Belfast civil servant, Kenneth Schimeld, fails when mercury-tilt switch bomb is spotted.

16 April. Bobby-trap bomb kills RUC man, Jack Donnelly, in west Belfast.

25 April. RUC Land Rover ambushed in Clonard district of west Belfast.

April. North Howard Street army base bombed.

27 April. Constable Gary Martin, injured in 16 April bombing, dies.

July. Soldier shot and wounded in Falls Road.

3 July. Sniper fire at Rev. Ian Paisley's entourage near the Markets.

10 July. Hugh O'Neill found shot dead in Ballymurphy, Belfast. INLA weapon used. Accidental death.

24 July. Bomb in van injures three near a brewery in west Belfast.

27 July. RUC man seriously wounded in sniper attack in Clonard district. Thirteen-year-old girl also injured.

31 July. Thomas Harpur, ex-RUC man, shot dead in Strabane.

29 September. Mark Alexander Scott, off-duty UDR man, shot dead in Springfield Road area.

16 October. William "Bucky" McCullough, member of UDA, shot dead near Shankill Road.

28 October. Edward Patrick Brogan, Derry found shot dead on rubbish tip. Suspected informer.

25 November. Bomb explodes at headquarters of 7th Signals Regiment in Herford, north-east Germany.

5 December. Harry Flynn, IRSP Ard-Chomhairle member and leading member of INLA, shot and wounded in Dublin on Steenson's orders.

(Thirty-eight deaths so far.)

1982

25 January. Seán Flynn and Bernard Dorrian shot in Short Strand area by Steenson faction.

29 January. John McKeague shot dead in east Belfast.

5 May. Bomb seriously injures soldier in Belfast.

12 May. Bomb explodes at home of Assistant Chief Constable Sam Bradley.

20 May. Attempt to kill Rev. William Beattie of DUP fails when bomb is spotted.

2 June. Patrick Smith killed accidentally by booby-trap bomb on bicycle in Lower Ormeau area of Belfast. INLA apologised.

11 June. Off-duty UDR man shot and wounded.

June–July. Fourteen bombs planted in Derry, injuring seventeen members of security forces, as well as civilians.

28 July. Policeman wounded in Derry by gunfire. Bombing attack against UDR man in Bellaghy, Co. Derry, fails.

2 August. UDR man seriously injured by booby-trap bomb near Queen's University, Belfast.

5 August. Assistant Chief Constable William Meharg, who had just resigned, escapes injury when a bomb explodes at his home.

27 August. Wilfred McIlvean, former member of UDR, killed by car bomb in Milford, Co. Armagh.

1 September. Belfast city councillor Billy Dickson of DUP shot and seriously wounded.

16 September. Two boys, Stephen Bennet and Kevin Valliday, die when a small bomb meant for a foot patrol explodes in Divis Flats.

20 September. Kevin Waller, a soldier injured in the Divis Flats blast, dies of his injuries. Bomb attack on Mount Gabriel radar station at Schull, Co. Cork.

25 September. Pensioner, William Nixon, shot dead in east Belfast.

27 September. Corporal Leon Bushe killed by booby-trap bomb in Belfast.

7 October. Elizabeth Chambers and UDR man Corporal Freddie Williamson die in Armagh in ambush.

17 October. Karen McKeown dies of wounds received in shooting in east Belfast on 25 September.

18 October. Bomb explodes at home of Ken Overend, Ulster Unionist Party candidate in assembly elections.

19 October. Former UDR man shot and wounded in Newry. Bomb blast at Unionist party headquarters in Belfast.

20 October. Bomb placed outside home of sister of James Molyneaux, leader of Ulster Unionist Party, is defused.

16 November. Reserve Constables Ronnie Irwin and Showden Corkery shot dead in Markethill, Co. Armagh.

24 November. Attempt on life of Judge Roy Watt fails.

6 December. Explosion at Droppin' Well in Ballykelly, Co. Derry, kills seventeen people. Eleven are soldiers, the other six civilians, including four women. Sixty-six people are injured in the blast, one of the worst in the history of the Troubles.

(Sixty-eight deaths.)

1983

16 May. Elizabeth Kirkpatrick, wife of informer, is kidnapped. (She is released on 25 August.)

6 May. Eric Dale, accused of being an informer, is murdered.

4 June. Andrew Stinson, a UDR man, shot dead in Co. Tyrone.

13 July. Éamonn McMahon and Peter Mackin killed because of dispute over stolen bankers' orders.

13 August. Policeman seriously wounded in Dungannon gun attack. Two INLA members, Gerald Mallon and Brendan Convery, die during the exchange of fire.

17 August. Murder attempt on RUC men outside Newry courthouse.

6 September. Constable John Wasson shot dead in Armagh.

12 September. Murder attempt on police outside St Joseph's School, Newry.

23 October. Former INLA member, Gerard "Sparky" Barkley, murdered.

4 November. Pub in Strabane bombed.

20 November. Victor Cunningham, David Wilson and Harold Brown, three members of Pentecostal church at Darkley, Co. Armagh, shot dead.

1984

20 January. Colin Houston, UDR man, shot dead in Dunmurry, Belfast.

28 January. RUC reserve constable seriously wounded in Kilkeel.

13 April. John George shot dead in west Belfast for alleged criminal activities.

15 June. Constable Michael Todd shot dead in west Belfast. An INLA member, Paul "Bonanza" McCann, also dies in the incident.

11 August. Ambush attempt on security forces fails in Dunmurry. Two arrested.

2 September. Paddy Bonner, a doorman, shot and seriously wounded in Derry; he later had a leg amputated.

28 September. Attempt to kill Co. Armagh UDR man fails.

18 October. Eighteen-year-old youth, Ed McGarrigle, shot and seriously

wounded in Strabane.

30 October. Man shot and wounded for "anti-social behaviour" in north Belfast.

December. Attempt to murder UDR man.

17 December. Attempt on life of Gregory Campbell in Derry fails. Bomb attack on British soldiers in Holywood, Co. Down.

(Eighty deaths.)

1985

January. Attempt on life of Rev. Ian Paisley fails.

24 February. Douglas McElhinney, ex-UDR man, shot dead in Derry.

23 May. Séamus Ruddy murdered near Paris by John O'Reilly's men.

23 June. Two policemen injured by bomb near pub in Banbridge.

9 August. Incendiary bomb attack forces evacuation of Belfast–Dublin train.

25 August. Peter Begley seriously injured after accidentally triggering booby-trap bomb in south Armagh.

9 September. James Burnett, accused of informing, shot dead near Dundalk.

28 September. Ex-UDR man injured in bomb attack in Derry.

29 September. Disc jockey loses hand in bomb blast at night-club in Newry.

24 October. RUC defuse 100 lb bomb in Derry.

11 November. 37 lb bomb defused outside Chelsea Barracks in London.

1986

5 April. Bomb explodes in pub in central Belfast, injuring two INLA bombers.

27 April. Car bomb defused in Belfast.

15 May. Sniper attack on RUC in Derry.

13 July. Newry youth given forty-eight hours to leave country after having his legs smashed with breeze-blocks for "anti-social behaviour".

28 August. Van bomb explodes outside Downpatrick RUC station. Bomb attack on Newry RUC station. Central Station bombed in Belfast.

29 August. Bomb explodes in centre of Antrim.

30 August. Pub bombed in Antrim.

22 September. Attempt to bomb British Legion hall in Killilea, Co. Down, fails.

28 September. Bomb attack on pub in Downpatrick fails.

14 October. RUC man wounded in north Belfast.

24 November. Bomb attack on home of Unionist Party Councillor Sam McCarney fails.

30 November. A 43-year-old woman, Esther Boyle, and her son, John, badly

beaten in their Newry home.

1987

1 January. 72-year-old woman shot and seriously wounded during attack on her son, a UDR man, in Bessbrook, Co. Armagh.

8 January. DUP Councillor David Calvert shot and seriously wounded.

20 January. John O'Reilly and "Ta" Power shot dead and Peter Stewart and Hugh Torney wounded in Rosnaree Hotel, Drogheda, as feud begins between INLA factions.

5 February. Tony McCluskey shot dead in revenge for Rosnaree shootings by O'Reilly faction, known as "INLA GHQ".

7 February. Iris Farley, mother of a UDR man, shot dead in attack on her son by INLA GHQ.

17 February. Michael Kearney shot dead in cross-fire during attack by Steenson-McAllister alliance, known as Army Council faction.

7 March. Thomas Maguire shot dead by Army Council faction.

14 March. Fergus Conlon, suspected informer, shot dead by GHQ faction. Gerard Steenson and Andrew McCarthy shot dead by GHQ faction in Springhill, west Belfast.

21 March. Emmanuel Gargan shot dead by Army Council faction in Lower Ormeau, Belfast. Kevin Barry O'Duffy shot dead by GHQ faction.

4 April. James McDaid shot dead.

1988

17 August. Fred Otley, a loyalist, shot dead.

3 November. RUC officer wounded in Waringstown, Co. Down.

24 December. RUC patrol fired on in Whiterock area.

1989

June. Bomb attack on international bowling venue in Bangor.

29 July–15 August. Three attacks on security forces in west Belfast. No injuries.

25 August. Two alleged drug dealers shot and wounded in Turf Lodge.

17 August–29 September. Five sniping attacks on security forces in Strabane and Armagh. No injuries.

1990

10 April. Attack on RUC man's house in Armagh, during which INLA member Martin Corrigan is killed.

12 November. Attempt to murder UDR sergeant in Strabane fails when Alex

Patterson, INLA member, is shot dead.

1991

30 June. Gerard Burns, suspected informer, shot dead.

27 November. Attempt to murder Laurence Kennedy, Conservative Party councillor, fails in Holywood, Co. Down. Gang arrested.

21 December. Robin Farmer, student, shot dead during attack on his father in Moy, Co. Tyrone. One arrested.

1992

April. Shooting attack on RUC checkpoint in west Belfast.

14 April. Michael Newman, recruiting sergeant, shot dead in Derby.

18 June. Two fire-bombs (out of twelve planted) go off in Leeds, causing £50,000 worth of damage.

24 August. Protestant youth shot and seriously wounded in north Belfast.

1 October. Protestant landscape gardener shot and seriously wounded in case of mistaken identity in south Belfast.

1 December. Protestant road-sweeper shot and seriously wounded in a case of mistaken identity.

24 December. Sniping attacks on Grosvenor Road army base in Belfast.

1993

14 January. John "Bunter" Graham, leading UVF member, shot and seriously wounded in Shankill Road.

22 January. Samuel Rock shot dead in north Belfast in a case of mistaken identity.

7 February. Attempt to steal explosives from west of England quarry foiled by police.

18 February. Attempt to murder off-duty RIR man fails in south Belfast.

30 April. Attempt to murder taxi driver in south Belfast fails.

18 May. Fifteen shots fired at west Belfast police station.

17 June. Ex-RUC man, John Murphy, shot dead in south Belfast hotel.

20 July. Man shot five times in Dunmurry, south Belfast. Mistaken identity.

7 September. Disabled loyalist seriously wounded after shooting in Shankill Road area.

1994

11 February. Protestant wounded in attack in north Belfast.

24 February. Jack Smyth, Protestant doorman, shot dead outside south Belfast bar. Allegations that he was in the UDA denied.

IPLO, 1986–1992

1986
10 November. Off-duty constable Derek Patterson shot dead in south Belfast.
29 November. Hand grenade attack on RUC station injures six constables.
22 December. Veteran INLA man Tom McCartan shot dead.

1987
January–March. INLA Feud. IPLO never issued any claims of responsibility for any killings during feud. Killings were carried out by members of different INLA factions, some of whom joined IPLO, and are dealt with in INLA chronology.
3 December. Loyalist George Seawright dies after being shot on the Shankill Road in November.

1988
4 August. Parcel bomb sent to Unionist politician, William McCrea.
12 August. Proxy bomb explodes near law courts in Belfast. Bomb defused in east Belfast.
19 August. Parcel bomb sent to Ken Maginnis.
7 September. Loyalist Billy Quee shot dead in north Belfast shop.
3 October. IPLO member, Henry McNamee, shot dead as alleged informer.

1989
18 February. Former loyalist prisoner, Stephen McCrea, shot dead in attack on loyalist club in Shankill area.
6 November. Robert Burns shot dead, mistaken for part-time member of security forces.

1990
14 March. Shots fired at security forces in west Belfast. Murder attempt in north Belfast fails.
20 March. Billy McClure, a Protestant, shot dead in north Belfast in retaliation for attacks on Catholics. Police say he had no paramilitary links.
15 July. William Sloss shot dead in south Belfast. Family denied loyalist connections.
August. Attempt on life of leading loyalist, "Chuck" Berry, fails.
11 September. Protestant shot and wounded on the Shankill Road.

1991

20 April. IPLO member loses three fingers in botched grenade attack on Bessbrook RUC station.

5 June. Eddie McIlwaine, former member of UVF Shankill Butchers gang, shot and wounded.

18 July. John McMaster, member of Royal Naval Reserve, shot dead in his shop in central Belfast.

3 September. Protestant labourer shot and wounded in north Belfast.

7 October. Protestant bar in south Belfast machine-gunned. Two injured.

10 October. Harry Ward, member of loyalist prisoners' welfare group, shot dead in bar in Shankill Road. Protestant wounded in Newry.

12 December. Fire-bomb attack on veterinary surgery in Newry, claiming it served British army. The claim was denied.

15 December. Colm Mahon, snooker club manager, shot dead after dispute at his city centre bar.

21 December. Barry Watson and Thomas Gorman shot dead in attack on Protestant pub in south Belfast.

1992

17 February. Seventeen-year-old Protestant, Andrew Johnston, shot dead in video store where he worked.

5 May. William Sergeant, 66-year-old Protestant pensioner, shot dead and two others wounded in attack on bar in north Belfast.

18 August. Jimmy Brown shot dead by gunman from rival IPLO faction in Clonard Street, west Belfast.

20 August. Security guard shot and seriously wounded at his home in Bessbrook.

27 August. Hugh McKibbin shot dead by same IPLO faction that killed Brown.

1 September. Michael Macklin shot dead in Whiterock area of west Belfast. A Dublin-based IPLO faction alleged he was involved in the killing of McKibbin. This was denied.

31 October. In a city-wide operation, the Provisional IRA move against the IPLO, killing Sam Ward and wounding dozens of others, forcing the group to disband.

(Twenty deaths.)

Bibliography

There has until now been no book devoted solely to the IRSP and INLA. What follows is a list of those books that deal with certain aspects of the history of these organisations.

Barril Paul, *Mission Très Speciale* (Presses de la Cité, Paris 1984).

Beau Jean-Michel, *L'Honneur d'un Gendarme* (Sand, Paris, 1989).

Clarke Liam, *Broadening the Battlefield: the H-blocks and the Rise of Sinn Féin* (Gill and Macmillan, Dublin, 1987).

Derogy Jacques & Pontaut Jean-Marie, *Enquête sur Trois Secrets d'État* (Robert Laffont, Paris, 1986).

Dunne Derek and Kerrigan Gene, *Round Up the Usual Suspects* (Magill, Dublin, 1984).

Holland Jack, *The American Connection: US Guns, Money and Influence in Northern Ireland* (Poolbeg, Dublin, 1989).

Plenel Edwy, *Le Part d'Ombre* (Stock, Paris, 1992).

Index